AMERICAN INTERNATIONAL LAW CASES

Fourth Series

2009

Volume 3

Oceana®
NEW YORK

INTRODUCTORY NOTE

In 2009, American courts dealt with a host of cases incorporating international law, including issues such as the federal government's foreign affairs power and human rights abuses in foreign countries. This year's edition of *AILC* includes cases involving these topics, along with dozens of others critical to understanding the current application of international law in domestic courts.

The force of the foreign affairs doctrine was felt last year when the Ninth Circuit Court of Appeals struck down two California statutes on the grounds that the statutes conflicted with the federal government's foreign affairs power. In the first case, *Von Saher v. Norton Simon Museum of Art at Pasadena*, the statute at issue provided a cause of action to recover artwork looted by the Nazis during World War II. The Ninth Circuit found that California exceeded its authority by allowing all Holocaust victims and their heirs to bring action against any museum or gallery located in the United States. Although the court found that regulating property is generally an activity reserved to the state, the statute's broad scope conflicted with the federal government's power over foreign affairs. In the second case, *Movsesian v. Victoria Versicherung AG*, the Ninth Circuit also struck down a California statute on similar grounds. The California statute at issue in *Movsesian* extended the statute of limitations for claims arising out of life insurance policies issued to Armenian Genocide victims. The statute was held unconstitutional because it conflicted with the executive branch's foreign policy of not providing legislative recognition for the Armenian Genocide. These two California cases demonstrate how a federal court struck down a statute even though the statute did not directly conflict with a treaty, executive agreement, or federal statute.

The Alien Tort Statute and Torture Victim Protection Act also produced a series of cases that dealt with human rights abuses occurring outside of the United States. In *Chavez v. Carranza*, the Sixth Circuit Court of Appeals decided in favor of plaintiffs for crimes committed by a former Salvadoran military officer during the civil war in El Salvador. The court found that a Salvadoran law which granted amnesty to the defendant was not applicable because the plaintiffs were bringing action in the United States. In *Saleh v. Titan Corp.*, the U.S. Court of Appeals for the District of Columbia Circuit discussed whether Alien Tort Statute claims against two private military contractors providing services to the United States at the Abu Ghraib military prison were barred by the federal governmental immunity defense exception. Finally, in *Arar v. Ashcroft*, the U.S. District Court for the Eastern District of New York dismissed an action brought by a Canadian citizen who was arrested by U.S. authorities in New York and deported to Syria, where he was held for a year before being released without charges. The plaintiff brought claims under the Torture Victim Protection Act and the Fifth Amendment against U.S. officials for violations of his rights under international law.

LIST OF SUBJECTS

LIST OF ABBREVIATIONS

Significant abbreviations appearing in *American International Law Cases, 2009* are listed below.

A., A.2d	Atlantic Reporter [1885–1938], *Id.,* 2d Series [1938–date].
App. Div.	Appellate Division Reports [N.Y. 1896–1955].
Bevans	Treaties and Other International Agreements of the United States of America [1776–1949], compiled under the direction of Charles I. Bevans.
B.R.	Bankruptcy Reporter [1979–date].
Cal., Cal. 2d	California Reports [1850–1934], *Id.,* 2d Series [1934–date].
Cal. App.	California Appellate Decisions [1905–1940].
Cal. Rptr.	California Reporter [1959–date].
Cir. (1st, 2d, etc.)	Numbered Circuits of United States Courts of Appeal.
C.M.R.	Court Martial Reports [1951–date].
[state] Ct. App.	Court of Appeals [s] (state)
Ct. Cl.	Court of Claims (U.S.) [1863–1982].
Ct. Int'l Trade or C.I.T.	Court of International Trade [1980–date].
Cust. Ct.	Customs Court (U.S.) [1938–1980].
D. (N.D., S.D., etc.)	District Court (N.D. Northern District, S.D. Southern District, etc.).
D.C.	District of Columbia.
E.A.S.	Executive Agreement Series (replaced in 1945 by T.I.A.S.).
F. App'x or Fed. App'x.	Federal Appendix [2001–date].
F., F.2d, F.3d	Federal Reporter [1910–date].
F.P.C.	Federal Power Commission Reports [1931–date].
F.R.D.	Federal Rules Decisions [1938–date].
F. Supp., F. Supp. 2d	Federal Supplement [1933–date].
Fed. Cir.	Federal Circuit.
Fed. Cl.	Federal Claims Reporter [1992–date].
I.L.M.	International Legal Materials.
L. Ed., L. Ed. 2d	Lawyers' Edition, United States Supreme Court Reports [1754–1956], *Id.,* 2d Series [1956–date].

ANTONIO M. MATABANG
v.
CARNIVAL CORPORATION

630 F. Supp. 2d 1361 (S.D. Fla. 2009)
Decided June 29, 2009

Howard Scott Grossman, Grossman Attorneys at Law, Boca Raton, F.L., for Plaintiff.

Theodore Livingston Shinkle, Gray Robinson, Melbourne, F.L., for Defendant.

ORDER AND REASONS

WILLIAM M. HOEVELER, Senior District Judge.

BEFORE the Court are two motions: (1) the plaintiffs motion for remand and (2) the defendant's motion to compel arbitration. For the reasons that follow, the motion for remand is GRANTED and the motion to compel arbitration is DENIED.

BACKGROUND

On New Year's Day of 2009, 25-year old Antonio Matabang Jr. ("Matabang") fell overboard from the Carnival M/V Sensation off the coast of Vero Beach, Florida and died at sea. Matabang was employed by Carnival as an entertainer under the terms of Carnival's "Revue Show Performer Contract." Paragraph 17 of the Contract requires employment disputes to be sent to mandatory arbitration in either London, Panama City, or Manilla, whichever is closest to the employee's home.

On April 14, 2009, Matabang's father, Antonio Matabang, Sr., ("plaintiff") filed this lawsuit against Carnival in state court in Miami Dade County. The plaintiff claims Carnival breached the Revue Show Performer Contract by refusing to pay Matabang's $50,000 death benefit without obtaining a legal release from the Matabang family.[1] Carnival removed the case on May 6, 2009, pursuant to

1 The Revue Show Performer Contract does not discuss death benefits. These details are found in the separate "Seafarer's Manual," which Carnival describes as an "advisory document"

"property located abroad." Matabang was hired as a singer, and his obligations had nothing to do with property.

A somewhat closer point is whether Matabang's employment agreement involves "performance . . . abroad." Several illuminating court of appeals cases provide a framework for deciding what constitutes performance abroad. *See Freudensprung v. Offshore Technical Services, Inc.*, 379 F.3d 327, 340 (5th Cir.2004) (Convention applied between U.S. citizen and U.S. corporation where the employment contract called for performance in waters off the coast of Nigeria); *Lander Company, Inc. v. MMP Investments, Inc.,* 107 F.3d 476, 481 (7th Cir.1997) (Convention applied between two U.S. companies where performance of contract was in Poland); *Jones v. Sea Tow Services, Inc.,* 30 F.3d 360, 366 (2nd Cir.1994) (Convention did not apply where performance was on Long Island and the only foreign element was the arbitration clause choice of law provision). Some district courts have considered whether job contracts envisage performance abroad. In *Millmaker v. Bruso,* 2008 WL 219551, at *3 (S.D.Texas 2008), the court considered a consulting agreement between two U.S. citizens that called for the consultant to work on projects related to the "development of oil and natural gas reserves in West Africa and other countries." The job would "include significant travel outside of the United States to, among others, West Africa, Europe, and Asia," and the consultant was required to obtain "legal documents and permits necessary to allow [work] in Africa, Europe, Japan, or Asia, including a passport, valid work permit, and medical certificates." *Id.* The employer agreed to pay for "any non-domestic flight (traveling to or from the United States)" and "all costs of foreign travel/medical/evacuation insurance." *Id.* Finally, only two "Covered Projects" were even listed in the agreement: "the Sudan visit" and "OPL 229, Offshore Nigeria." The court concluded that, "this Consultant Agreement envisages performance abroad from its opening clause to its concluding exhibit." *Id.* (internal punctuation omitted).[5] Therefore, the arbitration agreement fell within the New York Convention and the case was removable under § 205 of the Convention Act.

The district court in *Ensco Offshore Co. v. Titan Marine LLC,* 370 F. Supp 2d 594 (S.D.Texas 2005), considered an arbitration clause in a contract between two U.S. citizens for the salvage of an oil rig 90 miles off the Louisiana coast in the Gulf of Mexico. Titan, the salvor, agreed to salvage the legs of the rig and deliver them to Texas for repair. Titan argued that the contract "envisaged performance . . . abroad" because the rig was in international waters, and because the contract anticipated that a British-flagged support vessel would be used for the operation. *Id.* at 596. However, the district court found these international aspects too insignificant to establish federal jurisdiction under the Convention Act, concluding that "Congress

5 Foreign performance was also written into the contract and explicitly part of the legal relationship in *Freudensprung.* There, the employment contract expressly incorporated the terms of "any Work Order" issued to the employee. *Freudensprung,* 379 F.3d at 333. In Work Order No. 4, the employee agreed to work as a barge leaderman in West Africa. *Id.*

did not envision American companies with a dispute just off the Gulf Coast with eventual performance in Texas to be property, performance, or enforcement 'abroad.'" *Id.* at 600. Further, the *Ensco* court found no authority for the proposition that every "offshore" event connected to a contract is "abroad" for the purposes of the statute. "[T]he fact that the rig sat in international waters and would require work more than twelve miles off the coast of the United States," the court wrote, "is insufficient in and of itself to qualify this agreement under the exceptions outlined in § 202." *Id.* at 601. With respect to the British flag vessel, which was not a party to the contract, the court observed that, "as critical as [its] role may have been in the motivation of these two parties . . . the foreign element must involve the legal relationship in which the arbitration agreement arises." *Id.* The court held that the New York Convention did not apply.

The "legal relationship" in this case is defined by the Revue Show Performer Contract, which contains no references to performance abroad or any foreign state, apart from the arbitration clause. Even the choice-of-law clause is territorially neutral, stating only that disputes will be governed by "the laws of the flag of the vessel on which [Matabang] is assigned at the time the cause of action accrues." Although the contract requires "[a]ll performers [to] provide an up to date Passport," the only travel mentioned in the contract is Matabang's domestic roundtrip flight from Los Angeles to Orlando, payable by Carnival. In reality, the legal relationship embodied in the Performer Contract presents only a superficial connection to the Bahamas, where the Sensation visits twice a week. So far as the contract is concerned, Matabang is assigned to work on a vessel, not a specific international itinerary.

Even assuming the Sensation spends 80–85% of the time "in the Bahamas, in Bahamian waters and sailing on the high seas," as estimated in the declaration of Carnival employee Carlos Estrada,[6] this does not necessarily equate with a "reasonable relation with one or more foreign states" under § 202. Time on the high seas, which undoubtably accounts for much of the 80–85% of the time Sensation supposedly spends outside the United States, is arguably not time "abroad." *See Ensco,* 370 F.Supp.2d at 601. The *Ensco* court's comments on this point are useful and consistent with the purpose of the jurisdictional requirements in the Convention Act.[7] So far as it appears, Matabang wasn't even required to set foot on Bahamian

---

6 Plaintiff disagrees with this estimation.

7 From the full context of § 202 and the New York Convention, it is clear that "performance abroad" is more than a simple geographic requirement meaning, for example, beyond the airspace or territorial waters of the United States. Such a formulaic interpretation would raise unnecessary questions about the international character of all manner of domestic legal relationships that incidentally touch upon extra-domestic spaces. In testimony before the Senate Foreign Relations Committee on February 13, 1970, Richard Kearney, the Chairman of the Secretary of State's Advisory Committee of Private International Law explained that, "We have included in section 202 a requirement that any case concerning an agreement or award solely between U.S. citizens is excluded unless there is some important foreign element

III. PROCEDURE

1. Jurisdiction

E. Subject Matter*

* Cases are indexed under this subject. The full text of these cases is published in the **volume**-page indicated.

Respondent's account of his prison ordeal could, if proved, demonstrate unconstitutional misconduct by some governmental actors. But the allegations and pleadings with respect to these actors are not before us here. This case instead turns on a narrower question: Did respondent, as the plaintiff in the District Court, plead factual matter that, if taken as true, states a claim that petitioners deprived him of his clearly established constitutional rights. We hold respondent's pleadings are insufficient.

I.

Following the 2001 attacks, the FBI and other entities within the Department of Justice began an investigation of vast reach to identify the assailants and prevent them from attacking anew. The FBI dedicated more than 4,000 special agents and 3,000 support personnel to the endeavor. By September 18 "the FBI had received more than 96,000 tips or potential leads from the public." Dept. of Justice, Office of Inspector General, The September 11 Detainees: A Review of the Treatment of Aliens Held on Immigration Charges in Connection with the Investigation of the September 11 Attacks 1, 11–12 (Apr. 2003) (hereinafter OIG Report), http://www.usdoj.gov/oig/special/0306/full.pdf?bcsi_scan_61073EC0F74759AD0&bcsi_scan_filenamefull.pdf (as visited May 14, 2009, and available in Clerk of Court's case file).

In the ensuing months the FBI questioned more than 1,000 people with suspected links to the attacks in particular or to terrorism in general. *Id.*, at 1. Of those individuals, some 762 were held on immigration charges; and a 184-member subset of that group was deemed to be "of 'high interest'" to the investigation. *Id.*, at 111. The high-interest detainees were held under restrictive conditions designed to prevent them from communicating with the general prison population or the outside world. *Id.*, at 112–113.

Respondent was one of the detainees. According to his complaint, in November 2001 agents of the FBI and Immigration and Naturalization Service arrested him on charges of fraud in relation to identification documents and conspiracy to defraud the United States. *Iqbal v. Hasty*, 490 F.3d 143, 147–148 (CA2 2007). Pending trial for those crimes, respondent was housed at the Metropolitan Detention Center (MDC) in Brooklyn, New York. Respondent was designated a person "of high interest" to the September 11 investigation and in January 2002 was placed in a section of the MDC known as the Administrative Maximum Special Housing Unit (ADMAX SHU). *Id.*, at 148. As the facility's name indicates, the ADMAX SHU incorporates the maximum security conditions allowable under Federal Bureau of Prison regulations. *Ibid.* ADMAX SHU detainees were kept in lockdown 23 hours a day, spending the remaining hour outside their cells in handcuffs and leg irons accompanied by a four-officer escort. *Ibid.*

Respondent pleaded guilty to the criminal charges, served a term of imprisonment, and was removed to his native Pakistan. *Id.*, at 149. He then filed a *Bivens* action in the United States District Court for the Eastern District of New York against 34 current and former federal officials and 19 "John Doe" federal corrections officers. *See Bivens v. Six Unknown Fed. Narcotics Agents*, 403 U.S. 388, 91 S. Ct. 1999, 29 L. Ed. 2d 619 (1971). The defendants range from the correctional officers who had day-to-day contact with respondent during the term of his confinement, to the wardens of the MDC facility, all the way to petitioners—officials who were at the highest level of the federal law enforcement hierarchy. First Amended Complaint in No. 04-CV-1809 (JG)(JA), PP. 1011, App. to Pet. for Cert. 157a (hereinafter Complaint).

The 21-cause-of-action complaint does not challenge respondent's arrest or his confinement in the MDC's general prison population. Rather, it concentrates on his treatment while confined to the ADMAX SHU. The complaint sets forth various claims against defendants who are not before us. For instance, the complaint alleges that respondent's jailors "kicked him in the stomach, punched him in the face, and dragged him across" his cell without justification, *id.,* P. 113, App. to Pet. for Cert. 176a; subjected him to serial strip and body-cavity searches when he posed no safety risk to himself or others, *id.,* PP. 143–145, App. to Pet. for Cert. 182a; and refused to let him and other Muslims pray because there would be "[n]o prayers for terrorists," *id.,* P. 154, App. to Pet. for Cert. 184a.

The allegations against petitioners are the only ones relevant here. The complaint contends that petitioners designated respondent a person of high interest on account of his race, religion, or national origin, in contravention of the First and Fifth Amendments to the Constitution. The complaint alleges that "the [FBI], under the direction of Defendant MUELLER, arrested and detained thousands of Arab Muslim men . . . as part of its investigation of the events of September 11." *Id.,* P. 47, at 164a. It further alleges that "[t]he policy of holding post-September-11th detainees in highly restrictive conditions of confinement until they were 'cleared' by the FBI was approved by Defendants ASHCROFT and MUELLER in discussions in the weeks after September 11, 2001." *Id.,* P. 69, at 168a. Lastly, the complaint posits that petitioners "each knew of, condoned, and willfully and maliciously agreed to subject" respondent to harsh conditions of confinement "as a matter of policy, solely on account of [his] religion, race, and/or national origin and for no legitimate penological interest." *Id.,* P. 96, at 172a–173a. The pleading names Ashcroft as the "principal architect" of the policy, *id.,* P. 10, at 157a, and identifies Mueller as "instrumental in [its] adoption, promulgation, and implementation." *Id.,* P. 11, at 157a.

Petitioners moved to dismiss the complaint for failure to state sufficient allegations to show their own involvement in clearly established unconstitutional conduct. The District Court denied their motion. Accepting all of the allegations in respondent's complaint as true, the court held that "it cannot be said that there [is] no set of facts on which [respondent] would be entitled to relief as against" petitioners. *Id.,* at 136a–137a (relying on *Conley v. Gibson*, 355 U.S. 41, 78 S. Ct. 99, 2 L. Ed. 2d

to dismiss turned on an issue of law and rejected the defense of qualified immunity. It was therefore a final decision "subject to immediate appeal." *Ibid.* Respondent says that "a qualified immunity appeal based solely on the complaint's failure to state a claim, and not on the ultimate issues relevant to the qualified immunity defense itself, is not a proper subject of interlocutory jurisdiction." Brief for Respondent Iqbal 15 (hereinafter Iqbal Brief). In other words, respondent contends the Court of Appeals had jurisdiction to determine whether his complaint avers a clearly established constitutional violation but that it lacked jurisdiction to pass on the sufficiency of his pleadings. Our opinions, however, make clear that appellate jurisdiction is not so strictly confined.

In *Hartman v. Moore*, 547 U.S. 250, 126 S. Ct. 1695, 164 L. Ed. 2d 441 (2006), the Court reviewed an interlocutory decision denying qualified immunity. The legal issue decided in *Hartman* concerned the elements a plaintiff "must plead and prove in order to win" a First Amendment retaliation claim. *Id.*, at 257, n. 5, 126 S. Ct. 1695, 164 L. Ed. 2d 441. Similarly, two Terms ago in *Wilkie v. Robbins*, 551 U.S. 537, 127 S. Ct. 2588, 168 L. Ed. 2d 389 (2007), the Court considered another interlocutory order denying qualified immunity. The legal issue there was whether a *Bivens* action can be employed to challenge interference with property rights. 551 U.S., at 549, n. 4, 127 S. Ct. 2588, 168 L. Ed. 2d 389. These cases cannot be squared with respondent's argument that the collateral-order doctrine restricts appellate jurisdiction to the "ultimate issu[e]" whether the legal wrong asserted was a violation of clearly established law while excluding the question whether the facts pleaded establish such a violation. Iqbal Brief 15. Indeed, the latter question is even more clearly within the category of appealable decisions than the questions presented in *Hartman* and *Wilkie*, since whether a particular complaint sufficiently alleges a clearly established violation of law cannot be decided in isolation from the facts pleaded. In that sense the sufficiency of respondent's pleadings is both "inextricably intertwined with," *Swint v. Chambers County Comm'n*, 514 U.S. 35, 51, 115 S. Ct. 1203, 131 L. Ed. 2d 60 (1995), and "directly implicated by," *Hartman, supra*, at 257, n. 5, 126 S. Ct. 1695, 164 L. Ed. 2d 441, the qualified immunity defense.

Respondent counters that our holding in *Johnson*, 515 U.S. 304, 115 S. Ct. 2151, 132 L. Ed. 2d 238, confirms the want of subject-matter jurisdiction here. That is incorrect. The allegation in *Johnson* was that five defendants, all of them police officers, unlawfully beat the plaintiff. *Johnson* considered "the appealability of a portion of" the District Court's summary judgment order that, "though entered in a 'qualified immunity' case, determine[d] only" that there was a genuine issue of material fact that three of the defendants participated in the beating. *Id.*, at 313, 115 S. Ct. 2151, 132 L. Ed. 2d 238.

In finding that order not a "final decision" for purposes of § 1291, the *Johnson* Court cited *Mitchell* for the proposition that only decisions turning "'*on an issue of law*'" are subject to immediate appeal. 515 U.S., at 313, 115 S. Ct. 2151, 132 L. Ed. 2d 238. Though determining whether there is a genuine issue of material fact at summary judgment is a question of law, it is a legal question that sits near the law-fact divide. Or as we said in *Johnson*, it is a "fact-related" legal inquiry. *Id.*, at 314, 115 S. Ct. 2151, 132 L. Ed. 2d 238. To conduct it, a court of appeals may be required to consult a "vast pretrial record, with numerous conflicting affidavits, depositions, and other discovery materials." *Id.*, at 316, 115 S. Ct. 2151, 132 L. Ed. 2d 238. That process generally involves matters more within a district court's ken and may replicate inefficiently questions that will arise on appeal following final judgment. *Ibid.* Finding those concerns predominant, *Johnson* held that the collateral orders that are "final" under *Mitchell* turn on "abstract," rather than "fact-based," issues of law. 515 U.S., at 317, 115 S. Ct. 2151, 132 L. Ed. 2d 238.

The concerns that animated the decision in *Johnson* are absent when an appellate court considers the disposition of a motion to dismiss a complaint for insufficient pleadings. True, the categories of "fact-based" and "abstract" legal questions used to guide the Court's decision in *Johnson* are not well defined. Here, however, the order denying petitioners' motion to dismiss falls well within the latter class. Reviewing that order, the Court of Appeals considered only the allegations contained within the four corners of respondent's complaint; resort to a "vast pretrial record" on petitioners' motion to dismiss was unnecessary. *Id.*, at 316, 115 S. Ct. 2151, 132 L. Ed. 2d 238. And determining whether respondent's complaint has the "heft" to state a claim is a task well within an appellate court's core competency. *Twombly*, 550 U.S., at 557, 127 S. Ct. 1955, 167 L. Ed. 2d 929. Evaluating the sufficiency of a complaint is not a "fact-based" question of law, so the problem the Court sought to avoid in *Johnson* is not implicated here. The District Court's order denying petitioners' motion to dismiss is a final decision under the collateral-order doctrine over which the Court of Appeals had, and this Court has, jurisdiction. We proceed to consider the merits of petitioners' appeal.

III.

In *Twombly*, *supra*, at 553–554, 127 S. Ct. 1955, 167 L. Ed. 2d 929, the Court found it necessary first to discuss the antitrust principles implicated by the complaint. Here too we begin by taking note of the elements a plaintiff must plead to state a claim of unconstitutional discrimination against officials entitled to assert the defense of qualified immunity.

In *Bivens*—proceeding on the theory that a right suggests a remedy—this Court "recognized for the first time an implied private action for damages against federal officers alleged to have violated a citizen's constitutional rights." *Correctional Services Corp. v. Malesko*, 534 U.S. 61, 66, 122 S. Ct. 515, 151 L. Ed. 2d 456 (2001). Because implied causes of action are disfavored, the Court has been reluctant to extend *Bivens* liability "to any new context or new category of defendants." 534 U.S., at 68, 122 S. Ct. 515, 151 L. Ed. 2d 456. *See also Wilkie*, 551 U.S., at 549–550, 127 S. Ct. 2588, 168 L. Ed. 2d 389. That reluctance might well have disposed of respondent's First Amendment claim of religious discrimination. For while we have allowed a *Bivens* action to redress a violation of the equal protection component of the Due Process Clause of the Fifth Amendment, *see Davis v.*

legal conclusions. Threadbare recitals of the elements of a cause of action, supported by mere conclusory statements, do not suffice. *Id.*, at 555, 127 S. Ct. 1955, 167 L. Ed. 2d 929 (Although for the purposes of a motion to dismiss we must take all of the factual allegations in the complaint as true, we "are not bound to accept as true a legal conclusion couched as a factual allegation" (internal quotation marks omitted)). Rule 8 marks a notable and generous departure from the hyper-technical, code-pleading regime of a prior era, but it does not unlock the doors of discovery for a plaintiff armed with nothing more than conclusions. Second, only a complaint that states a plausible claim for relief survives a motion to dismiss. *Id.*, at 556, 127 S. Ct. 1955, 167 L. Ed. 2d 929. Determining whether a complaint states a plausible claim for relief will, as the Court of Appeals observed, be a context-specific task that requires the reviewing court to draw on its judicial experience and common sense. 490 F.3d at 157–158. But where the well-pleaded facts do not permit the court to infer more than the mere possibility of misconduct, the complaint has alleged—but it has not "show[n]"—"that the pleader is entitled to relief." Fed. Rule Civ. Proc. 8(a)(2).

In keeping with these principles a court considering a motion to dismiss can choose to begin by identifying pleadings that, because they are no more than conclusions, are not entitled to the assumption of truth. While legal conclusions can provide the framework of a complaint, they must be supported by factual allegations. When there are well-pleaded factual allegations, a court should assume their veracity and then determine whether they plausibly give rise to an entitlement to relief.

Our decision in *Twombly* illustrates the two-pronged approach. There, we considered the sufficiency of a complaint alleging that incumbent telecommunications providers had entered an agreement not to compete and to forestall competitive entry, in violation of the Sherman Act, 15 U.S.C. §1. Recognizing that §1 enjoins only anticompetitive conduct "effected by a contract, combination, or conspiracy," *Copperweld Corp. v. Independence Tube Corp.*, 467 U.S. 752, 775, 104 S. Ct. 2731, 81 L. Ed. 2d 628 (1984), the plaintiffs in *Twombly* flatly pleaded that the defendants "ha[d] entered into a contract, combination or conspiracy to prevent competitive entry . . . and ha[d] agreed not to compete with one another." 550 U.S., at 551, 127 S. Ct. 1955, 167 L. Ed. 2d 929 (internal quotation marks omitted). The complaint also alleged that the defendants' "parallel course of conduct . . . to prevent competition" and inflate prices was indicative of the unlawful agreement alleged. *Ibid.* (internal quotation marks omitted).

The Court held the plaintiffs' complaint deficient under Rule 8. In doing so it first noted that the plaintiffs' assertion of an unlawful agreement was a "'legal conclusion'" and, as such, was not entitled to the assumption of truth. *Id.*, at 555, 127 S. Ct. 1955, 167 L. Ed. 2d 929. Had the Court simply credited the allegation of a conspiracy, the plaintiffs would have stated a claim for relief and been entitled to proceed perforce. The Court next addressed the "nub" of the plaintiffs' complaint—the well-pleaded, nonconclusory factual allegation of parallel behavior—to determine whether it gave rise to a "plausible suggestion of conspiracy." *Id.*, at 565–566, 127 S. Ct. 1955, 167 L. Ed. 2d 929. Acknowledging that parallel conduct was consistent with an unlawful agreement, the Court nevertheless concluded that it did not plausibly suggest an illicit accord because it was not only compatible with, but indeed was more likely explained by, lawful, unchoreographed free-market behavior. *Id*., at 567, 127 S. Ct. 1955, 167 L. Ed. 2d 929. Because the well-pleaded fact of parallel conduct, accepted as true, did not plausibly suggest an unlawful agreement, the Court held the plaintiffs' complaint must be dismissed. *Id*., at 570, 127 S. Ct. 1955, 167 L. Ed. 2d 929.

B.

Under *Twombly's* construction of Rule 8, we conclude that respondent's complaint has not "nudged [his] claims" of invidious discrimination "across the line from conceivable to plausible." *Ibid.*

We begin our analysis by identifying the allegations in the complaint that are not entitled to the assumption of truth. Respondent pleads that petitioners "knew of, condoned, and willfully and maliciously agreed to subject [him]" to harsh conditions of confinement "as a matter of policy, solely on account of [his] religion, race, and/or national origin and for no legitimate penological interest." Complaint P. 96, App. to Pet. for Cert. 173a–174a. The complaint alleges that Ashcroft was the "principal architect" of this invidious policy, *id.*, P. 10, at 157a, and that Mueller was "instrumental" in adopting and executing it, *id.*, P. 11, at 157a. These bare assertions, much like the pleading of conspiracy in *Twombly*, amount to nothing more than a "formulaic recitation of the elements" of a constitutional discrimination claim, 550 U.S., at 555, 127 S. Ct. 1955, 167 L. Ed. 2d 929, namely, that petitioners adopted a policy "'because of,' not merely 'in spite of,' its adverse effects upon an identifiable group." *Feeney*, 442 U.S., at 279, 99 S. Ct. 2282, 60 L. Ed. 2d 870. As such, the allegations are conclusory and not entitled to be assumed true. *Twombly, supra*, 550 U.S., at 554–555, 127 S. Ct. 1955, 167 L. Ed. 2d 929. To be clear, we do not reject these bald allegations on the ground that they are unrealistic or nonsensical. We do not so characterize them any more than the Court in *Twombly* rejected the plaintiffs' express allegation of a "'contract, combination or conspiracy to prevent competitive entry,'" *id.*, at 551, 127 S. Ct. 1955, 167 L. Ed. 2d 929, because it thought that claim too chimerical to be maintained. It is the conclusory nature of respondent's allegations, rather than their extravagantly fanciful nature, that disentitles them to the presumption of truth.

We next consider the factual allegations in respondent's complaint to determine if they plausibly suggest an entitlement to relief. The complaint alleges that "the [FBI], under the direction of Defendant MUELLER, arrested and detained thousands of Arab Muslim men . . . as part of its investigation of the events of September 11." Complaint P. 47, App. to Pet. for Cert. 164a. It further claims that "[t]he policy of holding post-September-11th detainees in highly restrictive conditions of confinement until they were 'cleared' by the FBI was approved by Defendants ASHCROFT and MUELLER in discussions in the weeks after September 11, 2001." *Id.,* P. 69, at 168a. Taken as true, these allegations are

discovery process. *Twombly, supra*, at 559, 127 S. Ct. 1955, 167 L. Ed. 2d 929 ("It is no answer to say that a claim just shy of a plausible entitlement to relief can, if groundless, be weeded out early in the discovery process through careful case management given the common lament that the success of judicial supervision in checking discovery abuse has been on the modest side" (internal quotation marks and citation omitted)).

Our rejection of the careful-case-management approach is especially important in suits where Government-official defendants are entitled to assert the defense of qualified immunity. The basic thrust of the qualified-immunity doctrine is to free officials from the concerns of litigation, including "avoidance of disruptive discovery." *Siegert v. Gilley*, 500 U.S. 226, 236, 111 S. Ct. 1789, 114 L. Ed. 2d 277 (1991) (Kennedy, J., concurring in judgment). There are serious and legitimate reasons for this. If a Government official is to devote time to his or her duties, and to the formulation of sound and responsible policies, it is counterproductive to require the substantial diversion that is attendant to participating in litigation and making informed decisions as to how it should proceed. Litigation, though necessary to ensure that officials comply with the law, exacts heavy costs in terms of efficiency and expenditure of valuable time and resources that might otherwise be directed to the proper execution of the work of the Government. The costs of diversion are only magnified when Government officials are charged with responding to, as Judge Cabranes aptly put it, "a national and international security emergency unprecedented in the history of the American Republic." 490 F.3d at 179.

It is no answer to these concerns to say that discovery for petitioners can be deferred while pretrial proceedings continue for other defendants. It is quite likely that, when discovery as to the other parties proceeds, it would prove necessary for petitioners and their counsel to participate in the process to ensure the case does not develop in a misleading or slanted way that causes prejudice to their position. Even if petitioners are not yet themselves subject to discovery orders, then, they would not be free from the burdens of discovery.

We decline respondent's invitation to relax the pleading requirements on the ground that the Court of Appeals promises petitioners minimally intrusive discovery. That promise provides especially cold comfort in this pleading context, where we are impelled to give real content to the concept of qualified immunity for high-level officials who must be neither deterred nor detracted from the vigorous performance of their duties. Because respondent's complaint is deficient under Rule 8, he is not entitled to discovery, cabined or otherwise.

3.

Respondent finally maintains that the Federal Rules expressly allow him to allege petitioners' discriminatory intent "generally," which he equates with a conclusory allegation. Iqbal Brief 32 (citing Fed. Rule Civ. Proc. 9). It follows, respondent says, that his complaint is sufficiently well pleaded because it claims that petitioners discriminated against him "on account of [his] religion, race, and/or national origin and for no legitimate penological interest." Complaint P. 96, App. to Pet. for Cert. 172a–173a. Were we required to accept this allegation as true, respondent's complaint would survive petitioners' motion to dismiss. But the Federal Rules do not require courts to credit a complaint's conclusory statements without reference to its factual context.

It is true that Rule 9(b) requires particularity when pleading "fraud or mistake," while allowing "[m]alice, intent, knowledge, and other conditions of a person's mind [to] be alleged generally." But "generally" is a relative term. In the context of Rule 9, it is to be compared to the particularity requirement applicable to fraud or mistake. Rule 9 merely excuses a party from pleading discriminatory intent under an elevated pleading standard. It does not give him license to evade the less rigid—though still operative—strictures of Rule 8. See 5A C. Wright & A. Miller, Federal Practice and Procedure § 1301, p 291 (3d ed. 2004) ("[A] rigid rule requiring the detailed pleading of a condition of mind would be undesirable because, absent overriding considerations pressing for a specificity requirement, as in the case of averments of fraud or mistake, the general 'short and plain statement of the claim' mandate in Rule 8(a) . . . should control the second sentence of Rule 9(b)"). And Rule 8 does not empower respondent to plead the bare elements of his cause of action, affix the label "general allegation," and expect his complaint to survive a motion to dismiss.

V.

We hold that respondent's complaint fails to plead sufficient facts to state a claim for purposeful and unlawful discrimination against petitioners. The Court of Appeals should decide in the first instance whether to remand to the District Court so that respondent can seek leave to amend his deficient complaint.

The judgment of the Court of Appeals is reversed, and the case is remanded for further proceedings consistent with this opinion.

It is so ordered.

constructive notice, and neither question asked the parties or the Court to address the elements of such liability.

The briefing at the merits stage was no different. Ashcroft and Mueller argued that the factual allegations in Iqbal's complaint were insufficient to overcome their claim of qualified immunity; they also contended that they could not be held liable on a theory of constructive notice. Again they conceded, however, that they would be subject to supervisory liability if they "had actual knowledge of the assertedly discriminatory nature of the classification of suspects as being 'of high interest' and they were deliberately indifferent to that discrimination." Brief for Petitioners 50; *see also* Reply Brief for Petitioners 21–22. Iqbal argued that the allegations in his complaint were sufficient under Rule 8(a)(2) and *Twombly*, and conceded that as a matter of law he could not recover under a theory of *respondeat superior*. See Brief for Respondent Iqbal 46. Thus, the parties agreed as to a proper standard of supervisory liability, and the disputed question was whether Iqbal's complaint satisfied Rule 8(a)(2).

Without acknowledging the parties' agreement as to the standard of supervisory liability, the Court asserts that it must *sua sponte* decide the scope of supervisory liability here. *Ante*, at ____ – ____, 173 L. Ed. 2d, at 882–883. I agree that, absent Ashcroft and Mueller's concession, that determination would have to be made; without knowing the elements of a supervisory liability claim, there would be no way to determine whether a plaintiff had made factual allegations amounting to grounds for relief on that claim. See *Twombly*, 550 U.S., at 557–558, 127 S. Ct. 1955, 167 L. Ed. 2d 929. But deciding the scope of supervisory *Bivens* liability in this case is uncalled for. There are several reasons, starting with the position Ashcroft and Mueller have taken and following from it.

First, Ashcroft and Mueller have, as noted, made the critical concession that a supervisor's knowledge of a subordinate's unconstitutional conduct and deliberate indifference to that conduct are grounds for *Bivens* liability. Iqbal seeks to recover on a theory that Ashcroft and Mueller at least knowingly acquiesced (and maybe more than acquiesced) in the discriminatory acts of their subordinates; if he can show this, he will satisfy Ashcroft and Mueller's own test for supervisory liability. *See Farmer, supra*, at 842, 114 S. Ct. 1970, 128 L. Ed. 2d 811 (explaining that a prison official acts with "deliberate indifference" if "the official acted or failed to act despite his knowledge of a substantial risk of serious harm"). We do not normally override a party's concession, see, *e.g., United States v. International Business Machines Corp.*, 517 U.S. 843, 855, 116 S. Ct. 1793, 135 L. Ed. 2d 124 (1996) (holding that "[i]t would be inappropriate for us to [e]xamine in this case, without the benefit of the parties' briefing," an issue the Government had conceded), and doing so is especially inappropriate when, as here, the issue is unnecessary to decide the case, *see infra*, at ____, 173 L. Ed. 2d, at 894. I would therefore accept Ashcroft and Mueller's concession for purposes of this case and proceed to consider whether the complaint alleges at least knowledge and deliberate indifference.

Second, because of the concession, we have received no briefing or argument on the proper scope of supervisory liability, much less the full-dress argument we normally require. *Mapp v. Ohio*, 367 U.S. 643, 676–677, 81 S. Ct. 1684, 6 L. Ed. 2d 1081, 86 Ohio Law Abs. 513 (1961) (Harlan, J., dissenting). We consequently are in no position to decide the precise contours of supervisory liability here, this issue being a complicated one that has divided the Courts of Appeals. *See infra*, at ____ – ____, 173 L. Ed. 2d, at 893–894. This Court recently remarked on the danger of "bad decisionmaking" when the briefing on a question is "woefully inadequate," *Pearson v. Callahan*, 555 U.S. ___, ___, 129 S. Ct. 808, 172 L. Ed. 2d 565 (2009)), yet today the majority answers a question with no briefing at all. The attendant risk of error is palpable.

Finally, the Court's approach is most unfair to Iqbal. He was entitled to rely on Ashcroft and Mueller's concession, both in their petition for certiorari and in their merits briefs, that they could be held liable on a theory of knowledge and deliberate indifference. By overriding that concession, the Court denies Iqbal a fair chance to be heard on the question.

B.

The majority, however, does ignore the concession. According to the majority, because Iqbal concededly cannot recover on a theory of *respondeat superior*, it follows that he cannot recover under any theory of supervisory liability. *Ante*, at ____, 173 L. Ed. 2d, at 883. The majority says that in a *Bivens* action, "where masters do not answer for the torts of their servants," "the term 'supervisory liability' is a misnomer," and that "[a]bsent vicarious liability, each Government official, his or her title notwithstanding, is only liable for his or her own misconduct." *Ibid.* Lest there be any mistake, in these words the majority is not narrowing the scope of supervisory liability; it is eliminating *Bivens* supervisory liability entirely. The nature of a supervisory liability theory is that the supervisor may be liable, under certain conditions, for the wrongdoing of his subordinates, and it is this very principle that the majority rejects. *Ante*, at ____, 173 L. Ed. 2d, at 887 ("[P.]etitioners cannot be held liable unless they themselves acted on account of a constitutionally protected characteristic").

The dangers of the majority's readiness to proceed without briefing and argument are apparent in its cursory analysis, which rests on the assumption that only two outcomes are possible here: *respondeat superior* liability, in which "an employer is subject to liability for torts committed by employees while acting within the scope of their employment," Restatement (Third) of Agency § 2.04 (2005), or no supervisory liability at all. The dichotomy is false. Even if an employer is not liable for the actions of his employee solely because the employee was acting within the scope of employment, there still might be conditions to render a supervisor liable for the conduct of his subordinate. See, *e.g.*, *Whitfield v. Melendez-Rivera*, 431 F.3d 1, 14 (CA1 2005) (distinguishing between *respondeat superior* liability and supervisory liability); *Bennett v. Eastpointe*, 410 F.3d 810, 818

perceptions of the market." *Id.*, at 554, 127 S. Ct. 1955, 167 L. Ed. 2d 929. We held that in that sort of circumstance, "[a]n allegation of parallel conduct is . . . much like a naked assertion of conspiracy in a § 1 complaint: it gets the complaint close to stating a claim, but without some further factual enhancement it stops short of the line between possibility and plausibility of 'entitlement to relief.'" *Id.*, at 557, 127 S. Ct. 1955, 167 L. Ed. 2d 929 (brackets omitted). Here, by contrast, the allegations in the complaint are neither confined to naked legal conclusions nor consistent with legal conduct. The complaint alleges that FBI officials discriminated against Iqbal solely on account of his race, religion, and national origin, and it alleges the knowledge and deliberate indifference that, by Ashcroft and Mueller's own admission, are sufficient to make them liable for the illegal action. Iqbal's complaint therefore contains "enough facts to state a claim to relief that is plausible on its face." *Id.*, at 570, 127 S. Ct. 1955, 167 L. Ed. 2d 929.

I do not understand the majority to disagree with this understanding of "plausibility" under *Twombly*. Rather, the majority discards the allegations discussed above with regard to Ashcroft and Mueller as conclusory, and is left considering only two statements in the complaint: that "the [FBI], under the direction of Defendant MUELLER, arrested and detained thousands of Arab Muslim men . . . as part of its investigation of the events of September 11," Complaint P. 47, App. to Pet. for Cert. 164a, and that "[t]he policy of holding post-September-11th detainees in highly restrictive conditions of confinement until they were 'cleared' by the FBI was approved by Defendants ASHCROFT and MUELLER in discussions in the weeks after September 11, 2001," *id.*, P. 69, at 168a. See *ante*, at ____, 173 L. Ed. 2d, at 886. I think the majority is right in saying that these allegations suggest only that Ashcroft and Mueller "sought to keep suspected terrorists in the most secure conditions available until the suspects could be cleared of terrorist activity," *ante*, at ____, 173 L. Ed. 2d, at 887, and that this produced "a disparate, incidental impact on Arab Muslims," *ante*, at ____, 173 L. Ed. 2d, at 886. And I agree that the two allegations selected by the majority, standing alone, do not state a plausible entitlement to relief for unconstitutional discrimination.

But these allegations do not stand alone as the only significant, nonconclusory statements in the complaint, for the complaint contains many allegations linking Ashcroft and Mueller to the discriminatory practices of their subordinates. See Complaint P. 10, App. to Pet. for Cert. 157a (Ashcroft was the "principal architect" of the discriminatory policy); *id.*, P. 11 (Mueller was "instrumental" in adopting and executing the discriminatory policy); *id.*, P. 96, at 172a–173a (Ashcroft and Mueller "knew of, condoned, and willfully and maliciously agreed to subject" Iqbal to harsh conditions "as a matter of policy, solely on account of [his] religion, race, and/or national origin and for no legitimate penological interest").

The majority says that these are "bare assertions" that, "much like the pleading of conspiracy in *Twombly*, amount to nothing more than a 'formulaic recitation of the elements' of a constitutional discrimination claim" and therefore are "not entitled to be assumed true." *Ante*, at ____, 173 L. Ed. 2d, at 885 (quoting *Twombly, supra*, at 555, 127 S. Ct. 1955, 167 L. Ed. 2d 929). The fallacy of the majority's position, however, lies in looking at the relevant assertions in isolation. The complaint contains specific allegations that, in the aftermath of the September 11 attacks, the Chief of the FBI's International Terrorism Operations Section and the Assistant Special Agent in Charge for the FBI's New York Field Office implemented a policy that discriminated against Arab Muslim men, including Iqbal, solely on account of their race, religion, or national origin. See Complaint PP. 47–53, App. to Pet. for Cert. 164a–165a. Viewed in light of these subsidiary allegations, the allegations singled out by the majority as "conclusory" are no such thing. Iqbal's claim is not that Ashcroft and Mueller "knew of, condoned, and willfully and maliciously agreed to subject" him to a discriminatory practice that is left undefined; his allegation is that "they knew of, condoned, and willfully and maliciously agreed to subject" him to a particular, discrete, discriminatory policy detailed in the complaint. Iqbal does not say merely that Ashcroft was the architect of some amorphous discrimination, or that Mueller was instrumental in an ill-defined constitutional violation; he alleges that they helped to create the discriminatory policy he has described. Taking the complaint as a whole, it gives Ashcroft and Mueller "'fair notice of what the . . . claim is and the grounds upon which it rests.'" *Twombly*, 550 U.S., at 555, 127 S. Ct. 1955, 167 L. Ed. 2d 929 (quoting *Conley v. Gibson*, 355 U.S. 41, 47, 78 S. Ct. 99, 2 L. Ed. 2d 80 (1957) (omission in original)).

That aside, the majority's holding that the statements it selects are conclusory cannot be squared with its treatment of certain other allegations in the complaint as nonconclusory. For example, the majority takes as true the statement that "[t]he policy of holding post-September-11th detainees in highly restrictive conditions of confinement until they were 'cleared' by the FBI was approved by Defendants ASHCROFT and MUELLER in discussions in the weeks after September 11, 2001." Complaint P. 69, App. to Pet. for Cert. 168a; *see ante,* at ____, 173 L. Ed. 2d, at 886. This statement makes two points: (1) after September 11, the FBI held certain detainees in highly restrictive conditions, and (2) Ashcroft and Mueller discussed and approved these conditions. If, as the majority says, these allegations are not conclusory, then I cannot see why the majority deems it merely conclusory when Iqbal alleges that (1) after September 11, the FBI designated Arab Muslim detainees as being of "'high interest'" "because of the race, religion, and national origin of the detainees, and not because of any evidence of the detainees' involvement in supporting terrorist activity," Complaint PP. 48–50, App. to Pet. for Cert. 164a, and (2) Ashcroft and Mueller "knew of, condoned, and willfully and maliciously agreed" to that discrimination, *id.*, P. 96, at 172a. By my lights, there is no principled basis for the majority's disregard of the allegations linking Ashcroft and Mueller to their subordinates' discrimination.

I respectfully dissent.

FACTUAL BACKGROUND

CVI is the beneficial owner of certain bonds issued by the Republic of Argentina. One group of the bonds owned by CVI is governed by German law, and these bonds are denominated in Deutsche Marks and Euros ("the German bonds"). Each German bond was issued pursuant to its own offering circular. Section 13 of the offering circulars provides in part:

> (3) The Republic hereby irrevocably submits to the non-exclusive jurisdiction of the District Court (Landgericht) in Frankfurt am Main and any federal court sitting in the City of Buenos Aires as well as any appellate court of any thereof [sic], in any suit, action or proceeding against it arising out of or relating to these Bonds. The Republic hereby irrevocably waives—to the fullest extent it may effectively do so—the defense of an inconvenient forum to the maintenance of such suit or action or such proceeding and any present or future objection to such suit, action or proceeding whether on the grounds of venue, residence or domicile. The Republic agrees that a final judgment in any such suit, action or proceeding in the courts mentioned above shall be conclusive and may be enforced in other jurisdictions by suit on the judgment or any other method provided by law.
>
> (4) To the extent that the Republic has or hereafter may acquire any immunity (sovereign or otherwise) from jurisdiction of any court or from any legal process (whether through service or notice, attachment prior to judgment, attachment in aid of execution, execution or otherwise), with respect to itself or its revenues, assets or properties, the Republic hereby irrevocably waives such immunity in respect of its obligations under the Bonds to the extent it is permitted to do so under applicable law.[1]

The remainder of the bonds owned by CVI are denominated in United States dollars ("the U.S. bonds") and were issued pursuant to a Fiscal Agency Agreement ("FAA"). The FAA provides that Argentina will "pay interest" on the principal of the U.S. bonds "until the principal . . . is paid." It also sets forth periodic dates on which interest is due. The FAA contains an acceleration provision, which does not specify whether or not interest is due on the periodic dates after any acceleration.[2]

In December 2001, Argentina declared a moratorium on the payment of principal and interest on its foreign debt and stopped paying principal and interest on the bonds at issue here. In response to the default, on various dates in 2005 and 2006, CVI accelerated the bonds it owned, making the principal immediately due.

The instant lawsuit was filed in the Southern District on April 25, 2005. After various preliminary proceedings, the district court granted summary judgment in favor of CVI on the claims related to the U.S. bonds on May 17, 2006. Subsequently, on February 15, 2007, the district court held an oral argument on various open issues,

---

1 This language is taken from the Offering Circular governing the 8% Deutsche Mark Bonds of 1997/2009. The parties agree that every offering circular contains substantially identical provisions, insofar as is relevant to this appeal.

2 This provision governs the acceleration of the payment of principal upon certain events of default.

including Argentina's motion to dismiss the claims related to the German bonds for lack of subject matter jurisdiction and CVI's request for statutory prejudgment interest on certain interest payments it claimed were due after acceleration of the U.S. bonds.

At the oral argument, the district court ruled that it lacked subject matter jurisdiction over the claims relating to CVI's German bonds because Argentina was entitled to sovereign immunity with respect to those claims; the district court accordingly dismissed the German bond claims. Construing section 13(3) and (4) of the offering circulars, the district court concluded that Argentina had not explicitly waived its sovereign immunity in U.S. courts in section 13. Instead, it held that subsection 3 was a limited submission to the jurisdiction of courts in Frankfurt and Buenos Aires. The district court reasoned that "whatever [subsection 4] means it should not be read as reading out of this instrument the reference to Frankfurt and the city of Buenos Aires." Accordingly, while acknowledging that the language of subsection 4 was "very broad," the district court ultimately held that "where there is an expressed grant of jurisdiction in specific places . . . a general waiver of sovereign immunity [such as in subsection 4] does not mean that . . . suit can be brought any place in the world." Having found that Argentina did not waive its sovereign immunity to suit in U.S. courts, the district court dismissed the German bond claims and concomitantly denied CVI's motion for summary judgment on those claims.

As to CVI's request for prejudgment interest, the district court found that the FAA did not require the continued payment of interest after the principal was accelerated, because the act of accelerating the principal so that "[i]t is due now" is inconsistent with interest that "continue[s] to accrue quarterly" where the contract does not specifically provide that contractual interest continues to accrue. Accordingly, the district court only awarded prejudgment interest, at the contractual rate, for the entire amount of the principal after the date of acceleration and for interest payments that were due but unpaid prior to acceleration.

On March 16, 2007, the district court entered final judgment reflecting its rulings at the February 15, 2007 oral argument. This appeal followed.

DISCUSSION

On appeal, CVI challenges both the dismissal of the claims related to the German bonds and the denial of prejudgment interest on interest payments that would have come due after acceleration of the U.S. bonds.

A. Sovereign Immunity

1. Background Law and Standard of Review

The Foreign Sovereign Immunities Act ("FSIA") "is the sole source for subject matter jurisdiction over any action against a foreign state." *Kensington Int'l Ltd. v. Itoua*,

renounces to claim any immunity during any procedure relating to any arbitration decision handed down by an Arbitration Court"); *World Wide Minerals, Ltd. v. Republic of Kazakstan,* 353 U.S. App. D.C. 147, 296 F.3d 1154, 1162 & n.13 (D.C. Cir. 2002) (finding an "express waiver[] of sovereign immunity" where the waiver said "[i]n respect of any arbitration or legal action or proceedings arising out of or in connection with this Agreement, . . . [the Kazakhstan State Committee] hereby irrevocably agrees not to claim and hereby irrevocably waives . . . immunity for itself and the assets of the Republic of Kazakstan to the full extent permitted by the laws of such jurisdiction"). Any other result would stray from the plain meaning of the statutory language. *See United States v. Santos,* 541 F.3d 63, 67 (2d Cir. 2008) ("Statutory interpretation always begins with the plain language of the statute, assuming the statute is unambiguous." (internal quotation marks omitted)).

Despite Argentina's argument, *Argentine Republic v. Amerada Hess Shipping Corp.,* 488 U.S. 428, 109 S. Ct. 683, 102 L. Ed. 2d 818 (1989), does not require a contrary result. In *Amerada Hess*, the Supreme Court stated that it did not "see how a foreign state can waive its immunity under § 1605(a)(1) by signing an international agreement that contains no mention of a waiver of immunity to suit in United States courts or even the availability of a cause of action in the United States." *Id.* at 442–43. Argentina would have us read this language as a requirement that, for a waiver to satisfy the FSIA's explicitness requirement, it must mention the United States in some way. That is not the holding of *Amerada Hess.* The international agreements at issue in *Amerada Hess* were the Geneva Convention on the High Seas, Apr. 29, 1958, 13 U.S.T. 2312, and the Pan American Maritime Neutrality Convention, Feb. 20, 1928, 47 Stat. 1989—neither of which mentions waiving sovereign immunity at all, let alone in the United States. The offering circulars at issue here, which are contracts between Argentina and the bondholders, are far removed from multi-party international agreements and do discuss waiver of sovereign immunity to suit in *any* court, thereby indicating "waiver of immunity to suit in United States courts." *Amerada Hess*, 488 U.S. at 442–43. Accordingly, *Amerada Hess* does not control the outcome here.

There is likewise no support in our cases for Argentina's suggestion that the mention of specific, non-United States jurisdictions in subsection 3 of the offering circulars precludes a finding that Argentina waived its sovereign immunity to suit in the United States. Of course it is true that there will be cases in which, when a document mentions a non-U.S. jurisdiction, there will be no explicit waiver for FSIA purposes because it will be clear that there is no intent to waive sovereign immunity in United States courts. *See, e.g., Eaglet Corp. v. Banco Cent. De Nicar.,* 839 F. Supp. 232, 234 (S.D.N.Y. 1993) (finding no explicit waiver where jurisdictional clause stated "[t]his Agreement is governed by English law and therefore BCN submits to the nonexclusive jurisdiction of the English High Court of Justice"); *Atl. Tele-Network Inc. v. Inter-Am. Dev. Bank,* 251 F. Supp. 2d 126, 133 (D.D.C. 2003) (finding that a broad, non-geographically limited waiver of immunity, when "juxtapos[ed] immediately below a choice-of-law selection clause (specifying the law of Guyana) and above a forum-selection clause (specifying the courts of Guyana)," does not waive immunity in the United States). It is not true, however, that the mere mention of a non-U.S. jurisdiction will preclude a finding of waiver, because the statute requires only that the waiver be "explicit." As the waiver at issue here demonstrates, a waiver of sovereign immunity can be explicit even when other provisions of the document are applicable only to specific, non-United States jurisdictions.

Accordingly, because we find that Argentina explicitly waived its sovereign immunity to suits in the United States relating to the German bonds, we reverse the district court's dismissal of CVI's German bond claims.[5] In addition, because it is clear from the transcript of the proceeding before the district court that CVI's motion for summary judgment on the German bond-related claims was denied only because the district court dismissed those claims, we vacate the denial of CVI's summary judgment motion, so that the district court can consider, in the first instance, whether or not summary judgment would be appropriate on those claims.

B. Prejudgment Interest

Under *New York C.P.L.R.* § 5001, a creditor is entitled to prejudgment interest on all sums due, as of the date they became due. *N.Y. C.P.L.R. § 5001*; *see also Spodek v. Park Prop. Dev. Assocs.*, 96 N.Y.2d 577, 759 N.E.2d 760, 762, 733 N.Y.S.2d 674 (N.Y. 2001) (holding that "CPLR 5001(a) permits a creditor to recover prejudgment interest on unpaid interest and principal payments awarded from the date each payment became due"). While awards of interest are generally discretionary, "New York law does not permit the trial court to exercise any discretion where a party is entitled to [prejudgment interest] as a matter of right." *New Eng. Ins. Co. v. Healthcare Underwriters Mut. Ins. Co.,* 352 F.3d 599, 602–03 (2d Cir. 2003). We review the interpretation of a contract, which is a legal question, de novo. *Phillips v. Audio Active Ltd.,* 494 F.3d 378, 384 (2d Cir. 2007).

The parties agree that the district court correctly awarded CVI statutory prejudgment interest on the contractual interest payments that Argentina failed to make prior to acceleration of the principal of CVI's U.S. bonds, as well as on the entire amount of the principal starting on the date of acceleration. However, CVI argues that contractual interest payments continued to come due after acceleration, and therefore that the district court should have awarded CVI statutory prejudgment interest on the post-acceleration, unpaid interest payments.

The normal consequence of acceleration is that interest payments that would have been due in the future are no longer due, because, after acceleration, the entire

---

5 Because we find an explicit waiver of immunity, we do not reach CVI's arguments that other FSIA exceptions to sovereign immunity apply as well.

a result of their allision. At the time of the accident, MarMex owned and operated the ISLA AZTECA, and Protexa owned the TOTONACA. Both MarMex and Protexa are Mexican entities, and both the ISLA AZTECA and the TOTONACA were Mexican flagged vessels on the date of the allision. The allision occurred beyond Mexican territorial waters but within Mexico's exclusive economic zone ("EEZ"). Under the United Nations Convention on the Law of the Sea ("UNCLOS"), Mexico does not exercise full sovereignty over its EEZ, but rather has certain "sovereign rights" within the zone, including control over the economic exploitation and environmental protection of the sea's natural resources. *See* UNCLOS art. 56, Dec. 10, 1982, 1833 U.N.T.S. 397; 1 THOMAS J. SCHOENBAUM, ADMIRALTY & MAR. LAW § 2–16 (4th ed. 2004).[1]

Shortly after the allision, MarMex commenced a limitation action in Mexico under the Convention on Limitation of Liability for Maritime Claims (the "1976 Convention"), Nov. 19, 1976, 1456 U.N.T.S. 221, as codified in the Mexican Law of Navigation, and posted a bond of $427,460.97 to satisfy any claims arising out of the allision. Commencing a limitation action allows shipowners to avoid catastrophic liability for accidents at sea involving their vessels, capping potential damages based on some measure of the value of their ship and bringing multiple claimants into a single action. 2 SCHOENBAUM, *supra,* § 15–1. The United States is not party to the 1976 Convention, *id.,* but rather has its own Limitation of Liability Act, codified at 46 U.S.C. §§ 30501–30512 (2006). To date, Protexa has not filed a claim against MarMex in the Mexican limitation proceeding.

On July 28, 2005, Protexa[2] and its insurance underwriters filed suit against Mar Mex in federal district court in Galveston, Texas, attempting to hold MarMex liable for the alleged damage to the TOTONACA. MarMex eventually filed a motion to dismiss Protexa's suit on grounds of lack of subject matter jurisdiction, forum non conveniens, and international comity, but the district court denied the motion and allowed this case to proceed in the United States. Subsequently, the district court performed a conflicts of law analysis and ruled that Mexican substantive law, specifically Article 1913 of the Mexican Civil Code, would apply to the case, but also held that the limits to recovery established by the 1976 Convention were procedural and therefore were inapplicable in U.S. court.

For trial, the district court bifurcated the trial between liability and damages to allow the Fifth Circuit to provide guidance to the court before addressing damages. After a brief bench trial during which MarMex stipulated that the ISLA AZTECA

---

1 The United States has been a UNCLOS signatory for nearly three decades, but the Senate has not yet ratified the treaty. Nevertheless, the United States has declared that the provisions of UNCLOS establishing EEZs are declarative of customary international law. *See Mayaguezanos por la Salud y el Ambiente v. United States*, 198 F.3d 297, 304 n.14 (1st Cir. 1999).

2 Perforaciones Exploracion y Produccion ("PEP"), an affiliate of Protexa, initially filed suit against MarMex. However, when it became clear that Protexa was the real party in interest, and not PEP, the district court granted leave for the plaintiffs to amend their complaint, substituting Protexa for PEP.

had allided with the TOTONACA, the district court found that MarMex was liable to Protexa for the allision.

On appeal, MarMex asserts that this case should be dismissed for lack of subject matter jurisdiction, forum non conveniens, and international comity. It also argues that the district court erred when it concluded that the 1976 Convention is procedural and consequently may not be used to limit MarMex's liability in this case. We address these issues in turn.

II.

Whether a district court possesses subject matter jurisdiction is a question of law, reviewed de novo on appeal. *See Sandoz v. Cingular Wireless LLC,* 553 F.3d 913, 915 (5th Cir. 2008). 28 U.S.C. § 1333(1) provides that "[t]he district courts shall have original jurisdiction . . . of . . . [a]ny civil case of admiralty or maritime jurisdiction . . . ." We determine that the district court does have subject matter jurisdiction under section 1333 to resolve this dispute.

MarMex contends that subject matter jurisdiction under section 1333(1) cannot reach an allision that occurred in Mexico's EEZ, relying primarily on *Victory Carriers, Inc. v. Law*, 404 U.S. 202, 92 S. Ct. 418, 30 L. Ed. 2d 383 (1971). In *Victory Carriers,* the Supreme Court stated that "the maritime tort jurisdiction of the federal courts is determined by the locality of the accident and . . . maritime law governs only those torts occurring on the *navigable waters of the United States.*" *Id.* at 205 (emphasis added). However, the weight of authority, including the precedent of the Supreme Court, supports the view that there are no clear territorial limits to federal maritime tort jurisdiction. *See, e.g., Panama R. Co. v. Napier Shipping Co.*, 166 U.S. 280, 285, 17 S. Ct. 572, 41 L. Ed. 1004 (1897) ("[T]he law is entirely well settled . . . that torts originating within the waters of a foreign power may be the subject of a suit in a domestic court."); *Malay. Int'l Shipping Corp. v. Sinochem Int'l Co.,* 436 F.3d 349, 355–56 (3d Cir. 2006) (seizure of ship at Chinese port establishes admiralty jurisdiction), *rev'd on other grounds,* 549 U.S. 422, 127 S. Ct. 1184, 167 L. Ed. 2d 15 (2007); Coats v. *Penrod Drilling Corp.*, 61 F.3d 1113, 1117–19 (5th Cir. 1995) (finding admiralty jurisdiction over tort in territorial waters of United Arab Emirates); *Exxon Corp. v. Chick Kam Choo*, 817 F.2d 307, 311 (5th Cir. 1987) (finding that "admiralty jurisdiction over claims by Singapore plaintiffs on an alleged tort in Singapore" is "undoubted"), *rev'd on other grounds,* 486 U.S. 140, 108 S. Ct. 1684, 100 L. Ed. 2d 127 (1988). Consequently, we find MarMex's reliance on *Victory Carriers* to be unfounded. The statement in *Victory Carriers* appearing to limit jurisdiction to the navigable waters of the United States is dicta. *Victory Carriers* concerned whether jurisdiction under section 1333(1) reached an accident that occurred on a pier in Alabama, and did not address whether jurisdiction reaches the high seas or waters under the control of a foreign state. 404 U.S. at 203–04.

MarMex also argues that even if these cases are controlling, there can be no admiralty jurisdiction over maritime collisions unless the parties or their dispute have

unreasonable, we find that the district court did not abuse its discretion by denying a forum non conveniens dismissal.

IV.

MarMex also contends that the district court erred when it did not dismiss Protexa's suit out of respect for international comity. A district court's decision to exercise or decline jurisdiction in the face of possible international comity concerns is reviewed for abuse of discretion. *Seguros Del Estado, S.A. v. Scientific Games, Inc.*, 262 F.3d 1164, 1169 (11th Cir. 2001); *Jota v. Texaco, Inc.,* 157 F.3d 153, 160 (2d Cir. 1998). We conclude the district court did not abuse its discretion.

Comity "is the recognition which one nation allows within its territory to the legislative, executive or judicial acts of another nation, having due regard both to international duty and convenience, and to the rights of its own citizens or of other persons who are under the protection of its laws." *Hilton v. Guyot,* 159 U.S. 113, 164, 16 S. Ct. 139, 40 L. Ed. 95 (1895). Dismissal of a suit on international comity grounds may sometimes be appropriate when there is litigation pending in a foreign forum or, even absent such litigation, when allowing a case to proceed in the United States would intrude on the interests of a foreign government. *See Ungaro-Benages v. Dresdner Bank AG*, 379 F.3d 1227, 1238 (11th Cir. 2004).

MarMex relies on *Sequihua v. Texaco, Inc.* to suggest that this case should be dismissed out of deference to Mexican interests. 847 F. Supp. 61 (S.D. Tex. 1994). However, this case is readily distinguishable from *Sequihua,* where a district court dismissed a suit alleging pollution affecting a third of Ecuadorian territory after Ecuador had "expressed its strenuous objection to the exercise of jurisdiction." *Id.* at 63. Mexico has remained silent in this case, and while the TOTONACA was engaged in oil exploration at the time of the allision, it is unclear how the resolution of this private dispute by a U.S. court would impede Mexico's ability to exercise its sovereign rights over economic exploitation within its EEZ. *See* UNCLOS art. 56, *supra.*[4]

Additionally, MarMex has failed to cite any case where a U.S. court has deferred to a foreign limitation proceeding on international comity grounds. Limitation proceedings commenced under U.S. law only receive domestic recognition,

---

4 We note that *Sequihua* is inapposite in this case for another reason. In *Sequihua,* the district court relied on section 403 of the Restatement (Third) of the Foreign Relations Law of the United States to guide its analysis. 847 F. Supp. at 63. However, section 403 is not relevant to MarMex and Protexa's private law dispute, as section 403 concerns prescriptive jurisdiction, the authority of the United States to make its *public* law applicable extraterritorially. *See* RESTATEMENT (THIRD) OF THE FOREIGN RELATIONS LAW OF THE UNITED STATES pt. IV, ch. 1, subch. A introductory note ("[Section 403] concentrates on so-called public law—tax, antitrust, securities regulation, labor law, and similar legislation. . . . [T]he rules stated in [Section 403] do not necessarily apply to controversies unrelated to public law issues.").

Otal Invs. Ltd. v. M.V. Clary, 494 F.3d 40, 63 (2d Cir. 2007); *Matter of Bowoon Sangsa Co.*, 720 F.2d 595, 599 (9th Cir. 1983) ("Because a decree in limitation normally receives only domestic recognition, 'the courts of each country will apply local law on the question of limitation; no country will give effect to a foreign limitation decree as barring further suit.'" (internal brackets removed) (quoting GRANT GILMORE & CHARLES BLACK, THE LAW OF ADMIRALTY 945 (2d ed. 1975))), and although the 1976 Convention requires its signatories to defer to certain limitation proceedings abroad, the United States has not adopted the Convention. 2 SCHOENBAUM, *supra,* § 15–1 n.7. Given these considerations, the district court's decision not to defer to the Mexican limitation proceeding on comity grounds does not rise to being an abuse of discretion.[5]

V.

Finally, MarMex asserts that the district court erred in determining that the limits on liability established by the 1976 Convention and codified in Mexican law are procedural and thus cannot be applied in United States court. "This Court reviews questions of law, including conflicts of law questions, *de novo*." *Cantu v. Jackson Nat'l Life Ins. Co.,* 579 F.3d 434, 437 (5th Cir. 2009) (quoting *Abraham v. State Farm Mut. Auto. Ins. Co.,* 465 F.3d 609, 611 (5th Cir.2006)). Similarly, determinations of foreign law are reviewed de novo on appeal, and courts may consider information from any relevant source, including information not considered by the district court. *See* Fed. R. Civ. P. 44.1; *Grupo Protexa, S.A. v. All Am. Marine Slip,* 20 F.3d 1224, 1239 (5th Cir. 1994).

The leading case on conflicts of law in this area is Black *Diamond S.S. Corp. v. Robert Stewart & Sons, Ltd. (The Norwalk Victory)*, 336 U.S. 386, 69 S. Ct. 622, 93 L. Ed. 754 (1949). In *The Norwalk Victory,* the Supreme Court held that U.S. courts may apply a foreign limit on liability, but only when the limit is substantive and "attaches" to the right of recovery created by foreign law, as opposed to merely "provid[ing] procedural machinery by which claims otherwise created are . . . scaled down to their proportionate share of a limited fund." *Id.* at 396. MarMex argues that we should perform a "policy-based conflicts analysis" to determine which liability limit applies in this case, relying on a reading of *The Norwalk Victory* advanced in *Complaint of K.S. Line Corp.,* 596 F. Supp. 1268, 1270–72, 1274 (D. Alaska 1984). However, we have never adopted such an approach, finding instead that "United States courts 'must apply foreign limitation law if the substantive liability of the parties is governed by a foreign law *and* if the limitation law of the foreign country is such an integral part of the substantive law governing the action that it can be said to 'attach' to the substantive liability law.'" *Karim,* 265 F.3d at 270 (quoting *In re Korea Shipping Corp.*, 919 F.2d 601, 604–05

---

5 We do not mean to suggest that a district court could not properly exercise its discretion to dismiss a case under forum non conveniens when a party has commenced a foreign limitation action.

III. PROCEDURE

1. Jurisdiction

G. Diversity Jurisdiction

In 1992, the Republic of Argentina solicited bids from private companies for a thirty-year concession, which allowed the winning bidder to modernize and operate Buenos Aires' residential water and sewer system and collect fees for its use. Until then, a wholly government-owned company, Obras Sanitarias de la Nacion, had provided the services.

Aguas was the winning bidder. It consisted of a consortium of seven companies that included two multinational water companies, Suez, S.A., and Sociedad General de Aguas de Barcelona, S.A. On April 28, 1993, Aguas entered into the concession agreement with the Argentine government and was thereafter incorporated under the laws of Argentina. Under the terms of the concession, the Argentine government ceded to Aquas the right to possess and use certain assets necessary to the operation and maintenance of the water and sewer system, but expressly reserved title to the assets. Aguas provided water and sewer services to Buenos Aires from 1993 to 2006.

The concession was expected to require $4.1 billion in capital investments over its duration, but a substantial portion had to be invested early for modernization and expansion of the systems. Aguas secured financing, primarily by recourse to international capital markets, including the United States. On July 15, 2004, following a series of defaults on the loan agreements, Aguas restructured a number of these loans in two interim financial agreements ("IFA's"). Pursuant to these agreements, the lenders bought out some of Aguas's debt in exchange for payment of past-due interest according to a schedule of installments. The IFA's contained a New York forum selection clause and a *forum non conveniens* waiver (collectively "forum provisions"). They also contained a New York choice of law provision and a provision binding "successors and assigns."[2]

In January 2005, Aguas defaulted on the interest payments owed under the IFA's. Subsequently, in July 2005, Aquas initiated a contractually established procedure for the termination of the concession. Thereafter, on March 21, 2006, the Argentine government terminated the concession, alleging that Aguas had failed to meet its

(2d Cir. 1978) (en banc) ("The district court took the motion to dismiss on submission, based on the pleadings, affidavits and briefs of the parties—a practice long recognized as acceptable and followed from time immemorial in the busy Southern District of New York in determining forum non conveniens motions."); *Vanity Fair Mills, Inc. v. T. Eaton Co.*, 234 F.2d 633, 645 (2d Cir.) *cert. denied*, 352 U.S. 871, 77 S. Ct. 96, 1 L. Ed. 2d 76 (1956) ("[I]n determination of a motion to dismiss for forum non conveniens, the court may consider affidavits submitted by the moving and opposing parties.").

2 The IFA's differ somewhat with respect to the relevant provisions. One contains a New York choice of law provision, a forum selection clause providing that "any legal action, suit or proceeding against the Company or any Purchasing Sponsor arising out of or relating to this Agreement or the other Transaction Documents may be brought in the courts of the State of New York or of the United States of America for the Southern District of New York", a *forum non conveniens* waiver, and a provision binding successors. The second IFA contains substantially similar provisions save that it does not include a *forum non conveniens* waiver.

obligations under the concession, at least in part due to toxic levels of nitrates found in various water sources. The Argentine government temporarily assumed operation of the water and sewer facilities pursuant to an executive decree. It soon after assigned the concession to AySA, the appellee here, an entity incorporated on March 3, 2006 for that purpose.

The Argentine government currently owns ninety percent of AySA's stock while AySA's employees, virtually all of whom are former employees of Aguas, own the remaining ten percent pursuant to an employee stock ownership program. The assets transferred to AySA included not only the concession itself but physical assets that had been built, improved, or acquired with the money borrowed by Aguas. No payment was made to Aguas for the transfer of the assets, or to any of its lenders on the outstanding debt.

After the Argentine government terminated the concession with Aguas, Aguas filed for protection from its creditors on April 28, 2006. At the time of the district court's decision under review, Aguas's insolvency proceedings were pending in Argentina.

ALRG was formed under the laws of New York. It is composed of original and subsequent parties to various loan agreements with Aguas between 1998 and 2004. ALRG's constituent members include entities organized under the laws of Delaware, Germany, the Cayman Islands, the British Virgin Islands, and the Bahamas. On September 29, 2006, these various lenders assigned to ALRG their claims to unpaid amounts under financing agreements with Aguas. ALRG appears to hold no assets other than the claims based on the loan agreements.

On September 29, 2006, ALRG brought the present action against AySA to recover on the defaulted loans and IFA's.[3] ALRG's complaint alleged that AySA is "not entitled to step into Aguas'[s] shoes, yet disclaim Aguas'[s] loans" and is liable to ALRG for the full amount of Aguas's loans, unpaid interest, and other charges. Specifically, ALRG alleged that AySA: (i) as successor in interest to Aguas, breached the underlying loan agreements, which had been modified by the IFA's; and (ii) received a fraudulent transfer of Aguas's assets to AySA.

On March 3, 2008, the district court dismissed ALRG's claims against AySA on the ground of *forum non conveniens*. *See Aguas Lenders Recovery Group, LLC v. Suez S.A.*, 2008 U.S. Dist. LEXIS 16283, 2008 WL 612669 (S.D.N.Y. Mar. 3, 2008). The court reasoned that "district courts need not afford great deference to waivers of *forum non conveniens* upon non-signatories, even where the non-signatory is an alleged successor to the waiver." 2008 U.S. Dist. LEXIS 16283, [WL] at *4 (citing *Yung v. Lee*, 160 F. App'x 37, 40 (2d Cir. 2005)). It concluded that because neither party to the suit was a signatory to the IFA's and the defendant

3 The complaint included claims against Suez, S.A., and Sociedad General de Aguas de Barcelona, S.A. ALRG settled its claims with these two defendants prior to the district court order that is the subject of this appeal.

non-signatories); *Coastal Steel Corp. v. Tilghman Wheelabrator Ltd.,* 709 F.2d 190, 202–04 (3d Cir. 1983) (binding a non-signatory third-party beneficiary to a forum selection clause), *overruled on other grounds by Lauro Lines S.R.L. v. Chasser*, 490 U.S. 495, 109 S. Ct. 1976, 104 L. Ed. 2d 548 (1989); *TAAG Linhas Aereas de Angola v. Transam. Airlines, Inc.,* 915 F.2d 1351, 1354–55 (9th Cir. 1990) (applying *M/S Bremen* to enforce forum selection clause against non-signatory plaintiff); *Marano Enters. of Kansas v. Z-Teca Rests.,* L.P., 254 F.3d 753, 757–58 (8th Cir. 2001) (holding non-signatories were bound by forum selection clause because non-signatories were "closely related" to the signatory or had acquiesced to clause by voluntarily bringing suit with signatories); *Lipcon v. Underwriters at Lloyd's, London,* 148 F.3d 1285, 1299 (11th Cir. 1998) (holding non-signatories bound to forum selection clause on grounds that the non-signatories, who had provided letters of credit to signatories, had interests in the litigation that were "directly related to, if not predicated upon" those of the signatories (citation omitted)); *see also Hugel v. Corp. of Lloyd's,* 999 F.2d 206, 209 (7th Cir. 1993) ("In order to bind a non-party to a forum selection clause, the party must be 'closely related' to the dispute such that it becomes n' foreseeable' that it will be bound." (citations omitted)); *Bonny v. Soc'y of Lloyd's,* 3 F.3d 156, 162–63 (7th Cir. 1993) (subjecting non-contracting defendants to forum selection clause because integrally related to contracting defendants such that suit should be kept in a single forum). *Cf. Dayhoff Inc. v. H.J. Heinz Co.,* 86 F.3d 1287, 1297 & n.8 (3d Cir. 1996) (reversing district court's dismissal, on ground of forum selection clause, of all of plaintiff's claims as to non-signatories to those agreements, except for one Italian corporation who plaintiff alleged was successor to signatory).[4]

The successorship issue must, therefore, be resolved for purposes of applying *forum non conveniens*. As a threshold matter, the parties dispute whether the question is governed by the law of New York or of Argentina. ALRG urges that New York law applies but argues that its complaint contains factual allegations sufficient to support a theory of successorship under either New York or Argentine law.

---

4 In arguing to the contrary, defendants rely on two summary orders, *Yung v. Lee*, 160 F. App'x 37 (2d Cir. 2005), and *Acosta v. JPMorgan Chase & Co.*, 219 F. App'x 83 (2d Cir. 2007), which, of course, do not provide binding authority. *See Silivanch v. Celebrity Cruises, Inc.*, 333 F.3d 355, 370 n.11 (2d Cir. 2003) (noting that summary order disposition is not precedential).

Even if they were binding authority, however, neither decision would be dispositive of the present appeal. In *Yung*, the district court accorded a "strong favorable presumption" to the plaintiffs' choice of a New York forum to resolve a dispute. *See Yung*, 160 F. App'x at 40. While *Yung* cautioned against applying forum selection clauses to non-signatories, it did not involve a claim that the non-signatory defendants were successors in interest to a party to the contract. The appellants in *Yung* disputed only the level of deference accorded their choice under the traditional *forum non conveniens* analysis. *Id.*

Nor does *Acosta* lend support to AySA's claims. In that case, the successorship issue was never reached. The court concluded instead that the plaintiffs' claims did not arise out of the contract containing the relevant forum provision. *Acosta*, 219 F. App'x at 86 n.2.

In response, AySA contends that Argentine law applies, but that, in any event, no successorship finding is possible under the law of either Argentina or New York.

We intimate no view as to, *inter alia*, whether New York or Argentine law applies or whether the outcome on the merits depends upon the choice of law. For the reasons stated below, we believe that the present record is not sufficient to allow us to dispose of this case without factual findings by the district court, and it would be unwise for us to resolve legal issues that, after factual findings are made, may drop from the case.

Under New York law, the general rule is that an asset purchaser is not liable for the seller's debts. New York recognizes four common-law exceptions to this rule: "(1) a buyer who formally assumes a seller's debts; (2) transactions undertaken to defraud creditors; (3) a buyer who de facto merged with a seller; and (4) a buyer that is a mere continuation of a seller." *Cargo Partner AG v. Albatrans, Inc.,* 352 F.3d 41, 45 (2d Cir. 2003). Thus, for example, "when a successor firm acquires substantially all of the predecessor's assets and carries on substantially all of the predecessor's operations, the successor may be held to have assumed its predecessor's . . . liabilities, notwithstanding the traditional rule." *Nettis v. Levitt*, 241 F.3d 186, 193 (2d Cir. 2001), *overruled on other grounds by Slayton v. Am. Express Co.,* 460 F.3d 215 (2d Cir. 2006). Similarly, ALRG has submitted affidavits stating that under Argentine law, the transfer of a going concern to another commercial entity that provides the same "commercial activities . . . in the same building . . . [with] identical merchandise . . . directed to the same clients" may subject that entity to the liabilities of the predecessor.

ALRG argues that it has alleged a prima facie claim that AySA was a successor in interest to Aguas. Specifically, ALRG claims that Aguas's revenues were directly linked to Aguas's development of infrastructure and the expansion of the existing municipal water and sewer system in Buenos Aires, that the loans on which ALRG now seeks to recover were made to Aguas for this purpose, that infrastructure improvements were made for which Aguas was entitled to compensation under the terms of the concession, and that the Argentine government terminated the concession, Aguas's principal asset, and assumed control of Aguas under the name of AySA, in which it maintained a ninety percent ownership interest. In so doing, ALRG alleges that AySA assumed operating control of the facilities and infrastructure improvements, as well as business channels, to deliver, without interruption, the same services to Buenos Aires as Aguas. ALRG finds further support for its theory in an alleged continuity of both employees and management, of ten percent equity ownership through an employee stock ownership program, of assets, including customer lists and accounts receivable, and of contracts. Finally, ALRG notes that the agreements at issue expressly bind Aguas's "successors and assigns."

Under both New York and what little we know of Argentine law, the successor issue is highly fact-specific and, given the present record, cannot be resolved with

BOSTON TELECOMMUNICATIONS GROUP, INC.
v.
ROBERT WOOD

588 F.3d 1201 (9th Cir. 2009)
Decided December 9, 2009

Steven M. Cowley, Esq., Boston, Massachusetts, for plaintiffs-appellants Boston Telecommunications Group, Inc. and Roderick Marshall.

Susan K. Jamison, Esq., San Francisco, California, for defendant-appellee Robert Wood.

Before: J. Clifford Wallace, David R. Thompson and Sidney R. Thomas, Circuit Judges. Opinion by Judge Wallace.

WALLACE, Senior Circuit Judge:

Plaintiffs-appellants Boston Telecommunications Group, Inc. (BTG) and Roderick Marshall (collectively, Marshall) appeal from the judgment of dismissal of claims against defendant-appellee Robert Wood arising out of an allegedly fraudulent business venture. The district court dismissed the action on forum non conveniens grounds. We have jurisdiction over Marshall's appeal pursuant to 28 U.S.C. § 1291, and we reverse.

I.

The following are facts as alleged in Marshall's first amended complaint, except where otherwise stated. In late 1995 and early 1996, Marshall, a United States citizen, was living and working in Bratislava, Slovakia, providing legal services to various Slovak entities. During much of this time, he shared office space with Deloitte & Touche Slovakia, s.r.o. (Deloitte Slovakia), an entity providing consulting, auditing and other professional services. Marshall became acquainted with another American citizen, Robert Wood, who was then managing partner of Deloitte Slovakia.

Around April 1996, Wood began soliciting Marshall to invest in a business venture being pursued by a Deloitte Slovakia client, Global Cable Systems, Inc. (GCS), a Canadian company. Wood told Marshall that GCS was planning to acquire two

of personal jurisdiction, and Wood later attempted to "join" those motions. Mainas and GCS moved to dismiss on the grounds that there was a mandatory arbitration clause in the Partnership agreement between GCS and BTG. All defendants moved to dismiss on forum non conveniens grounds.

In 2003, the district court dismissed the claims against Mainas and GCS in favor of arbitration, and in 2004 dismissed the claims against the Deloitte entities and Wood for lack of personal jurisdiction. Having dismissed all claims, the district court did not address the forum non conveniens issue.

Marshall appealed and we affirmed the dismissals of Mainas, GCS and the Deloitte entities, but reversed the dismissal of Wood, reasoning that Wood had waived any personal jurisdiction defense by failing to raise it at the same time he brought his Rule 12(b)(5) motion. The case was remanded to the district court, with Wood the sole remaining defendant.

On remand, Wood renewed his motion to dismiss on forum non conveniens grounds. Marshall opposed that motion. The district court granted Wood's motion to dismiss on the conditions that (1) the courts of Slovakia accept the parties' agreement to toll the statute of limitations and (2) Wood accept service of process in Slovakia. Marshall now appeals.

III.

We have held that a district court considering a motion for dismissal on the ground of forum non conveniens must decide

> whether defendants have made a clear showing of facts which establish such oppression and vexation of a defendant as to be out of proportion to plaintiff's convenience, which may be shown to be slight or nonexistent. *Forum non conveniens* is an exceptional tool to be employed sparingly, not a doctrine that compels plaintiffs to choose the optimal forum for their claim.

Dole Food Co. v. Watts, 303 F.3d 1104, 1118 (9th Cir. 2002) (internal quotation marks, citations and alterations omitted).

A party seeking dismissal of an action on forum non conveniens grounds "must show two things: (1) the existence of an adequate alternative forum, and (2) that the balance of private and public interest factors favors dismissal." *Loya v. Starwood Hotels & Resorts Worldwide, Inc.,* 583 F.3d 656, 664 (9th Cir. 2009) (internal quotation marks and citation omitted). Here, Marshall does not question the district court's determination that Slovakia provides "an adequate alternative forum" for the case, and thus we will not address that portion of the district court's ruling.

Marshall urges, instead, that the district court incorrectly concluded that the balance of relevant private and public interest factors favored dismissal. In weighing the relevant private and public interest factors, "[o]rdinarily, a plaintiff's choice of forum will not be disturbed unless the 'private interest' and the 'public interest' factors strongly favor trial in a foreign country." *Lueck v. Sundstrand Corp.,* 236 F.3d 1137, 1145 (9th Cir. 2001).

We review the district court's dismissal in this action with the understanding that a determination of forum non conveniens "is committed to the sound discretion of the trial court" and "may be reversed only when there has been a clear abuse of discretion; where the court has considered all relevant public and private interest factors, and where its balancing of these factors is reasonable, its decision deserves substantial deference." *Creative Tech., Ltd. v. Aztech Sys. Pte., Ltd.,* 61 F.3d 696, 699 (9th Cir. 1995) (internal quotation marks and citation omitted); *see also Piper Aircraft Co. v. Reyno*, 454 U.S. 235, 257, 102 S. Ct. 252, 70 L. Ed. 2d 419 (1981).

IV.

We turn first to the private interest factors at issue in this case. The private interest factors to be weighed in a forum non conveniens inquiry are:

> (1) the residence of the parties and the witnesses; (2) the forum's convenience to the litigants; (3) access to physical evidence and other sources of proof; (4) whether unwilling witnesses can be compelled to testify; (5) the cost of bringing witnesses to trial; (6) the enforceability of the judgment; and (7) all other practical problems that make trial of a case easy, expeditious and inexpensive.

Lueck, 236 F.3d at 1145 (internal quotation marks and citations omitted).

With regard to the residence of the parties, BTG is a Delaware corporation with its principal place of business in Massachusetts; Marshall is a United States citizen who resides in New Hampshire; and Wood is a United States citizen. In 2003, in support of his initial motion to dismiss on forum non conveniens grounds, Wood averred that he had been working in Eastern Europe, particularly in Bratislava, since 1992. In February 2008, in support of his renewed motion to dismiss on forum non conveniens grounds, Wood stated that he was living in Albania and that his wife and children, although living in North Carolina, intended to move to Slovakia later that year. Wood averred he would divide his time between Slovakia and Albania after his family's relocation.

The district court held that the private interest factor of the parties' residences was neutral because the parties resided in neither of the potential forums (California or Slovakia). Marshall argues that the district court failed to give proper deference to his choice of forum. Although California is not Marshall's "home" forum, as he is a New Hampshire resident, Marshall is a United States citizen and resident suing in a United States forum. In that sense, Marshall asserts, he is suing in his "home" forum.

We have held that the mere "presence of American plaintiffs . . . is not in and of itself sufficient to bar a district court from dismissing a case on the ground of *forum non conveniens*." *Cheng v. Boeing Co.,* 708 F.2d 1406, 1411 (9th Cir. 1983). Moreover, in *Gemini Capital Group, Inc. v. Yap Fishing Corp.,* 150 F.3d 1088

For his part, Wood argues that at least fifteen witnesses who had either knowledge of the Bulgarian Venture or knowledge of Wood's character are located in Slovakia or "other nearby Central European countries."

The district court held that, because both sides "would be required to rely on procedures under the Hague Convention to obtain evidence" from at least some witnesses, and because "both sides would benefit from live testimony that would enable a factfinder to evaluate [witnesses'] demeanor," this private interest factor did not favor either party. The court also concluded that, because there was insufficient evidence regarding lodging and travel costs related to the two forums and because some witnesses would need to travel to court in either forum, the factor of the cost of bringing witnesses to trial was also neutral. The district court acknowledged that it had difficulty with this analysis, however, given that the parties provided much information that was either hearsay or insufficient to allow the court to understand fully why the various witnesses were important to the case.

The district court properly considered both the sources of proof that the plaintiff intended to use to present his case, and the proof that the defendant intended to use to defend himself. *See Lockman Found. v. Evangelical Alliance Mission*, 930 F.2d 764, 769–70 (9th Cir. 1991). The district court also appropriately pointed out that, in the context of allegations of fraud, it is particularly "desirable that the factfinder have the benefit of demeanor testimony of witnesses." *Id.* at 770, *quoting Fustok v. Banque Populaire Suisse,* 546 F. Supp. 506, 511 (S.D.N.Y. 1982). Nevertheless, we have cautioned that the focus for this private interest analysis "should not rest on the number of witnesses . . . in each locale" but rather the court "should evaluate the materiality and importance of the anticipated . . . witnesses' testimony and then determine their accessibility and convenience to the forum." *Lueck*, 236 F.3d at 1146 (internal quotation marks, citations and alteration omitted).

The record reflects that Marshall explained with specificity how several of the witnesses who could testify in California were important to his claims against Wood, and which witnesses were most vital to his case. In contrast, Wood argued, in conclusory fashion, that the various Slovakia- or Europebased witnesses "worked with and under him . . . on the professional engagements for [GCS]," "understood the relationship between him and Marshall," and "could help defend his professional, reputation for honesty, and character," without explaining who these witnesses were or what information each would have. Wood's declaration in support of the 2003 motion to dismiss on forum non conveniens grounds speaks to the witnesses "*identified by plaintiffs* in *their* Initial Disclosures . . . and information that *plaintiffs* allege the witnesses possess" (emphasis added), but sheds no further light on the relative importance of various witnesses to his defense. Similarly, Wood's supplemental disclosures, filed in April 2008, listed witnesses with a general statement that they were "expected to have relevant knowledge and information" regarding a long list of topics, but these disclosures failed to specify which witnesses would testify as to each topic.

This is a case in which witnesses are scattered around the globe. Whether the case is tried in Slovakia or California, both parties will likely be forced to depend on deposition testimony in lieu of live testimony for at least some witnesses. Wood, in asking for the extraordinary measure of dismissal on forum non conveniens grounds, needed to provide not simply the numbers of witnesses in each locale, but information sufficient to assist the court in assessing the "materiality and importance" of each witness. *Lueck*, 236 F.3d at 1146; *see also Gates Learjet Corp.*, 743 F.2d at 1335. A defendant need not specify in great detail the contents of each witness's testimony, but "must provide enough information to enable the District Court to balance the parties' interests." *Piper Aircraft*, 454 U.S. at 258. Here, the district court abused its discretion in holding that this private interest factor was neutral when Wood provided very little information that would have enabled the district court to understand why various witnesses were material to his defense. Moreover, although Wood stressed the need to present witnesses who worked on the Deloitte Valuation, his counsel acknowledged at oral argument that Marshall's fraud claims relating to the Deloitte Valuation are only one theory of fraud in this case. Marshall alleges fraud based not only on documents allegedly prepared by Deloitte, but also on Wood's alleged oral representations to Marshall on a wide variety of topics. On balance, the private interest factors relating to witnesses weigh against dismissal.

Neither party has argued that there would be any problem enforcing a judgment in either forum, and thus the district court properly concluded that the sixth public interest factor was neutral.

Finally, we consider any other "practical problems that make trial of a case easy, expeditious and inexpensive." Wood asserts that "[m]any, but by no means all, of the documents regarding the [GCS] venture into Bulgarian cable systems . . . were written in English." He stated in a declaration that "many other" relevant documents were not in English, including "[m]any records issued or maintained by the Deloitte Slovakia office," "[d]ocuments regarding the cable licenses," and "correspondence with potential lenders," which were in Slovak, Bulgarian, or Dutch and would therefore need to be translated if the case were to proceed in an American court. However, it is equally true that the numerous documents in languages other than Slovak would need to be translated for a Slovakian court. Similarly, evidence was before the district court that many potential witnesses were fluent in English, but some were fluent in Slovak. Thus, the district court properly concluded that the inconvenience and costs of translation for live witness testimony would likely affect both parties in either forum.

The district court ultimately held, however, that this final private interest factor favored dismissal because Marshall initially sought "to hold the Deloitte Defendants' [sic] liable for fraud on the theory that Wood was acting as their agent" and Marshall "did not back off this theory at the hearing on this matter," even though the Deloitte entities had been dismissed for lack of personal jurisdiction.

COMPANIA NAVIERA JOANNA SA
v.
KONINKLIJKE BOSKALIS WESTMINSTER NV

569 F.3d 189 (4th Cir. 2009)
Decided June 26, 2009

ARGUED: Mary Campbell Broughton, FOWLER RODRIGUEZ VALDES-FAULI, Mobile, Alabama, for Appellants.

Gordon D. Schreck, BUIST, MOORE, SMYTHE, MCGEE, PA, Charleston, South Carolina; Douglas M. Muller, MOORE & VAN ALLEN, PLLC, Charleston, South Carolina, for Appellees.

ON BRIEF: Antonio J. Rodriguez, Alanson T. Chenault, IV, FOWLER & RODRIGUEZ, New Orleans, Louisiana; Paul F. Tecklenburg, TECKLENBURG LAW FIRM, LLC, Charleston, South Carolina, for Appellants.

Adriane M. Belton, BUIST, MOORE, SMYTHE, MCGEE, PA, Charleston, South Carolina, for Appellee MSC Mediterranean Shipping Company SA.

Before NIEMEYER and SHEDD, Circuit Judges, and Thomas D. SCHROEDER, United States District Judge for the Middle District of North Carolina, sitting by designation.

Judge Niemeyer wrote the opinion, in which Judge Schroeder joined. Judge Shedd wrote a dissenting opinion.

OPINION

NIEMEYER, Circuit Judge:

During daylight hours on March 8, 2007, a large 107,849-ton containership, the *MSC Joanna*, owned by a Panamanian corporation and chartered by a Swiss corporation, collided with a 33,423-ton dredge, owned and chartered by Netherlands corporations, in Chinese territorial waters near the port of Tianjin, causing serious damage to both vessels. After Chinese authorities investigated the collision and legal proceedings began, with the arrest of both vessels, in the Tianjin Admiralty Court to resolve liability and damages, the Netherlands corporations commenced eight different actions in four separate district courts in the United States under

Boskalis also made the decision not to file a claim against the limitation fund in the Tianjin Admiralty Court, even though it knew of the Chinese court's admonition that claims had to be filed by June 30, 2007. As counsel for Boskalis acknowledged to the district court:

> The Court: Okay. So the Boskalis entities made a reasoned decision after being notified that there was a limitation of liability proceeding instituted in the courts of China not to participate and let the statute of limitations run?
>
> Counsel for Boskalis: That's correct, Your Honor.

Instead of proceeding in the Tianjin Admiralty Court, Boskalis sought to litigate its claims for damages against MSC Shipping in the United States. It acknowledges that it made this election because U.S. law would, according to its assessment, result in a larger limitation fund than the fund created under Chinese law. On May 4, 2007, it commenced an action against MSC Shipping for $326 million in damages in the Southern District of Texas. Because MSC Shipping was not found in that district, Boskalis proceeded under Admiralty Rule B and attached an unrelated vessel chartered by MSC Shipping, requiring MSC Shipping to file security for the release of that vessel. Rule B is designed to secure the appearance of the defendant and, through the attachment of defendant's assets, secure satisfaction of any judgment entered, up to the value of the assets. *See Swift & Co. Packers v. Compania Colombiana del Caribe, S.A.,* 339 U.S. 684, 693, 70 S. Ct. 861, 94 L. Ed. 1206 (1950). Because the amount filed by MSC Shipping to obtain release of its vessel was insufficient to pay Boskalis' $326-million damage claim, Boskalis filed seven additional Rule B claims in district courts in Texas, Louisiana, South Carolina, and Virginia, obtaining a total of 16 orders of attachment under Rule B to be executed against vessels chartered by MSC Shipping.

To avoid the continued attachment of its ships in the United States, MSC Shipping filed this limitation action pursuant to Admiralty Rule F and posted security of $111,348,810, based on the value of the *MSC Joanna* after the collision and pending freight, as required by United States law for calculating limitation liability. *See* 46 U.S.C. § 30505. Although MSC Shipping created a limitation fund, it asserted that its purpose in filing this action was to enjoin the eight actions filed by Boskalis and then to have this limitation action dismissed, contending that no court in the United States was a convenient forum to resolve the issues arising from the collision in China. MSC Shipping stated in its complaint:

> 20. Plaintiffs have initiated this proceeding as the result of Boskalis' filing of eight actions in four different U.S. District Courts seeking sixteen writs of attachment. Plaintiffs specifically reserve the right to assert the legal doctrine of *forum non conveniens* in this proceeding, and to file a motion to dismiss this proceeding on those grounds.
>
> 21. Plaintiffs also specifically reserve the right to assert that foreign law applies both to the determination of liabilities arising out of the Collision, and to all issues arising in connection with this limitation proceeding, said applicable law being that of the People's Republic of China.

After the district court enjoined Boskalis from proceeding in the other actions, MSC Shipping filed a motion to dismiss this action in favor of the proceedings in the Tianjin Admiralty Court, based on the doctrine of *forum non conveniens*. The district court granted the motion, even though Boskalis claimed that it could not prosecute its claim in the Tianjin Admiralty Court because it had let pass the time for filing claims there—a question of foreign law on which the parties disagree. The district court recognized that the doctrine of *forum non conveniens* presumes that an adequate alternative forum is available, but it also concluded that Boskalis could not assert the unavailability of an alternative forum when the unavailability was the product of Boskalis' own purposeful conduct. As the court observed:

> The Chinese maritime court established a June 30, 2007, deadline for filing claims in the limitation action. At the hearing, claimants' counsel acknowledged that they deliberately chose "not to participate in China." Thus, the only reason the Chinese forum is not available in this case is because claimants knowingly and purposefully opted to miss the deadline for filing their claims in that forum.

(Citations and footnote omitted). The court then addressed the inappropriateness of a United States court adjudicating Boskalis' claims, describing the lack of any nexus between the disputes and the United States. It stated:

> The United States has absolutely no connection to the events giving rise to this action. None of the parties is a United States entity or citizen. Neither vessel was registered in the United States. Neither vessel ever darkened the doorstep of a United States port. No member of either crew was a United States citizen. No United States citizens are fact witnesses. Most, if not all, of the potential witnesses speak a language other than English, requiring a plethora of translators if the case were retained by this court.
>
> * * *
>
> [And] [t]he most compelling public interest factor favoring dismissal may be the challenge of applying foreign law.

The court found that the only connection that Boskalis' claims have with the United States is "incredibly minor," *i.e.*, that "*other* vessels chartered by Mediterranean Shipping Co. regularly call on United States ports."

From the district court's order, dated November 2, 2007, dismissing this action under the doctrine of *forum non conveniens*, Boskalis appealed. On appeal, it contends (1) that the district court improperly allowed MSC Shipping to dismiss its own limitation of liability proceedings on the ground of *forum non conveniens*; (2) that the court erred in dismissing the action without finding that China was an available and adequate forum; and (3) that the court erred because no conditions were imposed "to maintain Boskalis' rights" in the Chinese courts such as having MSC Shipping not assert any limitation defenses in China.

II.

Boskalis' principal argument, which is procedural in nature, rests on its assertion that MSC Shipping cannot invoke the benefits of the limitation procedure in

charterer's liability for claims arising from "any embezzlement, loss, or destruction of any property, goods, or merchandise shipped or put on board the vessel, any loss, damage, or injury by collision, or any act, matter, or thing, loss, damage, or forfeiture, done, occasioned, or incurred, without the privity or knowledge of the owner [or charterer]" to the "value of the vessel and pending freight." 46 U.S.C. § 30505. Limiting the owner's liability to the value of his interest in the vessel and pending freight was intended to place investors in seashipping and navigation on equal footing with corporate investors in land-based enterprises.

> The great object of the law was to encourage shipbuilding and to induce capitalists to invest money in this branch of industry. Unless they can be induced to do so, the shipping interests of the country must flag and decline. Those who are willing to manage and work ships are generally unable to build and fit them. They have plenty of hardiness and personal daring and enterprise, but they have little capital. On the other hand, those who have capital, and invest it in ships, incur a very large risk in exposing their property to the hazards of the sea, and to the management of seafaring men, without making them liable for additional losses and damage to an indefinite amount. How many enterprises in mining, manufacturing, and internal improvements would be utterly impracticable if capitalists were not encouraged to invest in them through corporate institutions by which they are exempt from personal liability, or from liability except to a limited extent? The public interests require the investment of capital in shipbuilding, quite as much as in any of these enterprises.

Norwich Co. v. Wright, 80 U.S. 104, 121, 20 L. Ed. 585 (1871); *see also Black Diamond S.S. Corp. v. Robert Stewart & Sons, Ltd.*, 336 U.S. 386, 399, 69 S. Ct. 622, 93 L. Ed. 754 (1949) (Jackson, J., dissenting) (observing that the Limitation of Liability Act was "designed to encourage American capital to risk itself in shipping ventures where ships are but boards, sailors but men: . . . and then there is the peril of waters, winds, and rocks. In order that disaster at sea might not jeopardize the shipowner's other assets, Congress limited his liability . . . . This limitation serves much the same purpose for maritime ventures that the corporate fiction serves for the landsman's enterprises" (internal quotation marks and footnote omitted)).

Thus, upon receipt of a claim arising from damage at sea or a shipwreck, the owner or charterer of the vessel may commence an action under the Limitation of Liability Act by depositing a fund with the court for the benefit of all claimants equal to the value of the owner's interest in the vessel and pending freight at the end of the voyage or following any wreck. As in an analogous interpleader action or bankruptcy proceeding, the limitation of liability provisions authorize the court to enjoin all prosecutions of claims with respect to the matter other than claims against the fund. Thus, an owner or charterer may avoid a multiplicity of actions against it; resolve the issues raised in the multiplicity of actions in a single action; and limit its liability in the one action to the value of the vessel and pending freight. *See generally* 46 U.S.C. § 30511; Fed. R. Civ. P. Admiralty Rule F.

Complying with the requirements of the Limitation of Liability Act and Admiralty Rule F, MSC Shipping commenced this action against Boskalis by depositing with the court $111,348,810, the value of the *MSC Joanna* and pending freight. But its purpose in filing this action was not to have claims arising from the collision in China paid from the limitation fund but rather to protect itself from the multiplicity of actions filed by Boskalis against it *in the United States* relating to the collision. Boskalis contends that this use of the limitation-of-liability process amounted to a misuse and that the district court erroneously countenanced it by enjoining Boskalis' U.S. actions in favor of this action and then dismissing this action in favor of the Chinese proceedings under the doctrine of *forum non conveniens*.

In employing Admiralty Rule F in effect to collect all the actions filed in the United States into one action and have that one action serve as the forum for resolving MSC Shipping's *forum non conveniens* challenge to any U.S. litigation, MSC Shipping surely did not fulfill the full purpose of the Limitation of Liability Act, which includes the adjudication of claims against the fund. But it did take advantage of one purpose of the Act, that of enjoining multiple actions in favor of one action to resolve the disputes. Because the threshold question is where trials relating to the collision should take place, it never intended to have the fund used to pay claims. Nonetheless, it did create the fund in the U.S. court as required, and if it loses its *forum non conveniens* challenge, it will be required to litigate the claims in this case. MSC Shipping is thus gambling, just as Boskalis has gambled. But as with any gamble, the bettor must accept the risk of losing.

While there is a certain inconsistency in MSC Shipping's actions when considered within the "four corners" of a limitation-of-liability action, in the larger context, MSC Shipping was simply seeking to collect all of the cases in the United States relating to the Chinese collision and have them subjected to the test for determining whether they should be dismissed under the *forum non conveniens* doctrine. It announced its purpose for doing so at the outset. The alternative would have been for MSC Shipping to follow Boskalis around the country, as it filed each lawsuit seeking to attach assets of MSC Shipping, and, within each action, to make its *forum non conveniens* motion. Judicial efficiency for both parties, however, favors the course selected by MSC Shipping. The superficial inconsistency of filing an action and then seeking its dismissal does not in this context become intolerably inconsistent. The Supreme Court has specifically rejected the argument that the party initiating the limitation proceeding cannot then seek to have it dismissed. *See M/S Bremen*, 407 U.S. at 2, 19–20 (involving a circumstance where the party that initiated a limitations action then sought to dismiss it based on a contractual forum selection clause).

In the peculiar circumstances of this case, we conclude that MSC Shipping did not abuse the U.S. limitation of liability procedure; it complied with its requirements and was prepared to accept its outcome. Moreover, the fact that it filed a motion challenging all U.S. litigation under the *forum non conveniens* doctrine in the limitation of liability action that it filed was not an abuse of the process. If one accepts the conclusion that a foreign corporation's preference for U.S. law in resolving a dispute arising outside of the United States cannot alone serve as a valid basis for

of witnesses, procure relevant documents and other evidence, and provide translators for virtually every witness able to attend would administratively tax the court system, as would the effort at applying Chinese law.

These facts all weigh in favor of affirming the district court's ruling. Indeed none can be found to weigh in favor of trying this case in the United States. Boskalis can hardly maintain that its wish to apply U.S. limitation law is a sufficient reason to justify trying the case in the United States. *See Piper Aircraft*, 454 U.S. at 254–55. Thus, we conclude that the district court did not abuse its discretion in ordering dismissal of this action.

IV.

Boskalis contends that the Tianjin Admiralty Court is not an *available and adequate* alternative forum and that therefore the district court erred as a matter of law in dismissing this action in favor of that forum under the doctrine of *forum non conveniens*. It asserts:

> The district court committed an error of law by dismissing MSC's limitation proceeding in favor of an alternative forum that is neither available nor adequate. First, the court's attempt to create an exception to the availability requirement for fraud or bad faith is entirely without precedent in the doctrine of forum non conveniens. The doctrine of forum non conveniens is well defined, and does not include any such exception.
>
> * * *
>
> Even if such an exception did exist, it would be inapplicable here, as Boskalis did not act fraudulently or with bad faith, and the court did not find that it did. MSC commenced two limitations proceedings that were simultaneously open for claims, providing Boskalis with a choice of fora in which to proceed. Boskalis simply chose to proceed in Charleston rather than China. This decision was clearly not a product of fraud or bad faith, and thus should not be subject to the court's ill-founded exception to the availability requirement of forum non conveniens.

It is true that the doctrine of *forum non conveniens* can be applied only where another forum having jurisdiction is available at the time of the district court's decision to resolve the dispute. *See Piper Aircraft*, 454 U.S. at 254 n.22; *Kontoulas*, 745 F.2d at 315. An alternative forum exists "when the defendant is amenable to process in the other jurisdiction." *Piper Aircraft*, 454 U.S. at 254 n.22 (internal quotation marks omitted). We have held, however, that if the statute of limitations has expired in the alternative forum, the forum is not available, and the motion to dismiss based on *forum non conveniens* would not be appropriate. *Kontoulas*, 745 F.2d at 316. But a difference in the law in the two forums—even where the amount of potential recovery is drastically different—is not sufficient to bar application of the *forum non conveniens* doctrine. *See Piper Aircraft*, 454 U.S. at 254–55 (noting that unless plaintiffs would "be deprived of any remedy or treated unfairly," the alternative forum would not be considered inadequate).

In this case, MSC Shipping proffered evidence on the availability of the Chinese forum by noting that the forum had jurisdiction over the parties and over the vessels. With respect to whether a statute of limitations would bar a claim at the time the district court dismissed this action, MSC Shipping argued that Boskalis deliberately forfeited the availability of a forum on this basis by electing not to proceed in China and deliberately letting the time for filing claims in China pass. Boskalis nonetheless argues now that the time for filing had passed and that MSC Shipping cannot fulfill its burden of showing the availability of the Chinese forum.

In addition to showing that Boskalis deliberately forfeited the alternative forum, MSC Shipping also filed affidavits and copies of Chinese statutes to show that the statute of limitations had not in fact expired in China at the time it filed its motion to dismiss. It recognized that the notice issued by the Chinese court required that claims be filed in the limitation of liability action by June 30, 2007, but it provided interpretations issued by the Supreme People's Court of China that have noted that as long as the statute of limitations in a civil case is not raised as a defense, the court will not raise the issue *sua sponte*. Provisions of the Supreme People's Court on Several Issues Concerning the Application of Statutes of Limitation During the Trial of Civil Cases (promulgated by the Supreme People's Court, Aug. 21, 2008, effective Sept. 1, 2008), art. 3. MSC Shipping also showed that Chinese legal scholars have noted that China's system is not a strictly statutory system and that judges are given sufficient leeway to effectuate a just outcome. *See* Feng Jinwei & Zhang Decai, Statute of Limitations: Law and Realty, China L. & Prac., Dec. 2000–Jan. 2001 (stating that "judge(s) will usually take into consideration the facts of the particular case when deciding whether to strictly enforce the time limits . . . . They do not believe it is fair to decide against the rights holder simply because it has failed to exercise its rights in time" and noting that attempts at settlements or mediation will often be considered sufficient to satisfy the statute of limitations).

While it is thus not clear whether a statute of limitations would have indeed barred Boskalis' claim against the limitation fund in China, the overriding fact in this case remains that Boskalis has *elected not to proceed in China*—presumably based on its assessment that it is unlikely to benefit substantially in doing so—and accordingly has *deliberately* allowed any deadline for filing claims there to pass. As counsel acknowledged candidly to the district court, Boskalis "made a reasoned decision after being notified that there was a limitation of liability proceeding instituted in the courts of China not to participate and let the statute of limitations run." And based on that acknowledgment, the district court found that Boskalis "knowingly and purposefully opted to miss the deadline for filing their claims in [China]" because Boskalis chose "not to participate in China." The district court therefore ruled that "[a] party should not be allowed to assert the unavailability of an alternative forum when the unavailability is a product of its own purposeful conduct."

We agree with the district court. In circumstances as these, a claimant should not be heard to complain that an available forum, having jurisdiction over the parties

in *Piper Aircraft*, the Supreme Court noted that even though Scottish law did not afford recovery to the plaintiffs based on strict liability, as did U.S. law, and even though the damages might be smaller, these differences did not indicate that a Scottish forum was an inadequate forum. An inadequate forum based on substantive law arises "where the alternative forum does not permit litigation of the subject matter of the dispute." *Id.* at 254 n.22. The Court summarized that a district court may reject an alternative forum as inadequate based on a difference in law *when the claimant "will be deprived of any remedy or treated unfairly." Id.* at 255 (emphasis added).

In this case, the Chinese forum provides a remedy, and moreover one that is completely analogous to the remedy provided by a U.S. forum *i.e.* affording the trial of claims made against a limitation fund—albeit computing the limitation fund through a different, but not necessarily less adequate method. If Boskalis were to succeed on its argument that the difference in the method of computing a limitation fund is an appropriate basis for finding inadequacy, it would have to conclude likewise that an admiralty court in The Netherlands, where it is based, and in most other seafaring nations would also not be adequate forums, inasmuch as The Netherlands maritime law, as well as the law of most other seafaring nations, applies the same method of computing the limitation fund as does the Chinese maritime law. *See* LLMC, 16 I.L.M. 606 (The Netherlands as signatory). Also, there is no indication that a Chinese admiralty court would treat Boskalis "unfairly." *See also Sinochem Int'l*, 549 U.S. at 432–36 (applying *forum non conveniens* doctrine in favor of a Chinese admiralty court).

We conclude that the district court did not abuse its substantial discretion in concluding that the District of South Carolina was not an appropriate forum in which to litigate the issues of liability and damages for a collision that occurred in China between ships owned by foreign corporations, particularly in view of its conclusion—which is supported by the record—that "[t]he United States has absolutely no connection to the events giving rise to this action."

We do, however, modify the district court's judgment to make it conditional on MSC Shipping's not raising or asserting a defense based on a statute of limitations or court-imposed deadline in response to any claim made by Boskalis against MSC Shipping in China. *See Calavo Growers of California v. Generali Belgium*, 632 F.2d 963, 968 n.6 (2d Cir. 1980) ("[I]t is advisable to make any dismissal conditional in nature").

V.

The increasingly integrated markets served by global shipping cry for an increasingly coherent application of maritime law for the resolution of maritime disputes. Just as maritime law grew dramatically during the Middle Ages with the new growth of international trade, to become a reasonably homogenous compilation of principles, so now maritime law demands refinement such that it becomes imbued in application with yet greater mutual respect of seafaring nations for each nation's application of maritime law. More than ever, parties need a system that responds predictably and fairly to maritime disputes arising from international shipping and trade. Thus, without hesitation, the Supreme Court deferred to the Guangzhou Admiralty Court in China to resolve a dispute over the legitimacy of a bill of lading that led to the arrest in China of a ship that carried steel coils from Philadelphia to China. Likewise, we readily affirm application of the doctrine of *forum non conveniens* in deference to the Tianjin Admiralty Court to resolve the liability and damages for a collision occurring in Chinese waters between ships of foreign nations when the Chinese authorities investigated the collision, the Chinese court arrested both ships involved to aid disposition of the claims made to that court, and no U.S. financial interests are directly implicated.

It will, at the same time, also become increasingly important to the U.S. justice system for district courts to exercise their jurisdiction with care when presented with suits between non-Americans over collisions that occur in foreign waters simply because the application of U.S. law is desired. U.S. courts should be ready to rely on their wide discretion and decline to exercise jurisdiction when doing so will avoid the danger of U.S. courts becoming a place for resolving a maritime dispute only because U.S. law might provide a more favorable outcome for one of the litigants. The circumstances of this case provide a prime example of when a U.S. court should show restraint. We accordingly affirm the judgment of the district court, subject to the condition we imposed in Part IV.

AFFIRMED AS MODIFIED

announce in its complaint that it would move to dismiss this action, it only reserved the right to do so. *See* MSC Shipping Compl. at P 20. Therefore, if the equities are at all relevant to determining whether MSC Shipping could move to dismiss its own action on *forum non conveniens* grounds, they do not appear to favor MSC Shipping.

III.

A.

Even assuming MSC Shipping could properly move to dismiss its own action on *forum non conveniens* grounds, the district court abused its discretion in granting MSC Shipping's motion because it did so without first concluding that an alternative forum was available at the time of its dismissal. *See United States v. Delfino*, 510 F.3d 468, 470 (4th Cir. 2007) ("A district court abuses its discretion when it . . . commits an error of law."). As noted above, both Supreme Court and Fourth Circuit precedents require a district court to determine that an alternative forum is available at the time of its decision before it can dismiss an action on *forum non conveniens* grounds. *Piper*, 454 U.S. at 254 n.22; *Kontoulas*, 745 F.2d at 315–16. Controlling case law also makes it clear that the party who moves for a dismissal on *forum non conveniens* grounds bears the "heavy burden of showing" that an alternative forum is available. *Kontoulas*, 745 F.2d at 316; *see also Sinochem*, 549 U.S. at 430 (stating that the defendant bears the "heavy burden"). As the majority acknowledges, an alternative forum is not available if, among other things, the statute of limitations in the alternative forum has expired. *Maj. Op.*, at 20; *see also Kontoulas*, 745 F.2d at 316.

Here, the parties dispute whether a statute of limitations or its equivalent rendered the Chinese forum unavailable at the time of the district court's ruling. According to Boskalis, the deadline for commencing or joining an action against MSC Shipping in China passed on June 30, 2007, which was before the district court's decision. In response, MSC Shipping argues that China does not always follow filing deadlines and therefore *might* permit Boskalis to join or commence an action against it notwithstanding the expiration of the June 30 deadline. *See* Appellees' Br. 26. However, Chinese maritime procedure law and the notices issued by the Tianjin Maritime Court support Boskalis's position. *See* J.A. 105, 326, 333–34. Thus, on this record, MSC Shipping clearly has not carried its heavy burden of showing that the Chinese forum was available at the time of the district court's decision. Therefore, Supreme Court and Fourth Circuit case law provide that this case cannot be dismissed on *forum non conveniens* grounds. *See Piper*, 454 U.S. at 254 n.22; *see also Kontoulas*, 745 F.2d at 315–16.

However, the majority does not require MSC Shipping to meet its burden. Instead, after noting the parties' differing positions with respect to the availability of the Chinese forum, the majority simply states that it is "not clear whether a statute of limitations would have indeed barred Boskalis' claim against the limitation fund in China." *Maj. Op.*, at 21–22. In other words, the majority finds that it is not clear whether MSC Shipping has carried its burden of showing the availability of the Chinese forum. Nonetheless, the majority affirms the district court's decision by adopting an exception to the *forum non conveniens* doctrine, holding that an alternative forum does not need to be available in this case because Boskalis could have joined the Chinese proceeding before the June 30 deadline expired. I do not agree with the majority that we should adopt and apply such an exception because, as noted above, both Supreme Court and Fourth Circuit case law clearly require that an alternative forum be available before a case can be dismissed on *forum non conveniens* grounds. *See, e.g., Piper*, 454 U.S. at 254 n.22; *see also Kontoulas*, 745 F.2d at 315–16. The majority's decision thus represents a dramatic change from current law.

In addition to being a required element of the *forum non conveniens* analysis, the availability requirement serves a vital purpose and thus should not be lightly discarded. The Supreme Court has repeatedly instructed that "federal courts have a strict duty to exercise the jurisdiction that is conferred upon them by Congress." *Quackenbush v. Allstate Ins. Co.*, 517 U.S. 706, 716, 116 S. Ct. 1712, 135 L. Ed. 2d 1 (1996); *see also Deakins v. Monaghan*, 484 U.S. 193, 203, 108 S. Ct. 523, 98 L. Ed. 2d 529 (1988) ("[T]he federal courts have a virtually unflagging obligation to exercise their jurisdiction." (quotation marks omitted)). The *forum non conveniens* doctrine represents one of the narrow exceptions to this general requirement because it allows a court to dismiss an action even if, as here, subject matter jurisdiction is entirely proper. *See Gulf Oil,* 330 U.S. at 504. However, one of the reasons why we can use the *forum non conveniens* doctrine to dismiss an action—even when we have jurisdiction—is because the doctrine's availability requirement helps ensure that a tribunal in some alternative forum will be able to address the merits of the parties' dispute. *See id.* at 504–09; *cf. Burford v. Sun Oil Co.,* 319 U.S. 315, 332–34, 63 S. Ct. 1098, 87 L. Ed. 1424 (1943) (stating that a state court's concurrent jurisdiction counsels in favor of abstention). Indeed, "if no other forum is available . . . it would be exceedingly harsh to dismiss for forum non conveniens." *Veba-Chemie A.G. v. M/V Getafix*, 711 F.2d 1243, 1248 (5th Cir. 1983).

B.

To the extent some courts have created a "bad faith" exception to the availability requirement—under which a party's conduct can eliminate the requirement that an alternative forum be available—and to the extent there is a suggestion that Boskalis's past conduct places this case within that exception, there is nothing in the record to support such a view. Both United States and Chinese law provided Boskalis with options for attempting to recover losses associated with the collision, and Boskalis simply elected not to pursue a remedy in China. Similar decisions are made by litigants all the time when they decide whether and where to commence an action, and this alone does not show any bad faith by Boskalis.

ANNICK JOELLE PIERRE-LOUIS
v.
NEWVAC CORPORATION

584 F.3d 1052 (11th Cir. 2009)
Decided October 8, 2009

Donald L. McCune, Jr., Mary Schivao, Motley Rice, LLC, Mt. Pleasant, SC, Lexi Hazam, Lieff, Cabraser, Heimann & Bernstein, San Francisco, CA, Jorge Emilio Silva, Silva & Silva, Coral Gables, FL, Philip D. Parrish, Phillip D. Parrish, P.A., South Miami, FL, for Appellants.

Alan I. Mendelsohn, Donald J. Kassilke, Sher & Blackwell, LLP, Washington, DC, Joseph Thompson Thornton, Beverly D. Eisenstadt, Thornton, Davis & Fein, PA, Miami, FL, John Shelton Penton, Jr., Cole, Scott & Kissane, P.A., West Palm Beach, FL, Henry M. Knoblock, Stephen Coxhead, Knoblock, Dohner, Kim & Copeland, South Miami, FL, for Appellees.

Thomas M. Bondy, Douglas N. Letter, Sharon Swingle, U.S. Dept. of Justice, Civ. Div., App. Staff, Washington, DC, for Amici Curiae, U.S.

Before BARKETT and HULL, Circuit Judges, and QUIST,* District Judge.

* Honorable Gordon J. Quist, United States District Judge for the Western District of Michigan, sitting by designation.

BARKETT, Circuit Judge:

This consolidated appeal arises from several wrongful death actions brought by the survivors of passengers killed in the crash of a McDonnell Douglas MD-82 aircraft, operating as West Caribbean Airways Flight 708, in the mountains of Venezuela. All of the appellants/cross-appellees, plaintiffs in the proceedings below ("Plaintiffs"), are natural persons and residents of Martinique, a Department of the Republic of France, and represent the deceased passengers of Flight 708.[1] The appellees/cross-appellants, defendants below ("Defendants"), are (1) West

1 The crew members of Flight 708 are not plaintiffs in this action and have filed a separate action in the Southern District of Florida.

[Chapter V], be subject to the rules of this Convention, the former for the whole of the carriage contemplated in the contract, the latter solely for the carriage which it performs."

In turn, Article 45 provides that a plaintiff may bring an action for damages under the Convention against the actual carrier or the contracting carrier, or against both together or separately, and Article 46 specifies the fora in which a plaintiff may bring such a suit. Article 46 provides that "[a]ny action for damages contemplated in Article 45 must be brought, at the option of the plaintiff, in the territory of one of the States Parties, either before a court in which an action may be brought against the contracting carrier, as provided in Article 33, or before the court having jurisdiction at the place where the actual carrier has its domicile or its principal place of business." The district court found that Newvac and/or Go 2 Galaxy was the "contracting carrier" for the flight at issue, and thus the lawsuit was filed in an appropriate forum pursuant to the Convention.[6]

The district court next found, however, that although it had jurisdiction, the Convention did not preclude application of forum non conveniens. In so holding, the district court relied on Article 33(4) of the Convention, which provides that "[q]uestions of procedure shall be governed by the law of the court seised of the case." The district court reasoned that because the doctrine of forum non conveniens is part of United States civil procedure, the Convention unambiguously permits its application in accordance with the law of the forum. The district court also concluded that the shared expectation of the states party to the Convention was that those states which recognized the doctrine could continue to apply it. We find no error in these conclusions.

When interpreting a treaty, we begin with the words of the treaty in the context in which the words are used. *Volkswagenwerk Aktiengesellschaft v. Schlunk,* 486 U.S. 694, 699, 108 S.Ct. 2104, 100 L.Ed.2d 722 (1988). Plaintiffs concede that the starting point of treaty interpretation is the relevant text and recognize that the treaty expressly provides that "[q]uestions of procedure" are governed by the law of the forum in which the case is validly brought. They argue, however, that because the Convention does not specifically affirm the availability of forum non conveniens, it should not be permitted in cases arising under it. We find this argument untenable for two reasons. First, there is no dispute that forum non

6 Newvac challenges this holding on cross-appeal. We find no merit to this contention. The district court properly concluded that because "Newvac knowingly assumed the responsibility to supply the aircraft and crew, and to otherwise conduct itself as a carrier, for the transportation of Globe Trotter's customers," it was a "contracting carrier" within the meaning of Article 39 of the Montreal Convention. The court correctly rejected Newvac's argument that because the actual passengers were not known to Newvac at the time it contracted with Globe Trotter, Newvac could not be a "contracting carrier" under the Convention. The Newvac-Globe Trotter contract clearly provided that Globe Trotter would procure passengers for the flights and tour packages that would be supplied by Newvac and that, once the passengers had been procured, Globe Trotter would forward their information to Newvac so Newvac could issue the relevant travel documents, including individual passenger tickets.

conveniens is a "question[] of procedure" under U.S. law and thus it clearly falls within the ambit of Article 33(4). Second, under Plaintiffs' theory, all state procedural rules would have to be specifically enumerated in order to be applicable under the Convention, and we do not believe the Convention's drafters intended such an absurd result.

Plaintiffs further argue that to permit the application of forum non conveniens would undermine the purpose and implementation of the Convention's jurisdictional provisions, which have already enumerated the five "convenient" jurisdictions for purposes of adjudicating international carrier liability. Although we acknowledge Plaintiffs' concerns, we think the purpose of the Convention is adequately safeguarded under traditional forum non conveniens analysis. As the district court pointed out, forum non conveniens would permit dismissal under the Convention only if the alternative forum was authorized to hear the case under Article 33(1) or (2) and was "demonstrably the more appropriate venue."

We therefore find no ambiguity or limitation in the express language of Article 33(4), which states in no uncertain terms that questions of procedure—which can only reasonably be read to include *all* questions of procedure—are governed by the rules of the forum state.[7] As the district court correctly noted, the doctrine of forum non convenience is "firmly entrenched in the procedural law of the United States." In addition, we are satisfied that a district court may—where appropriate—exercise its discretion to apply forum non conveniens, without interfering with the implementation of the Convention, so long as another Convention jurisdiction is available and can more conveniently adjudicate the claim.[8]

II.

Having found that the Convention is not a bar to the application of forum non conveniens, we turn to Plaintiffs' alternative argument that the district court abused its discretion in applying it here. As noted, a party seeking dismissal for forum non conveniens must demonstrate:

(1) that an adequate alternative forum is available,

(2) that relevant public and private interests weigh in favor of dismissal, and

---

7 The two cases on which Plaintiffs principally rely, Hosaka v. United Airlines, Inc., 305 F.3d 989 (9th Cir.2002), and Milor v. British Airways, Plc., [1996] Q.B. 702 (Eng.C.A.), are distinguishable and do not, as Plaintiffs suggest, create an ambiguity in Article 33(4). Among other distinguishing factors, both cases involved interpretation of the Warsaw Convention, a predecessor to the Montreal Convention drafted in 1929, at which time forum non conveniens, in its current form, was not recognized under U.S. law. Indeed, the Hosaka court explicitly noted that it was not addressing the applicability of forum non conveniens under the (at the time un-ratified) Montreal Convention.

8 Contrary to Plaintiffs' assertions, we think the drafting history of the Convention is clear that it was the shared intent of the states party that each state could continue to apply its procedural rules, including forum non conveniens.

cannot be implied in an action in Martinique nor that evidence pertaining to such third-party claims is not available in Martinique.[11] Although access to U.S. manufacturers' evidence is admittedly somewhat more difficult in a foreign forum as opposed to the United States, the district court did not abuse its discretion in finding that this burden—which is Defendants alone to bear in any event—was outweighed by the inconvenience to both parties of accessing damages evidence in Martinique, respecting over a hundred decedents and their beneficiaries.

Public interest considerations include factors such as (1) the forum's interest in entertaining the suit; (2) court congestion and jury duty generated by the lawsuit; (3) the desirability of having localized controversies decided at home; and (4) the difficulty in determining applicable law and applying foreign law. *La Seguridad,* 707 F.2d at 1307. The district court likewise did not abuse its discretion in determining that these factors weigh in favor of Martinique as the proper forum for Plaintiffs' claims.

As the district court pointed out, although the United States has an interest in deterring the alleged tortious conduct of Newvac and other U.S. third-party defendants, that interest is outweighed by Martinique's interest in adjudicating actions that aim to redress injuries to its citizens.[12] Moreover, any deterrent impact on Newvac is not eliminated merely because damages are determined in Martinique rather than in the United States. Therefore, the United States' interest in adjudicating Plaintiffs' claims does not justify the enormous commitment of time—both of the court and of jurors—and other judicial resources that would be consumed by the presentation of live testimony and documentary evidence in a foreign language.

---

that Plaintiffs' choice of forum would prejudice their ability to implead third parties, and the Supreme Court agreed that it was more convenient to resolve all claims in one forum. Here, of course, Defendants have proposed the alternative forum.

11 Plaintiffs argue that it is not their burden to demonstrate that evidence regarding third-party claims will be accessible in Martinique, Leon v. Million Air, 251 F.3d 1305, 1311 (11th Cir.2001), and that the district court impermissibly shifted the burden of persuasion to Plaintiffs to demonstrate why Martinique would be inconvenient to them. While it is true as a matter of law that Defendants bear the burden of persuasion on forum non conveniens, we are not persuaded by this argument. The district court's observation that Plaintiffs would not be inconvenienced by litigating third-party claims in Martinique did not impermissibly shift the burden to Plaintiffs but instead was simply one of many factors to be weighed in assessing the various private interests of the litigants. And, we agree with the district court that the relative ease of access to third-party evidence, unlike damages evidence, ultimately will be of concern only to Defendants.

12 Plaintiffs argue that Martinique has a state interest in ensuring that the rights of its citizens to their choice of forum under the Montreal Convention are respected. They further argue that the United States has a significant interest in deterring corporate misconduct like that of Newvac, which continues to act as a contracting carrier under U.S. laws. Again, while we acknowledge the competing public interests at work in this analysis, we do not believe the district court abused its discretion in crediting the undeniable interest of Martinique in redressing injuries to its citizens.

Finally, the district court found that although litigating third-party claims in Martinique would be more convenient in a U.S. forum than in Martinique, the burden of translation in Martinique with respect to these claims is not as great as the burden of presenting French damages evidence in the United States. This is so because the Martinique court designated to hear Montreal Convention claims does so in writing only and will not hear testimony. Thus, Defendants will not bear the burden of translating live testimony in Martinique as both parties would in the United States.[13]

In sum, the district court did not err in determining that the Montreal Convention does not preclude the use of forum non conveniens in U.S. courts nor did it abuse its discretion in dismissing Plaintiffs' claims on forum non conveniens grounds.

AFFIRMED.

---

13 We are not persuaded by Plaintiffs' argument that the district court erred in failing to consider the fact that Defendants made no argument that the congestion factor supports dismissal. The failure of Defendants to make an argument on this issue is not fatal to their forum non conveniens argument if, as the district court determined, other factors clearly support a dismissal.

non conveniens grounds. Vivendi S.A. is a French corporation. Vivendi Holding is a Delaware corporation.

Vivendi filed suit against Deutsche Telekom AG, T-Mobile International AG, T-Mobile Deutschland GmbH, T-Mobile USA, Inc. (collectively T-Mobile), and Zygmunt Solorz-Zak (Solorz) in the Western District of Washington, asserting a claim under the Racketeer Influenced and Corrupt Organizations Act, 18 U.S.C. § 1962, and a claim for common-law fraud. Deutsche Telekom, T-Mobile Deutschland, and T-Mobile International are German corporations. T-Mobile USA is a Delaware corporation with its principal place of business in Bellevue, Washington. Solorz is a Polish citizen.

FACTUAL AND PROCEDURAL BACKGROUND

The facts in this case, spanning ten years of European business transactions and litigation, could be difficult to follow. Therefore, we relate here only those facts essential to the disposition of this appeal.[3]

I. The Battle for Control of Polska Telefonia

In 1999, both T-Mobile Deutschland and Vivendi S.A. took an interest in the Polish wireless telephone company, Polska Telefonia Cyfrowa Sp. z o.o. (Polska Telefonia). At the time, Polish law precluded foreign investors from holding more than 49% of the shares of any Polish telecommunications company.[4] The German company T-Mobile Deutschland, which at the time held a 22.5% interest in Polska

---

Vivendi S.A. and Vivendi Holding, gave the parties notice that Vivendi Holding also intended to appeal.

Federal Rule of Appellate Procedure 3(c)(1)(A) mandates that the notice of appeal "specify the party or parties taking the appeal by naming each one in the caption or body of the notice, but an attorney representing more than one party may describe those parties with terms such as 'all plaintiffs,' 'the defendants,' 'the plaintiffs A, B, et al.,' or 'all defendants except X.'" Vivendi S.A.'s notice of appeal makes no mention of Vivendi Holding, and no Ninth Circuit case law holds that the CADS suffices to give notice of an intent to appeal.

However, the Supreme Court has held that courts should "liberally construe the requirements of Rule 3. Thus, when papers are technically at a variance with the letter of Rule 3, a court may nonetheless find that the litigant has complied with the rule if the litigant's action is the functional equivalent of what the rule requires." *Smith v. Barry*, 502 U.S. 244, 247, 112 S. Ct. 678, 116 L.Ed.2d 678 (1992) (holding that the filing of an opening brief within the time period for filing a notice of appeal could constitute notice of appeal). Here, the CADS was filed simultaneously with the notice of appeal, it listed Vivendi Holding as a plaintiff, and it refers to the principal issues the "plaintiffs" propose to raise on appeal. *Cf.* Fed. R. App.P. 3(c)(1)(A) (permitting a notice of appeal to identify the parties by referring to them collectively). Therefore, we grant Vivendi S.A.'s motion to add Vivendi Holding as an appellant.

3 Because this is an appeal from an order granting a motion to dismiss, the facts are taken from Vivendi's Third Amended Complaint.

4 The Polish government terminated this limitation in 2001.

Telefonia, acquired an additional 26.5% interest from other shareholders, for a total of 49%.

While T-Mobile Deutschland was buying up shares, so was Vivendi S.A., a French corporation. To facilitate its intended takeover of Polska Telefonia, Vivendi S.A. partnered with a Polish company, Elektrim S.A. Vivendi S.A. and Elektrim established a joint venture that operated through a holding company called Telco. Over time, Vivendi S.A. invested $2.5 billion to acquire a 51% interest in Telco. Pursuant to the joint venture agreement, Elektrim transferred its 37.1% interest in Polska Telefonia to Telco, along with an additional interest it acquired from other shareholders, for a total of 51% of the Polska Telefonia stock.

On December 7, 2000, T-Mobile Deutschland initiated arbitration against Elektrim in Vienna. T-Mobile Deutschland claimed that Elektrim's transfer of its shares to Telco materially breached Polska Telefonia's shareholder agreement.[5] The shareholder agreement bound all Polska Telefonia shareholders and provided certain shareholders, including T-Mobile Deutschland, the option to buy the shares of any shareholder who materially breached the agreement.

In 2003, while the arbitration was pending, Solorz purchased a controlling interest in Elektrim, which at the time held a joint venturer's interest in Telco's Polska Telefonia shares. Vivendi alleges that Solorz secretly agreed to help T-Mobile Deutschland gain control of Polska Telefonia. To this end, Elektrim terminated its joint venture agreement with Vivendi S.A. Vivendi S.A. and Elektrim, however, retained their joint ownership of Telco.

On November 26, 2004, the Vienna arbitration panel held that Elektrim's transfer of its shares to Telco was ineffective because Elektrim transferred its shares to Telco without the consent of all of the members of Polska Telefonia's Board of Directors, as required by the Polska Telefonia shareholder agreement. The panel further held that, if Elektrim did not recover its shares from Telco within two months, Elektrim would be in material breach of the shareholder agreement, thus triggering T-Mobile Deutschland's options to buy Elektrim's shares. A Warsaw Regional Court granted Elektrim's petition for recognition of the arbitral award.

Relying on this recognition order, T-Mobile Deutschland and Elektrim took over the Polska Telefonia management board. Elektrim and T-Mobile Deutschland then secured an order from the Warsaw Regional Court changing the Polish government's official share register to show Elektrim alone, and not Vivendi S.A., as the owner of the Telco shares.

In February 2005, Everest, a Miami-based company, purchased Elektrim bonds. By this time, however, Vivendi alleged Solorz used his controlling interest in

5 T-Mobile Deutschland alleged that the transfer of Elektrim's Polska Telefonia shares to Telco constituted a material breach of the shareholder agreement because the transfer violated Poland's limit on foreign ownership of telecommunications companies.

[4] The only allegations Vivendi asserts that connect this action to the United States are the use of "U.S. wires" in various conversations and e-mail exchanges between the parties and the appointment to Polska Telefonia's board of Thomas Winkler, the Chief Financial Officer of T-Mobile International, a German corporation, "who upon information and belief conducted business in the United States at T-Mobile USA's Seattle, Washington headquarters." Notably, Vivendi has alleged no facts that show that Winkler took any action from Seattle—or, for that matter, from anyplace else—specifically with respect to T-Mobile's allegedly fraudulent acquisition of Polska Telefonia. Instead, these allegations are incidental to the substance of Vivendi's complaint and involve only tenuous connections to the United States. These allegations do not establish plausibly that a U.S. entity participated in the alleged fraud and thus fail to show that the plaintiffs' fraud claims are connected to a U.S. business entity. *See Ashcroft v. Iqbal*, 129 S. Ct. 1937, 1949, 173 L.Ed.2d 868 (2009) ("To survive a motion to dismiss, a complaint must contain sufficient factual matter, accepted as true, to 'state a claim to relief that is plausible on its face.'" (quoting *Bell Atl. Corp. v. Twombly*, 550 U.S. 544, 570, 127 S. Ct. 1955, 167 L.Ed.2d 929 (2007))). Therefore, the district court did not err when it granted Vivendi S.A.'s choice of forum little deference.

[5] Likewise, the choice of forum of Vivendi S.A.'s American co-plaintiff, Vivendi Holding, deserves reduced deference because the district court found that Vivendi had engaged in forum shopping. Vivendi alleges that Vivendi Holding, as the assignee of Everest's purchase of Elektrim's bonds, was prevented from maximizing its interest in the Elektrim bonds. Everest's Elektrim bonds, however, are related only incidentally to the fraud Vivendi alleges T-Mobile and Solorz colluded to commit against Vivendi S.A. In short, Elektrim was required to pay bondholders, including Everest, an "equity kicker" equal to 25% of the net asset value of Elektrim in excess of 160 million euros. Solorz began stripping Elektrim's assets, however, which undermined the value of the equity kicker. The injunction issued by the bankruptcy court halted this asset-stripping and thus preserved the value of the equity kicker, but when Elektrim—fraudulently, so Vivendi alleges—sold its Polska Telefonia shares to T-Mobile Deutschland, the bankruptcy court lifted the injunction. Ultimately, Vivendi alleges only that, had Everest known about Elektrim's transfer of its Polska Telefonia shares and had T-Mobile Deutschland not issued misleading press releases over U.S. wires, "Everest would have blown the whistle on the withdrawal of the [Polish] bankruptcy petition."

[6] Most significantly, however, Vivendi Holding did not acquire Everest's Elektrim bonds and was not added as a plaintiff until after T-Mobile filed its first motion to dismiss for *forum non conveniens,* seven months after Vivendi S.A. originally had filed suit. Vivendi even concedes that Vivendi Holding acquired the Elektrim bonds for the purpose of, among others, strengthening its U.S. connections to the case.

Vivendi also stated it chose to file its action in the United States because the United States offers "proper discovery" and favorable law. The district court concluded that, because Vivendi was engaging in forum shopping, its choice of forum was entitled to little deference. A determination that a party is forum shopping turns on issues of that party's intent; it is a finding of fact to which we owe deference unless the trial court abused its discretion in making such a determination.

[7] We hold that such eleventh-hour efforts to strengthen connections with the United States allow the district court to reduce the deference due a plaintiff's choice of forum. As the Second Circuit explained,

> the more it appears that the plaintiff's choice of a U.S. forum was motivated by forum-shopping reasons—such as attempts to win a tactical advantage resulting from local laws that favor the plaintiff's case, the habitual generosity of juries in the United States or in the forum district, the plaintiff's popularity or the defendant's unpopularity in the region, or the inconvenience and expense to the defendant resulting from litigation in that forum—the less deference the plaintiff's choice of forum commands

Iragorri v. United Techs. Corp., 274 F.3d 65, 72 (2d Cir.2001) (en banc). In this case, Vivendi admitted that Vivendi Holding acquired Everest's bonds "in part to strengthen [Vivendi's] case." Given this concession and the actions Vivendi has filed across Europe, the district court did not abuse its discretion when it concluded that Vivendi was engaging in forum shopping by filing suit in the United States.[10]

[8] Therefore, the district court was within its discretion to grant little deference to the choice of forum of this foreign plaintiff.

II. Balance of Factors

[9] When considering a motion to dismiss for *forum non conveniens*, the district court must weigh the following private interest factors: "the ease of access to sources of proof; compulsory process to obtain the attendance of hostile witnesses, and the cost of transporting friendly witnesses; other problems that interfere with an expeditious trial . . .; and the ability to enforce the judgment." *Leetsch v. Freedman*, 260 F.3d 1100, 1103-04 (9th Cir.2001) (internal quotation marks, internal citations, and alterations omitted). The district court also must consider factors affecting the public interest, such as

> (1) administrative difficulties flowing from court congestion; (2) imposition of jury duty on the people of a community that has no relation to the litigation; (3) local

10 Of course, a suspicion that a plaintiff engaged in forum shopping does not obligate a district court to reduce the deference it pays to a plaintiff's choice of forum. A competent attorney, as part of his ethical obligation to represent his client with reasonable diligence, *see* Model Rule of Professional Conduct 1.3, is obligated to consider various fora and to choose the best forum in which to file a client's complaint. However, in a case like this, where the plaintiff already had filed dozens of actions in European courts and arbitration tribunals before adding a new plaintiff, admittedly (at least in part) to justify its choice of forum, and then commenced this action in a forum unrelated to the events underlying the alleged fraud, the district court did not abuse its discretion when it gave Vivendi's choice of forum less deference based on Vivendi's complex forum shopping.

III. PROCEDURE

3. Choice of Law/Conflict of Laws*

* Cases are indexed under this subject. The full text of these cases is published in the **volume**-page indicated.

I.

Petitioner, an inmate in New York's Attica Correctional Facility, commenced two § 1983 actions against several correction employees alleging that they violated his civil rights in connection with three prisoner disciplinary proceedings and an altercation. Proceeding *pro se*, petitioner filed his claims in State Supreme Court and sought punitive damages and attorney's fees. The trial court dismissed the actions on the ground that, under N. Y. Correct. Law Ann. § 24 (West 1987) (hereinafter Correction Law § 24), it lacked jurisdiction to entertain any suit arising under state or federal law seeking money damages from correction officers for actions taken in the scope of their employment. The intermediate appellate court summarily affirmed the trial court. 35 App. Div. 3d 1290, 826 N.Y.S.2d 542 (2006).

The New York Court of Appeals, by a 4-to-3 vote, also affirmed the dismissal of petitioner's damages action. The Court of Appeals rejected petitioner's argument that Correction Law § 24's jurisdictional limitation interfered with § 1983 and therefore ran afoul of the Supremacy Clause of the United States Constitution. The majority reasoned that, because Correction Law § 24 treats state and federal damages actions against correction officers equally (that is, neither can be brought in New York courts), the statute should be properly characterized as a "neutral state rule regarding the administration of the courts" and therefore a "valid excuse" for the State's refusal to entertain the federal cause of action. 9 N.Y.3d 481, 487, 881 N.E.2d 180, 183, 184, 851 N.Y.S.2d 84 (2007) (quoting *Howlett v. Rose*, 496 U.S. 356, 369, 372, 110 S. Ct. 2430, 110 L. Ed. 2d 332 (1990) (internal quotation marks omitted)). The majority understood our Supremacy Clause precedents to set forth the general rule that so long as a State does not refuse to hear a federal claim for the "sole reason that the cause of action arises under federal law," its withdrawal of jurisdiction will be deemed constitutional. 9 N.Y.3d, at 488, 881 N. E. 2d, at 184. So read, discrimination *vel non* is the focal point of Supremacy Clause analysis.

In dissent, Judge Jones argued that Correction Law § 24 is not a neutral rule of judicial administration. Noting that the State's trial courts handle all other § 1983 damages actions, he concluded that the State had created courts of competent jurisdiction to entertain § 1983 suits. In his view, "once a state opens its courts to hear section 1983 actions, it may not selectively exclude section 1983 actions by denominating state policies as jurisdictional." *Id.*, at 497, 881 N. E. 2d, at 191.

Recognizing the importance of the question decided by the New York Court of Appeals, we granted certiorari. 554 U.S. ___, 128 S. Ct. 2938, 171 L. Ed. 2d 863 (2008). We now reverse.

---

be the supreme Law of the Land; and the Judges in every State shall be bound thereby, any Thing in the Constitution or Laws of any State to the Contrary notwithstanding."

II.

Motivated by the belief that damages suits filed by prisoners against state correction officers were by and large frivolous and vexatious, New York passed Correction Law § 24.[3] The statute employs a two-step process to strip its courts of jurisdiction over such damages claims and to replace those claims with the State's preferred alternative. The provision states in full:

> "1. No civil action shall be brought in any court of the state, except by the attorney general on behalf of the state, against any officer or employee of the department, in his personal capacity, for damages arising out of any act done or the failure to perform any act within the scope of employment and in the discharge of the duties by such officer or employee.
>
> "2. Any claim for damages arising out of any act done or the failure to perform any act within the scope of employment and in the discharge of the duties of any officer or employee of the department shall be brought and maintained in the court of claims as a claim against the state."

Thus, under this scheme, a prisoner seeking damages from a correction officer will have his claim dismissed for want of jurisdiction and will be left, instead, to pursue a claim for damages against an entirely different party (the State) in the Court of Claims—a court of limited jurisdiction.[4] *See* N. Y. Const., Art. VI, § 9; N. Y. Ct. Clms. Law Ann. § 9 (West 1989) (hereinafter Court of Claims Act).

For prisoners seeking redress, pursuing the Court of Claims alternative comes with strict conditions. In addition to facing a different defendant, plaintiffs in that Court are not provided with the same relief, or the same procedural protections, made available in § 1983 actions brought in state courts of general jurisdiction. Specifically, under New York law, plaintiffs in the Court of Claims must comply with a 90-day notice requirement, Court of Claims Act § 9; are not entitled to a jury trial, § 12; have no right to attorney's fees, § 27; and may not seek punitive damages or injunctive relief, *Sharapata v. Town of Islip*, 56 N. Y. 2d 332, 334, 437 N.E.2d 1104, 1105, 452 N.Y.S.2d 347 (1982).

We must decide whether Correction Law § 24, as applied to § 1983 claims, violates the Supremacy Clause.

---

3 The New York Attorney General described Correction Law § 24 as "further[ing] New York's legitimate interest in minimizing the disruptive effect of prisoner damages claims against correction employees, many of which are frivolous and vexatious." Brief in Opposition 10; *see also Arteaga v. State*, 72 N.Y.2d 212, 219, 527 N.E.2d 1194, 1198, 532 N.Y.S.2d 57 (1988) ("In carrying out their duties relating to security and discipline in the difficult and sometimes highly stressful prison environment, correction employees . . . should not be inhibited because their conduct could be the basis of a damage claim").

4 Although the State has waived its sovereign immunity from liability by allowing itself to be sued in the Court of Claims, a plaintiff seeking damages against the State in that court cannot use § 1983 as a vehicle for redress because a State is not a "person" under § 1983. *See Will v. Michigan Dep't of State Police*, 491 U.S. 58, 66, 109 S. Ct. 2304, 105 L. Ed. 2d 45 (1989).

IV.

While our cases have uniformly applied the principle that a State cannot simply refuse to entertain a federal claim based on a policy disagreement, we have yet to confront a statute like New York's that registers its dissent by divesting its courts of jurisdiction over a disfavored federal claim in addition to an identical state claim. The New York Court of Appeals' holding was based on the misunderstanding that this equal treatment of federal and state claims rendered Correction Law § 24 constitutional. 9 N.Y.3d, at 489, 881 N. E. 2d, at 185 ("Put simply, because Correction Law § 24 does not treat section 1983 claims differently than it treats related state law causes of action, the Supremacy Clause is not offended"). To the extent our cases have created this misperception, we now make clear that equality of treatment does not ensure that a state law will be deemed a neutral rule of judicial administration and therefore a valid excuse for refusing to entertain a federal cause of action.

Respondents correctly observe that, in the handful of cases in which this Court has found a valid excuse, the state rule at issue treated state and federal claims equally. In *Douglas v. New York,* N. H. & H. R. Co., 279 U.S. 377, 49 S. Ct. 355, 73 L. Ed. 747 (1929), we upheld a state law that granted state courts discretion to decline jurisdiction over state and federal claims alike when neither party was a resident of the State. Later, in *Herb v. Pitcairn,* 324 U.S. 117, 65 S. Ct. 459, 89 L. Ed. 789 (1945), a city court dismissed an action brought under the Federal Employers' Liability Act (FELA), 45 U.S.C. § 51 et seq., for want of jurisdiction because the cause of action arose outside the court's territorial jurisdiction. We upheld the dismissal on the ground that the State's venue laws were not being applied in a way that discriminated against the federal claim. 324 U.S., at 123, 65 S. Ct. 459, 89 L. Ed. 789. In a third case, *Missouri ex rel. Southern R. Co. v. Mayfield*, 340 U.S. 1, 71 S. Ct. 1, 95 L. Ed. 3 (1950), we held that a State's application of the *forum non conveniens* doctrine to bar adjudication of a FELA case brought by nonresidents was constitutionally sound as long as the policy was enforced impartially. *Id.*, at 4, 71 S. Ct. 1, 95 L. Ed. 3. And our most recent decision finding a valid excuse, *Johnson v. Fankell*, 520 U.S. 911, 117 S. Ct. 1800, 138 L. Ed. 2d 108 (1997), rested largely on the fact that Idaho's rule limiting interlocutory jurisdiction did not discriminate against § 1983 actions. *See id.*, at 918, 117 S. Ct. 1800, 138 L. Ed. 2d 108.

Although the absence of discrimination is necessary to our finding a state law neutral, it is not sufficient. A jurisdictional rule cannot be used as a device to undermine federal law, no matter how evenhanded it may appear. As we made clear in *Howlett*, "[t]he fact that a rule is denominated jurisdictional does not provide a court an excuse to avoid the obligation to enforce federal law if the rule does not reflect the concerns of power over the person and competence over the subject matter that jurisdictional rules are designed to protect." 496 U.S., at 381, 110 S. Ct. 2430, 110 L. Ed. 2d 332. Ensuring equality of treatment is thus the beginning, not the end, of the Supremacy Clause analysis.

In addition to giving too much weight to equality of treatment, respondents mistakenly treat this case as implicating the "great latitude [States enjoy] to establish the structure and jurisdiction of their own courts." *Id.*, at 372, 110 S. Ct. 2430, 110 L. Ed. 2d 332. Although Correction Law § 24 denies state courts authority to entertain damages actions against correction officers, this case does not require us to decide whether Congress may compel a State to offer a forum, otherwise unavailable under state law, to hear suits brought pursuant to § 1983. The State of New York has made this inquiry unnecessary by creating courts of general jurisdiction that routinely sit to hear analogous § 1983 actions. New York's constitution vests the state supreme courts with general original jurisdiction, N. Y. Const., Art. VI, § 7(a), and the "inviolate authority to hear and resolve all causes in law and equity." *Pollicina v. Misericordia Hospital Medical Center,* 82 N. Y. 2d 332, 339, 624 N.E.2d 974, 977, 604 N.Y.S.2d 879 (1993). For instance, if petitioner had attempted to sue a police officer for damages under § 1983, the suit would be properly adjudicated by a state supreme court. Similarly, if petitioner had sought declaratory or injunctive relief against a correction officer, that suit would be heard in a state supreme court. It is only a particular species of suits—those seeking damages relief against correction officers—that the State deems inappropriate for its trial courts.[6]

We therefore hold that, having made the decision to create courts of general jurisdiction that regularly sit to entertain analogous suits, New York is not at liberty to shut the courthouse door to federal claims that it considers at odds with its local policy.[7] A State's authority to organize its courts, while considerable, remains

6 While we have looked to a State's "common-law tort analogues" in deciding whether a state procedural rule is neutral, *see Felder v. Casey*, 487 U.S. 131, 146, n. 3, 108 S. Ct. 2302, 101 L. Ed. 2d 123 (1988), we have never equated "analogous claims" with "identical claims." Instead, we have searched for a similar claim under state law to determine whether a State has established courts of adequate and appropriate jurisdiction capable of hearing a § 1983 suit. *See Testa v. Katt*, 330 U.S. 386, 388, 394, 67 S. Ct. 810, 91 L. Ed. 967 (1947); *Martinez v. California*, 444 U.S. 277, 283–284, n. 7, 100 S. Ct. 553, 62 L. Ed. 2d 481 (1980) ("[W]here the same *type* of claim, if arising under state law, would be enforced in the state courts, the state courts are generally not free to refuse enforcement of the federal claim" (emphasis added)). Section 1983 damages claims against other state officials and equitable claims against correction officers are both sufficiently analogous to petitioner's § 1983 claims.

7 The dissent's contrary view is based on its belief that "States have unfettered authority to determine whether their local courts may entertain a federal cause of action." *Post*, at ____, 173 L. Ed. 2d, at 937 (opinion of Thomas, J.). But this theory of the Supremacy Clause was raised and squarely rejected in *Howlett.* Respondents in that case "argued that a federal court has no power to compel a state court to entertain a claim over which the state court has no jurisdiction as a matter of state law." 496 U.S., at 381, 110 S. Ct. 2430, 110 L. Ed. 2d 332; *see also* Brief for National Association of Counties et al. as *Amici Curiae* in *Howlett* v. *Rose*, O. T. 1989, No. 89-5383, pp. 11–13 ("[S]tate courts are under no obligation to disregard even-handed jurisdictional limitations that exclude both state and federal claims"). We declared that this argument had "no merit" and explained that it ignored other provisions of the Constitution, including the *Full Faith and Credit Clause* and the Privileges and Immunities Clause, which compel States to open their courts to causes of action over which they would normally lack jurisdiction. *See* 496 U.S., at 381–382, 110 S. Ct. 2430, 110 L. Ed. 2d 332; *see also Hughes v. Fetter*, 341 U.S.

DISSENT

Justice Thomas, with whom The Chief Justice, Justice Scalia, and Justice Alito join as to Part III, dissenting.

The Court holds that New York Correction Law Annotated § 24, which divests New York's state courts of subject-matter jurisdiction over suits seeking money damages from correction officers, violates the Supremacy Clause of the Constitution, Art. VI, cl. 2, because it requires the dismissal of federal actions brought in state court under 42 U.S.C. § 1983. I disagree. Because neither the Constitution nor our precedent requires New York to open its courts to § 1983 federal actions, I respectfully dissent.

I.

Although the majority decides this case on the basis of the Supremacy Clause, *see ante*, at ____ – ____, 173 L. Ed. 2d, at 928–932, the proper starting point is Article III of the Constitution. Article III, § 1, provides that "[t]he judicial Power of the United States, shall be vested in one supreme Court, and in such inferior Courts as the Congress may from time to time ordain and establish." The history of the drafting and ratification of this Article establishes that it leaves untouched the States' plenary authority to decide whether their local courts will have subject-matter jurisdiction over federal causes of action.

The text of Article III reflects the Framers' agreement that the National Government needed a Supreme Court. There was sharp disagreement at the Philadelphia Convention, however, over the need for lower federal courts. Several of the Framers, most notably James Madison, favored a strong central government that included lower federal tribunals. Under the Virginia Plan, the Constitution would have established a "National Judiciary . . . to consist of one or more supreme tribunals, and of inferior tribunals to be chosen by the National Legislature." 1 Records of the Federal Convention of 1787, p. 21 (M. Farrand ed. 1911) (hereinafter Farrand). A revised version of the proposal, which stated that the National Judiciary would "'consist of One supreme tribunal, and of one or more inferior tribunals,'" was approved on June 4, 1787. *Id.*, at 95.

The following day, however, John Rutledge raised an objection to "establishing any national tribunal except a single supreme one." *Id.*, at 119. He proposed striking the language providing for the creation of lower federal courts because state courts were "most proper" for deciding "all cases in the first instance." *Ibid.* According to Rutledge, "the right of appeal to the supreme national tribunal [was] sufficient to secure the national rights [and] uniformity of Judgm[en]ts," and the lower federal courts were thus an "unnecessary encroachment" on the sovereign prerogative of the States to adjudicate federal claims. *Id.*, at 124. Madison nonetheless defended the Virginia Plan. He countered that "inferior [federal] tribunals . . . dispersed throughout the Republic" were necessary to meet the needs of the newly formed government: "An effective Judiciary establishment commensurate to the legislative authority [is] essential. A Government without a proper Executive [and] Judiciary would be the mere trunk of a body without arms or legs to act or move." *Ibid.* But despite Madison's objections, Rutledge's motion prevailed. *See id.*, at 125.

Madison and James Wilson soon thereafter proposed alternative language that "'empowered [Congress] to institute inferior tribunals.'" *Ibid.* This version moderated the original Virginia Plan because of the "distinction between establishing such tribunals absolutely, and giving a discretion to the Legislature to establish or not establish [inferior federal courts]." *Ibid.* Over continued objections that such courts were an unnecessary expense and an affront to the States, the scaled-back version of the Virginia Plan passed. *Ibid.*

On June 15, 1787, however, the New Jersey Plan was introduced. Although it did not directly challenge the decision to permit Congress to "institute" inferior federal courts, the plan, among other things, required state courts to adjudicate federal claims. *Id.,* at 125, 243. In particular, the plan provided that, except for cases of impeachment (over which the Supreme Court would have original jurisdiction), "all punishments, fines, forfeitures [and] penalties . . . shall be adjudged by the Common law Judiciar[ies] of the State in which any offence contrary to the true intent [and] meaning of [federal law] shall have been committed or perpetrated, with liberty of commencing in the first instance all suits [and] prosecutions for that purpose in the superior Common law Judiciary in such State, subject nevertheless, for the correction of all errors, both in law [and] fact in rendering judgment, to an appeal to the Judiciary of the U[nited] States." *Id.*, at 243, 244.

The introduction of the New Jersey Plan reignited the debate over the need for lower federal courts. In light of the plan's provision for mandatory state-court jurisdiction over federal claims, Pierce Butler "could see no necessity for such tribunals." 2 *id.,* at 45. Luther Martin added that lower federal courts would "create jealousies [and] oppositions in the State tribunals, with the jurisdiction of which they will interfere." *Id.*, at 45–46. But Nathaniel Ghorum responded that inferior federal tribunals were "essential to render the authority of the Nat[ional] Legislature effectual." *Id.*, at 46. Edmund Randolph bluntly argued that "the Courts of the States can not be trusted with the administration of the National laws." *Ibid.* George Mason suggested that, at the very least, "many circumstances might arise not now to be foreseen, which might render such a power absolutely necessary." *Ibid.* Roger Sherman also "was willing to give the power to the Legislature," even though he "wished them to make use of the State Tribunals whenever it could be done . . . with safety to the general interest." *Ibid.*

At the conclusion of this debate, the New Jersey Plan, including its component requiring state-court consideration of federal claims, was defeated and the Madison-Wilson proposal was delivered to the Committee of Detail, *see id.*, at 133. The Committee amended the proposal's language to its current form in Article III, which gives Congress the power to "ordain and establish" inferior federal courts.

22 U.S. 738, 9 Wheat. 738, 821, 6 L. Ed. 204 (1824); *see also Stearns v. United States*, 22 F. Cas. 1188, 1192, F. Cas. No. 13341 (No. 13, 341) (DC Vt. 1835) (Thompson, J.) (Article III does not give Congress authority to "compel a state court to entertain jurisdiction in any case; they are not inferior courts in the sense of the constitution; they are not ordained by congress. State courts are left to consult their own duty from their own state authority and organization"). "The states, in providing their own judicial tribunals, have a right to limit, control, and restrict their judicial functions, and jurisdiction, according to their own mere pleasure." *Mitchell v. Great Works Milling & Mfg. Co.,* 17 F. Cas. 496, 499, F. Cas. No. 9662 (No. 9,662) (CCD Me. 1843) (Story, J.). In short, there was "a very clear intimation given by the judges of the Supreme Court, that the state courts were not bound in consequence of any act of congress, to assume and exercise jurisdiction in such cases. It was merely permitted to them to do so as far, as was compatible with their state obligations." Kent 375; *see also id.*, at 377 (explaining that the Constitution "permits state courts which are competent for the purpose, and have an inherent jurisdiction adequate to the case, to entertain suits in the given cases").

Under our federal system, therefore, the States have unfettered authority to determine whether their local courts may entertain a federal cause of action. Once a State exercises its sovereign prerogative to deprive its courts of subject-matter jurisdiction over a federal cause of action, it is the end of the matter as far as the Constitution is concerned.

The present case can be resolved under this principle alone. New York Correction Law Annotated § 24, P1 (West 1987) (NYCLA) provides that "[n]o civil action shall be brought in any court of the state, except by the attorney general on behalf of the state, against any officer or employee of the department, in his personal capacity, for damages arising out of any act done or the failure to perform any act within the scope of the employment and in the discharge of the duties by such officer or employee." The majority and petitioner agree that this statute erects a jurisdictional bar that prevents the state courts from entertaining petitioner's claim for damages under § 1983. *See ante*, at ____, 173 L. Ed. 2d, at 927 (agreeing that "a prisoner seeking damages from a correction officer will have his claim dismissed for want of jurisdiction"); Brief for Petitioner 21 ("Every New York court must immediately dismiss such suits for lack of jurisdiction, regardless of merit"). Because New York's decision to withdraw jurisdiction over § 1983 damages actions—or indeed, over any claims—does not offend the Constitution, the judgment below should be affirmed.

II.

The Court has evaded Article III's limitations by finding that the Supremacy Clause constrains the States' authority to define the subject-matter jurisdiction of their own courts. *See ante*, at ____ – ____, 173 L. Ed. 2d, at 928–929. In particular, the Court has held that "the Federal Constitution prohibits state courts of general jurisdiction from refusing" to entertain a federal claim "solely because the suit is brought under a federal law" as a "state may not discriminate against rights arising under federal laws." McKnett *v. St. Louis & San Francisco R. Co.,* 292 U.S. 230, 233–234, 54 S. Ct. 690, 78 L. Ed. 1227 (1934). There is no textual or historical support for the Court's incorporation of this antidiscrimination principle into the *Supremacy Clause.*

A.

1.

The *Supremacy Clause* provides that "[t]his Constitution, and the Laws of the United States which shall be made in Pursuance thereof . . . shall be the supreme Law of the Land; and the Judges in every State shall be bound thereby, any Thing in the Constitution or Laws of any State to the Contrary notwithstanding." Art. VI, cl. 2. Under this provision, "[t]he laws of the United States are laws in the several States, and just as much binding on the citizens and courts thereof as the State laws are. . . . The two together form one system of jurisprudence, which constitutes the law of the land for the State." *Claflin*, 93 U.S., at 136–137, 23 L. Ed. 833; *see also Gregory v. Ashcroft*, 501 U.S. 452, 460, 111 S. Ct. 2395, 115 L. Ed. 2d 410 (1991); *Robb v. Connolly*, 111 U.S. 624, 637, 4 S. Ct. 544, 28 L. Ed. 542 (1884). Thus, a valid federal law is substantively superior to a state law; "if a state measure conflicts with a federal requirement, the state provision must give way." *Swift & Co. v. Wickham*, 382 U.S. 111, 120, 86 S. Ct. 258, 15 L. Ed. 2d 194 (1965). As a textual matter, however, the *Supremacy Clause* does not address whether a state court must entertain a federal cause of action; it provides only a rule of decision that the state court must follow if it adjudicates the claim. *See* R. Berger, Congress v The Supreme Court 245 (1969) (The *Supremacy Clause* only "'enacts what the law shall be'. . . . [I]t defines the governing 'supreme law,' and *if* a State court *has* jurisdiction, it commands that that law shall govern").

The Supremacy Clause's path to adoption at the Convention confirms this focus. Its precursor was introduced as part of the New Jersey Plan. *See* 1 Farrand 245 ("[A]ll Acts of . . . Cong[ress] made by virtue [and] in pursuance of the powers hereby . . . vested in them . . . shall be the supreme law of the respective States so far forth as those Acts . . . shall relate to the said States or their Citizens"); *ibid.* ("[T]he Judiciary of the several States shall be bound thereby in their decisions, any thing in the respective laws of the Individual States . . . notwithstanding"). But, as explained above, *see supra*, at ____ – ____, 173 L. Ed. 2d, at 934–935, the New Jersey Plan also included an entirely separate provision that addressed state-court jurisdiction, which would have required all federal questions to "b[e] determined in the first instance in the courts of the respective states." 3 Farrand 287. These two provisions of the New Jersey Plan worked in tandem to require state courts to entertain federal claims and to decide the substantive dispute in favor of federal law if a conflict between the two arose.

to complain" "until they refuse to exercise" the jurisdiction granted over federal claims).[5]

The supremacy of federal law, therefore, is not impugned by a State's decision to strip its local courts of subject-matter jurisdiction to hear certain federal claims. Subject-matter jurisdiction determines only whether a court has the power to entertain a particular claim—a condition precedent to reaching the merits of a legal dispute. *See Steel Co. v. Citizens for Better Environment,* 523 U.S. 83, 94, 118 S. Ct. 1003, 140 L. Ed. 2d 210 (1998) ("Without jurisdiction the court cannot proceed at all in any cause. Jurisdiction is power to declare the law, and when it ceases to exist, the only function remaining to the court is that of announcing the fact and dismissing the cause" (internal quotation marks omitted)). Although the line between subject-matter jurisdiction over a claim and the merits of that claim can at times prove difficult to draw, *see Arbaugh v. Y & H Corp.*, 546 U.S. 500, 513–515, 126 S. Ct. 1235, 163 L. Ed. 2d 1097 (2006), *see also Bell v. Hood,* 327 U.S. 678, 682, 66 S. Ct. 773, 90 L. Ed. 939 (1946), the distinction is crucial in the Supremacy Clause context. If the state court does not reach the merits of the dispute for lack of statutory or constitutional jurisdiction, the preeminence of federal law remains undiminished.

Accordingly, the superiority of federal law as a substantive matter does not trigger an obligation on States to keep their courts jurisdictionally neutral with respect to federal and state-law claims. "The federal law in any field within which Congress is empowered to legislate is the supreme law of the land in the sense that it may supplant state legislation in that field, but not in the sense that it may supplant the existing rules of litigation in state courts. Congress has full power to provide its own courts for litigating federal rights. The state courts belong to the States."

---

5 The majority contends that the Full Faith and Credit Clause and the Privileges and Immunities Clause support its view of the Supremacy Clause because each "compel[s] States to open their courts to causes of action over which they would normally lack jurisdiction." *Ante*, at ____, n. 7, 173 L. Ed. 2d, at 931 (citing *Howlett v. Rose*, 496 U.S. 356, 381–382, 110 S. Ct. 2430, 110 L. Ed. 2d 332 (1990)). But the majority has it backwards. The *Full Faith and Credit Clause* and the Privileges and Immunities Clause include a textual prohibition on discrimination that the Supremacy Clause lacks. See Art. IV, § 1 ("Full Faith and Credit shall be given in each State to the public Acts, Records, and judicial Proceedings of every other State"); Art. IV, § 2 ("The Citizens of each State shall be entitled to all Privileges and Immunities of Citizens in the several States"). The Framers' decision to address state-to-state discrimination in these two clauses without taking similar steps with respect to federal-state relations governed by the Supremacy Clause aligns with reasons given for abandoning the Articles of Confederation, see The Federalist No. 42, p. 292 (E. Bourne ed. 1947) (J. Madison) (describing the Full Faith and Credit Clause as "an evident and valuable improvement on the clause relating to this subject in the articles of Confederation"), and the principle of dual sovereignty that the Constitution preserves, *see Texas v. White*, 74 U.S. 700, 7 Wall. 700, 725, 19 L. Ed. 227 (1869). Accordingly, contrary to the majority's supposition, there are in fact strong "reason[s] to treat the Supremacy Clause differently," *ante*, at ____, n. 7, 173 L. Ed. 2d, at 931, from the Full Faith and Credit and Privileges and Immunities Clauses.

Brown v. Gerdes, 321 U.S. 178, 193, 64 S. Ct. 487, 88 L. Ed. 659 (1944) (Frankfurter, J., concurring).

2.

The Court was originally faithful to this conception of federal supremacy. In *Claflin*, the Court concluded that because the federal statute under consideration did not deprive the state court of jurisdiction, the state court was competent to resolve the claim. *See* 93 U.S., at 136–137, 23 L. Ed. 833 ("[R]ights, whether legal or equitable, acquired under the laws of the United States, may be prosecuted in the United States courts, or in the State courts, competent to decide rights of the like character and class; subject, however, to this qualification, that where a right arises under a law of the United States, Congress may, if it see[s] fit, give to the Federal courts exclusive jurisdiction"). But the Court was careful to also explain that the Constitution did not impose an obligation on the States to accept jurisdiction over such claims. *See id.*, at 137, 23 L. Ed. 833 (explaining that there "is no reason why the State courts should not be open for the prosecution of rights growing out of the laws of the United States, to which their jurisdiction is competent, and not denied"). The Constitution instead left the States with the choice—but not the obligation—to entertain federal actions. *See id.*, at 139, 23 L. Ed. 833 ("[W]here no direction is given [from Congress] on the subject, it was assumed, in our early judicial history, that the State courts retained their usual jurisdiction concurrently with the Federal Courts invested with jurisdiction in like cases").

Then in *Second Employers' Liability Cases*, 223 U.S. 1, 32 S. Ct. 169, 56 L. Ed. 327 (1912), the Court applied the rule set forth in *Claflin* and correctly rejected a Connecticut court's refusal to enforce the 1908 Federal Employers' Liability Act (FELA), 45 U.S.C. § 51 et seq. FELA neither provided for exclusive federal jurisdiction nor attempted to require state courts to entertain claims brought under it. *See* 223 U.S., at 54–55, 32 S. Ct. 169, 56 L. Ed. 327. Therefore, the statute was enforceable "as of right, in the courts of the States *when their jurisdiction, as prescribed by local laws, is adequate to the occasion.*" *Id.*, at 55, 32 S. Ct. 169, 56 L. Ed. 327 (emphasis added). Connecticut had not deprived its courts of subject-matter jurisdiction over FELA claims; thus, the state court's refusal to hear the claim was "not because the ordinary jurisdiction of the Superior Courts, as defined by the constitution and laws of the State, was deemed inadequate or not adapted to the adjudication of such a case." *Ibid.* Rather, the state court took the position that "it would be inconvenient and confusing for the same court, in dealing with cases of the same general class, to apply in some the standards of right established by the congressional act and in others the different standards recognized by the laws of the State." *Id.*, at 55–56, 32 S. Ct. 169, 56 L. Ed. 327.

The Court's reversal of such a decision is compatible with the original understanding of Article III and the *Supremacy Clause*. Because there was no question that the state court had subject-matter jurisdiction under state law to adjudicate the federal claim, *id.*, at 57, 32 S. Ct. 169, 56 L. Ed. 327, the Court correctly observed

ejected Connecticut's refusal to adjudicate the federal
ly noted, the "existence of the jurisdiction creates an
cise it, and that its exercise may be onerous does not
tion." *Id.*, at 58, 32 S. Ct. 169, 56 L. Ed. 327.

oyers' suggested that the *Supremacy Clause* could pre-
ed the local court of subject-matter jurisdiction over the
Second Employers' Court took exactly the opposite
'[W]e deem it well to observe that there is not here
ongress to enlarge or regulate the jurisdiction of state
on of the duty of such a court, when its ordinary juris-
al laws is appropriate to the occasion." *Id.*, at 56–57, 32

The Court again confronted this issue in *Douglas v. New York*, N. H. & H. R. Co., 279 U.S. 377, 49 S. Ct. 355, 73 L. Ed. 747 (1929). There, the Court considered whether a New York court was required to hear a claim brought under FELA. Unlike the Connecticut court in *Second Employers'*, however, the New York court did not have jurisdiction under state law to entertain the federal cause of action. 279 U.S., at 386–387, 49 S. Ct. 355, 73 L. Ed. 747. As a result, this Court upheld the state-court ruling that dismissed the claim. The Court explained that FELA did "not purport to require State Courts to entertain suits arising under it, but only to empower them to do so, so far as the authority of the United States is concerned. It may very well be that if the Supreme Court of New York [was] given no discretion, being otherwise competent, it would be subject to a duty. But there is nothing in the Act of Congress that purports to force a duty upon such Courts as against an otherwise valid excuse." *Id.*, at 387–388, 49 S. Ct. 355, 73 L. Ed. 747. In other words, because the New York court lacked subject-matter jurisdiction under state law, it was not "otherwise competent" to adjudicate the federal claim.

In sum, *Claflin, Second Employers'*, and *Douglas* together establish that a state court's inability to entertain a federal claim because of a lack of state-law jurisdiction is an "otherwise valid excuse" that in no way denies the superiority of federal substantive law. It simply disables the state court from adjudicating a claim brought under that federal law.

3.

It was not until five years after *Douglas* that the Court used the *Supremacy Clause* to strike down a state jurisdictional statute for its failure to permit state-court adjudication of federal claims. *See McKnett*, 292 U.S. 230, 54 S. Ct. 690, 78 L. Ed. 1227.

mpted to compel states to
eral Constitution prohibits
o solely because the suit is
n by the Alabama court is
ed. The plaintiff is cast out
y not discriminate against
. Ct. 690, 78 L. Ed. 1227.

ot be reconciled with the
onnecticut court in *Second*
lulge its own bias against
to hear a federal claim over
which it had subject-matter jurisdiction. Rather, like the New York court decision affirmed in *Douglas*, the Alabama court's dismissal merely respected a jurisdictional barrier to adjudication of the federal claim imposed by state law. The fact that Alabama courts were competent to hear similar state-law claims should have been immaterial. Alabama had exercised its sovereign right to establish the subject-matter jurisdiction of its courts. Under *Claflin* and its progeny, that legislative judgment should have been upheld.

Despite *McKnett*'s infidelity to the Constitution and more than a century of Supreme Court jurisprudence, the Court's later decisions have repeated *McKnett*'s declaration that state jurisdictional statutes must be policed for antifederal discrimination. *See, e.g., Testa v. Katt*, 330 U.S. 386, 394, 67 S. Ct. 810, 91 L. Ed. 967 (1947) ("It is conceded that this same type of claim arising under Rhode Island law would be enforced by that State's courts. . . . Under these circumstances the State courts are not free to refuse enforcement of petitioners' claim"); *Howlett v. Rose*, 496 U.S. 356, 375, 110 S. Ct. 2430, 110 L. Ed. 2d 332 (1990) ("[W]hether the question is framed in pre-emption terms, as petitioner would have it, or in the obligation to assume jurisdiction over a 'federal' cause of action, . . . the Florida court's refusal to entertain one discrete category of § 1983 claims, when the court entertains similar state-law actions against state defendants, violates the Supremacy Clause"). The outcome in these cases, however, can be reconciled with first principles notwithstanding the Court's stated reliance on *McKnett*'s flawed interpretation of the Supremacy Clause.[6]

---

6 Other decisions also have articulated this antidiscrimination principle. *See, e.g., Johnson v. Fankell*, 520 U.S. 911, 117 S. Ct. 1800, 138 L. Ed. 2d 108 (1997); *Missouri ex rel. Southern*

In *Testa*, the Court struck down the Rhode Island Supreme Court's refusal to entertain a claim under the federal Emergency Price Control Act. There was no dispute that "the Rhode Island courts [had] jurisdiction adequate and appropriate under established local law to adjudicate this action." 330 U.S., at 394, 67 S. Ct. 810, 91 L. Ed. 967, and n. 13. The Rhode Island court nevertheless declined to exercise that jurisdiction under its decision in *Robinson v. Norato*, 71 R. I. 256, 258, 43 A.2d 467, 468 (1945), which had relied on a "universally acknowledged" doctrine "of private international law" as a basis for refusing to adjudicate federal "penal" claims. Because the Rhode Island Supreme Court had invoked this common-law doctrine despite the existence of state-law statutory jurisdiction over the federal claims, this Court correctly ruled that the state court's "policy against enforcement . . . of statutes of other states and the United States which it deems penal, [could not] be accepted as a 'valid excuse.'" 330 U.S., at 392–393, 67 S. Ct. 810, 91 L. Ed. 967

Testa thus represents a routine application of the rule of law set forth in *Second Employers'*: As long as jurisdiction over a federal claim exists as a matter of state law, state-court judges cannot *sua sponte* refuse to enforce federal law because they disagree with Congress' decision to allow for adjudication of certain federal claims in state court. *See* 330 U.S., at 393, 67 S. Ct. 810, 91 L. Ed. 967 ("[A] state court cannot 'refuse to enforce the right arising from the law of the United States because of conceptions of impolicy or want of wisdom on the part of Congress in having called into play its lawful powers'" (quoting *Minneapolis & St. Louis R. Co. v. Bombolis*, 241 U.S. 211, 222, 36 S. Ct. 595, 60 L. Ed. 961 (1916)).[7]

R. Co. v. Mayfield, 340 U.S. 1, 71 S. Ct. 1, 95 L. Ed. 3 (1950); *Herb v. Pitcairn*, 324 U.S. 117, 65 S. Ct. 459, 89 L. Ed. 789 (1945); *Miles v. Illinois Central R. Co.*, 315 U.S. 698, 62 S. Ct. 827, 86 L. Ed. 1129 (1942). The outcomes in these cases nonetheless preserved state-court jurisdictional autonomy. In *Johnson* and *Herb*, the Court sustained the state-court dismissals of the federal claims as nondiscriminatory. *See Johnson, supra*, at 918–920, 117 S. Ct. 1800, 138 L. Ed. 2d 108; *Herb, supra*, at 123, 65 S. Ct. 459, 89 L. Ed. 789 . In *Mayfield*, the Court never decided whether the state court had jurisdiction over the relevant federal claim; rather, it remanded the case to the Missouri Supreme Court based on the state court's possibly erroneous interpretation of federal law at issue in that case. *See* 340 U.S., at 4–5, 71 S. Ct. 1, 95 L. Ed. 3. Finally, in *Miles*, the Court struck down a Tennessee decision that enjoined a citizen of that State from pursuing a FELA action in Missouri state court "on grounds of inequity." 315 U.S., at 702, 62 S. Ct. 827, 86 L. Ed. 1129. The Court correctly held that, so long as jurisdiction existed under Missouri law, the Tennessee court could not rely on its own notions of "inequity" to thwart the vindication of a federal right in state court. *Ibid.*

7 Despite suggestions to the contrary, *see ante*, at ____, 173 L. Ed. 2d, at 928; *Howlett v. Rose,* 496 U.S. 356, 110 S. Ct. 2430, 110 L. Ed. 2d 332 (1990), the Court's decision in *Bombolis*, 241 U.S. 211, 36 S. Ct. 595, 60 L. Ed. 961, which held that the Seventh Amendment does not require a unanimous jury verdict when federal civil claims are adjudicated in state court, provides no support for the antidiscrimination principle. As quoted above, the Court (in dicta) accurately summarized the holding of *Second Employers'*. *See* 241 U.S., at 222, 36 S. Ct. 595, 60 L. Ed. 961. The Court also reiterated that before a state court owes a duty to enforce federal law, it must have subject-matter jurisdiction over the claim under state law. *See id.*, at 221, 36 S. Ct. 595, 60 L. Ed. 961 ("[L]awful rights of the citizen, whether arising from

In *Howlett*, the Court likewise correctly struck down a Florida Supreme Court decision affirming the dismissal of a § 1983 suit on state-law sovereign immunity grounds. *See* 496 U.S., at 361, 375–381, 110 S. Ct. 2430, 110 L. Ed. 2d 332. The Florida court had interpreted the State's statutory "waiver of sovereign immunity" not to extend to federal claims brought in state court. *Id.*, at 361, 110 S. Ct. 2430, 110 L. Ed. 2d 332 (citing Fla. Stat. § 768.28 (1989)). According to the state court, absent a statutory waiver, Florida's pre-existing common-law sovereign immunity rule provided a "blanket immunity on [state] governmental entities from federal civil rights actions under § 1983" brought in Florida courts. 496 U.S., at 364, 110 S. Ct. 2430, 110 L. Ed. 2d 332. Based on this rule, the Florida Supreme Court affirmed the dismissal with prejudice of the § 1983 suit against the state officials. *See id.*, at 359, 110 S. Ct. 2430, 110 L. Ed. 2d 332; *see also Howlett v. Rose*, 537 So. 2d 706, 708 (Fla. App. 1989) (concluding that Florida's "common law immunity" rule barred "the use of its courts for suits against the state in those state courts").

No antidiscrimination rule was required to strike down the Florida Supreme Court's decision. Even though several Florida courts had concluded that the defense of sovereign immunity was jurisdictional, *see* 496 U.S., at 361, n. 5, 110 S. Ct. 2430, 110 L. Ed. 2d 332, "[t]he force of the *Supremacy Clause* is not so weak that it can be evaded by mere mention of the word 'jurisdiction,'" *id.*, at 382–383, 110 S. Ct. 2430, 110 L. Ed. 2d 332. That is, state courts cannot evade their obligation to enforce federal law by simply characterizing a statute or common-law rule as "jurisdictional"; the state law must in fact operate in a jurisdictional manner. No matter where the line between subject-matter jurisdiction and the merits is drawn, *see supra*, at ____, 173 L. Ed. 2d, at 940, Florida's "common law immunity" rule crossed it.

First, because the Florida Supreme Court had dismissed the § 1983 lawsuit with prejudice, its decision was on the merits. *Cf. Semtek Int'l Inc. v. Lockheed Martin Corp.*, 531 U.S. 497, 505, 121 S. Ct. 1021, 149 L. Ed. 2d 32 (2001) ("'With prejudice' is an acceptable form of shorthand for 'an adjudication upon the merits'" (quoting 9 C. Wright, A. Miller, & E. Cooper, Federal Practice and Procedure § 2373, p. 396, n 4 (1981))). Second, Florida's sovereign immunity rule violated the *Supremacy Clause* by operating as a state-law defense to a federal law. *See Martinez v. California*, 444 U.S. 277, 284, n. 8, 100 S. Ct. 553, 62 L. Ed. 2d 481 (1980) ("'[P]ermitt[ing] a state immunity defense to have controlling effect'" over

---

a legitimate exercise of state or national power . . . are concurrently subject to be enforced in the courts of the State or nation when such rights come within the general scope of the jurisdiction conferred upon such courts by the authority, State or nation, creating them"); *id.*, at 222, 36 S. Ct. 595, 60 L. Ed. 961 (explaining that state courts are "charged with the duty to safeguard and enforce the right of every citizen without reference to the particular exercise of governmental power from which the right may have arisen, if only the authority to enforce such right comes generally within the scope of the jurisdiction conferred by the government creating them").

a federal claim violates the *Supremacy Clause*). Resolving a federal claim with preclusive effect based on a state-law defense is far different from simply closing the door of the state courthouse to that federal claim. The first changes federal law by denying relief on the merits; the second merely dictates the forum in which the federal claim will be heard.

In the end, of course, "the ultimate touchstone of constitutionality is the Constitution itself and not what we have said about it." *Graves v. New York ex rel. O'Keefe*, 306 U.S. 466, 491–492, 59 S. Ct. 595, 83 L. Ed. 927, 1939–1 C.B. 129 (1939) (Frankfurter, J., concurring). And contrary to *McKnett*, the Constitution does not require state courts to give equal billing to state and federal claims. To read the *Supremacy Clause* to include an anti-discrimination principle undermines the compromise that shaped Article III and contradicts the original understanding of Constitution. There is no justification for preserving such a principle. But even if the Court chooses to adhere to the antidiscrimination rule as part of the *Supremacy Clause* inquiry, the rule's infidelity to the text, structure, and history of the Constitution counsels against extending the principle any further than our precedent requires. *Cf. United States v. Lopez*, 514 U.S. 549, 584–585, 115 S. Ct. 1624, 131 L. Ed. 2d 626 (1995) (Thomas, J., concurring); *see infra*, at ____ – ____, 173 L. Ed. 2d, at 948–952.

B.

Although the *Supremacy Clause* does not, on its own force, pre-empt state jurisdictional statutes of any kind, it may still pre-empt state law once Congress has acted. Federal law must prevail when Congress validly enacts a statute that expressly supersedes state law, *see Sprietsma v. Mercury Marine*, 537 U.S. 51, 62–63, 123 S. Ct. 518, 154 L. Ed. 2d 466 (2002); *United States v. Locke*, 529 U.S. 89, 109, 120 S. Ct. 1135, 146 L. Ed. 2d 69 (2000), or when the state law conflicts with a federal statute, *see American Telephone & Telegraph Co. v. Central Office Telephone, Inc.*, 524 U.S. 214, 118 S. Ct. 1956, 141 L. Ed. 2d 222 (1998); *Florida Lime & Avocado Growers, Inc. v. Paul*, 373 U.S. 132, 83 S. Ct. 1210, 10 L. Ed. 2d 248 (1963). NYCLA § 24 does not fall prey to either category of pre-emption.[8]

---

8 Because 42 U.S.C. § 1983 does not pre-empt NYCLA § 24, there is no need to reach the more difficult question of whether Congress has the delegated authority under the Constitution to require state courts to entertain a federal cause of action. *Compare Printz v. United States*, 521 U.S. 898, 907, 117 S. Ct. 2365, 138 L. Ed. 2d 914 (1997) (suggesting that Congress' authority in this regard was "perhaps implicit in one of the provisions of the Constitution [Article III, § 1], and was explicit in another [Article VI, cl. 2]"); Prakash, Field Office Federalism, 79 VA. L. REV. 1957, 2032 (1993) ("As a matter of original understanding, the Founding Generation understood that state courts could be commandeered to enforce federal law"), with *Prigg v. Pennsylvania*, 41 U.S. 539, 16 Pet. 539, 615, 10 L. Ed. 1060 (1842) (concluding that state courts could not "be compelled to enforce" the 1793 Fugitive Slave Act); Collins 45 (concluding as an original matter that "states did not have to accept unwanted federal civil and criminal judicial business, and that Congress could not compel them to do so").

First, federal law does not expressly require New York courts to accept jurisdiction over § 1983 suits. Under § 1983, any state official who denies "any citizen of the United States or other person within the jurisdiction thereof . . . any rights, privileges, or immunities secured by the Constitution and laws, shall be liable to the party injured in an action at law, suit in equity, or other proper proceeding for redress." The statute addresses who may sue and be sued for violations of federal law. But it includes no substantive command requiring New York to provide a state judicial forum to a § 1983 plaintiff. *See Felder v. Casey*, 487 U.S. 131, 158, 108 S. Ct. 2302, 101 L. Ed. 2d 123 (1988) (O'Connor, J., dissenting) ("Section 1983 . . . creates no substantive law. . . . Its purpose, as we have repeatedly said, 'was to interpose the *federal courts* between the States and the people, as guardians of the people's federal rights'" (quoting *Patsy v. Board of Regents of Fla.,* 457 U.S. 496, 503, 102 S. Ct. 2557, 73 L. Ed. 2d 172 (1982))). Like FELA, therefore, § 1983 does not "enlarge or regulate the jurisdiction of state courts." *Second Employers'*, 223 U.S., at 56, 32 S. Ct. 169, 56 L. Ed. 327.[9]

Second, NYCLA § 24 does not conflict with § 1983. *See Wyeth v. Levine*, 555 U.S. ___, ___, 129 S. Ct. 1187, 1210, 173 L. Ed. 2d 51, 76 (2009) (Thomas, J., concurring in judgment) (explaining that the Court has alternatively described the standard for conflict pre-emption as "physical impossibility" and "direct conflict" (citations omitted)). As explained above, Congress did not grant § 1983 plaintiffs a "right" to bring their claims in state court or "guarantee" that the state forum would remain open to their suits. *See id.*, at ___ , 129 S. Ct. 1187, 173 L. Ed. 2d 51 Moreover, Congress has created inferior federal courts that have the power to adjudicate all § 1983 actions. And this Court has expressly determined that § 1983 plaintiffs do not have to exhaust state-court remedies before proceeding in federal court. *See Patsy*, *supra*, at 516, 102 S. Ct. 2557, 73 L. Ed. 2d 172.

Therefore, even if every state court closed its doors to § 1983 plaintiffs, the plaintiffs could proceed with their claims in the federal forum. *See*, *e.g., Felder*, *supra*, at 160, 108 S. Ct. 2302, 101 L. Ed. 2d 123 (O'Connor, J., dissenting) ("Every plaintiff has the option of proceeding in federal court, and the Wisconsin statute has not the slightest effect on that right"). And because the dismissal of § 1983 claims from state court pursuant to NYCLA § 24 is for lack of subject-matter jurisdiction, *see supra*, at ____ – ____, 173 L. Ed. 2d, at 937, it has no preclusive effect on claims refiled in federal court, *see Allen v. McCurry,* 449 U.S. 90, 94, 105, 101 S. Ct. 411, 66 L. Ed. 2d 308 (1980) (requiring "a final judgment on the merits"

---

9 The history surrounding § 1983's enactment also supports this conclusion. *See Felder v. Casey*, 487 U.S. 131, 158, 108 S. Ct. 2302, 101 L. Ed. 2d 123 (1988)(O'Connor, J., dissenting) ("[T] he original version of § 1983 provided that the federal courts would have exclusive jurisdiction of actions arising under it. This fact is conclusive proof that the Congress which enacted § 1983 over 100 years ago, could not possibly have meant thereby to alter the operation of state courts in any way . . . . Abandoning the rule of exclusive federal jurisdiction over § 1983 actions, and thus restoring the tradition of concurrent jurisdiction . . . did not leave behind a pre-emptive grin without a statutory cat" (internal quotation marks and citations omitted)).

before a § 1983 would be barred in federal court under the doctrine of claim preclusion), and thus does not alter the substance of the federal claim. Any contention that NYCLA § 24 conflicts with § 1983 therefore would be misplaced.

The Court nevertheless has relied on an expansive brand of "conflict" pre-emption to strike down state-court procedural rules that are perceived to "burde[n] the exercise of the federal right" in state court. *Felder*, 487 U.S., at 141, 108 S. Ct. 2302, 101 L. Ed. 2d 123. In such cases, the Court has asked if the state-law rule, when applied "to § 1983 actions brought in state courts [is] consistent with the goals of the federal civil rights laws, or does the enforcement of such a requirement instead 'stand as an obstacle to the accomplishment and execution of the full purposes and objectives of Congress'?" *See id.*, at 138, 108 S. Ct. 2302, 101 L. Ed. 2d 123 (quoting *Hines v. Davidowitz*, 312 U.S. 52, 67, 61 S. Ct. 399, 85 L. Ed. 581 (1941)). There has been no suggestion in this case, however, that NYCLA § 24 is a procedural rule that must be satisfied in order to bring the § 1983 action in state court. *See supra*, at ____ – ____, 173 L. Ed. 2d, at 937; *infra*, at ____, 173 L. Ed. 2d, at 948; *see also ante*, at ____, n. 9, 173 L. Ed. 2d, at 932. As explained above, petitioner's claim was not procedurally deficient; the state court simply lacked the power to adjudicate the claim. *See supra*, at ____ – ____, 173 L. Ed. 2d, at 937. Thus, the *Felder* line of cases is inapplicable to this case.

But even if there were such a claim made in this case, the *Supremacy Clause* supplies this Court with no authority to pre-empt a state procedural law merely because it "burdens the exercise" of a federal right in state court. "Under the *Supremacy Clause*, state law is pre-empted only by federal law 'made in Pursuance' of the Constitution, Art. VI, cl. 2 —not by extratextual considerations of the purposes underlying congressional inaction," such as a desire to ensure that federal law is not burdened by state-law procedural obligations. *Wyeth*, 555 U.S., at ___, 129 S. Ct. 1187, 173 L. Ed. 2d 51 (Thomas, J., concurring in judgment). A sweeping approach to pre-emption based on perceived congressional purposes "leads to the illegitimate—and thus, unconstitutional—invalidation of state laws." *Id.*, at __, 129 S. Ct. 1187, 1217, 173 L. Ed. 2d 51, 85. I cannot agree with the approach employed in *Felder* "that pre-empts state laws merely because they 'stand as an obstacle to the accomplishment and execution of the full purposes and objectives' of federal law . . . as perceived by this Court." 555 U.S., at ___, 129 S. Ct. 1187, 1217, 173 L. Ed. 2d 51, 85

III.

Even accepting the entirety of the Court's precedent in this area of the law, however, I still could not join the majority's resolution of this case as it mischaracterizes and broadens this Court's decisions. The majority concedes not only that NYCLA § 24 is jurisdictional, but that the statute is neutral with respect to federal and state claims. Nevertheless, it concludes that the statute violates the *Supremacy Clause* because it finds that "equality of treatment does not ensure that a state law will be deemed a neutral rule of judicial administration and therefore a valid excuse for refusing to entertain a federal cause of action." *Ante*, at ____ – ____, 173 L. Ed. 2d, at 930. This conclusion is incorrect in light of Court precedent for several reasons.

A.

The majority mischaracterizes this Court's precedent when it asserts that jurisdictional neutrality is "the beginning, not the end, of the *Supremacy Clause* analysis." *Ante*, at ____ – ____, 173 L. Ed. 2d, at 930. As explained above, *see supra*, at ____ – ____, 173 L. Ed. 2d, at 938–946, "subject to only one limitation, each State of the Union may establish its own judicature, distribute judicial power among the courts of its choice, [and] define the conditions for the exercise of their jurisdiction and the modes of their proceeding, to the same extent as Congress is empowered to establish a system of inferior federal courts within the limits of federal judicial power." *Brown*, 321 U.S., at 188, 64 S. Ct. 487, 88 L. Ed. 659 (Frankfurter, J., concurring). That "one limitation" is the neutrality principle that the Court has found in the *Supremacy Clause*. *See id.*, at 189, 64 S. Ct. 487, 88 L. Ed. 659 ("The only limitation upon the freedom of a State to define the jurisdiction of its own courts is that . . . [it] must treat litigants under the Federal act as other litigants are treated" (internal quotation marks omitted)); *Herb v. Pitcairn*, 324 U.S. 117, 123, 65 S. Ct. 459, 89 L. Ed. 789 (1945) ("The freedom of the state courts so to decide is, of course, subject to the qualification that the cause of action must not be discriminated against because it is a federal one"). Here, it is conceded that New York has deprived its courts of subject-matter jurisdiction over a particular class of claims on terms that treat federal and state actions equally. *See ante*, at ____ – ____. ____ – ____, 173 L. Ed. 2d, at 925–926, 929–931. That is all this Court's precedent requires. *See supra*, at ____, ____ – ____, 173 L. Ed. 2d, at 937, 943.

The majority's assertion that jurisdictional neutrality is not the touchstone because "[a] jurisdictional rule cannot be used as a device to undermine federal law, no matter how even-handed it may appear," *ante*, at ____, 173 L. Ed. 2d, at 930, reflects a misunderstanding of the law. A jurisdictional statute simply deprives the relevant court of the power to decide the case altogether. *See* 10A C. Wright, A. Miller, & M. Kane, Federal Practice and Procedure § 2713, p. 239 (3d ed. 1998) ("If the court has no jurisdiction, it has no power to enter a judgment on the merits and must dismiss the action"); Restatement (Second) of Judgments § 11, p. 108 (1980) (defining subject-matter jurisdiction as a court's "authority to adjudicate the type of controversy involved in the action"). Such a statute necessarily operates without prejudice to the adjudication of the matter in a competent forum. *See supra*, at ____ – ____, 173 L. Ed. 2d, at 940–941. Jurisdictional statutes therefore by definition are incapable of undermining federal law. NYCLA § 24 no more undermines § 1983 than the amount-in-controversy requirement for federal diversity jurisdiction undermines state law. *See* 28 U.S.C. § 1332. The relevant law (state or federal) remains fully operative in both circumstances. The sole consequence of the jurisdictional barrier is that the law cannot be enforced in one particular judicial forum.[10]

As a result, the majority's focus on New York's reasons for enacting this jurisdictional statute is entirely misplaced. *See ante*, at ____ – ____, 173 L. Ed. 2d, at 929–930. The States "remain independent and autonomous within their proper sphere of authority." *Printz v. United States*, 521 U.S. 898, 928, 117 S. Ct. 2365, 138 L. Ed. 2d 914 (1997). New York has the organic authority, therefore, to tailor the jurisdiction of state courts to meet its policy goals. *See Fay v. Noia*, 372 U.S. 391, 466–467, 83 S. Ct. 822, 9 L. Ed. 2d 837 (1963) (Harlan, J., dissenting) ("The right of the State to regulate its own procedures governing the conduct of litigants in its courts, and its interest in supervision of those procedures, stand on the same constitutional plane as its right and interest in framing 'substantive' laws governing other aspects of the conduct of those within its borders").

It may be true that it was "Congress' judgment that *all* persons who violate federal rights while acting under color of state law shall be held liable for damages." *Ante*, at ____ – ____, 173 L. Ed. 2d, at 929. But Congress has not enforced that judgment by statutorily requiring the States to open their courts to *all* § 1983 claims. *See* n 8, *supra*. And this Court has "never held that state courts must entertain § 1983 suits." *National Private Truck Council, Inc. v. Oklahoma Tax Comm'n*, 515 U.S. 582, 587, n. 4, 115 S. Ct. 2351, 132 L. Ed. 2d 509 (1995). Our decisions have held only that the States cannot use jurisdictional statutes to discriminate against federal claims. Because NYCLA § 24 does not violate this command, any policy-driven reasons for depriving jurisdiction over a "federal claim in addition to an identical state claim," *ante*, at ____, 173 L. Ed. 2d, at 930, are irrelevant for purposes of the *Supremacy Clause*.

---

10 If by asserting that state law is not permitted to "undermine federal law," *ante*, at ____, 173 L. Ed. 2d, at 930, the majority instead is arguing that NYCLA § 24 is a procedural rule that too heavily "burdens the exercise of the federal right" in state court, *see Felder*, 487 U.S., at 141, 108 S. Ct. 2302, 101 L. Ed. 2d 123, its argument is equally misplaced. First, the majority concedes that NYCLA § 24 is not a state procedural rule. *See* ante, at ____, n. 8, 173 L. Ed. 2d, at 932. Second, applying the reasoning of *Felder* to a jurisdictional statute like NYCLA § 24 would overrule all of the Court's decisions upholding state laws that decline jurisdiction over federal claims, and would virtually ensure that in future cases, no state jurisdictional rule will be upheld as constitutional. By simply rendering a federal claim noncognizable in state court, a statute depriving a state court of subject-matter jurisdiction (even under the terms and conditions permitted by this Court's precedent) will always violate *Felder*'s command that a state rule must not undermine the "remedial objectives" of a federal claim, *see* 487 U.S., at 138, 108 S. Ct. 2302, 101 L. Ed. 2d 123. The jurisdictional statute also will unavoidably implicate *Felder*'s concern that a state rule should not inevitably produce a different outcome depending on whether a claim is asserted in state or federal court, *see ibid.* A state jurisdictional statute necessarily will result in a different outcome in state court, where it will cause dismissal of the federal claim, than in federal court, where that claim will be heard. It is for this reason that the Court has been careful to keep its examination of state jurisdictional statutes and state procedural rules in different categories.

This Court's decision in *Howlett* is not to the contrary. Despite the majority's assertion, *Howlett* does not stand for the proposition "that a State cannot employ a jurisdictional rule 'to dissociate itself from federal law because of disagreement with its content or a refusal to recognize the superior authority of its source.'" *Ante*, at ____, 173 L. Ed. 2d, at 928 (quoting *Howlett*, 496 U.S., at 371, 110 S. Ct. 2430, 110 L. Ed. 2d 332). As an initial matter, the majority lifts the above quotation—which was merely part of a passage explaining that a "State may not discriminate against federal causes of action," *id.*, at 372, 110 S. Ct. 2430, 110 L. Ed. 2d 332—entirely out of context. *Howlett*'s reiteration of *McKnett's* neutrality command, which is all the selected quotation reflects, *see* 496 U.S., at 372–373, 110 S. Ct. 2430, 110 L. Ed. 2d 332, offers no refuge to the majority in light of its concession that NYCLA § 24 affords "equal treatment" to "federal and state claims." *Ante*, at ____, 173 L. Ed. 2d, at 930.

Howlett instead stands for the unremarkable proposition that States may not add immunity defenses to § 1983. *See* ante, at ____, n. 5, 173 L. Ed. 2d, at 929 (explaining that *Howlett* held that "a Florida school board could [not] assert a state-law immunity defense in a § 1983 action brought in state court" because "the 'elements of, and the defenses to, a federal cause of action are defined by federal law'" (quoting 496 U.S., at 375, 110 S. Ct. 2430, 110 L. Ed. 2d 332)). A state law is not jurisdictional just because the legislature has "denominated" it as such. *Id.*, at 381, 110 S. Ct. 2430, 110 L. Ed. 2d 332. As the majority observes, the State's "invocation of 'jurisdiction'" cannot "trump" the "*Supremacy Clause* inquiry," *ante*, at ____ – ____, 173 L. Ed. 2d, at 931–932. The majority, therefore, is correct that a state court's decision "to nullify a federal right or cause of action [that it] believe[s] is inconsistent with [its] local policies" cannot evade the *Supremacy Clause* by hiding behind a jurisdictional label, *ante*, at ____, 173 L. Ed. 2d, at 928, because "the *Supremacy Clause* cannot be evaded by formalism," *ante*, at ____, 173 L. Ed. 2d, at 932. Rather, a state statute must in fact *operate* jurisdictionally: It must deprive the court of the power to hear the claim and it must not preclude relitigation of the action in a proper forum. *See supra*, at ____ – ____, 173 L. Ed. 2d, at 949–950. *Howlett* proved the point by striking down a state-law immunity rule that bore the jurisdictional label but operated as a defense on the merits and provided for the dismissal of the state court action with prejudice. *See* 496 U.S., at 359, 110 S. Ct. 2430, 110 L. Ed. 2d 332; *supra*, at ____ – ____, 173 L. Ed. 2d, at 945–046.

But the majority's axiomatic refrain about jurisdictional labels is entirely unresponsive to the issue before the Court—*i.e.,* whether NYCLA § 24 operates jurisdictionally. Unlike the Florida immunity rule in *Howlett*, NYCLA § 24 is not a defense to a federal claim and the dismissal it authorizes is without prejudice. *See* 9 N.Y.3d 481, 490, 881 N.E.2d 180, 186, 851 N.Y.S.2d 84 (2007) (explaining that "the Legislature did nothing more than exercise its prerogative to establish the subject matter jurisdiction of state courts" and that "litigants like plaintiff can use the federal courts to pursue section 1983 claims" against correction officers).

For this reason, NYCLA § 24 is not merely "denominated" as jurisdictional—it actually is jurisdictional. The New York courts, therefore, have not declared a "category" of § 1983 claims to be "'frivolous'" or to have "'no merit'" in order to "'relieve congestion'" in the state-court system. *See ante*, at ____ – ____, 173 L. Ed. 2d, at 929 (quoting *Howlett, supra*, at 380, 110 S. Ct. 2430, 110 L. Ed. 2d 332). These courts have simply recognized that they lack the power to adjudicate this category of claims regardless of their merit.

The majority's failure to grapple with the clear differences between the immunity rule at issue in *Howlett* and NYCLA § 24 proves that its decision is untethered from precedent. And more broadly, the majority's failure to account for the important role of claim preclusion in evaluating whether a statute is jurisdictional undermines the important line drawn by this Court's decisions between subject-matter jurisdiction and the merits. *See Marrese v. American Academy of Orthopaedic Surgeons*, 470 U.S. 373, 382, 105 S. Ct. 1327, 84 L. Ed. 2d 274 (1985) ("With respect to matters that were not decided in the state proceedings . . . claim preclusion generally does not apply where 'the plaintiff was unable to . . . seek a remedy because of the limitations on the subject matter jurisdiction of the courts'" (quoting Restatement (Second) of Judgments § 26(1)(c)(1982))); *see also Arbaugh*, 546 U.S., at 514–516, 126 S. Ct. 1235, 163 L. Ed. 2d 1097; *Steel Co.*, 523 U.S., at 94, 118 S. Ct. 1003, 140 L. Ed. 2d 210.

The majority's principal response is that NYCLA § 24 "is effectively an immunity statute cloaked in jurisdictional garb." *Ante*, at ____, 173 L. Ed. 2d, at 932. But this curious rejoinder resurrects an argument that the majority abandons earlier in its own opinion. *See* ante, at ____, n. 5, 173 L. Ed. 2d, at 929. The majority needs to choose. Either it should definitively commit to making the impossible case that a statute denying state courts the power to entertain a claim without prejudice to its reassertion in federal court is an immunity defense in disguise, or it should clearly explain why some other aspect of *Howlett* controls the outcome of this case. This Court has required Congress to speak clearly when it intends to "upset the usual constitutional balance of federal and state powers." *Gregory*, 501 U.S., at 460, 111 S. Ct. 2395, 115 L. Ed. 2d 410. It should require no less of itself.

At bottom, the majority's warning that upholding New York's law "would permit a State to withhold a forum for the adjudication of any federal cause of action with which it disagreed as long as the policy took the form of a jurisdictional rule" is without any basis in fact. *Ante*, at ____, n. 9, 173 L. Ed. 2d, at 932. This Court's jurisdictional neutrality command already guards against antifederal discrimination. A decision upholding NYCLA § 24, which fully adheres to that rule, would not "circumvent our prior decisions." *Ibid.* It simply would adhere to them.[11]

---

11 The majority also suggests that allowing jurisdictional neutrality to be the test "would create a blind spot in the *Supremacy Clause*" because a procedural rule that too heavily burdens a federal cause of action would be struck down as unconstitutional while "a State could express its disagreement with (and even open hostility to) a federal cause of action, declare a desire to

B.

The majority also incorrectly concludes that NYCLA § 24 is not a neutral jurisdictional statute because it applies to a "narrow class of defendants," *ante*, at ____, 173 L. Ed. 2d, at 929, and because New York courts "hear the lion's share of all other § 1983 actions," ante, at ____, 173 L. Ed. 2d, at 932. A statute's jurisdictional status does not turn on its narrowness or on its breadth. *See Arbaugh*, *supra*, at 515, n. 11, 126 S. Ct. 1235, 163 L. Ed. 2d 1097. Rather, as explained above, a statute's jurisdictional status turns on the grounds on which the state-law dismissal rests and the consequences that follow from such rulings. No matter how narrow the majority perceives NYCLA § 24 to be, it easily qualifies as jurisdictional under this established standard. Accordingly, it is immaterial that New York has chosen to allow its courts of general jurisdiction to entertain § 1983 actions against certain categories of defendants but not others (such as correction officers), or to entertain § 1983 actions against particular defendants for only certain types of relief.

Building on its assumption that a statute's jurisdictional status turns on its scope, the majority further holds that "having made the decision to create courts of general jurisdiction that regularly sit to entertain analogous suits, New York is not at liberty to shut the courthouse door to federal claims that it considers at odds with its local policy." *Ante*, at ____, 173 L. Ed. 2d, at 931. But whether two claims are "analogous" is relevant only for purposes of determining whether a state jurisdictional statute discriminates against federal law. This inquiry necessarily requires an evaluation of the similarities between *federal* and *state* law claims to assess whether state-court jurisdiction is being denied to a federal claim simply because of its federal character.

---

thwart its enforcement, and achieve that goal by removing the disfavored category of claims from its courts' jurisdiction." *Ante*, at ____, n. 8, 173 L. Ed. 2d, at 932. This is incorrect for at least two reasons. First, as explained above, a State may permissibly register its hostility to federal law only by subjecting analogous state-law claims to equally disfavored treatment. *See supra*, at ____ – ____, 173 L. Ed. 2d, at 943–944. Hostility to federal law is thus irrelevant under this Court's precedent—the *Supremacy Clause* is concerned only with whether there is antifederal discrimination. Second, the majority obscures important differences between procedural rules, like the notice-of-claim rule at issue in *Felder*, and neutral jurisdictional statutes like NYCLA § 24. Unlike a neutral jurisdictional statute, which merely prevents a state court from entertaining a federal claim, failure to comply with a state procedural rule will result in dismissal of a federal claim with prejudice. *See Felder*, 487 U.S., at 151, 108 S. Ct. 2302, 101 L. Ed. 2d 123 (explaining that the State's "outcome-determinative law must give way when a party asserts a federal right in state court"). Contrary to the majority's assertion, therefore, it is not that state courts with "unconstitutionally burdensome procedural rules did not go far enough"—it is instead that they went too far by placing an insurmountable procedural hurdle in the plaintiff's path that led to a judgment against him on the merits. *Ante*, at ____, n. 8, 173 L. Ed. 2d, at 932. As a result, the Court's assessment of whether a state procedural rule too heavily burdens a federal right does not have any bearing on the Court's continued adherence to the neutrality principle as the sole determinant in evaluating state-law jurisdictional statutes.

In contrast, the majority limits its analysis to state-law claims, finding discrimination based solely on the fact that state law provides jurisdiction in state court for claims against state officials who serve in "analogous" roles to the correction officers. *See ante*, at ____, 173 L. Ed. 2d, at 931. The majority's inquiry is not probative of antifederal discrimination, which is the concern that first led this Court in *McKnett* to find a Supremacy Clause limitation on state-court jurisdictional autonomy. Consequently, there is no support for the majority's assertion that New York's decision to treat police officers differently from correction officers for purposes of civil litigation somehow violates the Constitution. *See ante*, at ____, 173 L. Ed. 2d, at 930–031.

Worse still, the majority concludes that § 1983 claims for damages against "other state officials" are "sufficiently analogous to petitioner's § 1983 claims" to trigger a *Supremacy Clause* violation. *Ante*, at ____ – ____, 173 L. Ed. 2d, at 930–932, and n. 6. Under this reasoning, if a State grants its trial courts jurisdiction to hear § 1983 claims for damages against *any* state official, the State's decision to deny those courts the power to entertain some narrower species of § 1983 claims—even on jurisdictionally neutral terms—*a fortiori* violates the *Supremacy Clause*. The majority's assurance that its holding is applicable only to New York's "unique scheme" thus rings hollow. *Ante*, at ____, 173 L. Ed. 2d, at 932. The majority is forcing States into an all-or-nothing choice that neither the Constitution nor this Court's decisions require. *See FERC v. Mississippi*, 456 U.S. 742, 774, n. 4, 102 S. Ct. 2126, 72 L. Ed. 2d 532 (1982) (Powell, J., concurring in part and dissenting in part) ("It would not be open to us to insist on adjudication in a state court of a federal claim arising beyond the jurisdiction of the local court" (internal quotation marks omitted)).

Indeed, the majority's novel approach breaks the promise that the States still enjoy "'great latitude . . . to establish the structure and jurisdiction of their own courts.'" Ante, at ____, 173 L. Ed. 2d, at 930 (quoting *Howlett*, 496 U.S., at 372, 110 S. Ct. 2430, 110 L. Ed. 2d 332). It cannot be that New York has forsaken the right to withdraw a particular class of claims from its courts' purview simply because it has created courts of general jurisdiction that would otherwise have the power to hear suits for damages against correction officers. The *Supremacy Clause* does not fossilize the jurisdiction of state courts in their original form. Under this Court's precedent, States remain free to alter the structure of their judicial system even if that means certain federal causes of action will no longer be heard in state court, so long as States do so on nondiscriminatory terms. *See Printz*, 521 U.S., at 906, n. 1, 117 S. Ct. 2365, 138 L. Ed. 2d 914. (explaining that "the States obviously regulate the 'ordinary jurisdiction' of their courts"); *Johnson v. Fankell*, 520 U.S. 911, 922, n. 13, 117 S. Ct. 1800, 138 L. Ed. 2d 108 (1997) ("We have made it quite clear that it is a matter for each State to decide how to structure its judicial system"). Today's decision thus represents a dramatic and unwarranted expansion of this Court's precedent.

IV.

"[I]n order to protect the delicate balance of power mandated by the Constitution, the *Supremacy Clause* must operate only in accordance with its terms." *Wyeth*, 555 U.S., at ___, 129 S. Ct. 1187, 1206, 173 L. Ed. 2d 51, 72 (Thomas, J., concurring in judgment). By imposing on state courts a duty to accept subject-matter jurisdiction over federal § 1983 actions, the Court has stretched the *Supremacy Clause* beyond all reasonable bounds and upended a compromise struck by the Framers in Article III of the Constitution. Furthermore, by declaring unconstitutional even those laws that divest state courts of jurisdiction over federal claims on a non-discriminatory basis, the majority has silently overturned this Court's unbroken line of decisions upholding state statutes that are materially indistinguishable from the New York law under review. And it has transformed a single exception to the rule of state judicial autonomy into a virtually ironclad obligation to entertain federal business. I respectfully dissent.

RAFAL RUDNICKI
v.
WPNA 1490 AM

Case No. 04 C 5719, 2009 U.S. Dist. LEXIS 115236 (N.D. Ill. 2009)
Decided December 10, 2009

MEMORANDUM OPINION AND ORDER

REBECCA R. PALLMEYER, District Judge.

Plaintiff Rafal Rudnicki, a Polish radio news correspondent, accuses Defendants, a Chicago-area radio station and its owners, of committing copyright infringement by broadcasting Plaintiff's radio reports without his permission. Before the court are the parties' motions for summary judgment. Defendants move for summary judgment on all claims because, they contend, Plaintiff cannot establish a copyrightable interest in the reports or any measure of damages. Plaintiff moves for partial summary judgment on the issue of whether six specific recordings of Rudnicki's work—only a portion of the several broadcasts at issue in this case—were properly registered pursuant to the United States Copyright Act. 17 U.S.C. §101, et seq. The court also addresses Defendant's motion to strike certain affidavits.

BACKGROUND

Plaintiff Rudnicki is a Polish national residing in Brussels, Belgium. (Rudnicki Dep. 10/16/06, 11:4-10). At all relevant times, Rudnicki was a radio news correspondent covering European Union issues for RadioZET, a major Polish broadcast network. (Rudnicki Aff. ¶ 1, Ex. J to Pl.'s 56.1 Resp.; Def. 56.1 Resp. ¶ 7.) The parties dispute whether Rudnicki should be characterized as an employee of RadioZET, but they agree that Rudnicki and RadioZET entered into a "Cooperation Agreement" in 2003 that obligated Rudnicki to provide no less than 40 pieces of journalistic correspondence to RadioZET each month in exchange for reimbursement of healthcare and business expenses and remuneration in the amount of 120 Polish zlotych (the plural form of zloty) per piece of correspondence. (Def.'s 56 Stat. ¶ 12–14; Pl's 56.1 Resp. ¶ 12–14.)[1] In addition to his work on behalf of

1 A copy of the Cooperation Agreement, drafted in Polish, is in the record. The parties present the court with conflicting English translations, for which they offer contradictory interpretations.

RadioZET, Plaintiff also collaborated with and provided news reports to WNVR, a Chicago-area radio station, apparently with RadioZET's knowledge and consent. (Rudnicki Dep. 03/13/09, 142–44.) At least one of the reports Defendants allegedly infringed was prepared for WNVR by Rudnicki. (Def.'s 56 Stat. ¶ 34; Pl's 56.1 Resp. ¶ 34.)

Defendant WPNA 1490 AM ("WPNA") is a radio station based in Oak Park, Illinois that purports to serve a diverse audience of ethnic communities, including the large Chicago-area Polish community.[2] (Def.'s 56 Stat. ¶ 3-4.) WPNA is operated by Defendant Alliance Communications, Inc. ("Alliance"), a corporation which is organized under Illinois law and maintains its principal place of business in Illinois. (Def. 56 Stat. ¶ 3.) Both WPNA and Alliance are owned by Defendant Polish National Alliance ("PNA"), a fraternal insurance benefit association with its principal place of business in Illinois. (Def. 56 Stat. ¶ 2-4.)

In his initial complaint, Plaintiff alleged that, on 26 different occasions in 2004, WPNA broadcast audio recordings of Rudnicki's news reports during the station's morning show, which is broadcast from approximately 7:00 a.m. until 9:00 a.m. (Def.'s 56 Stat. ¶ 9; Pl's 56.I Resp. ¶ 9.) In support of his 2004 claims, Rudnicki submitted an affidavit stating that he listened to recordings of WPNA broadcasts provided to him by his attorney and identified 26 instances in which the recordings included his reports. (Rudnicki Aff. ¶ 4-11, Ex. J to Pl.'s 56.1 Resp.) Each of the reports had been first broadcast on RadioZET in Poland and made available on RadioZET's website. (*Id.* at ¶ ¶ 4, 8, 12.) According to Rudnicki, the reports played on WPNA were in Rudnicki's voice and reproduced verbatim, except for the elision of Rudnicki's sign-on and sign-off at the beginning and end of each report. (*Id.*) Rudnicki claims that he never gave anyone at WPNA permission to use or reproduce his reports. (*Id.* at ¶ 11.)

Plaintiff later amended his complaint to add 27 occasions in 2006 when, he alleges, WPNA again aired news reports by Rudnicki, again without his permission, this time on an afternoon news program hosted by Slawomiz Budzik. (Def.'s 56 Stat. ¶ 10; Pl's 56.1 Resp. ¶ 10.) In a deposition, Budzik testified that, though he did not recall specifically broadcasting Rudnicki's work on his show, Budzik did

---

(Ex. B Def 56 Stat.; Ex. H to Pl.'s 56.1 Resp.) The main area of dispute is the translation of § 5 of the agreement, titled "License," which describes the rights possessed by RadioZET and by Rudnicki in the news report recordings. Plaintiff's translation of this provision refers to RadioZET's ownership of "economic rights" in the recordings. Defendant's version translates the same provision as transferring primary "copyrights" to RadioZET. The parties agree that the Agreement does not contain an explicit territorial limitation on the designation of rights between the parties, but they differ on the significance of this lack of specificity. (Def.'s 56 Stat. ¶ 16; Pl.'s 56.1 Resp. ¶ 16)

2 With over one million residents claiming Polish ancestry, Chicago is often said to have a larger Polish population than any city other than Warsaw, Poland. The Polish language is spoken in neighborhoods throughout the city. *See* America the Diverse, USA TODAY WEEKEND MAGAZINE (May 15, 2005).

occasionally use material from RadioZET's website on the air because he believed this material was not copyrighted. (Budzik Dep. 28:6-15.)

In early September 2006, Rudnicki sought U.S. copyright protection for six of his reports. (Def. 56 Stat. ¶ 31; Pl's 56.1 Resp. ¶ 31.) The United States Copyright Office issued Rudnicki a Certificate of Registration on September 5, 2006. (Ex. 4, Pl's 56.1 Stat.) The certificate describes the copyrighted work as "News Reports and Analysis of Rafal Rudnicki" and lists Rafal Rudnicki as the author, performer, and copyright claimant of the work. (*Id.*) Attached to the certificate is a compact disc, which contains the Polish-language recordings of six news reports. (*Id.*) The certificate itself does not specify exactly which "news reports and analysis" it refers to nor does it identify the date the news reports were first recorded or broadcast. (*Id.*) There is no dispute between the parties, however, as to which of Rudnicki's reports were recorded on the disc that he deposited with the Copyright Office; the deposited reports concern events in the late summer of 2006, including (1) a story outlining the Polish Prime Minister's visit to Brussels, (2) a story on the commitment of European troops to Lebanon, (3) a story on state aid to Polish shipyards, (4) a story on meetings between the European Commission President and the Polish Prime Minister, (5) a story on the Polish Prime Minster's schedule while in Brussels, and (6) a story on security at European airports. (Ex. J, to Def's 56 Stat.; Ex. B to Ex. I to Def's 56 Stat.; Pl's 56.1 Stat. ¶ 10.) Rudnicki prepared and recorded the reports himself before sending them to RadioZET and WNVR. In five of the six deposited reports, Rudnicki refers to himself as a correspondent for RadioZET. (Ex. B to Ex. I to Def's 56 Stat.) In the remaining one, he refers to himself as a correspondent for a WNVR news show. (*Id.*) All of the reports pertain to information that was of public interest and import in Poland at the time of the initial broadcasts. (Def. 56.1 ¶ 32; Pl's 56.1 Resp. ¶ 8.) Rudnicki did not remember the exact date that each deposited report was composed and broadcast, but he believed they were all broadcast (either by RadioZET in Poland or by WNVR in Chicago) some time in August 2006. (Rudnicki Dep. 03/13/09, 25:10-14, 32:2-8.)

Complete copies of the allegedly infringing WPNA broadcasts, which were stored by the radio station on digital audio tapes (DAT), are not in the record. While it appears that both parties had unimpeded access to the relevant WPNA broadcast recordings at some point, the recordings are currently inaccessible. According to Alan Kearns, the technician that Defendants placed in charge of preserving the broadcast recordings, the only machine capable of playing the master DAT recordings ceased working during the course of this litigation. (Kearns Dep. 06/10/09, 9:13-23.) Kearns explained that the machine's loading mechanism malfunctioned and its electrical system was severely damaged by power glitches at WPNA's Oak Park facility. (*Id.* at 29–31.) There is no indication that either party has made any effort to obtain access to another machine capable of playing the master tapes or to produce full and complete copies of the master tapes in some other format.

In lieu of the original WPNA broadcast recordings, the parties present contradictory affidavits of persons claiming to have first-hand knowledge of the

DAT recordings. Defendants present the affidavit of Emily Lecszczynski, a PNA employee responsible for overseeing operations at WPNA. (Lecszczynski Aff.¶ 1, Ex. L to Def. 56 Stat.) Lecszczynski stated that she reviewed the DAT recordings and determined that none of the reports Rudnicki deposited with the Copyright Office "aired on WPNA 1490 on the times stated" in Plaintiff's amended complaint. (*Id.* ¶ 11.) Lecszczynski also reviewed 14 WPNA broadcasts copied from the DAT recordings by Plaintiff's attorneys prior to the machine malfunction. From that review, Lecszczynski reported, she determined that none of the WPNA broadcasts "matched" Rudnicki's deposited reports. (*Id.* at ¶ 14.) Lecszczynski further stated that she had never personally heard any recording of WPNA's afternoon news show in which Rudnicki's deposited reports appeared. (*Id.* ¶ 15). Attached to Lecszczynski's affidavit are discs containing copies of the broadcast recordings that she reviewed, six reports she acknowledges Rudnicki deposited with the Copyright Office, and 14 clips of WPNA broadcasts provided by Plaintiff's attorneys. (*Id.*, Ex.'s A, B, and C.)

In response, Plaintiff submitted the affidavit of Anna Roclawska, a legal assistant employed by Plaintiff's counsel. Roclawska stated that she also reviewed the original DAT recordings maintained by the Defendants and identified more than 40 occasions between late July 2006 and mid-October 2006 when Rudnicki's reports aired on WPNA's afternoon news program. (Roclawska, Aff. ¶ 1-8, Ex. J to Pl's 56.1 Resp.) Roclawska says the reports were in Rudnicki's voice and reproduced verbatim, except for the deletion of Rudnicki's sign-off. (*Id.* at ¶ 13.) According to Roclawska, recordings of the six reports that Rudnicki deposited with the Copyright Office aired during WPNA's afternoon news program on August 17, 18, 25, 28, 29 and 30, 2006. (*Id.* at ¶ 12.)

In May 2007, Plaintiff moved in limine to bar any argument that Rudnicki's 2006 works were not properly registered with the United States Copyright Office under 17 U.S.C. § 411. Plaintiff's motion effectively sought a declaration that the reports were properly registered and therefore appropriate bases for claims for statutory damages and recovery of attorney's fees. (Docket Entry 76.) In support of the motion, Plaintiff attached the certificate issued by the Copyright Office. He did not, however, attach the deposited disc, nor did he otherwise specify precisely which of Rudnicki's reports were deposited with the Copyright Office. (*Id.*) In his motion, Plaintiff argued that the registration certificate acted as a blanket registration for all of Rudnicki's works composed in the 90 days prior to his application. Judge Moran of this court rejected that contention and observed that

> at most, the only broadcasts that are registered and thus eligible for statutory damages and attorney's fees, are the six broadcasts that were submitted with the registration application. But, because plaintiff has submitted no evidence as to the identity of those six broadcasts, we cannot grant his motion with respect to those broadcasts.

Rudnicki v. WPNA 1490 AM, 580 F. Supp. 2d 690, 694 (N.D. Ill 2008).

Plaintiff now seeks summary judgment on the issue of whether the six broadcasts that were submitted to the Register of Copyrights have been properly registered. This time, Plaintiff presents the disc containing recordings of the six broadcasts and Defendants' apparent agreement on the contents of the disc, as demonstrated by Defendants' Rule 56 statement and exhibits. (Def. 56.1 ¶ 32; Ex. J, to Def's 56 Stat.; Ex. B to Ex. I to Def's 56 Stat.) For their part, Defendants move for summary judgment on all claims and seek to strike certain affidavits relied on by Plaintiff in opposition.

For the reasons explained here, the court grants Plaintiff's motion for partial summary judgment, grants Defendants' motion to strike, and reserves ruling on Defendants' motion for summary judgment.

DISCUSSION

I. Defendants' Motion to Strike

Before addressing the motions for summary judgment, the court turns to Defendants' motion to strike three affidavits relied on by Plaintiff. The contested affidavits are that of Anna Roclawska, who reviewed the DAT recordings for Plaintiff's counsel, and those of Malgorzata Moszczenska and Kimila Ceran, senior employees of RadioZET who describe the assignment of rights under Rudnicki's Cooperation Agreement with their network.

Defendants seek to exclude Roclawska's affidavit because she was never disclosed as a potential witness in accordance with FED.R.CIV.P. 26, and because Roclawska failed to attach copies of the WPNA radio broadcasts to her affidavit in accordance with FED.R.CIV.P. 56(e)(1). Plaintiff argues that Roclawska's statement is proper rebuttal testimony offered in response to the affidavit of Emily Lecszczynski and used to demonstrate the contents of the DAT recordings of the WPNA broadcasts.

The only complete and original recording of the relevant WPNA broadcasts—on which both Lecszczynski and Roclawska base their testimony—is in Defendants' possession. The original DAT recordings are being stored in a supply closet at a WPNA recording facility in Oak Park. (Kearns Dep. 5-6.) Both parties have had physical access to the DAT tapes, but the audio recordings have been effectively inaccessible since no later than June 2009 because the only available machine capable of playing the DAT recordings is broken. The recordings themselves are apparently intact and could be played if the machine were repaired or another machine were found. The motions and responses the court now considers were filed in August 2009, and it does not appear from the record that either party made an effort to repair the disabled machine or to obtain a replacement prior to filing.

Roclawska's affidavit sets forth the content of the DAT recordings she reviewed before the machine broke down. The need for disclosing Roclawska as a potential witness was understandably not anticipated by Plaintiff, as need for her affidavit presumably arose only after the unexpected inaccessibility of the original recordings. The court assumes the parties will ultimately find another method for presenting the original recordings should the case proceed to trial, obviating the need for Roclawska's testimony. In the meantime, Plaintiff's reliance on Roclawska's testimony is justified given the circumstances. The court's consideration of Roclawska's affidavit is also harmless to Defendants, who have had unlimited access to the original recordings since the initiation of this lawsuit and who would still have unimpeded access had they maintained or repaired the machinery needed to play the recordings. Offering the recordings as an exhibit to Roclawska's affidavit, as Defendants would require, would serve no purpose in light of the parties' current inability to play them. Roclawska's personal knowledge of the DAT recordings she heard is sufficient to establish their contents for purposes of the motions now before the court. The motion to strike her affidavit is denied.

Defendants next object to the affidavits of Malgorzata Moszczenska and Kimila Ceran, both senior RadioZET employees. (Ceran Aff. ¶ 1-3, Ex. C. Pl.'s 56.1 Resp.; Moszczenska Aff. ¶ 1-3, Ex. B. Pl.'s 56.1 Resp.) Neither Moszczenska nor Ceran were disclosed to Defendants as potential witnesses during discovery. Their affidavits have been produced now by Plaintiff to rebut Defendants' contention that Rudnicki transferred his copyrights to RadioZET and therefore lacks standing to bring this lawsuit. Both Moszczenska and Ceran state that the assignment of rights in Rudnicki's work to RadioZET under the Cooperation Agreement was limited to the country of Poland and that RadioZET was aware of and acquiesced in Rudnicki's collaboration with WNVR in Chicago. (Ceran Aff. ¶ 4-6, Ex. C. Pl.'s 56.1 Resp.; Moszczenska Aff. ¶ 4-6, Ex. B. Pl.'s 56.1 Resp.)

Plaintiff asserts that he did not initially intend to call anyone from RadioZET to testify and could not have anticipated Defendants' standing argument. Since Plaintiff offers the Ceran and Moszczenska affidavits only to rebut Defendants' standing theory, Plaintiff contends, his failure to disclose Moszczenska or Ceran did not run afoul of FED. R. CIV. P. 26(a). Whatever the merits of that argument, the court finds Defendants were adequately "on notice" prior to the close of discovery that Moszczenska and Ceran potentially had information that was pertinent to this matter. *See Gutierrez v. AT&T Broadband, LLC*, 382 F.3d 725, 732 (7th Cir 2004). In an October 2006 deposition, Rudnicki identified Moszczenska as his superior at RadioZET and Ceran as the person with whom he negotiated the terms of his Cooperation Agreement. (Rudnicki Dep. 10/16/06, 56:14-23, 37–38.) When Defendants elected to pursue their theory that Rudnicki contractually transferred his copyright to RadioZET, Defendants were well aware that Moszczenska and Ceran might have had knowledge of this matter. Although a party has a general duty to supplement its Rule 26(a) disclosures, it is not required to do so when information has "otherwise been made known to the other parties during the discovery process." FED.R.CIV.P.26(e)(1), (2); *see also David v. Caterpillar, Inc.*, 324 F.3d 851, 856 (7th Cir. 2003). That test is met here: for many months,

Defendants have known the identity of Moszczenska and Ceran and what they are likely to know about Rudnicki's relationship with RadioZET. Accordingly, the court declines to strike the affidavits of Moszczenska or Ceran on this basis.

In the alternative, Defendants seek to exclude certain paragraphs of the Moszczenska and Ceran affidavits because they are not based on personal knowledge, are conclusory, or constitute hearsay.[3] Two paragraphs, which are identical in both affidavits, specifically purport to characterize the legal meaning of the Cooperation Agreement and RadioZET's knowledge with regard to that agreement. The parties agree that the Cooperation Agreement itself does not include any explicit limitation of its application to the territory of Poland. The affiants assert, however, that (1) "[a]t all relevant times, Rafal Rudnicki's contract with RadioZET was limited to the country of Poland," and (2) "RadioZET was always aware and had knowledge that Rafal Rudnicki had the right to his works, including works provided to RadioZET, in any country or location outside Poland." (Ceran Aff. ¶ 4-5, Ex. C. Pl.'s 56.1 Resp.; Moszczenska Aff. ¶ 4-5, Ex. B. Pl.'s 56.1 Resp.)

Though Moszczenska and Ceran are senior employees of RadioZET, neither one was a signatory to the Cooperation Agreement and neither one sets out any facts in her affidavit that supports her interpretation of the contract. Neither affidavit describes what role, if any, either affiant played in drafting or negotiating the contract. Instead, both attest to "administering" the contract, which the court supposes to mean only that the affiants oversaw Rudnicki's performance of his obligations. (Ceran Aff. ¶ 3, Ex. C. Pl.'s 56.1 Resp.; Moszczenska Aff. ¶ 3, Ex. B. Pl.'s 56.1 Resp.)

"A supporting or opposing affidavit must be made on personal knowledge, set out facts that would be admissible in evidence, and show the affiant is competent to testify on the matters stated." FED. R. CIV. P. 56(e). Although personal knowledge may include reasonable inferences, those inferences must be "grounded in observations or other first-hand personal experience. They must not be flights of fancy, speculations, hunches, intuitions, or rumors about matters remote from that experience." *Visser v. Packer Eng'g Assoc.*, 924 F.2d 655, 659 (7th Cir. 1991)(en banc). If Moszczenska and Ceran have any personal knowledge or experience that permits them to interpret the contract or that supports an inference as to how RadioZET understands its contractual entitlements, they have failed to sufficiently attest to that knowledge in their affidavits. Accordingly, the court grants Defendants'

3 Defendants also seek to strike the paragraphs because the affidavits fail to attach a sworn copy of the agreement. This objection has no merit. Sworn copies of the Agreement, drafted in Polish, are in the record. (Ex. G to Pl.'s 56.1 Resp.; Ex. B1 to Def.'s 56 Stat.) The parties' dueling interpretations of the agreement derive, in part, from their contradictory English translations. Presumably, Moszczenska and Ceran speak Polish and their understanding of the agreement is derived from the Polish version, which is not in dispute and which is already part of the record.

motion in part. Paragraphs four and five of both the Moszczenska and Ceran affidavits will be stricken from the record.

Paragraph six, which is also identical in both affidavits, is another matter, however. That paragraph describes RadioZET's awareness of Rudnicki's association with a United States broadcasting entity (WNVR). As Rudnicki's supervisors, Moszczenska and Ceran would have personal knowledge of what information was available to RadioZET and how RadioZET administered and enforced its Cooperation Agreement with Rudnicki. Defendants' objection to paragraph six is overruled.

Defendants' motion to strike is granted with respect to paragraphs four and five of the affidavits from Moszczenska and Ceran and otherwise denied.

II. Summary Judgment Standard

Summary judgment "should be rendered if the pleadings, the discovery and disclosure materials on file, and any affidavits show that there is no genuine issue as to any material fact and that the moving party is entitled to judgment as a matter of law." FED. R. Civ. P. 56(c); *Celotex Corp. v. Catrett*, 477 U.S. 317, 322 (1986); *Jackson v. Kotter*, 541 F.3d 688, 697 (7th Cir. 2008). In determining whether a genuine issue of material fact exists, a court must consider the evidence in the light most favorable to the nonmoving party. *Lee v. Young*, 533 F.3d 505, 509 (7th Cir. 2008); *Adickes v. S.H Kress & Co.*, 398 U.S. 144, 157 (1970). At the same time, a party opposing summary judgment must present evidence from which the jury could reasonably find for the non-moving party. *Rozskowiak v. Village of Arlington Hts.*, 415 F.3d 608, 612 (7th Cir. 2005)(and cases cited therein). When considering dueling motions for summary judgment, the court requires each movant to satisfy FED. R. Civ. P. 56's requirements to prevail on its motion. *Int'l Bhd. of Elec. Workers, Local 176 v. Balmoral Racing Club, Inc.*, 293 F.3d 402, 404 (7th Cir. 2002).

III. Choice of Law

This case involves journalistic works by a Polish national that were created in Belgium, broadcast in Poland, and allegedly infringed in the United States. The Berne Convention, 1986 U.S.T. 160, to which the United States, Poland, and Belgium are all signatories, applies to international copyright protections. Under the Convention, the law of the signatory country with the closest relationship to the international work at issue governs determination of copyright ownership. *Itar-Tass Russian News Agency v. Russian Kurier, Inc.*, 153 F.3d 82, 90–91 (2nd Cir. 1998). In this case, the parties agree that Poland is the country with the closest relationship to the news reports; though he resides in Belgium, the author is a Polish national, and the works were first broadcast and intended for public consumption in Poland. The relevant law governing ownership rights, therefore, is Poland's Law on Copyright and Related Rights of February 4, 1994 (hereafter referred to as "Poland's Copyright Law"). The definitive English translation of Poland's Copyright Law, and the one on which the court relies for purposes of this decision, is found on the website of the United Nations Educational, Scientific, and Cultural Organization (UNESCO).[4] For infringement issues, such as the scope of protection or recovery, the relevant law is that of the country where the alleged infringement occurred. *Itar-Tass Russian News Agency*, 153 F.3d at 91–92. Thus, in this case, the United States Copyright Act governs infringement issues.

IV. Ownership of News Under Polish Law

Defendants first argue for the dismissal of all claims because, they contend, Poland's Copyright Law does not protect Rudnicki's news reports. There is no factual dispute that the reports in question include information that was of public interest and import in Poland. On this basis, Defendants contend, Article 4 of Poland's Copyright Law precludes Rudnicki's claimed ownership interest. Article 4 reads: "The copyright shall not cover . . . simple press information."

In the court's view, Defendants read the provision too broadly. The exemption of "simple press information" is not a blanket exemption that precludes any copyright protection for news reports. Rather, the court reads this provision as consistent with similar provisions in both the United States Copyright Act, 17 U.S.C. §102(b),[5]and the Berne Convention, Art. 2(8).[6] These provisions are commonly interpreted to exclude raw facts from copyright protection while preserving protections for the manner in which the facts are presented. As one commentator has observed: "Under both American copyright law and international copyright agreements, the 'news of the day' belongs to the public. Once that 'news' is communicated, however, American law provides that copyright subsists in the expression that embodies the news." Eric Easton, *Who Owns 'the First Draft of History?': Reconsidering Copyright in News, 27 Colum.* J. L. & Arts 521, 524 (2004).

In short, copyright protection does not extend to raw facts themselves, but does extend to certain expressions and arrangements of facts. *Cf. Feist Publ'ns, Inc. v.*

---

4 The parties have presented the court with inconsistent English translations of the relevant Polish law. Under the circumstances, the court believes the UNESCO translation is the most reliable version available. The court therefore disregards the parties' versions. The full UNESCO translation is available at: http://portal.unesco.org/culture/en/files/30304/11420011803pl_copyright_2005_en.pdf/pl_copyright_2005_en.pdf (last visited on Dec. 9, 2009).

5 17 U.S.C. §102(b) provides that, "[i]n no case does copyright protection . . . extend to any idea, procedure, process, system, method of operation, concept, principle, or discovery . . ." News, in the abstract, meaning the raw information that makes up the news, has been held to be encompassed by this provision. *See Harper & Row Publishers, Inc. v. Nation Enters.*, 471 U.S. 539, 557 (1985).

6 Art. 2(8) of the Berne Convention excludes "news of the day" and "miscellaneous facts having the character of mere items of press information."

Rural Tel. Serv. Co., 499 U.S. 340, 347–48 (holding that, while facts are part of the public domain, only a "minimal degree of creativity" in selection and arrangement is necessary for copyright protection). Defendants have not explained why this court should interpret Poland's Copyright Law to substantially deviate from this generally-recognized principle. Whether Rudnicki's work is sufficiently original and creative to warrant protection under the laws of Poland and the United States is disputed.

Defendant's contention that Article 4 of Poland's Copyright Law contains a blanket exclusion of all news-related material is further belied by Article 25 of the law, which specifically addresses the rights of the press. Article 25 reads, in part: "It shall be permitted, for informative purposes, to disseminate through the press, radio and television the materials . . . which have been already disseminated . . . [including] (a) reports on current events, [and] (b) updates on political, economic or religious issues, unless further dissemination thereof has been expressly prohibited . . . " While the language outlining reproduction of press reports is permissive, Article 25 goes on to identify several instances in which authors of press reports "shall have the right to obtain remuneration for the use of their works . . . ." Notably, the provision specifically recognizes that authors of political, economic, and religious updates are entitled to remuneration. The Polish Copyright Law does not define what constitutes an "update on political, economic, or religious issues," but as the court reads this term, it could include a journalistic work that addresses social concerns and contains a modicum of creativity or analysis. Taken as a whole, Article 25 demonstrates that the drafters of the Polish law intended to protect both the free flow of information and the right of members of the press to be compensated in exchange for their creative efforts.

Though the vast majority of the allegedly infringed reports are not in the record, the six items of Rudnicki's work currently before the court, which include elements of analysis and reporting on political events, appear to fall within Article 25's "updates on political issues" language. As such, Poland's Copyright Law appears to vest Rudnicki or his assignees with the right to obtain remuneration for the use of his journalistic work.[7] At a minimum, there are disputes of fact precluding summary judgment in favor of Defendants on this basis.

V. Rudnicki's Standing to Bring Suit

Defendants next argue that Rudnicki lacks standing to bring this lawsuit because he has contractually transferred his rights in his reports to RadioZET. Under 17 U.S.C. § 501(b), only "[t]he legal or beneficial owner of an exclusive right under a copyright is entitled . . . to institute an action for any infringement of that

7 Further, Article 34 of Poland's Copyright Law requires proper attribution and identification of author and source in order for a work's reproduction to fall within a permitted use. According to Rudnicki and Roclawska, WPNA deleted Rudnicki's name from the broadcast reports. That fact would defeat any argument that Defendants' use was permissible under Polish law.

particular right committed while he or she is the owner of it." This requirement applies even when the work at issue was produced abroad and ownership is to be determined by foreign law. *Itar-Tass Russian News Agency*, 153 F.3d at 91. Accordingly, Rudnicki's standing to bring an action for infringement under American law depends on whether he currently possesses an exclusive right under copyright.

The distribution of rights between Rudnicki and RadioZET is defined by § 5 of Rudnicki's employment contract, called the Cooperation Agreement. That provision reads:

> Each and every time the Correspondence medium (carrier) is delivered or the Correspondence is broadcast live by RadioZET, RadioZET acquires the author's economic rights[8] to such Correspondence, including the unlimited, in time and space, right to manage and exploit the Correspondence in the following areas of exploitation: (i) recording and multiplying, in particular on magnetic tapes, CDs, and computer disks, (ii) entering into computer memory, (iii) selling; (iv) reproducing in public, replaying, broadcasting, or re-transmitting; (v) dissemination in the form of a digital recording on the internet. As of the moment of copyright transfer, RadioZET also acquires the ownership right to media (carriers) the Correspondence has been recorded on.

(Cooperation Agreement [English], Ex. H. to Pl's 56.1 Resp.) Defendants claim this provision transfers all of Rudnicki's cognizable rights in the reports to RadioZET, thus depriving Rudnicki of the ability to maintain this lawsuit. Plaintiff counters that the agreement is, in fact, a grant of a limited license to RadioZET with an implicit territorial limitation. Plaintiff contends the contract transfers Rudnicki's economic rights to RadioZET only for uses within the territory of Poland, leaving to Rudnicki full rights to his work everywhere else in the world. Rudnicki points to RadioZET's awareness of his work with Chicago-area station WNVR to corroborate this interpretation.

The contractual provision contains no explicit limitation to Polish territory, but Plaintiff urges the court to read such a limitation into the agreement as implicit under Polish law. In support, Plaintiff directs the court to Article 66 of Poland's Copyright Law, which reads: "Unless provided otherwise therein, a license contract shall authorize the use of the work for five years within the territory of the state in which the licensee has its seat." Defendants respond that this provision is inapplicable because the agreement does explicitly "provide otherwise." Specifically, the Cooperation Agreement unambiguously provides that RadioZET's

8 The original agreement was drafted exclusively in Polish. The Defendants' translation would translate this term as "copyrights." After reviewing Poland's copyright law, however, the court has determined that Polish law distinguishes between "moral" and "economic" rights, a distinction that supports Plaintiff's translation. For the purpose of considering Defendants' motion for summary judgment, the court adopts Plaintiff's proffered translation of the contract.

rights are "unlimited, in time and space," effectively indicating that the contract is intended to apply forever and everywhere.

The court agrees. In interpreting written contracts, a court initially determines, as a matter of law, whether the contract is ambiguous or unambiguous.[9] *See Grun v. Pneumo Abex Corp.*, 163 F.3d 411, 420 (7th Cir. 1998) citing *Ryan v. Chromalloy American Corp.*, 877 F.2d 598, 602 (7th Cir. 1989). If the contract is unambiguous, the court is to construe it as a matter of law. *U.S. Fire Ins. Co. v. Pressed Steel Tank Co.*, 852 F.2d 313, 316 (7th Cir. 1988). Construction of an unambiguous contract is therefore a question of law, for which summary judgment is particularly appropriate. *Grun*, 163 F.3d at 419. The phrase "unlimited in time and space" as used in the Cooperation Agreement is unambiguous. In plain terms, it means the transfer of rights described applies at all times and in all places. As the court reads the contract, the "unlimited in time and space" language does not modify the general term "economic rights," but describes instead a subset of economic, management, and exploitation rights that are specifically enumerated in § 5. These are the rights to control the work for purposes of (i) recording and multiplying, in particular on magnetic tapes, CDs, and computer disks; (ii) entering into computer memory; (iii) selling; (iv) reproducing in public, replaying, broadcasting, or re-transmitting; and (v) dissemination in the form of a digital recording on the internet. The agreement transfers total ownership rights in these five enumerated areas to RadioZET. The enumerated rights encompass substantially the rights that are typically protected under American copyright law. *See* 17 U.S.C. § 106 (granting the copyright owner exclusive rights to (1) reproduce the work, (2) prepare derivative works, (3) sell the work, (4) perform the work, (5) display the work, and (6) perform the work by digital audio transmission). Assuming the English translation adequately captures the language of the original Polish draft, the contract transfers a substantial portion of Rudnicki's copyright to RadioZET.

The challenge for an American court in discerning the distribution of rights under the language of the Cooperation Agreement is that, unlike copyright law in the United States, Polish law distinguishes between "moral" rights and "economic" rights in the same copyright.[10] Article 16 of Poland's Copyright Law recognizes "moral rights" that "protect the link between the author and his work." Under Article 16, moral rights are unlimited in time and cannot be waived or transferred by contract. They include the rights "to have the contents and form of the author's work inviolable and properly used" and the right "to control the manner of using the work."

---

9 The parties have not suggested that Polish law rules of contract construction are inconsistent with these standards.

10 In American law, "[c]reators of certain artistic works are entitled (along the lines of the European approach to moral rights) to control how their work is presented or altered by others," but this entitlement is considered distinct from traditional copyright protections. *Bretford Mfg., Inc. v. Smith System Mfg. Corp.* 419 F.3d 576, 581 (7th Cir. 2005) (holding that a manufacturer's table was not a work of visual art and, therefore, the manufacturer was not entitled to dictate buyer's use of the product).

Moral rights are distinct from economic rights, which are governed by Article 41 of Poland's Copyright Law. That article makes clear that "economic rights" in a copyright are transferable and that the holder of economic rights in copyrighted work is entitled to remuneration for its use. As this court understands Polish law, the holder of moral rights is entitled to equitable relief, such as an injunction preventing certain uses of a work, and the holder of economic rights is entitled to monetary recovery for the value of infringed work. (Compare Article 78 with Article 79.) In this case, while Rudnicki retains nontransferable moral rights to his work under Polish law, he does not have an "exclusive right" under a copyright that is cognizable under 17 U.S.C. § 501(b). Rudnicki has relinquished substantial elements of the copyright, such as the right to receive remuneration for the use of his work, to RadioZET. And because the Agreement specifically provides that this transfer of rights is unlimited in time and space, Polish law does not provide Rudnicki with an implicit term permitting him to exercise economic rights in his copyright outside Poland.

Plaintiff challenges this conclusion, urging that RadioZET's performance under the contract demonstrates that RadioZET initially understood the agreement not to apply beyond the territory of Poland. Alternatively, Plaintiff argues, RadioZET effectively waived its contractual entitlement to enforce Rudnicki's economic rights outside of Poland. Rudnicki's testimony and the non-excluded statements of Malgorzata Moszczenska and Kimila Ceran do reflect that RadioZET acknowledged Rudnicki's ability to work with WNVR in the United States. This apparent accommodation by RadioZET is not sufficient by itself, however, to demonstrate a transfer of ceded economic rights back to Rudnicki under either Polish or American law. *See* Poland's Copyright Law, Art. 53 ("A contract for the transfer of author's economic rights shall be made in writing under the pain of nullity."); 17 U.S.C. §204(a)("A transfer of copyright ownership . . . is not valid unless an instrument of conveyance, or a note or memorandum of the transfer, is in writing and signed by the owner of the rights conveyed . . ."). Under the plain terms of the Cooperation Agreement, RadioZET became the legal owner of Rudnicki's economic rights in his reports as soon as he transferred the reports to RadioZET's possession. "Each and every time the Correspondence medium (carrier) is delivered or the Correspondence is broadcast live by RadioZET, RadioZET acquires the author's economic rights." (Cooperation Agreement [English], Ex. H. to Pl's 56.1 Resp.) Rudnicki presents no evidence to establish that RadioZET understood the contract to mean anything other than what is indicated by that plain language. Nor does Rudnicki present sufficient evidence, even when viewed in the light most favorable to Plaintiff, that RadioZET transferred its ownership interest back to Rudnicki when it permitted him to work simultaneously for WNVR.

The court therefore grants Defendants' motion for summary judgment on the issue of standing without prejudice. Rudnicki will have leave within 30 days from the issuance of this opinion to seek an assignment of the economic rights in his works from RadioZET. Should Rudnicki obtain the assignment, the court will entertain further argument on his standing to enforce a copyright on reports "delivered" to or "broadcast live" by RadioZET prior to the alleged infringement.[11]Because the court's resolution of certain other issues may be helpful in determining how the parties will proceed, the court addresses the remainder of the parties' arguments briefly below.

VI. Entitlement to Damages

Under 17 U.S.C. § 504, an infringer may be liable for either "the copyright owner's actual damages and any additional profits of the infringer" or statutory damages. Defendants seek summary judgment on the ground that, assuming he has standing to proceed here, Plaintiff has failed to demonstrate that he is entitled to either actual or statutory damages.

In his deposition, Rudnicki admitted that he incurred no economic losses as a result of Defendants' infringement. (Rudnicki Dep. 10/16/06 161:3-163:8.) Defendants suggest that Rudnicki's admission forecloses the possibility of any recovery of actual damages. Recovery of actual damages may, however, be based on the value of the infringing use to the infringer so long as the amount is not based on "undue speculation." *McRoberts Software, Inc. v. Media 100, Inc.*, 329 F.3d 557 (7th Cir. 2003). The value of the infringing use to the infringer can be determined in part through a "determination of what a willing buyer would have been reasonably required to pay to a willing seller for plaintiff['s] work." *Deltak, Inc. v. Advanced Systems, Inc.*, 767 F.2d 357, 362 (7th Cir. 1985)(quoting *Sid & Marty Krofft Televison Productions v. McDonald's Corp.*, 562 F.2d 1157, 1174 (9th Cir. 1977)).

In this case, a non-speculative value of Rudnicki's reports is discernable, based on the price paid by willing buyers. Rudnicki was paid 120 Polish zlotych per piece of correspondence by RadioZET. At the 2006 exchange rate (1 USD to 3.1 zlotych),[12] that amounts to roughly $38.71 per report. Also, WNVR paid Rudnicki $20 for each report that he filed for that station. (Pl.'s 56.1 Resp. at ¶ 20.)

---

11 Assuming Rudnicki is able to obtain an assignment, such an effort still might serve only to postpone the ultimate dismissal of his claims. Civil actions under the Copyright Act are time-barred if they are not brought within three years of the alleged act of infringement. 17 U.S.C.A. § 507(b). "Because each act of infringement is a distinct harm, the statute of limitations bars infringement claims that accrued more than three years before suit was filed but does not preclude infringement claims that accrued with the statutory period." *Bridgeport Music, Inc. v. Diamond Time, Ltd.*, 371 F.3d 883, 899 (6th Cir. 2004). As far as the court is aware, the last alleged act of infringement in this case occurred in August 2006. Were RadioZET to bring its own infringement action today, its claims would be likely be time-barred. Assuming Rudnicki obtains an assignment, it is unclear whether the claims brought on RadioZET's behalf would relate back to Rudnicki's complaint or whether his action would otherwise act to toll the statute of limitations. In the event a deeper consideration of this issue becomes necessary, the court invites the parties to file briefs addressing the matter.

12 Currency exchange rates can be found in The CIA World Factbook, which is available online at: https://www.cia.gov/library/publications/the-world-factbook/last visited December 9, 2009.

These numbers indicate that the market value of Rudnicki's correspondence was roughly $20 to $38 per report. Assuming WPNA infringed in every instance alleged in Rudnicki's 2004 and 2006 complaints (53 incidents in total), WPNA would have committed an infringing use with a market value inside the range of roughly $1,060 to $2,014. Whatever the wisdom of pursuing a federal lawsuit for such a sum, the amount of recoverable actual damages under this calculation is not unduly speculative. Assuming Plaintiff obtained an assignment and proved infringement, he could recover a non-speculative amount of actual damages.

As a plaintiff may recover either actual or statutory damages under the Copyright Act, it is unnecessary for the court to consider Defendants' arguments as to why Rudnicki is not entitled to statutory damages. Defendants are not entitled to summary judgment on this basis.

VII. Registration with the Copyright Office

Finally, Plaintiff moves for partial summary judgment on the issue of whether the six works that Rudnicki deposited with the United States Copyright Office were properly registered under the Copyright Act. Plaintiff emphatically argues that he seeks "only a limited ruling" that the works were registered and "does not seek a determination that [Rudnicki] is entitled to statutory damages" or attorneys' fees for infringement of the six works. (Pl's Reply at 1.) In light of the limited nature of Plaintiff's motion, the court will not address whether Plaintiff is entitled to statutory damages or attorney's fees under 17 U.S.C. § 504 except to observe that Plaintiff has not yet established to the court's satisfaction that any such entitlement exists.[13] Responding to Plaintiff's previous motion in limine on this issue, Judge Moran observed that all that 17 U.S.C. § 408(b)(3) requires for the valid registration of works published outside the United States is the deposit of "one complete copy or phonorecord" of the works and payment of a registration fee. *Rudnicki*, 580 F. Supp. 2d at 692. On that basis, Judge Moran rejected Plaintiff's argument that Rudnicki somehow broadly registered all of his works by sending a sample of six reports to the Copyright Office. The court reserved judgment, however, on the six deposited works because Plaintiff had failed to identify precisely which reports had been properly deposited. *Id.* at 694.

---

13 In five of the six reports deposited with the Copyright Office, Rudnicki signs off by indicating that he is an agent of RadioZET. (Ex. 4, Pl's 56.1 Stat.) Assuming these reports were delivered to RadioZET as they appear to have been, RadioZET owns the economic rights to them under the terms of its contract with Rudnicki. Claims for these five items will be dismissed should Plaintiff fail to obtain a valid assignment of RadioZET's rights. It is unclear from the record whether RadioZET also owns economic rights to the sixth report on the disc, which was apparently aired on WNVR. In addition, questions of fact remain as to when these works were first published and whether the works were registered within a period that would permit Rudnicki to recover statutory damages. Under the Copyright Act, no award for statutory damages or attorneys fees may be made for "any infringement of copyright commenced after first publication of the work and before the effective date of the registration, unless such registration is made within three months after the first publication of the work." 17 U.S.C. § 412.

Plaintiff now submits to the court a copy of the disc and transcripts of the six works that Rudnicki deposited with the Copyright Office. The filings of both parties acknowledge the contents of the disc.[14] As there is no material dispute that the six listed works were submitted to the United States Copyright Office and a certificate of registration was subsequently issued to Plaintiff by the Copyright Office, the court finds the six works were properly registered pursuant to the United States Copyright Act. It is immaterial that the alleged infringement in this case occurred prior to effective registration or the works. That issue is relevant to Rudnicki's claim for statutory damages for infringement, not to the question of whether he properly registered the works.

Accordingly, Plaintiff's motion for partial summary judgment is granted. The court finds Rudnicki registered the six works with the United States Copyright Office. The court makes no finding as to whether Rudnicki may recover statutory damages or attorneys' fees for infringement of these works.

CONCLUSION

For the reasons stated, Defendants' motion to strike [168] is granted in part and denied in part. Paragraphs four and five of the affidavits of Malgorzata Moszczenska and Kimila Ceran are stricken. The court grants Defendant's motion for summary judgment [140] without prejudice to reconsideration, should Plaintiff succeed in obtaining an assignment of rights from RadioZET. Should he fail to do so, Defendants will be entitled to summary judgment on all claims relating to reports owned by RadioZET. Plaintiff's motion for partial summary judgment on the issue of registration is granted [143]. The court finds six items of Rudnicki's work were properly registered with the United States Copyright Office, but renders no judgment as to the availability of statutory damages or attorneys' fees under the United States Copyright Act.

---

14 As described earlier, the deposited reports are (1) a story outlining the Polish Prime Minister's visit to Brussels, (2) a story on the commitment of European troops to Lebanon, (3) a story on state-aid to Polish shipyards, (4) a story on meetings between the European Commission President and the Polish Prime Minister, (5) A story on the Polish Prime Minster's schedule while in Brussels, and (6) a story on security at European airports. (Ex. J, to Def's 56 Stat.; Ex. B to Ex. I to Def's 56 Stat.; Pl's 56.1 Stat. ¶ 10).

III. PROCEDURE

4. Discovery

COMPANIA DEL BAJO CARONI (CAROMIN), C.A.
v.
BOLIVARIAN REPUBLIC OF VENEZUELA

341 Fed. Appx. 722 (2d Cir. 2009)
Decided August 14, 2009

APPEARING FOR APPELLANTS: NATHAN SCHWED (Yoav M. Griver, on the brief), Zeichner Ellman & Krause LLP, New York, New York.

APPEARING FOR APPELLEES: RONALD E.M. GOODMAN (Paul S. Reichler, Janis H. Brennan, Ara B. Gershengorn, on the brief), Foley Hoag LLP, Washington, D.C.

PRESENT: REENA RAGGI, DEBRA ANN LIVINGSTON, Circuit Judges, EDWARD R. KORMAN, District Judge.*

* District Judge Edward R. Korman of the United States District Court for the Eastern District of New York, sitting by designation.

SUMMARY ORDER

UPON DUE CONSIDERATION, IT IS HEREBY ORDERED, ADJUDGED, AND DECREED that the judgment of the district court entered on May 1, 2008, is AFFIRMED.

Plaintiffs appeal the dismissal of their action for lack of subject matter jurisdiction pursuant to Fed. R. Civ. P. 12(b)(1) and the Foreign Sovereign Immunities Act of 1976 (FSIA), 28 U.S.C. §§ 1330, 1602–1611. "The standard of review applicable to district court decisions regarding subject matter jurisdiction under the FSIA is clear error for factual findings and *de novo* for legal conclusions." *In re Terrorist Attacks* on Sept. 11, 2001, 538 F.3d 71, 79 (2d Cir. 2008) (internal quotation marks omitted). Where, as here, a plaintiff challenges a district court's denial of jurisdictional discovery, our standard of review is abuse of discretion. *Id.* We assume the parties' familiarity with the facts and the record of prior proceedings, which we reference only as necessary to explain our decision.

1. Denial of Discovery

Plaintiffs' contention that they were improperly denied "focused discovery" of jurisdictional facts, Appellants' Br. at 37, is lacking in merit. The district court denied plaintiffs' discovery request because, *inter alia,* plaintiffs failed to identify "specific facts or statements that [they] could challenge through additional jurisdictional discovery." *Compania Del Bajo Caroni (Caromin) v. Bolivarian Republic of Venezuela (Caromin v. Venezuela)*, 556 F. Supp. 2d 272, 282–83 (S.D.N.Y. 2008). This decision fell within the district court's discretion and was consistent with the rule that "in the FSIA context, discovery should be ordered circumspectly and only to verify allegations of specific facts crucial to an immunity determination.*"* *EM Ltd. v. Republic of Argentina*, 473 F.3d 463, 486 (2d Cir. 2007) (internal quotation marks omitted).

2. Denial of Rebuttal

Plaintiffs further complain that the district court unfairly refused to afford them an opportunity to rebut—in writing or orally—arguments and factual allegations asserted by defendants for the first time on reply. A district court enjoys broad discretion (1) to consider arguments made for the first time in a reply brief, *see Ruggiero v. Warner-Lambert Co.,* 424 F.3d 249, 252 (2d Cir. 2005); (2) to rely on evidence submitted with the reply papers, *see id.;* and (3) to decide dispositive motions on written submissions without oral argument, *see Dotson v. Griesa*, 398 F.3d 156, 159 (2d Cir. 2005); *AD/SAT, Div. of Skylight, Inc. v. Associated Press*, 181 F.3d 216, 226 (2d Cir. 1999). We identify no abuse of discretion here.

First, the district court did not err by refusing to allow plaintiffs to submit papers rebutting arguments and evidence presented in defendants' reply papers. The general theory raised in those papers, that Minister Ramirez's purported signature on the alleged waiver was a forgery created through mechanical fabrication, was indisputably known to plaintiffs. As the district court explained, "[g]iven that the central question from the outset was the authenticity of a signature on a *duplicate* document, the possibility of 'mechanical fabrication' lay at the forefront of the instant controversy." *Caromin v. Venezuela*, 556 F. Supp. 2d at 283 n.40. Indeed, the district court "raised this precise concern at [an] August 22, 2007 conference." *Id.* Moreover, after defendants' reply papers were filed on November 20, 2007, plaintiffs did nothing for more than a month. When they eventually did act on January 4, 2008, it was merely to request that the district court grant leave for their counsel to withdraw without any mention of any difficulty with the reply papers. The district court granted this request almost immediately, but only "on condition that[, *inter alia,*] the pending motion to dismiss is treated as fully submitted." *Caromin v. Venezuela,* No. 07 Civ. 3179, Order at 1–2 (S.D.N.Y. January 7, 2008) ("Jan. 7 Order"). Plaintiffs' first complaint regarding the content of defendants' reply papers did not occur until February 5, 2008, roughly two-and-a-half months after defendants submitted the offending papers.

Under these circumstances, the district court's actions did not amount to an abuse of discretion.

Second, the district court did not deny plaintiffs an opportunity to respond orally to defendants' arguments. Rather, plaintiffs forfeited argument by their own actions. The motion to dismiss was fully submitted and oral argument scheduled for January 24, 2008, when plaintiffs discharged their counsel and sought an adjournment of argument. As previously noted, the district court granted plaintiffs' discharged counsel's leave to withdraw, but only "on condition that the pending motion to dismiss is treated as fully submitted and that oral argument will proceed as scheduled (unless if plaintiffs are unrepresented on [that day], it will be cancelled)." Jan. 7 Order at 1–2. Consistent with this order, no oral argument was held on January 24, 2008, because new counsel for plaintiffs did not file a notice of appearance until February 5, 2008. When, on that date, counsel requested an extension of time to prepare for the oral argument (that had already been cancelled), the district court acted within its discretion in denying the application "as unwarranted and in violation of the conditions of granting the plaintiffs' motion to substitute counsel." February 25 Order at 4.

3. Destruction of Records

Plaintiffs contend that the district court erred in failing to draw an adverse inference against defendants for the loss or destruction of original records. Plaintiffs, however, did not raise this argument before the district court. Accordingly, we will not consider it on appeal. *See In re Nortel Networks Corp. Sec. Litig.,* 539 F.3d 129, 132 (2d Cir. 2008).

4. Assignment of Burden

Plaintiffs argue that the district court erred "by placing upon Caromin the burden of proving beyond all doubt the genuineness of the documents." Appellants' Br. at 44 (internal quotation marks omitted). This argument misunderstands the district court's opinion, which states clearly that while plaintiffs met "their burden of production on the waiver issue, . . . defendants have succeeded in establishing, by a preponderance of the evidence, the lack of a genuine and authentic waiver of sovereign immunity." *Caromin v. Venezuela*, 556 F. Supp. 2d at 278. The district court's thorough opinion unmistakably indicates that it did not improperly shift the burden of persuasion to plaintiffs, but rather considered the "totality of the evidence presented" and concluded that it was "more probable than not" that Minister Ramirez did not execute a waiver of sovereign immunity. *Id.* at 281.

5. Failure to Hold Evidentiary Hearing

Finally, plaintiffs submit that the district court erred by resolving disputed issues of fact without holding an evidentiary hearing. The decision to hold an evidentiary hearing, however, is ordinarily left to the discretion of the district court. *See Zappia*

Middle East Constr. Co. v. Emirate of Abu Dhabi, 215 F.3d 247, 253 (2d Cir. 2000). Moreover, plaintiffs failed to request an evidentiary hearing from the district court. As a result, we need not consider this argument on appeal. *See In re Nortel Networks*, 539 F.3d at 2.

We have considered defendant's other arguments on appeal and conclude that they are without merit. Accordingly, we AFFIRM the judgment of the district court.

FRONTERA RESOURCES AZERBAIJAN CORPORATION
v.
STATE OIL COMPANY OF THE AZERBAIJAN REPUBLIC

582 F.3d 393 (2d Cir. 2009)
Decided September 28, 2009

JAMES E. BERGER, Paul Hastings Janofsky & Walker, LLP, New York, NY, for Petitioner-Appellant.

JOHN D. WINTER, Patterson Belknap Webb & Tyler LLP, New York, NY, for Respondent-Appellee.

Before: WALKER, PARKER, and RAGGI, Circuit Judges.

JOHN M. WALKER, JR.

JOHN M. WALKER, JR., *Circuit Judge*:

Petitioner-Appellant Frontera Resources Azerbaijan Corporation ("Frontera") appeals from the dismissal by the United States District Court for the Southern District of New York (Richard J. Holwell, Judge) of its petition to enforce a Swedish arbitration award against Respondent-Appellee State Oil Corporation of the Azerbaijan Republic ("SOCAR"). The district court granted SOCAR's motion to dismiss for want of personal jurisdiction. *See Frontera Res. Azer. Corp. v. State Oil Co. of the Azer. Republic*, 479 F. Supp. 2d 376, 388 (S.D.N.Y. 2007). We conclude that SOCAR is not entitled to the Due Process Clause's jurisdictional protections if it is an agent of the Azerbaijani state. Accordingly, we vacate and remand for the district court to reconsider its analysis.

BACKGROUND

Frontera and SOCAR are two companies in the oil industry. Frontera is based in the Cayman Islands, and SOCAR is based in and owned by the Republic of Azerbaijan ("Azerbaijan"). In November 1998, the parties entered into a written agreement (the "Agreement") under which Frontera developed and managed oil deposits in Azerbaijan and delivered oil to SOCAR. In 2000, a dispute arose over SOCAR's refusal to pay for some of this oil, and in response, Frontera allegedly sought to sell oil that was supposed to be sold to SOCAR to parties outside of

Azerbaijan instead. In November 2000, after instructing local customs authorities to block Frontera's oil exports, SOCAR seized the oil.

In March 2002, the bank that had financed Frontera's involvement in Azerbaijan foreclosed on its loan, forcing Frontera to assign its rights in the project to the bank. In July 2002, the bank settled its claims with SOCAR. Frontera, however, continued to seek payment for both previously delivered and seized oil. Based on its settlement with the bank, SOCAR denied liability to Frontera.

After Frontera and SOCAR were unable to settle their dispute amicably, Frontera served SOCAR in July 2003 with a request for arbitration as per the Agreement. In January 2006, after a hearing on the merits with full participation by both parties, a Swedish arbitral tribunal awarded Frontera approximately $1.24 million plus interest.

On February 14, 2006, Frontera filed a petition in the Southern District of New York to confirm the award pursuant to Article II(2) of the Convention on the Recognition and Enforcement of Foreign Arbitral Awards ("New York Convention"), *opened for signature* June 10, 1958, 21 U.S.T. 2517, 330 U.N.T.S. 38, *implemented at* 9 U.S.C. § 207. The district court dismissed the petition for lack of personal jurisdiction, on the basis that SOCAR had insufficient contacts with the United States to meet the Due Process Clause's requirements for the assertion of personal jurisdiction. The district court questioned the soundness of according due process protections to SOCAR, a company owned by Azerbaijan, but nonetheless applied the traditional due process test based on our precedent in *Texas Trading & Milling Corp. v. Federal Republic of Nigeria,* 647 F.2d 300 (2d Cir. 1981). The district court also declined to find quasi in rem jurisdiction over SOCAR, because Frontera had not identified specific SOCAR assets within the court's jurisdiction. The district court denied jurisdictional discovery and dismissed Frontera's petition. This appeal followed.

DISCUSSION

Frontera contends (1) that a court does not need personal jurisdiction over a party in order to confirm a foreign arbitral award against that party, and (2) that *Texas Trading* should be overruled, because the Due Process Clause's protections should not apply to foreign states or their instrumentalities. Frontera also challenges the district court's denial of jurisdictional discovery.

I. Personal Jurisdiction over SOCAR

When considering a district court's dismissal for lack of personal jurisdiction, we review its factual findings for clear error and its legal conclusions *de novo*. *See Sunward Elecs., Inc. v. McDonald,* 362 F.3d 17, 22 (2d Cir. 2004).

Generally, personal jurisdiction has both statutory and constitutional components. A court must have a statutory basis for asserting jurisdiction over a defendant, see Grand River Enters. Six Nations, Ltd. v. Pryor, 425 F.3d 158, 165 (2d Cir. 2005), and the Due Process Clause typically also demands that the defendant, if "not present within the territory of the forum, . . . have certain minimum contacts with it such that the maintenance of the suit does not offend 'traditional notions of fair play and substantial justice.'" *Int'l Shoe Co. v. Washington*, 326 U.S. 310, 316, 66 S. Ct. 154, 90 L. Ed. 95 (1945) (quoting *Milliken v. Meyer*, 311 U.S. 457, 463, 61 S. Ct. 339, 85 L. Ed. 278 (1940)). The parties do not challenge the district court's reliance on the Foreign Sovereign Immunities Act ("FSIA"), 28 U.S.C. § 1608(a), as the statutory basis for jurisdiction over SOCAR. *See Frontera,* 479 F. Supp. 2d at 379–80; *see* also Argentine Republic v. Amerada Hess Shipping Corp., 488 U.S. 428, 439, 109 S. Ct. 683, 102 L. Ed. 2d 818 (1989) (stating that the FSIA "provides the sole basis for obtaining jurisdiction over a foreign state in federal court"). This appeal instead is focused on the Due Process Clause's place in the district court's analysis.

The district court dismissed Frontera's petition because it concluded that SOCAR's contacts with the United States were insufficient to meet the Due Process Clause's demands for personal jurisdiction. Frontera contends that this was in error both because personal jurisdiction is not necessary for the requested relief, and because SOCAR is not entitled to the Due Process Clause's protections. We address each argument in turn.

A. The Need for Jurisdiction

Frontera argues that a district court does not need personal jurisdiction over a respondent to confirm a foreign arbitral award against that party. Yet, Frontera contends, the district court's dismissal of its petition "necessarily rest[ed] upon an assumption" that personal jurisdiction over SOCAR was indispensable. (Appellant's Br. at 38.)

We read the district court's decision differently. Although the district court considered whether it could assert personal jurisdiction over SOCAR, it did not make that question dispositive. Instead, after finding SOCAR's contacts with the United States insufficient to establish personal jurisdiction, the district court examined whether it had jurisdiction over any of SOCAR's assets, because "in the absence of minimum contacts, quasi in rem jurisdiction may be exercised to attach property to collect a debt." *Frontera*, 479 F. Supp. 2d at 387. Thus, by suggesting that the district court required personal jurisdiction, Frontera misunderstands the framework of the court's analysis. And to the extent that Frontera's challenge is to the district court's requirement of *either* personal or quasi in rem jurisdiction, it is without merit.

We have previously avoided deciding whether personal or quasi in rem jurisdiction is required to confirm foreign arbitral awards pursuant to the New York Convention. *See Dardana Ltd. v. A.O. Yuganskneftegaz*, 317 F.3d 202, 207 (2d Cir. 2003). However, the numerous other courts to have addressed the issue have each required personal or quasi in rem jurisdiction. *See, e.g., Telcordia Tech Inc.*

v. Telkom SA Ltd., 458 F.3d 172, 178–79 (3d Cir. 2006); *Glencore Grain Rotterdam B.V. v. Shivnath Rai Harnarain Co.*, 284 F.3d 1114, 1120–22 (9th Cir. 2002); *Base Metal Trading, Ltd. v. OJSC "Novokuznetsky Aluminum Factory"*, 283 F.3d 208, 212–13 (4th Cir. 2002); *see also Transatl. Bulk Shipping Ltd. v. Saudi Chartering S.A.*, 622 F. Supp. 25, 27 (S.D.N.Y. 1985).

Frontera contends that none of these courts addressed the precise argument it advances here: that there is no "positive statutory or treaty basis" for such a jurisdictional requirement.[1] (Appellant's Reply Br. at 11.) The federal statute that implements the New York Convention requires a court to confirm an award "unless it finds one of the grounds for refusal or deferral of recognition or enforcement of the award specified in the said Convention." 9 U.S.C. § 207. Article V of the New York Convention "provides the exclusive grounds for refusing confirmation," *Yusuf Ahmed Alghanim & Sons, W.L.L. v. Toys "R" Us, Inc.*, 126 F.3d 15, 20 (2d Cir. 1997), and specifies seven grounds for refusing to enforce an arbitral award, none of which include a lack of jurisdiction over the respondent or the respondent's property, *see* New York Convention at art. 5, 21 U.S.T. at 2517. Frontera accordingly argues that we cannot impose a jurisdictional requirement if the Convention does not already have one. We disagree.

Unlike "state courts[,] [which] are courts of general jurisdiction[,] . . . federal courts are courts of limited jurisdiction which thus require a specific grant of jurisdiction." *Foxhall Realty Law Offices, Inc. v. Telecomm. Premium Servs., Ltd.*, 156 F.3d 432, 435 (2d Cir. 1998) (citing *Sheldon v. Sill*, 49 U.S. (8 How.) 441, 449, 12 L. Ed. 1147 (1850)). "The validity of an order of a federal court depends upon that court's having jurisdiction over both the subject matter and the parties." *Ins. Corp. of Ir., Ltd. v. Compagnie des Bauxites de Guinee*, 456 U.S. 694, 701, 102 S. Ct. 2099, 72 L. Ed. 2d 492 (1982). While the requirement of subject matter jurisdiction "functions as a restriction on federal power," *id.* at 702, the need for personal jurisdiction is fundamental to "the court's power to exercise control over the parties," *Leroy v. Great W. United Corp.*, 443 U.S. 173, 180, 99 S. Ct. 2710, 61 L. Ed. 2d 464 (1979). "Some basis must be shown, whether arising from the respondent's residence, his conduct, his consent, the location of his property or otherwise, to justify his being subject to the court's power." *Glencore Grain*, 284 F.3d at 1122 (quoting *Transatl. Bulk Shipping*, 622 F. Supp. at 27).

Because of the primacy of jurisdiction, "jurisdictional questions ordinarily must precede merits determinations in dispositional order." S*inochem Int'l Co. v. Malay. Int'l Shipping Corp.*, 549 U.S. 422, 431, 127 S. Ct. 1184, 167 L. Ed. 2d 15 (2007). "[T]he items listed in Article V as the exclusive defenses . . . pertain to *substantive*

---

1 This position is not as novel as Frontera suggests. The Ninth Circuit rejected an identical argument in *Glencore Grain. See* 284 F.3d at 1121 ("[I]t is not significant in the least that the . . . [New York] Convention lacks language requiring personal jurisdiction over the litigants. We hold that neither the Convention nor its implementing legislation removed the district courts' obligation to find jurisdiction over the defendants in suits to confirm arbitration awards.").

matters rather than to procedure." *Monegasque de Reassurances S.A.M. v. Nak Naftogaz of Ukr.,* 311 F.3d 488, 496 (2d Cir. 2002) (emphasis added). Article V's exclusivity limits the ways in which one can challenge a request for confirmation, but it does nothing to alter the fundamental requirement of jurisdiction over the party against whom enforcement is being sought.

Frontera argues that the Supreme Court suggested otherwise in *Shaffer v. Heitner*, 433 U.S. 186, 97 S. Ct. 2569, 53 L. Ed. 2d 683 (1977), in the following footnote:

> Once it has been determined by a court of competent jurisdiction that the defendant is a debtor of the plaintiff, there would seem to be no unfairness in allowing an action to realize on that debt in a State where the defendant has property, whether or not that State would have jurisdiction to determine the existence of the debt as an original matter.

Id. at 210 n.36. But while this footnote indicated, in dicta, that a court might not need jurisdiction over a respondent's person when enforcing a debt—"the *Shaffer* principle" that Frontera makes much of, (Appellant's Br. at 46)—it nonetheless assumed that such a court would still have jurisdiction over the respondent's property. And in this regard, the district court's approach in no way conflicted with *Shaffer*. The district court did not view its lack of personal jurisdiction over SOCAR as fatal to Frontera's petition; instead, the court then appropriately considered whether it could assert jurisdiction over SOCAR's property.

We therefore hold that the district court did not err by treating jurisdiction over either SOCAR or SOCAR's property as a prerequisite to the enforcement of Frontera's petition. The district court may, however, have given the Constitution's Due Process Clause an unwarranted place in its analysis, which we discuss next.

B. SOCAR's Rights Under the Due Process Clause

The district court recognized that our precedent *Texas Trading* compelled it to hold that SOCAR possessed rights under the Due Process Clause, thus requiring that jurisdiction over SOCAR meet the minimum contacts requirements of *International Shoe*. The district court, however, questioned *Texas Trading's* soundness. These doubts were well-founded.

The Due Process Clause famously states that "no *person* shall be . . . deprived of life, liberty or property without due process of law." U.S. Const. amend. V (emphasis added). In *Texas Trading*, we held that a foreign state was a "person" within the meaning of the Due Process Clause, and that a court asserting personal jurisdiction over a foreign state must—in addition to complying with the FSIA—therefore engage in "a due process scrutiny of the court's power to exercise its authority" over the state. 647 F.2d at 308, 313 ("[T]he [FSIA] cannot create personal jurisdiction where the Constitution forbids it."). *Texas Trading* reached this conclusion without much analysis, while also noting that cases on point were "rare." *Id.* at 313. The FSIA had been enacted only five years earlier, and pre-FSIA suits against foreign states were generally supported by quasi in rem jurisdiction. *Id.* Subsequently, we applied *Texas Trading* not only to foreign states but also to their agencies and instrumentalities. *See, e.g., Seetransport Wiking Trader Schiffarhtsgesellschaft MBH & Co. v. Navimpex Centrala Navala*, 989 F.2d 572, 579–80 (2d Cir. 1993) (applying *Texas Trading* to a foreign trading company wholly owned by Romania that "promoted ship sales through its governmental office in Manhattan").

Since *Texas Trading*, however, the case law has marched in a different direction. In *Republic of Argentina v. Weltover, Inc.*, the Supreme Court "assum[ed], without deciding, that a foreign state is a 'person' for purposes of the Due Process Clause," 504 U.S. 607, 619, 112 S. Ct. 2160, 119 L. Ed. 2d 394 (1992), but then cited *South Carolina v. Katzenbach,* 383 U.S. 301, 323–24, 86 S. Ct. 803, 15 L. Ed. 2d 769 (1966), which held that "States of the Union are not 'persons' for purposes of the Due Process Clause," 504 U.S. at 619. *Weltover* did not require deciding the issue because Argentina's contacts satisfied the due process requirements, *see id.* at 619 & n.2, but the Court's implication was plain: If the "States of the Union" have no rights under the Due Process Clause, why should foreign states?

After *Weltover*, we noted that "we are uncertain whether [*Texas Trading*] remains good law." *Hanil Bank v. PT Bank Negara Indon.*, 148 F.3d 127, 134 (2d Cir. 1998). But we went no further in *Hanil Bank* because the due process requirements were satisfied in that case. *See id.* The instant case is different, however, as only the Due Process Clause prevented the district court from asserting personal jurisdiction over SOCAR.

In *Price v. Socialist People's Libyan Arab Jamahiriya*, 294 F.3d 82, 352 U.S. App. D.C. 284 (D.C. Cir. 2002), the D.C. Circuit reasoned that because "the word 'person' in the context of the Due Process Clause of the Fifth Amendment cannot, by any reasonable mode of interpretation, be expanded to encompass the States of the Union," *Katzenbach*, 383 U.S. at 323, "absent some compelling reason to treat foreign sovereigns more favorably than 'States of the Union,' it would make no sense to view foreign states as 'persons' under the Due Process Clause," 294 F.3d at 96. The *Price* court found no such reason, *see id.* at 95–100, and we find that case's analysis persuasive. As the *Price* court noted, the States of the Union "both derive important benefits [from the Constitution] and must abide by significant limitations as a consequence of their participation [in the Union]," *id.* at 96,[2] yet a "'foreign State lies outside the structure of the Union,'" *id.* (quoting *Principality of Monaco v. Mississippi*, 292 U.S. 313, 330, 54 S. Ct. 745, 78 L. Ed. 1282 (1934)).

---

2 *Price* compared U.S. Const. art. I, § 10 (prohibiting specific acts by the States), with *id.* at art. IV, § 4 ("The United States shall guarantee to every State in this Union a Republican form of Government, and shall protect each of them against Invasion; and on Application of the Legislature, or of the Executive (when the Legislature cannot be convened) against domestic Violence."), and *id.* at art. VI, cl. 2 ("This Constitution, and the Laws of the United States which shall be made in Pursuance thereof ... shall be the supreme Law of the Land; and the Judges in every State shall be bound thereby, any Thing in the Constitution or Law of the State to the Contrary notwithstanding."). 294 F.3d at 96.

If the States, as sovereigns that are part of the Union, cannot "avail themselves of the fundamental safeguards of the Due Process Clause," Price, 294 F.3d at 97, we do not see why foreign states, as sovereigns wholly outside the Union, should be in a more favored position. This is particularly so when the Supreme Court has "[n]ever . . . suggested that foreign nations enjoy rights derived from the Constitution," and when courts have instead "relied on principles of comity and international law to protect foreign governments in the American legal system." *Id.* For the reasons discussed by the *Price* court in its thorough opinion, we "are unwilling to interpret the Due Process Clause as conferring rights on foreign nations that States of the Union do not possess." *Id.* at 99. Thus, we hold that the district court erred, albeit understandably in light of *Texas Trading*, by holding that foreign states and their instrumentalities are entitled to the jurisdictional protections of the Due Process Clause.

SOCAR argues otherwise by defending not *Texas Trading's* reasoning but its significance as precedent. And, to be sure, our court's decisions are binding until overruled by us sitting *en banc* or by the Supreme Court, *United States v. Wilkerson*, 361 F.3d 717, 732 (2d Cir. 2004), neither of which has happened to *Texas Trading*. "We do, however, recognize an exception to this general rule where there has been an intervening Supreme Court decision that casts doubt on our controlling precedent." *Gelman v. Ashcroft,* 372 F.3d 495, 499 (2d Cir. 2004) (internal quotation marks omitted). Although *Weltover* arguably casts sufficient doubt on *Texas Trading* to justify its overruling by this panel, *see Hanil Bank*, 148 F.3d at 134, we have nonetheless circulated this opinion to all active members of our court, and none has objected to our departure from *Texas Trading. See United States v. Parkes*, 497 F.3d 220, 230 n.7 (2d Cir. 2007) (describing our "mini-en banc" process). Accordingly, to the extent that Texas Trading conflicts with our holding today that foreign states are not "persons" entitled to rights under the Due Process Clause, it is overruled.

Simply overruling *Texas Trading*, however, and holding that a sovereign state does not enjoy due process protections does not decide the precise question in this case, because SOCAR is not a sovereign state, but rather an instrumentality or agency of one. Frontera contends that, because the FSIA treats foreign states and their agencies and instrumentalities identically, *see Kensington Int'l Ltd. v. Itoua,* 505 F.3d 147, 153 (2d Cir. 2007) (citing 28 U.S.C. § 1603(a)), we should treat SOCAR just as we would treat Azerbaijan for constitutional purposes. The simple fact that SOCAR is deemed a foreign state as a *statutory* matter, however, does not answer the *constitutional* question of SOCAR's due process rights. SOCAR may indeed lack due process rights like a foreign state, but similar statutory treatment will not be the reason.

However, if the Azerbaijani government "exerted sufficient control over" SOCAR "to make it an agent of the State, then there is no reason to extend to [SOCAR] a constitutional right that is denied to the sovereign itself." *TMR Energy Ltd. v. State Prop. Fund of Ukr.,* 411 F.3d 296, 301, 366 U.S. App. D.C. 320 (D.C. Cir. 2005).

Although "government instrumentalities established as juridical entities distinct and independent from their sovereign should normally be treated as such," this presumption can be overcome if the state so "extensively control[s]" the instrumentality "that a relationship of principal and agent is created," or if "adher[ing] blindly to the corporate form . . . would cause . . . injustice." *First Nat'l City Bank v. Banco Para El Comercio Exterior de Cuba* ("*Bancec*"), 462 U.S. 611, 626–27, 629, 632, 103 S. Ct. 2591, 77 L. Ed. 2d 46 (1983); *see also Zappia Middle E. Constr. Co. v. Emirate of Abu Dhabi*, 215 F.3d 247, 252 (2d Cir. 2000) ("While the presumption of separateness is a strong one, it may be overcome if a corporate entity is so extensively controlled by the sovereign that the latter is effectively the agent of the former, or if recognizing the corporate entity as independent would work a fraud or injustice."). Although *Bancec* asked when a state instrumentality can be treated like its state for "the attribution of liability," *id.* at 622 n.11, we think, as the D.C. Circuit did in *TMR Energy*, that *Bancec's* analytic framework is also applicable when the question is whether the instrumentality should have due process rights to which the state is not entitled. *See TMR Energy*, 411 F.3d at 301; *see also, e.g., Walter Fuller Aircraft Sales, Inc. v. Republic of the Phil.*, 965 F.2d 1375, 1382 (5th Cir. 1992) ("The broader principles upon which *Bancec* was based . . . are undoubtedly relevant whenever a plaintiff seeks to disregard a foreign government instrumentality . . . ."). Accordingly, if SOCAR is an agent of the Azerbaijani state, as recognized in *Bancec* and subsequent cases, then, like Azerbaijan, SOCAR lacks due process rights.

The district court did not decide whether SOCAR is an agent of the state because *Texas Trading* rendered the question unnecessary and, unsurprisingly, there was scant briefing on the issue. SOCAR suggests that the parties' lack of focus on the question should be fatal to Frontera's position, because Frontera "bears the burden of proving that the corporate entity should not be presumed distinct from a sovereign or sovereign entity." *Zappia*, 215 F.3d at 252. But the *Bancec* analysis and Frontera's related burden were not relevant until our decision today, nor did Frontera argue that *Bancec* should apply. *Cf. Brooklyn Legal Servs. Corp. v. Legal Servs. Corp.*, 462 F.3d 219, 232 (2d Cir. 2006) ("It is our role to ensure that in making factual findings, the district court applies the proper legal test and applies it correctly."). Moreover, using the parties' inattention to SOCAR's relationship with Azerbaijan to decide that SOCAR is not an agent of the state would still not resolve this appeal. We would then have to determine whether SOCAR, as a corporation owned by a foreign state but not the state's agent, was entitled to the Due Process Clause's protections.

In *TMR Energy*, the D.C. Circuit called this last question "far from obvious." 411 F.3d at 302 n.*. The *TMR Energy* court observed that "'aliens receive constitutional protections [only] when they have come within the territory of the United States and developed substantial connections with this country.'" *Id.* (quoting *United States v. Verdugo-Urquidez*, 494 U.S. 259, 271, 110 S. Ct. 1056, 108 L. Ed. 2d 222 (1990)) (alteration in *TMR Energy*). The Supreme Court has gone so far as to accord due process protections to privately owned foreign corporations. *See Helicopteros Nacionales de Colombia, S.A. v. Hall,* 466 U.S. 408, 418–19, 104 S. Ct. 1868, 80 L. Ed. 2d 404 (1984); *see also, e.g., Bank Brussels Lambert v. Fiddler Gonzalez & Rodriguez*, 171 F.3d 779, 784 (2d Cir. 1999); *Metro. Life Ins. Co. v. Robertson-Ceco Corp.*, 84 F.3d 560, 571 (2d Cir. 1996). Whether, and to what extent, it would do so for state-owned foreign corporations has not been decided. And, given the present posture of this litigation, it would be premature for us to address this question without hearing first from the court below. *See Farricielli v. Holbrook,* 215 F.3d 241, 246 (2d Cir. 2000) (per curiam) ("It is our settled practice to allow the district court to address arguments in the first instance."). Accordingly, we choose to remand so that in the first instance the district court can determine, in light of *Texas Trading's* demise and *Bancec's* new relevance to this context, (1) whether SOCAR is an agent of Azerbaijan, and if not, (2) whether SOCAR is entitled to the protections of the Due Process Clause.

II. Jurisdictional Discovery

Frontera also argues that the district court erred by rejecting its request for limited discovery of SOCAR's contacts with the United States. We review the district court's decision for an abuse of discretion. *See Jazini v. Nissan Motor Co.*, 148 F.3d 181, 186 (2d Cir. 1998). This issue is relevant only if the Due Process Clause protects SOCAR, which is for the district court to determine on remand.

"A district court has wide latitude to determine the scope of discovery," *In re "Agent Orange" Prod. Liab. Litig.,* 517 F.3d 76, 103 (2d Cir. 2008), and is typically within its discretion to deny jurisdictional discovery when "the plaintiff [has] not made out a prima facie case for jurisdiction," *Best Van Lines, Inc. v. Walker*, 490 F.3d 239, 255 (2d Cir. 2007) (citing cases). Assuming for the moment that SOCAR has the jurisdictional protections of the Due Process Clause, to establish jurisdiction Frontera must show that SOCAR had "continuous and systematic general business contacts" with the United States, *Metro. Life Ins. Co.,* 84 F.3d at 568 (quoting *Helicopteros*, 466 U.S. at 416), a highly fact-sensitive "contextual inquiry" with no one factor having "talismanic significance," *id.* at 570–71.

Frontera argued that SOCAR's production-sharing contracts with several U.S. oil companies and loan agreement with "a syndicate that included [a] U.S. bank" brought it within the district court's jurisdiction. *Frontera*, 479 F. Supp. 2d at 386. Frontera also alleged that "it is highly likely that at least a portion of [SOCAR's] oil and gas revenues are processed through U.S.-based banks." *Id.* at 386–87 (alteration in original). The district court dismissed this latter allegation as "conclusory," and then found the rest of Frontera's claims insufficient to demonstrate a prima facie case for jurisdiction, reasoning that "[t]he fact that American oil companies and one bank have entered into contracts with SOCAR for oil production in Azerbaijan does not demonstrate a continuous and systematic presence in the United States." *Id.* "In the absence of any prima facie showing of personal jurisdiction," the district court found it "inappropriate to subject SOCAR to the burden and expense of discovery" and denied Frontera's request. *Id.* at 387.

Frontera contends that our decision in *Seetransport* demonstrates that the district court's denial was erroneous. In *Seetransport,* we held that a foreign company's "deliberate[]" solicitations of business through U.S.-based representatives "with a fair measure of permanence or continuity" met the minimum requirements for general personal jurisdiction. 989 F.2d at 580. Frontera argues that SOCAR's contracts with U.S. oil and financial companies "were likely the product of the type of 'deliberate solicitations'" found sufficient in *Seetransport, see id.*, and that the district court should therefore have granted jurisdictional discovery. (Appellant's Br. at 54–55.) But this is pure speculation on Frontera's part.

Seetransport addressed solicitations that were "deliberate[,] and not occasional[] or casual[]," with the record establishing the defendant's use of a New York office. 989 F.2d at 580. Here, the fact that SOCAR has relationships with American companies, without more, could just as easily be the result of occasional or casual solicitations, or solicitations outside the United States. Thus, because Frontera has not pointed to anything in the record that suggests otherwise, we will not disturb the district court's discretionary decision not to allow discovery. *See Best Van Lines*, 490 F.3d at 255 ("We conclude that the district court acted well within its discretion in declining to permit discovery because the plaintiff had not made out a prima facie case for jurisdiction."). The district court is free to consider further discovery requests in light of the questions it must decide on remand.

III. Forum Non Conveniens

Finally, SOCAR asks us to affirm the district court's dismissal on the alternate basis of *forum non conveniens*. Having dismissed for want of jurisdiction, the district court expressly declined to address this argument. Following "our settled practice" of allowing district courts to address arguments in the first instance, *Farricielli*, 215 F.3d at 246, we express no view on SOCAR's *forum non conveniens* argument, which it is free to raise again on remand.

CONCLUSION

For the foregoing reasons, we VACATE the district court's dismissal of Frontera's petition and REMAND for further proceedings.

III. PROCEDURE

5. Court of International Trade

AECTRA REFINING AND MARKETING, INC.
v.
UNITED STATES

565 F.3d 1364 (Fed. Cir. 2009)
Decided May 8, 2009

Michael F. Mitri, Phelan & Mitri, of Norwalk, Connecticut, argued for plaintiff-appellant. With him on the brief was John J. Galvin, Galvin & Mlawski, of New York, New York.

Tara K. Hogan, Trial Attorney, Commercial Litigation Branch, Civil Division, United States Department of Justice, of Washington, DC, argued for defendant-appellee. With her on the brief were Jeanne E. Davidson, Director, and Todd M. Hughes, Deputy Director.

Before MICHEL, Chief Judge, MAYER and DYK, Circuit Judges.

DYK, *Circuit Judge*.

Aectra Refining and Marketing, Inc. ("Aectra") unsuccessfully sought a refund from United States Customs and Border Protection ("Customs") of import taxes and fees paid on products that were subsequently used to produce exported goods. Such refund claims are known as claims for "drawback." Aectra then filed suit in the Court of International Trade, which rejected Aectra's drawback claim as untimely. The trade court held that the three-year limitations period imposed by 19 U.S.C. § 1313(r)(1) had not been suspended by 2004 legislation and that Aectra had not completed its claim within the three-year limitations period because it had not timely provided Customs with a calculation of the taxes and fees it sought. *Aectra Ref. & Mktg. Inc. v. United States*, 533 F. Supp. 2d 1318, 1326 (Ct. Int'l Trade 2007). We affirm.

BACKGROUND

Between January 1987 and June 1997, Aectra imported into the United States certain petroleum products upon which customs duties, Merchandise Processing Fee ("MPF"), and Harbor Maintenance Tax ("HMT") were paid.[1] Aectra exported

---

1 In its Complaint, Aectra makes passing reference to an additional category of fees and taxes, the Environmental Tax imposed under 26 U.S.C. § 4611. On appeal the government contends,

drawback-eligible finished petroleum products between May 1987 and December 1997. In general, under the current statute, Customs is required to provide a refund (drawback) of 99% of "any duty, tax, or fee imposed under Federal law upon entry or importation" of imported merchandise if that merchandise (or a "commercially interchangeable" substitute) is subsequently "exported, or . . . destroyed under customs supervision; and . . . is not used within the United States before such exportation or destruction." 19 U.S.C. § 1313(j), (p) (2006). Aectra's exported petroleum products always qualified for drawback (even under earlier versions of the statute), and under the current statute, MPF and HMT (each of which is a "duty, tax, or fee imposed . . . upon entry or importation") are also eligible to be refunded. However, the drawback eligibility of MPF and HMT (as opposed to customs duties) under the earlier statute was disputed at the time of Aectra's exports. The question is whether Aectra made a timely claim for refund of MPF and HMT.

By statute, claims for drawback generally must be filed and completed within a three-year limitations period accruing from the date of export:

> A drawback entry and all documents necessary to complete a drawback claim, including those issued by the Customs Service, shall be filed or applied for, as applicable, *within 3 years after the date of exportation* or destruction of the articles on which drawback is claimed . . . . Claims not completed within the 3-year period shall be considered abandoned. No extension will be granted unless it is established that the Customs Service was responsible for the untimely filing.

19 U.S.C. § 1313(r)(1) (2006) (emphasis added); 19 C.F.R. § 191.51(e)(1) (2008).

The statute requires timely filing of both the "drawback entry," which is defined by regulation as "the document containing a description of, and other required information concerning, the exported or destroyed article on which drawback is claimed," 19 C.F.R. § 191.2(k), and all documents necessary to complete the "drawback claim," which is "the drawback entry and related documents required by regulation which together constitute the request for drawback payment," *id.* § 191.2(j). Customs has promulgated regulations addressing what is necessary to "complete" a claim; under the regulations, a claimant must supply various documents and certificates specified in 19 C.F.R. § 191.51(a) and "correctly calculate the amount of drawback due" under *id.* § 191.51(b)(1). Claims for drawback may be altered or amended prior to liquidation of the drawback entry ("liquidation" being the final calculation by Customs of drawback due on an entry, *see id.* § 159.1), provided that the amendment is made within the three-year limitations period. *Id.* § 191.52(c).

---

and Aectra apparently does not dispute, that there is no evidence that Aectra actually paid that tax on the goods in question.

Between August 1997 and June 1998, Aectra timely filed ten entries claiming drawback of the customs duties paid on the petroleum products.[2] For the "total drawback claimed" on each of the ten drawback entry forms, Aectra listed only the specific amount of customs duty paid on that entry. None of the ten forms included a request for drawback of the MPF or HMT paid on that entry or any calculations indicating the amount of MPF or HMT sought. Aectra states that it did not include calculations for MPF or HMT because Customs regulations at the time provided that neither MPF nor HMT was eligible for drawback under the statute.[3]

Although the regulations did not allow MPF and HMT claims, Aectra admits that it was aware that Customs's position regarding the recoverability of MPF and HMT was being actively challenged in 1997 and 1998. *See, e.g., Texport Oil Co. v. United States*, 1 F. Supp. 2d 1393, 22 CT. INT'L TRADE 118 (Ct. Int'l Trade 1998), *rev'd*, 185 F.3d 1291 (Fed. Cir. 1999). Aectra offers no explanation for why it did not include protective claims for MPF and HMT in its ten drawback claims other than its belief that such claims would not be successful at the administrative level. Subsequent to the original filing of those claims (but at a time when Aectra's claims could have been timely amended or re-filed), in July 1999 a panel of this court in *Texport Oil Co. v. United States*, 185 F.3d 1291, 1296 (Fed. Cir. 1999), held that MPF was recoverable but HMT was not. However, efforts continued in other cases to secure en banc reconsideration of *Texport's* holding as to HMT, *see, e.g., George E. Warren Corp. v. United States,* 341 F.3d 1348, 1351–52 (Fed. Cir. 2003), and efforts to change the *Texport* decision as to HMT legislatively proceeded as well. In 2004, Congress amended 19 U.S.C. § 1313(j) to permit drawback of HMT. Miscellaneous Trade and Technical Corrections Act of 2004, Pub. L. No. 108-429, § 1557(b), 118 Stat. 2434, 2579 ("2004 Trade Act").[4] Aectra contends that the amendment applies to the claims in question.

Although Aectra never sought to formally amend its claims within the three-year period, Aectra itself recognized that a claim could be filed even before the 2004 Trade Act (allowing recovery of HMT) was enacted on December 3, 2004.

---

2 The first five entries were later lawfully re-filed in December 1999 pursuant to a temporary suspension of the three-year limitations period accompanying a June 25, 1999 amendment to the drawback statute, as discussed below. *See* Miscellaneous Trade and Technical Corrections Act of 1999, Pub. L. No. 106-36, § 2420(e), 113 Stat. 127, 179 ("1999 Trade Act").

3 Specifically, 19 C.F.R. § 191.3(b) (1998), entitled "Duties and fees subject or not subject to drawback," stated that "Duties and fees not subject to drawback include: (1) Harbor maintenance [tax] . . . [and] (2) Merchandise processing fee."

4 The revised language provides that "any duty, tax, or fee imposed under Federal law *upon entry or importation*" is now eligible for drawback, 19 U.S.C. § 1313(j) (2006) (emphasis added), rather than only "any duty, tax, or fee imposed under Federal law *because of its importation*," 19 U.S.C. § 1313(j) (2000) (emphasis added). The parties agree that the statute as amended by the 2004 Trade Act now permits drawback of HMT (which is a charge imposed *upon* importation, though not *because* of importation), in addition to customs duties and MPF. *See Aectra*, 533 F. Supp. 2d at 1323.

On February 2, 2004, Aectra filed a protest contesting Customs's failure to refund the MPF and HMT paid on the ten entries.[5] On or about February 6, 2004, Customs denied the protest without elaboration. Aectra understood the grounds for denial to be its failure to include a timely request for HMT and MPF in its original filings.

On July 23, 2004 (still before the statute was amended), Aectra filed a summons in the Court of International Trade under 28 U.S.C. § 1581(a), contesting the denial of its protest. Aectra ultimately offered three main theories for why Customs had incorrectly rejected the request for drawback of MPF and HMT. First, Aectra argued in essence that the 2004 Trade Act suspended the three-year limitations period as to HMT. Second, Aectra argued that even if the three-year limitations period applied, its original drawback claims, despite their lack of an explicit request for MPF and HMT, were sufficient to include a claim for MPF and HMT. Third, Aectra argued that it was not required to file a claim for MPF and HMT because such a claim would have been futile. On cross motions for summary judgment, the trade court rejected Aectra's arguments and granted the government's motion, affirming Customs's denial of the claim. *Aectra*, 533 F. Supp. 2d at 1327.

Aectra timely appealed, and we have jurisdiction under 28 U.S.C. § 1295(a)(5). "We review the Court of International Trade's grant of summary judgment de novo, including by deciding de novo the proper interpretation of governing statutes and regulations." *Shinyei Corp. of Am. v. United States,* 524 F.3d 1274, 1282 (Fed. Cir. 2008).

DISCUSSION

I.

On appeal, Aectra contends that the 2004 Trade Act suspended the three-year limit on HMT drawback claims imposed by 19 U.S.C. § 1313(r)(1). As previously noted, prior to the 2004 amendment, § 1313(j) stated that "any duty, tax, or fee imposed under Federal law [upon imported merchandise] *because of its importation* . . . shall be refunded as drawback" if the merchandise is exported or destroyed unused. 19 U.S.C. § 1313(j) (2000) (emphasis added). In *Texport,* this court held that MPF was a "duty, tax, or fee" imposed "because of . . . importation" and therefore was eligible for drawback; in contrast, we held that HMT was not similarly subject to drawback because it was a general charge "assessed against all shipments, regardless of whether they are imports." 185 F.3d at 1296. The 2004 Trade Act made clear that HMT was recoverable by eliminating the requirement that a charge be imposed "because of" importation, instead more broadly allowing drawback of any duty, tax, or fee imposed "*upon* entry" of merchandise. 2004 Trade Act, § 1557(a), 118 Stat. at 2579 (emphasis added). The legislative history indicates

5 On or about November 28, 2003, Customs approved in its initial liquidation the refund of 99% of the total drawback amount sought by Aectra for each entry (i.e., 99% of the customs duties that had been paid).

that the amendment was designed to clarify prior law that 19 U.S.C. § 1313(j) had been intended to permit recovery of HMT, *see* S. Rep. No. 108-28, at 173 (2003), and that the contrary *Texport* decision had been in error.[6]

The basis for Aectra's argument as to the timeliness of its claims is the effective date provision of the 2004 Trade Act, which provides:

> (b) EFFECTIVE DATE.—The amendments made by this section shall take effect on the date of the enactment of this Act [Dec. 3, 2004], and shall apply to any drawback claim filed on or after that date *and to any drawback entry filed before that date if the liquidation of the entry is not final on that date.*

2004 Trade Act, § 1557(b), 118 Stat. at 2579 (emphasis added).

The first clause of the provision plainly applies prospectively to claims filed after December 3, 2004, and is inapplicable to Aectra. Aectra argues that the second (emphasized) clause of the provision must be read as permitting recovery of the HMT paid on any drawback entry filed before December 3, 2004, but not finally liquidated as of that date.[7] Thus, Aectra contends that its February 2004 protest containing a claim for HMT—though made well beyond the close of the three-year limitations period—is nonetheless a timely claim.[8] Aectra urges that the trade court's contrary reading of the statute "creates an absurd result," for it "gives meaning only to the first clause," while rendering "the retroactive second clause of the effective date provision . . . superfluous." Pl.-Appellant's Br. 9, 12.

We disagree. It is first important to recognize that the 2004 Trade Act amendment was not designed to create a new right to drawback for HMT, but rather to clarify that HMT was always subject to drawback under the statute. Read in that light,

---

6 As noted in the report:

> *Explanation of provision*
>
> The provision amends Section 313(j) of the Tariff Act of 1930 (19 U.S.C. 1313(j)) to clarify that the Harbor Maintenance Tax (HMT) is a fee eligible for drawback under the statute.
>
> *Reason for Change*
>
> The Committee believes that the U.S. Court of Appeals for the Federal Circuit erred in overturning the U.S. Court of International Trade's ruling . . . that Section 313(j) . . . allows drawback of the Harbor Maintenance Tax. *Section 313(j) allows for drawback of any duty, tax, or fee imposed under Federal law because of its importation. The Committee believes allowing for drawback of the Harbor Maintenance Tax is consistent with original Congressional intent.*

S. Rep. No. 108-028, at 173 (2003) (final emphasis added).

7 While the entries were liquidated by Customs in 2003, the liquidation did not become final because the liquidation determination was timely protested. *See* 19 U.S.C. § 1514.

8 On appeal, Aectra at points appears to suggest that the 2004 Trade Act applies to both MPF and HMT, rather than to only HMT. This court, however, had already confirmed that MPF was eligible for drawback under the pre-amendment statute several years earlier. *See Texport*, 185 F.3d at 1296. There is thus no basis in the 2004 Trade Act upon which to argue that it suspended 19 U.S.C. § 1313(r)(1) with regard to MPF.

it was not unreasonable to assume that Congress would limit the right to those who had previously attempted to claim it within the three-year limitations period, absent some contrary language in the statute. Nothing in the text of the statute states or suggests that it was intended to waive the normal three-year limit imposed by 19 U.S.C. § 1313(r)(1). Given that Congress is presumed to enact legislation with knowledge of the law and a newly-enacted statute is presumed to be harmonious with existing law and judicial concepts, *see Cannon v. Univ. of Chi.,* 441 U.S. 677, 696-98, 99 S. Ct. 1946, 60 L. Ed. 2d 560 (1979), the absence of any statement that the statute was designed to modify the limitations period for drawback claims is telling.

Contrary to Aectra's argument, the Court of International Trade's reading of the statute renders no part of the text surplusage. Under the plain language of the statute, the first and second clauses of the effective date provision apply the amendments of the 2004 Trade Act to two distinct categories. The first clause applies prospectively to new drawback "claims" filed on or after December 3, 2004, which may seek drawback on exports made within the previous three years. There is no dispute that this clause does not apply to Aectra's drawback claims, which were filed before that date.

The second clause covers certain drawback "entries" filed before December 3, 2004, but not yet finally liquidated on that date. This clause applies the 2004 Trade Act's amendments to unliquidated entries that already included a timely protective request for HMT. This clause is necessary to make clear that such unliquidated entries were entitled to the benefit of the amendments, since the pre-amendment statute in effect at the time those entries would have been filed did not allow recovery of HMT. Although it is the case that Aectra's ten entries are not within this clause, the second clause of the effective-date provision is not rendered surplusage by that fact.

Moreover, when Congress intends to suspend the three-year limit imposed by § 1313(r), it has done so explicitly. Just five years before the 2004 Trade Act was passed, for example, Congress enacted the 1999 Trade Act. That statute made certain technical amendments to 19 U.S.C. § 1313(p), easing the recovery of drawback "for petroleum products where a party other than the exporter is the importer," because the difficulty of tracing specific imported petroleum to specific exported products had "often made it economically unfeasible to seek drawback claims." S. Rep. No. 106-2, at 70 (1999) (report of the Senate Finance Committee); *see* 1999 Trade Act, § 2420, 113 Stat. at 178–79. Section 2420(e) of the 1999 Trade Act applied the amendments retroactively and expressly suspended the three-year limit imposed by 19 U.S.C. § 1313(r), creating a six-month grace period in which otherwise untimely claims could be filed or re-filed to obtain relief under the amended statute:

> EFFECTIVE DATE.—The amendments made by this section shall take effect as if included in the amendment made by . . . the [1993] North American Free Trade

> Agreement Implementation Act. For purposes of section 632(b) of that Act [providing that the NAFTA Implementation Act amendments applied to any entry filed after 1988 or unliquidated as of the Act's passage], *the 3-year requirement set forth in section 313(r) of the Tariff Act of 1930 shall not apply* to any drawback claim filed within 6 months after the date of the enactment of this Act for which that 3-year period would have expired.

1999 Trade Act, § 2420(e), 113 Stat. at 179 (emphasis added).

We agree with the Court of International Trade that the 2004 Trade Act did not eliminate the three-year claim completion limit imposed by 19 U.S.C. § 1313(r)(1).

II.

Alternatively, Aectra argues that § 1313(r)(1) requires only that a "drawback entry and all documents necessary to complete a drawback claim" be submitted within three years. The statute does not expressly require that a calculation of the amount of tax and fee drawback claimed be submitted along with the entry document in order to "complete" a claim. Aectra thus maintains that even if the three-year limit does apply, Aectra's "drawback claims for import duty recoveries can be found 'complete' for § 1313(r)(1) purposes" because the drawback entries themselves were timely filed within three years of export. Pl.-Appellant's Br. 23.

Aectra is correct that the drawback statute itself does not explicitly state that a calculation of taxes and fees sought must be included with the drawback entry as one of the "documents necessary to complete a drawback claim." 19 U.S.C. § 1313(r)(1). The payment of drawback, however, is expressly conditioned—by statute—upon compliance with regulations promulgated by the Secretary of the Treasury. *Id.* § 1313(l); *see also id.* § 1624; *United States v. Lockheed Petroleum Servs., Ltd.,* 709 F.2d 1472, 1474 (Fed. Cir. 1983). One such regulation, 19 C.F.R. § 191.51 (1998), is directly applicable here. At the time the relevant entries were filed, that regulation provided:

> § 191.51 Completion of drawback claims.
>
> (a) *General.* (1) *Complete claim.* Unless otherwise specified, a complete drawback claim under this part shall consist of the drawback entry on Customs Form 7551 . . . and evidence of exportation or destruction under subpart G of this part.
>
> . . .
>
> (b) *Drawback due. Drawback claimants are required to correctly calculate the amount of drawback due.* The amount of drawback requested on the drawback entry is generally to be 99 percent of the import duties eligible for drawback. (For example, if $1,000 in import duties are eligible for drawback less 1 percent ($10), the amount claimed on the drawback entry should be for $990. Claims exceeding 99 percent (or 100% when 100% of the duty is available for drawback) will not be paid until the calculations have been corrected by the claimant.) Claims for less than 99 percent (or 100% when 100% of the duty is available for drawback) will be paid as filed, unless the claimant amends the claim in accordance with § 191.52(c).

19 C.F.R. § 191.51 (1998) (final emphasis added).[9] Under the "correctly calculate" requirement of paragraph (b) of the regulation, a "complete" claim for purposes of the three-year limit of 19 U.S.C. § 1313(r)(1) must include a correct calculation of the amount of drawback due.

The question, therefore, is what a "correct" calculation entails. In Aectra's view, because the Customs regulations in effect at the time specified that both MPF and HMT were ineligible for drawback, *see* 19 C.F.R. § 191.3(b) (1998), a correct calculation required calculating only the amount of customs duties to be refunded, not the amount of taxes and fees.[10] It bolsters its argument by pointing out that paragraph (b) makes mention of "duty," and contains no reference to calculation of taxes and fees. Moreover, Aectra reads paragraph (b) as stating that "[c]laims exceeding 99 percent" of "duties" would be rejected, thus requiring rejection of claims for 99 percent of duties plus taxes and fees. Thus, Aectra argues, its ten claims were "complete" within the meaning of the regulation despite the fact that they included no calculation of (and indeed made no mention of) the amounts of MPF and HMT that Aectra now claims.

We are aware of no authoritative administrative construction of the "correctly calculate" requirement of 19 C.F.R. § 191.51(b) (1998), but we think that on its face the phrase "correctly calculate the amount of drawback due" requires a claimant to include an accurate calculation of the entire amount that it seeks to be refunded under the drawback statute. The purpose of the "correctly calculate" requirement is plain enough from the face of the regulation; it is to allow Customs to carry out its mandate to process drawback claims under the statute in an efficient and accurate manner. This purpose is served by requiring a claimant to put Customs on notice of the total amount sought. It is equally clear that this purpose is defeated by allowing the untimely filing of incomplete claims. Under Aectra's theory, a claimant could submit a partial claim for duty that would be fully paid by Customs as requested, and then institute a second proceeding, perhaps years later, requesting

9 In 2001, Customs amended 19 C.F.R. § 191.51(b), noting that the closing parenthesis following the fourth sentence was a typographical error. Instead, that parenthesis should have followed the third sentence, such that the third sentence would conclude "should be for $990.)" Technical Amendments to the Customs Regulations, T.D. 01-14, 35 *Cust. B. & Dec.* 59, 62 (Jan. 3, 2001). This change has no significance for present purposes.

10 Following *Texport*, 19 C.F.R. § 191.3 was eventually amended in 2001 to acknowledge that MPF was eligible for drawback. *Merchandise Processing Fee Eligible To Be Claimed as Unused Merchandise Drawback*, 66 Fed. Reg. 9647, 9649 (Feb. 9, 2001); *see also Merchandise Processing Fees Eligible To Be Claimed as Certain Types of Drawback Based on Substitution of Finished Petroleum Derivatives*, 69 Fed. Reg. 60,082 (Oct. 7, 2004); Merhcandise [*sic*] *Processing Fee Eligible To Be Claimed as Unused Merchandise Drawback*, 67 Fed. Reg. 48,547 (July 25, 2002). Although a new paragraph was also added as 19 C.F.R. § 191.51(b)(2) with specific information as to how to calculate the MPF drawback, the amendment did not alter the existing text imposing the basic requirement that the drawback claimant "correctly calculate the amount of drawback due." *See* 19 C.F.R. § 191.51(b)(1) (2001). No relevant further amendment has been made following passage of the 2004 Trade Act.

by protest an additional amount, thereby plainly increasing the cost and complexity of processing the claim. The regulation seeks instead to promote the orderly administration of the drawback system by requiring that a complete calculation of the drawback sought be presented within the statutory period.

Indeed, during the Notice and Comment period that preceded adoption of § 191.51(b) in 1998, Customs recognized the analogous administrative problems that would be created if Customs were required on its own to make a refund of the maximum permissible amount, even if the claim were for a lesser amount. As Customs noted, "adoption of the procedure suggested . . . would create an untenable administrative burden for Customs in its processing of drawback claims." *Drawback*, 63 Fed. Reg. 10,970, 10,988 (Mar. 5, 1998). Likewise, allowing claimants to submit claims piecemeal after the three-year completion window has passed would detract from the ability of Customs to "effectively carry out its duties," including preventing circumvention of the three-year statutory limit of 19 U.S.C. § 1313(r)(1). *Aectra*, 533 F. Supp. 2d at 1326.

In short, we think the first sentence of 19 C.F.R. § 191.51(b) (1998) in effect at the time Aectra filed its claims required a correct calculation of whatever amount a claimant sought to recover, not merely a calculation of the customs duties to be refunded. The remainder of paragraph (b), which does refer specifically to duty, does not limit the requirement of the first sentence but simply discusses the calculation requirement as applied to the duty component of a drawback claim. The second sentence of (b) notes that the drawback due is "generally" to be 99 percent of the import duties eligible; it does not state an absolute rule. Likewise, the fourth sentence similarly concerns duty, stating that claims "exceeding 99 percent (or 100% when 100% of the duty is available for drawback) will not be paid until the calculations have been corrected by the claimant." *Id.* § 191.51(b). The better reading of these statements is that they do not limit the general requirement imposed by the first sentence of paragraph (b), which requires a claimant to properly set forth the total amount sought (from whatever category of duty, tax, or fee) as drawback.[11]

III.

Aectra argues that it was not required to make claims for MPF and HMT at the time its drawback entries were filed because such claims would have been futile. However, futility does not excuse the failure to file a proper claim for limitations purposes. A claimant is generally required to file a complete and specific claim within the limitations period, even if the government authority to whom the claim is presented is certain to dispute the validity of the claim. In *United States v. Clintwood Elkhorn Mining Co.*, for example, the Supreme Court held that a refund suit for a tax imposed in violation of the Export Clause, filed beyond the applicable

11 In its reply brief Aectra argues that claims for MPF and HMT were "implicit" in its timely filing requesting a refund of customs duties. Pl.-Appellant's Reply Br. 11. We see no basis for such an argument.

period of limitations, was barred where the claimant had failed to first present a timely administrative claim to the Internal Revenue Service. 128 S. Ct. 1511, 1515, 170 L. Ed. 2d 392 (2008). This was so even though there was little if any reason to believe that the claim for a refund of the tax would have been granted by the IRS. *See id.* at 1515, 1520; *see also Frazer v. United States*, 288 F.3d 1347, 1354–55 (Fed. Cir. 2002) (noting that possible futility of filing action and "considerable doubt" about viability of claims did not justify failure to satisfy statute of limitations); *Boling v. United States*, 220 F.3d 1365, 1374 (Fed. Cir. 2000) ("It is true that during the period between the decision in *Ballam* [which made the claim appear futile] and its subsequent reversal in *Owen*, any claim by the plaintiffs for compensation would have been difficult. However, this difficulty does not justify tolling the statute of limitations."). *See generally Computervision Corp. v. United States*, 445 F.3d 1355, 1363–73 (Fed. Cir. 2006) (discussing exceptions to limitations periods in the internal revenue context).

Our decision in *George E. Warren*, 341 F.3d at 1348, is not to the contrary. In that case, Warren paid duty, HMT, and Environmental Tax ("ET") on imported petroleum, and later exported drawback-eligible substitute merchandise. *Id.* at 1349. Warren timely submitted drawback claims for the duty, which Customs paid as submitted, but failed to include in those claims an express request for HMT or ET. *Id.* at 1349–50. Shortly thereafter—but still within three years of the date of export—Warren filed a protest seeking drawback of HMT and ET. *Id.* Customs denied the protest on the merits, ruling that no additional refund would be issued on the entries because HMT was not recoverable under the drawback statute. *Id.; see also George E. Warren Corp. v. United States*, 201 F. Supp. 2d 1366, 1368, 26 Ct. Int'l Trade 486 (Ct. Int'l Trade 2002). We held that the Court of International Trade properly exercised jurisdiction over the denial of the importer's protest despite the fact that the HMT and ET requests were first made by protest, and that Warren was not required to engage in the futile exercise of re-filing new claims for HMT and ET in light of Customs's previous denial of recovery of those taxes on the specific entries at issue. *George E. Warren*, 341 F.3d at 1351.

As Aectra concedes, *George E. Warren* "rested on jurisdictional grounds inapplicable here" and consequently "it was unnecessary for the *Warren* court to address the effect of § 1313(r)(1) [which imposed the three-year limitations period] on those refund requests." Appellant's Br. 24. Aectra's reliance on George E. Warren is thus misplaced, as our opinion in that case does not suggest that a party may be excused from a failure to comply with the statute of limitations by arguing futility.[12]

---

12 Aectra's reliance on our decision in *Texport*, 185 F.3d at 1291, is similarly misplaced. The issue of whether the importer's claims for HMT and MPF were timely made was not raised by Customs in that appeal, and *Texport* is not binding authority with regard to an issue it neither discussed nor squarely decided. *See Boeing N. Am., Inc. v. Roche,* 298 F.3d 1274, 1282 (Fed. Cir. 2002).

In any event, even if George E. Warren were viewed as relevant to the limitations issue, that case dealt with the unique circumstance in which Congress in 1999 extended the three-year statute of limitations after Customs (in acting on a protest) had denied the requested refunds; at most we held that under such circumstances the filing of a new claim in the extended limitations period was unnecessary since Customs already had notice of the claim. No comparable circumstances exist here since Customs was never presented with, and therefore never addressed, Aectra's claim for HMT during the limitations period.

In sum, we agree with the Court of International Trade that a complete claim under 19 C.F.R. § 191.51(b) (1998) requires a calculation of the total amount of drawback sought even if the claim would have been rejected by Customs. Here, Aectra did not preserve its claim for taxes and fees by timely providing Customs with a calculation of the amount sought under § 191.51(b).

IV.

We turn briefly to Aectra's final argument. Aectra notes that 19 U.S.C. § 1313(r)(1) permits an "extension" of the three-year limit when "the Customs Service was responsible for the untimely filing." It contends that because the Customs regulations in effect at the time it filed its claims did not recognize drawback of MPF and HMT, *see* 19 C.F.R. § 191.3(b) (1998), "it is incontestable that Customs was responsible for any perceived 'untimely filing' of Aectra's requests for tax and fee drawback." Appellant's Br. 28.

The provision of § 1313(r)(1) allowing extensions for Customs delay is not applicable here, as Aectra's failure to file a protective claim for taxes and fees cannot fairly be attributed to the agency.

CONCLUSION

In summary, we agree with the Court of International Trade that the 2004 Trade Act did not suspend the three-year limit imposed by 19 U.S.C. § 1313(r)(1) and that a complete claim under 19 C.F.R. § 191.51(b) (1998) requires a claimant to calculate not only the amount of duty but also the amount of taxes and fees sought as drawback. Because Aectra's drawback claims were not completed with such a calculation within three years of export of the underlying goods, Customs properly denied Aectra's February 2004 request for drawback of MPF and HMT. Accordingly, the judgment of the Court of International Trade is affirmed.

AFFIRMED

COSTS

No costs.

AGRO DUTCH INDUSTRIES LIMITED
v.
UNITED STATES

589 F.3d 1187 (Fed. Cir. 2009)
Decided December 15, 2009

Richard P. Schroeder, Trial Attorney, Commercial Litigation Branch, Civil Division, United States Department of Justice, of Washington, DC, argued for defendant-appellee. With him on the brief were Michael F. Hertz, Acting Assistant Attorney General, Jeanne E. Davidson, Director, and Patricia M. McCarthy, Assistant Director.

Before RADER, BRYSON, and LINN, Circuit Judges.

BRYSON, *Circuit Judge*.

The government appeals from a decision of the Court of International Trade ordering the reliquidation of certain imported entries by plaintiff Agro Dutch Industries, Ltd. At issue is whether liquidation of the entries by Customs and Border Protection after the court issued an injunction against liquidation but before the injunction took effect rendered the case moot. The trial court held that the case was not moot, and we affirm.

I.

On July 12, 2002, the Department of Commerce published the final results of its second administrative review of an antidumping duty order imposing duties on preserved mushrooms from India. 67 Fed. Reg. 46,172. Commerce assigned Agro Dutch, a foreign producer and exporter, an antidumping duty of 27.80 percent.

Agro Dutch sought review of Commerce's determination by filing an action in the Court of International Trade on July 19, 2002. On September 26, 2002, Agro Dutch moved for a preliminary injunction, pursuant to 19 U.S.C. § 1516a(c), to prevent liquidation of its covered entries during the pendency of the action. Although Agro Dutch's request occurred after the expiration of the 30-day deadline under Rule 56.2 of the Rules of the United States Court of International Trade, which provides that a party may file a motion to enjoin liquidation "within 30 days after service of the complaint, or at such later time, for good cause shown," the government nevertheless consented to Agro Dutch's request for an injunction.

On October 1, 2002, the trial court granted Agro Dutch's consent motion and issued an order enjoining liquidation. By its terms, the injunction was to become effective five days after service on particular Commerce and Customs officials.

According to the government, which requested the five-day delay in the effective date of the injunction, the purpose of the delay was to avoid "an inadvertent violation" of the injunction by "ensuring that the appropriate Government officials receive notice" and by "providing the Government with the time needed to keep the entries from being . . . liquidated." Agro Dutch served the injunction on the pertinent government officials three days after it was issued.

Meanwhile, on August 23, 2002, Commerce had issued liquidation instructions to Customs based on the July 12 Final Results. On October 4, 2002, the same day on which Agro Dutch served the injunction on the appropriate government officials, Customs acted on those instructions and liquidated nearly all of Agro Dutch's entries.

After extensive additional proceedings that are not relevant here, the trial court remanded the matter to Commerce for a redetermination of Agro Dutch's antidumping duty margin. Commerce then issued a redetermination that lowered Agro's antidumping duty rate from 27.80 percent to 1.54 percent. The trial court sustained that duty rate. Agro Dutch then moved to amend the judgment, requesting reliquidation of the previously liquidated entries at the reduced rate of 1.54 percent.

The trial court granted the motion in part, ordering that the effective date of the injunction be amended to the date the injunction was issued, October 1, 2002, and directing that the relevant entries be reliquidated at the lower duty rate. *Agro Dutch Indus. Ltd. v. United States,* No. 02-499, 2008 Ct. Intl. Trade LEXIS 116, at *10 (Ct. Int'l Trade Oct. 17, 2008). The court rejected the argument that this court's decisions in *SKF USA, Inc. v. United States*, 512 F.3d 1326, 246 Fed. Appx. 692 (Fed. Cir. 2008), and *Zenith Radio Corp. v. United States,* 710 F.2d 806 (Fed. Cir. 1983), barred the reliquidation of the entries on the ground that the liquidation rendered the action before the court moot.

The trial court noted that, unlike in *SKF*, the court entered its injunction before the subject entries were liquidated. Moreover, the court observed that the liquidation of Agro Dutch's entries occurred as a result of "what might best be charitably described as 'inadvertence'" and that the parties had intended that liquidation would be enjoined during the pendency of the court action. The court therefore reasoned that backdating the injunction would "comport with the parties' intention." The court added that not granting relief would result in "manifest injustice" to the non-party importer of record, which was likely to be rendered insolvent unless the entries were reliquidated at the proper, lower duty rate.

II.

On appeal, the government argues that the trial court lacked jurisdiction to entertain Agro Dutch's challenge regarding the entries that were liquidated prior to the effective date of the injunction. Relying principally on the *Zenith* case, the government argues that the October 4 liquidations rendered Agro Dutch's claims moot, and that the trial court was powerless to order reliquidation or to amend the injunction *nunc pro tunc*.

In *Zenith*, the trial court refused to issue a preliminary injunction to prevent liquidation, on the ground that the movant had not established a likelihood of irreparable injury. We reversed. Under the statutory scheme that governs judicial review of Commerce's annual review determinations, we held that challenged entries must be liquidated at the disputed duty rate unless liquidation is enjoined. 710 F.2d at 810 (discussing 19 U.S.C. §§ 1516a(c) and 1516a(e)). From the absence of any statutory provision allowing subsequent reliquidation if a challenge is successful, we inferred that "[o]nce liquidation occurs, a subsequent decision by the trial court on the merits of [a] challenge can have no effect on the dumping duties assessed." *Id.* We therefore concluded that the movant had established a likelihood of irreparable injury because liquidation would eliminate its only available remedy: the reassessment of dumping duties in accordance with a corrected duty rate. *Id.* at 810, 812.

Subsequent case law has interpreted *Zenith* to establish a general rule that, at least in the context of judicial review under 19 U.S.C. § 1516a, liquidation moots a party's claims pertaining to the liquidated entries. *See, e.g., SKF*, 512 F.3d at 1329 ("The *Zenith* rule renders a court action moot once liquidation occurs."); *Yancheng Baolong Biochemical Prods. Co. v. United States*, 406 F.3d 1377, 1381 (Fed. Cir. 2005) ("As this court held in [*Zenith*], if there is no injunction, liquidation is automatic under 19 U.S.C. § 1516a(e) and § 1516a(c)(1), and any decision on the merits of a liquidation challenge after liquidation has taken place is without effect."); *Cambridge Lee Indus., Inc. v. United States*, 916 F.2d 1578, 1579 (Fed. Cir. 1990) ("Once an entry has been liquidated, the duties paid cannot be recovered even if the payor subsequently prevails in its challenge to the antidumping order.").

In *SKF*, we vacated a judgment affirming a redetermination of antidumping duties, where the covered entries had been deemed liquidated by operation of law prior to the redetermination. 512 F.3d at 1328, 1332. In that case, the government had consented to the importer's request for an injunction preventing liquidation during the pendency of the action in the trial court. *Id.* at 1328. However, before the trial court issued the injunction, the importer's entries became subject to 19 U.S.C. § 1504(d), which provides that if Customs has not liquidated an entry within six months of receiving notification that Commerce has completed its annual review, any unliquidated entries will be "treated as having been liquidated" at the amount of duty deposited by the importer at the time of import. 512 F.3d at 1329. We held that under the *Zenith* rule the deemed liquidation rendered the importer's claims moot in the absence of an injunction. *Id.* Although the trial court ultimately granted an injunction several months after the deemed liquidation, we concluded that "[t]o allow backdating of an injunction on liquidation that the court granted after the covered entries were liquidated would undermine the rule of *Zenith*." *Id.* at 1332.

The government relies on *SKF* to argue that the trial court violated the rule of *Zenith* when it backdated Agro Dutch's injunction to eliminate the five-day period before the injunction went into effect. In *SKF*, however, we emphasized the complete absence of an issued injunction, as the trial court had failed to "decide whether it [would] exercise its equitable power to grant relief" before the liquidation occurred. *Id.* In the present case, the trial court considered Agro Dutch's motion, determined that relief should be granted, and issued a valid injunction—all before liquidation occurred. Moreover, unlike the deemed liquidation in *SKF*, Customs affirmatively liquidated Agro Dutch's entries, despite the government's awareness of the injunction.

While the *Zenith* rule ordinarily renders moot court actions in which liquidation has already occurred, we have acknowledged that there are exceptions to that general rule.[1] valid injunction. *See Yancheng*, 406 F.3d at 1377, 1381–82 (Fed. Cir. 2005) (upholding the trial court's contempt ruling against the government when liquidation violated an injunction that remained in effect through appeal); Shinyei, 355 F.3d at 1312 (declining "to find that the statute [imposing finality upon liquidations] as a whole was intended to preclude judicial enforcement of court orders after liquidation"). The government does not suggest that the *Zenith* rule would moot Agro Dutch's claim if the liquidation had taken place after the injunction became effective. Moreover, like the Court of International Trade, we believe that when liquidation violates an injunction, not only does the trial court retain jurisdiction, but a broad array of remedies (including reliquidation) is available to the court to rectify the unlawful liquidation. See Allegheny *Bradford Corp. v. United States*, 342 F. Supp. 2d 1162, 1171, 28 Ct. Int'l Trade 603 (Ct. Int'l Trade 2004) (ordering refund of monies exacted pursuant to the enjoined liquidation in order to purge contempt and ordering reliquidation upon a final decision on the underlying action); *AK Steel Corp. v. United States,* 281 F. Supp. 2d 1318, 1323, 27 Ct. Int'l

1 We have recognized several situations in which the Zenith rule does not deprive the trial court of jurisdiction to address the merits of an antidumping duty determination. *See Shinyei Corp. of Am. v. United States*, 524 F.3d 1274 (Fed. Cir. 2008) (entries that were deemed liquidated by operation of law may be reliquidated in action brought under the Administrative Procedure Act ("APA") to challenge Commerce's liquidation instructions); *Gerdau Ameristeel Corp. v. United States*, 519 F.3d 1336, 1343 (Fed. Cir. 2008) (liquidation did not moot challenge to dumping margins because of an issue having ongoing legal consequences relating to the possible revocation of the underlying antidumping order); *Shinyei Corp. of Am. v. United States*, 355 F.3d 1297 (Fed. Cir. 2004) (an APA action challenging Commerce's liquidation instructions is not rendered moot by liquidation). Moreover, while acknowledging that this court has consistently applied the *Zenith* rule in the context of judicial review under 19 U.S.C. § 1516a, we have also noted that "the rule's effect may run counter to a congressional intent to facilitate judicial review of Commerce determinations." *SKF*, 512 F.3d at 1329.

TRADE 1382 (Ct. Int'l Trade 2003) (ordering that the matter be returned to the status quo ante and declaring liquidations null and void *ab initio*, where entries were liquidated through an illegal act of Customs in violation of a preliminary injunction); *LG Elecs. U.S.A., Inc. v. United States*, 991 F. Supp. 668, 675, 21 CT. INT'L TRADE 1421 (Ct. Int'l Trade 1997) (finding that liquidations in violation of a valid preliminary injunction had no legal effect and ordering reliquidation in accordance with Commerce's instructions and the court's rulings).

The *Zenith* rule would also not apply if liquidation occurred because of a clerical or typographical error in the injunctive order that was contrary to the purpose of the injunction and the parties' intent. Courts enjoy broad discretion to correct clerical errors in previously issued orders in order to conform the record to the intentions of the court and the parties. *See R. Ct. Int'l Trade* 60(a); Fed. R. Civ. P. 60(a) ("The court may correct a clerical mistake or a mistake arising from oversight or omission whenever one is found in a judgment, order, or other part of the record . . . on motion or on its own, with or without notice."); *see also Robert Lewis Rosen Assocs., Ltd. v. Webb,* 473 F.3d 498, 504–05 & n.11 (2d Cir. 2007) (trial court properly corrected an omission from a judgment to conform with the court's original intent); *Robi v. Five Platters, Inc.,* 918 F.2d 1439, 1445–46 (9th Cir. 1990) (district court did not abuse its discretion by amending the judgment to clarify its original intention to cancel certain trademarks); *Pattiz v. Schwartz,* 386 F.2d 300 (8th Cir. 1968) (where the intent of the parties was to apply a stipulation to an amended complaint rather than the original complaint, trial court had authority to issue an order that would reflect the intent of the parties and the court).

As a general matter, a court of equity may exercise its sound discretion to modify an injunctive order when modification is necessary to achieve the order's intended purpose and does not otherwise result in prejudice to a party. *See United States v. United Shoe Mach. Corp.,* 391 U.S. 244, 252, 88 S. Ct. 1496, 20 L. Ed. 2d 562 (1968) (if the district court's injunctive decree did not accomplish its intended goals, "the [d]istrict [c]ourt should modify the decree so as to achieve the required result with all appropriate expedition"); *see also Regal Knitwear Co. v. NLRB,* 324 U.S. 9, 15, 65 S. Ct. 478, 89 L. Ed. 661 (1945). The trial court's discretion is not limited to the correction of clerical or typographical errors but encompasses the correction of errors needed to comport the order with the original understandings and intent of the court and the parties.

As the trial court found, it was the purpose of the injunction and the understanding and intent of all the parties to suspend liquidation pending a decision on the merits of Agro Dutch's challenge. As issued by the trial court on October 1, 2002, the injunction contained a grace period delaying the effective date of the injunction until five days after it was served on the appropriate government officials.[2]

2 Even if the appropriate government officials had been served on October 1, the injunction would not have taken effect until October 8, after the liquidation of Agro Dutch's entries

However, the five-day window was apparently added only to ensure against subjecting Customs officials to contempt sanctions for an inadvertent liquidation. It was not intended to give the government free rein to liquidate the subject entries before the injunction took effect. As counsel for the government conceded at oral argument, the five-day window was not intended to allow the government to "rush in" to liquidate the relevant entries and thereby avoid the effect of the injunction. Thus, as the government has acknowledged and the trial court has found, the five-day grace period was not intended to allow the government an opportunity to effect liquidation if it moved quickly.

Pointing to Agro Dutch's delay of more than 30 days after service of the complaint before seeking an injunction, the government argues that if Agro Dutch had acted more promptly, it could have prevented the case from becoming moot.[3] That assertion is belied, however, by the fact that the government consented to the injunction even though Agro Dutch had delayed in seeking it. Moreover, counsel for the government maintained at oral argument that liquidation during the five-day window would have deprived the trial court of jurisdiction even if Agro Dutch had filed its request for an injunction within the 30-day period after serving the complaint. Thus, the government is not relying upon Agro Dutch's lack of timeliness as a basis for its legal position that liquidation prior to the effective date of the injunction renders moot any challenge with respect to the liquidated entries.

We agree with the trial court that there is no reason to upset the court's and the parties' clear intentions by applying the rule of *Zenith* to this case. By amending the effective date of the injunction and ordering reliquidation, the trial court gave full effect to the purposes underlying both the injunction and the five-day window provision. Under the court's final order, Agro Dutch's claim would proceed on the merits, and no contempt proceedings would be instituted against government officials for the inadvertent liquidation.

The government argues that upholding the trial court's decision would create uncertainty regarding the finality of antidumping duties imposed by the government. We have observed that the rule of *Zenith* is designed to promote finality for antidumping duties and related liquidations. As noted by this court in *SKF*,

---

took place on October 4. Therefore, the fact that it took Agro Dutch three days to serve the injunction is irrelevant to our reasoning, which focuses upon the effect of Customs' act of liquidating the entries during the five-day period between the injunction's issuance and its effective date.

3 The government asserts that if Agro Dutch had not waited past the 30-day deadline Commerce would not have issued the liquidation instructions that were ultimately implemented during the window prior to the injunction's effective date. However, this argument is undermined by the government's acknowledgement, in oral argument, that Commerce is not required to delay issuing liquidation instructions upon the filing of a timely motion for a preliminary injunction.

liquidation is "designed to close the books on an importer's entries" and reflects a "decision that an importer's liability has been finalized." 512 F.3d at 1329.

While finality is an important goal, the interest in finality must give way in the face of a more compelling interest in this case: namely, effecting the intent of the parties and the court to prevent a premature liquidation while judicial review is ongoing. Granting relief in this case is unlikely to give rise to any real uncertainty because the parties specifically contemplated that Agro Dutch's challenge to the Final Results would go forward. No valid interest in finality is served by foreclosing judicial review in a case such as this one, where the parties and trial court agreed that finality was not warranted, and where an injunction was entered for the very purpose of preventing the antidumping duty from becoming final.

While the government argues that affirming the trial court's decision will "turn[] what generally is a relatively cooperative endeavor into an adversarial one," we think the opposite is the case. The endeavor would be more likely to become adversarial if we were to allow liquidation during the five-day notice period to render moot a challenge to the antidumping duty determination, in contravention of the parties' express intent. Foreign importers are far more likely to trust and cooperate with the government if they can be confident that grace periods in issued injunctions cannot be exploited. Under the result urged by the government, in which liquidation occurring during the period after issuance and before the effective date of an injunction would be unchallengeable, it seems unlikely that any party challenging an antidumping duty in the future would agree to the government's request for a postponement of the effective date of the injunction.

For the foregoing reasons, we hold that the trial court did not abuse its discretion in amending the judgment to effect the parties' intent to prevent liquidation and allow adjudication of the merits of this dispute.

AFFIRMED.

AMANDA FOODS (VIETNAM) LTD.
v.
UNITED STATES

647 F. Supp. 2d 1368 (C.I.T. 2009)
Decided September 29, 2009

Mayer Brown LLP (Matthew J. McConkey and Jeffery C. Lowe) for Plaintiff Amanda Foods (Vietnam) Ltd.

Picard Kentz & Rowe LLP (Andrew W. Kentz and Nathaniel M. Rickard), Washington, DC, for Consolidated Plaintiff and Defendant-Intervenor Ad Hoc Shrimp Trade Action Committee.

Thompson Hine LLP (Matthew R. Nicely and Christopher M. Rassi) and Winston & Strawn LLP (Valerie S. Ellis and William H. Barringer), Washington, DC, for Consolidated Plaintiff's Ca Mau Seafood Joint Stock Company; Cadovimex Seafood Import-Export and Processing JointStock Company; Cafatex Fishery Joint Stock Corporation; Can Tho Agricultural and Animal Products Import Export Company; Coastal Fisheries Development Corporation; C.P. Vietnam Livestock Co., Ltd.; Cuulong Seaproducts Company; Danang Seaproducts Import Export Corporation; Investment Commerce Fisheries Corporation; Minh Hai Export Frozen Seafood Processing Joint-Stock Company; Minh Hai Joint-Stock Seafoods Processing Company; Ngoc Sinh Private Enterprise; Nha Trang Fisheries Joint Stock Company; Nha Trang Seaproduct Company; Phu Cuong Seafood Processing & ImportExport Co., Ltd.; Sao Ta Foods Joint Stock Company; Soc Trang Aquatic Products and General Import-Export Company; Thuan Phuoc Seafoods and Trading Corporation; UTXI Aquatic Products Processing Company; Viet Foods Co., Ltd.; Kim Anh Co., Ltd.; Phuong Nam Co., Ltd.

Tony West, Assistant Attorney General; Jeanne E. Davidson, Director; Franklin E. White, Jr., Assistant Director, Commercial Litigation Branch, Civil Division, United States Department of Justice (Stephen C. Tosini), and, of counsel, Jonathan Zielinski, Office of Chief Counsel for Import Administration, Department of Commerce for Defendant United States.

Thompson Hine LLP (Matthew R. Nicely and Christopher M. Rassi), Washington, DC, for Defendant-Intervenors Camau Frozen Seafood Processing Import Export Corporation; Grobest & I-Mei Industrial (Vietnam) Co., Ltd.; Minh Phu Seafood Corporation; Minh Qui Seafood Co., Ltd.; Minh Phat Seafood Co., Ltd.

OPINION AND ORDER

POGUE, Judge.

In this consolidated action, Plaintiffs seek review of the *Final Results* issued by the Department of Commerce ("the Department" or "Commerce") in the second administrative review ("Second Review") of the antidumping ("AD") order covering warmwater shrimp from the Socialist Republic of Vietnam. *See Certain Frozen Warmwater Shrimp From the Socialist Republic of Vietnam,* 73 Fed.Reg. 52,273 (Dep't Commerce Sept. 9, 2008) (final results and final partial rescission of antidumping duty administrative review) ("*Final Results*"),[1] and accompanying Issues & Decision Memorandum, A-552-802, 2d AR 02/01/06-01/31/07 (Sept. 2, 2008), Admin. R. Pub. Doc. 231, *available at* http:// ia.i ta.doc.gov/frn/summary/vietnam/E8-20927-1.pdf (last visited Sept. 23, 2009) ("*Issues & Decision Mem.*").[2]

Three questions are before the court. First, whether Commerce's selection of Bangladesh as the surrogate country[3] for the Second Review was supported by substantial evidence on the record[4]; second, whether Commerce's decision to value raw shrimp based on the surrogate value data contained in an intergovernmental agency study, Network of Aquaculture Centres in Asia-Pacific, *Evaluation of the Impact of the Indian Ocean Tsunami and the U.S. Anti-Dumping Duties on the Shrimp Farming Sector of South and South-East Asia: Case Studies in Vietnam,*

---

1 The *Final Results* cover entries of the subject merchandise made from February 1, 2006 through January 31, 2007, the period of review ("POR").

2 The *Issues & Decision Mem.* was adopted by and incorporated into the *Final Results. Final Results,* 73 Fed. Reg. at 52,273.

3 Vietnam has a non-market economy ("NME"). Generally, in an NME, because of limitations on the availability of data, Commerce may not be able to determine the normal or fair market value of products as it would in a market economy ("ME"). Consequently, Commerce derives the normal value of such products by aggregating the "best available" information with respect to factors utilized to produce the merchandise in "a market economy country or countries considered to be appropriate by [the Department]," i.e., a "surrogate" country. Tariff Act of 1930 § 773(c)(1), as amended, 19 U.S.C. § 1677b(c)(1).

4 *See Dorbest Ltd. v. United States,* 30 CIT 1671, 1676 462 F.Supp.2d 1262, 1268 (2006) ("If the question is whether Commerce *may* use a particular piece of data, whether Commerce *may* use a factor in weighing the choice between two data sources, or what weight Commerce *may* attach to such a factor, the question is legal. . . . If the question is whether Commerce *should* have used a particular piece of data, when viewed among alternative available data, or what weight Commerce *should* attach to a price or data, the question is factual." (emphasis in original) (citations omitted)).

Indonesia and Bangladesh (2006), http://library.enaca.org/shrimp/publications/NACAStudy.pdf ("NACA Study"), is supported by substantial evidence on the record; and, third, whether Commerce's assignment—as reasonable for Plaintiffs—of a separate or "all others" rate of either 4.30% or 4.57% was supported by substantial evidence on the record.

After specifying the controlling standard of review and summarizing the background of this dispute, the court will discuss each issue in turn.

STANDARD OF REVIEW

When it reviews the agency's final determinations in an administrative review of an AD duty order, the court will uphold all agency determinations, findings, or conclusions, except those not supported by substantial evidence on the record or otherwise not in accordance with law. Tariff Act of 1930 § 516A(b)(1)(B)(i), as amended, 19 U.S.C. § 1516a (b)(1)(B)(i) (2006).[5]

In reviewing whether Commerce's decisions are unsupported by substantial evidence, the court assesses whether the agency action is reasonable given the record as a whole. *See Nippon Steel Corp. v. United States,* 458 F.3d 1345, 1351 (Fed. Cir.2006). Substantial evidence is "such relevant evidence as a reasonable mind might accept as adequate to support a conclusion." *Consol. Edison Co. v. NLRB,* 305 U.S. 197, 229, 59 S.Ct. 206, 83 L.Ed. 126 (1938). While "the possibility of drawing two inconsistent conclusions from the evidence does not prevent an administrative agency's findings from being supported by substantial evidence," *Matsushita Elec. Indus. Co. v. United States,* 750 F.2d 927, 933 (Fed.Cir.1984) (citation omitted), the "substantiality of evidence must [also] take into account whatever in the record fairly detracts from its weight." *Universal Camera Corp. v. NLRB,* 340 U.S. 474, 488, 71 S.Ct. 456, 95 L.Ed. 456 (1951); *Gerald Metals, Inc. v. United States,* 132 F.3d 716, 720 (Fed.Cir. 1997) (explaining that the substantial evidence standard requires that contradictory record evidence be taken into account).

BACKGROUND

At the request of Plaintiff Ad Hoc Shrimp Trade Action Committee ("AHSTAC") and twenty-two individual exporters, Commerce, in April 2007, initiated the Second Review. *See Certain Frozen Warmwater Shrimp From the Socialist Republic of Vietnam and the People's Republic of China,* 72 Fed.Reg. 17,095, 17,096 (Dep't Commerce Apr. 6, 2007) (notice of initiation of administrative reviews of antidumping orders).

For this POR, eighteen of the twenty-three respondent Plaintiffs now before us requested review, while representatives of the domestic industry requested review for all twenty-three respondent Plaintiffs plus several other respondents.

---

5 Further citation to the Tariff Act of 1930 is to Title 19 of the U.S.Code, 2006 edition.

Rather than reviewing all respondents, Commerce limited the "mandatory respondents" for the Second Review to two companies—Camimex and Minh Phu Group.[6] Selection of Respondents Memorandum, A-552-802, 2d AR 02/01/06-01/31/07 (July 18, 2007), Admin. R. Pub. Doc. 102, at 7. These two companies were both mandatory respondents in the original investigation, but neither had been reviewed in the first administrative review.

As part of its review, because Vietnam is an NME, Commerce sent interested parties a letter asking for comments on surrogate country selection and information relating to the valuation of factors of production. Letter to Interested Parties, A-552-802, 2d AR 02/01/06-01/31/07 (Aug. 3, 2007), Admin. R. Pub. Doc. 110 ("*Letter to Interested Parties*"). This memorandum identified five countries from a surrogate country list that Commerce deemed to be equally economically comparable to Vietnam for administrative review purposes: Bangladesh, Pakistan, India, Sri Lanka, and Indonesia. *Id.* Attach. I at 2. Because Commerce's regulations specify that it will normally value all factors of production, except for labor, by using data from a single surrogate country, 19 C.F.R. § 351.408(c)(2),[7] Commerce's letter was preliminary to its choice from the list of five.

Responding to Commerce's letter, Camimex and Minh Phu Group submitted comments in favor of selecting Bangladesh and offered certain surrogate value data, including the NACA Study data from Bangladesh.[8] Minh Phu & Camimex's Surrogate Country & Value Submission, A-552-802, 2d AR 02/01/06-01/31/07 (Oct. 26, 2007), Admin. R. Pub. Doc. 147. Petitioners, in turn, requested that India serve as the surrogate country, and also offered certain publicly available surrogate value data from India. Letter from Pet'rs, A-552-802, 2d AR 02/01/06-01/31/07 (Oct. 26, 2007), Admin. R. Pub. Doc. 149.

---

6 *See* 19 U.S.C. § 1677f-1(c)(2) ("If it is not practicable to make individual weighted average dumping margin determinations . . . because of the large number of exporters or producers involved in the investigation or review, the administering authority may determine the weighted average dumping margins for a reasonable number of exporters or producers by limiting its examination to—

> (A) a sample of exporters, producers, or types of products that is statistically valid based on the information available to the administering authority at the time of selection, or
>
> (B) exporters and producers accounting for the largest volume of the subject merchandise from the exporting country that can be reasonably examined.")

7 In relevant part, 19 C.F.R. § 351.408(c) reads:

> (c) *Valuation of factors of production.* For purposes of valuing the factors of production. . . under section 773(c)(1) of the Act the following rules will apply:
>
> . . .
>
> (2) *Valuation in a single country.* Except for labor, as provided in paragraph (d)(3) of this section, the Secretary normally will value all factors in a single surrogate country.

8 Commerce had used Bangladesh as the surrogate country in the original, underlying, investigation, in the first administrative review, and in a new shipper review under this AD order.

In the *Preliminary Results* of the review, Commerce chose Bangladesh as the surrogate country, and used data from the NACA Study to value Bangladeshi raw shrimp. *See Certain Frozen Warmwater Shrimp from the Socialist Republic of Vietnam,* 73 Fed.Reg. 12,127, 12,133–34 (Dep't Commerce Mar. 6, 2008) (preliminary results, preliminary partial rescission and final partial rescission of the second antidumping duty administrative review) ("*Preliminary Results*").

To respond to the *Preliminary Results,* Plaintiff AHSTAC filed a case brief addressing, among other issues, the use of Bangladesh as a surrogate country and the use of the NACA Study data to value Bangladeshi raw shrimp. Pet'rs' Br., A-552-802, 2d AR 02/01/06-01/31/07 (May 7, 2008), Admin. R. Pub. Doc. 215, at 3, 6–8. Rejecting AHSTAC's claim, Commerce continued with its decision to use Bangladesh as the surrogate country and to use data from the NACA Study to provide surrogate values. *Issues & Decision Mem.* at 4–5; *see also Final Results,* 73 Fed.Reg. at 52,273 (listing no change from Preliminary Results in this regard).

Also in its *Preliminary Results,* Commerce calculated *de minimis* dumping margins for mandatory respondents Camimex and Minh Phu Group and granted all Plaintiffs separate rate status.[9] *Preliminary Results,* 73 Fed.Reg. at 12,135. At this time, Commerce assigned all separate rate companies the average of Camimex and Minh Phu Group's margins—a *de minimis* rate. *Id.*

In its *Final Results,* Commerce maintained *de minimis* rates for Camimex and Min Phu Group, but, rather than averaging the two mandatory respondents' rates and using the resulting average for the separate rate companies, Commerce assigned to the separate rate companies the most recent rate that each had received in a prior proceeding. Specifically, the Department applied the rate that the separate rate companies had received in the original investigation, based on sales made prior to the imposition of the dumping order, except that separate rate companies that had been examined in the First Administrative Review, and which received a different rate in that review, were assigned the rate they received in the First Review. *Final Results* at 52,275–76. This resulted in Vietnam Fish-One Company, Limited ("Fish One") and Grobest being assigned a zero rate (the rate received by these companies in the First Review); Minh Hai Joint-Stock Seafoods Processing Company being assigned a 4.30% rate (the rate received by this company in the original investigation, based on its own data); while all other Plaintiffs were assigned a rate of 4.57% (the rate received by these companies in the original investigation).

9 *See Decca Hospitality Furnishings, LLC v. United States,* 29 CIT 920, 921, 391 F. Supp. 2d 1298, 1300 (2005) ("While Commerce presumes that all companies [operating in an NME] are under state-control, a company may rebut this presumption, and therefore qualify for an antidumping duty rate separate from the PRC-wide rate, if it demonstrates *de jure* and *de facto* independence from government control."). Companies qualifying for such a "separate" rate are referred to as having "separate rate status."

DISCUSSION

I. Selection of Surrogate Country

The first issue before the court is Commerce's choice of Bangladesh as a surrogate ME country. As noted above, the selection of surrogate ME countries in the valuation of NME factors of production is regulated by 19 U.S.C. § 1677b(c)(1), which requires that the valuation be based on "the best available information regarding the values of such factors in a market economy country or countries considered to be appropriate by the administering authority." With regard to the choice of an "appropriate" country, the statute specifies two criteria that Commerce must use in its analysis. Specifically:

> [Commerce] shall utilize, to the extent possible, the prices or costs of factors of production in one or more market economy country that are—
>
> (A) at a level of economic development comparable to that of the nonmarket economy country, and
>
> (B) significant producers of comparable merchandise.

19 U.S.C. § 1677b(c)(4).

For purposes of determining whether a surrogate country is at a comparable level of economic development, Commerce's regulations specify that per capita income is to be given prominence. *See* 19 C.F.R. § 351.408(b) ("*Economic Comparability.* In determining whether a country is at a level of economic development comparable to the nonmarket economy [country] . . . , the Secretary will place primary emphasis on *per capita* GDP as the measure of economic comparability.").[10]

Procedurally, in selecting a surrogate country, Commerce, as a matter of policy, follows a four-step process. First, Commerce compiles a list of countries that are at a level of economic development "comparable" to the country being investigated. Secondly, Commerce ascertains which, if any, of those countries produce comparable merchandise. Third, from the resulting list of countries, Commerce then determines which, if any, of the countries are significant producers of the comparable merchandise. Finally, Commerce evaluates the reliability and availability of the data from the countries that are significant producers. *See Import Administration Policy Bulletin 04.1: Non-Market Economy Surrogate Country Selection Process* (Dep't Commerce Mar. 1, 2004), *available at* http://ia.ita.doc.gov/policy/bull04-1.html (last visited Sept. 23, 2009) ("Policy Bulletin").

Following this process in the Second Review, Commerce, as noted above, prepared a list of five possible surrogate countries and then stated that, for purposes of the review, Commerce would consider all five to be "equally economically comparable" to Vietnam. This list included Pakistan, India, Sri Lanka, and Indonesia,

---

10 No party challenges Commerce's use of per capita Gross National Income ("GNI") as a proxy for per capita GDP.

in addition to Bangladesh, the country eventually chosen as the surrogate country. *See Letter to Interested Parties,* Admin. R. Pub. Doc. 110, Attach. I at 2; *Issues & Decision Mem.* 4.

AHSTAC challenges this determination, noting that the countries on Commerce's list do not have equal *per capita* GDP; nor are they equally distant from Vietnam by this measure. In particular, India, the potential surrogate country favored by AHSTAC, appears to be closer to, and thus more "comparable" to Vietnam in this regard than is Bangladesh. *See Letter to Interested Parties,* Admin. R. Pub. Doc. 110, Attach. I at 2.

In response, Commerce and Defendant-Intervenors argue, correctly, that Commerce is not required to select more than one surrogate country, 19 C.F.R. § 351.408(c)(2), and that Commerce may give significant weight to data quality in determining an appropriate surrogate country. *See Globe Metallurgical, Inc. v. United States,* Slip Op. 08-105, 2008 WL 4417187, at *3–4, 2008 Ct. Intl. Trade LEXIS 105, at *10–11 (CIT Oct. 1, 2008) (concluding that Commerce acted reasonably in selecting a surrogate country based on its superior quality of available data relative to other comparable market economies). However, this response provides no support for Commerce's determination of economic comparability. Even assuming, *arguendo,* that Commerce has provided evidence of data superiority that could, if accepted by the court,[11] support the selection of Bangladesh as the surrogate country over India, this is not a basis for assuming that Bangladesh and India are equally comparable to Vietnam in terms of *per capita* GDP.

Nor has Commerce explained why the difference between Bangladesh and Vietnam, in *per capita* GDP, is not relevant in this case or why the difference in economic similarity to Vietnam is outweighed by the differences in quality of data between Bangladesh and India. Rather, without explanation, Commerce has adopted a policy of treating all countries on the surrogate country list as being equally comparable to Vietnam. As Commerce's chosen designation has not been supported by any justification or evidence at all, it is not supported by substantial evidence. *See Bowman Transp., Inc. v. Arkansas-Best Freight Sys., Inc.,* 419 U.S. 281, 285, 95 S.Ct. 438, 42 L.Ed.2d 447 (1974) (explaining that, even under the narrower arbitrary and capricious standard of review, the agency must examine the relevant data and articulate a satisfactory explanation for its action, including a "rational connection between the facts found and the choice made" (quoting *Burlington Truck Lines, Inc. v. United States,* 371 U.S. 156, 168, 83 S.Ct. 239, 9 L.Ed.2d 207 (1962))).[12]

11 Whether this evidence is sufficient and should be accepted by the court is a substantial part of the second question before the court. For now, however, we will assume a positive answer to this question.

12 Moreover, a reviewing court should not attempt itself to make up for such deficiencies; "we may not supply a reasoned basis for the agency's action that the agency itself has not given." *Bowman,* 419 U.S. at 285–86, 95 S.Ct. 438 (citing *SEC v. Chenery Corp.,* 332 U.S. 194, 196,

Finally, Commerce's designation of equal economic comparability prevents the court from determining whether the selection of Bangladesh, as opposed to India, on the basis of the purportedly better data, is reasonable considering the record as a whole.

The Department argues that this court's decision in *Fujian Lianfu Forestry Co. v. United States,* 638 F.Supp.2d 1325 (CIT 2009), rejected "an identical challenge to Commerce's surrogate country selection methodology to that raised by Ad Hoc." (Def.'s Notice of Subsequent Authority 2.) But *Fujian Lianfu Forestry* is distinguishable, as a comparison of the level of explanation provided by Commerce in each case indicates.

In *Fujian Lianfu Forestry,* the court upheld, as supported by substantial evidence, Commerce's treatment of all potential surrogate countries on its surrogate country list as equally economically comparable to the NME at issue in that case, despite the "parties' arguments that India[the chosen surrogate country]'s GNI (USD 620) was too disparate from China[the NME]'s (USD 1290) for India to be considered 'economically comparable.'" *Fujian Lianfu Forestry,* 638 F.Supp.2d 1325, 1348–49. In support of its determination in that case, Commerce had offered the following explanation:

> While the Department's regulations at 19 CFR 351.408 instruct the Department to consider per capita income when determining economic comparability, neither the statute nor the Department's regulations define the term 'economic comparability.' As such, the Department does not have a set range within which a country's GNI per capita could be considered economically comparable. In the context of the World Development Report, which contains approximately 180 countries and territories, the difference in GNI per capita between India and the PRC is minimal. As previously stated in the Surrogate Country Selection Memo, 'while the difference between the PRC's USD1290 per capita GNI and India's USD620 per capita GNI in 2004 seems large in nominal terms, seen in the context of the spectrum of economic development across the world, the two countries are at a fairly similar stage of development.' For example, in the World Development Report the four countries immediately higher than China in per capita GNI were Egypt (which was on the list of potential surrogate countries), Morocco, Columbia [*sic*], and Bosnia. Their per capita GNIs were higher than China's by USD20, USD230, USD710, and USD750, respectively. India's GNI per capita was only USD670 lower than China's. Therefore, the Department disagrees with the contention that India is no longer ecomoically comparable to the PRC.

Id. (quoting Issues & Decision Mem. for 2004–2005 Admin. Rev. of Wooden Bedroom Furniture from the People's Republic of China, A-570-890, AR 06/24/04-12/31/05 (Aug. 8, 2007), *available at* http:// ia.ita.doc.gov/frn/summary/prc/E7-16584-1.pdf (last visited Sept. 23, 2009)).

---

67 S.Ct. 1575, 91 L.Ed. 1995 (1947)); *Atchison, Topeka & Santa Fe Ry. v. Wichita Bd. of Trade,* 412 U.S. 800, 807, 93 S.Ct. 2367, 37 L.Ed.2d 350 (1973)(plurality)("[T]he agency must set forth clearly the grounds on which it acted.").

Here, in contrast to *Fujian Lianfu Forestry,* Commerce has failed to provide more than conclusory reasoning for why the GNI discrepancy between Vietnam and the countries on the Surrogate Country List did not affect the Department's comparability determination. Rather, as noted above, Commerce devised its Surrogate Country List without explanation and, again without explanation, adopted a policy of treating all countries on this list as being equally comparable to Vietnam.[13] Significantly, the Department's Policy Bulletin states that each Surrogate Country Memorandum must explain how the chosen country satisfies each element of the statutory criteria. In accordance with the Department's own policy, therefore, the Surrogate Country Memorandum must explain why its chosen surrogate country is at a level of economic development comparable to Vietnam. *See* 19 U.S.C. § 1677b(c)(4)(A). The memorandum in this case does not do so. *See Second Antidumping Duty Administrative Review of Certain Frozen Warmwater Shrimp from the Socialist Republic of Vietnam: Selection of a Surrogate Country,* A-552-802, 2d AR 02/01/06-01/31/07 (Feb. 28, 2008), Admin. R. Pub. Doc. 186, at 6–7. Accordingly, the court cannot find on this record that Commerce's surrogate country selection is supported by substantial evidence.

For these reasons the court must remand this issue to Commerce so that it may: 1) explain why it is justified in treating all the countries on the surrogate country list as equally comparable to Vietnam, despite their differences in *per capita* GDP, or 2) explain why the difference in comparability to Vietnam in *per capita* GDP between India and Bangladesh is small enough that it may be outweighed by superior quality of the Bangladeshi data, providing a reasoned basis for the determination of such superiority, or 3) otherwise reconsider its determination in accordance with this opinion.

II. Use of NACA Study

The second issue before the court is whether Commerce's decision to value raw shrimp based on the surrogate value data contained in the NACA Study, *supra,* is supported by substantial evidence on the record.[14] In making this selection, Commerce rejected data submitted by the petitioners, specifically a price quote for Indian shrimp submitted by affidavit and a public list of ranged shrimp prices from an Indian shrimp processor. Plaintiffs claim that the Bangladeshi data is inferior to the Indian data, and that Commerce should have, therefore, used the Indian data in the valuation of raw shrimp.

In considering the validity of proposed surrogate values, Commerce seeks to weigh the specificity, the accuracy, and the contemporaneity of the proposed data.

---

13 As the court's opinion in *Fujian Lianfu Forestry* was not issued until August 10, 2009, we will not assume that Plaintiff was on notice of the Department's position at the time of the administrative proceeding here.

14 Commerce's selection of the NACA study was, to some degree, based on its selection of Bangladesh as the surrogate country. *See supra.*

See Preliminary Results, 73 Fed.Reg. at 12,134. In making such evaluations Commerce considers (1) whether the surrogate value is product-specific; (2) whether the surrogate value is representative of a range of prices within the POR; (3) whether a surrogate value is a non-export value; and (4) whether the surrogate value is tax exclusive. *See, e.g., Polyethylene Retail Carrier Bags from the People's Republic of China,* 69 Fed.Reg. 34,125 (Dep't Commerce June 18, 2004)(final determination of sales at less than fair value), and accompanying Issues & Decision Memorandum, A-570-886 (June 18, 2004), *available at* http://ia.ita.doc.gov/frn/summary/prc/04-13815-1.pdf (last visited Sept. 23, 2009) 44; *Manganese Metal from the People's Republic of China,* 60 Fed.Reg. 31,282, 31,284 (Dep't Commerce June 14, 1995) (preliminary determination of sales at less than fair value); *accord Dorbest,* 30 CIT at 1686, 462 F.Supp.2d at 1276.

As noted above, in making its selection, Commerce is required to select "the best available information regarding the values of such factors in a market economy country or countries." 19 U.S.C. § 1677b(c)(1). Because "best available information" is not defined in the statute, Commerce has significant discretion in making this determination. *See Nation Ford Chem. Co. v. United States,* 166 F.3d 1373, 1377 (Fed.Cir.1999). Nonetheless, for Commerce's conclusion to be supported by substantial evidence, the court must be satisfied that, viewing the record as a whole, a reasonable mind could conclude that Commerce chose the best available information. *See Dorbest,* 30 CIT at 1676–77, 462 F.Supp.2d at 1269.

For the court to conclude that a reasonable mind would support Commerce's selection of the NACA Study as the best available information, Commerce needed to justify its selection. *See Olympia Indus., Inc. v. United States,* 22 CIT 387, 390, 7 F.Supp.2d 997, 1001 (1998) ("Commerce has an obligation to review all data and then determine what constitutes the best information available or, alternatively, to explain why a particular data set is not methodologically reliable."). In doing so, Commerce must "conduct a fair *comparison* of the data sets on the record" with regard to its announced method or criteria. *Allied Pac. Food (Dalian) Co. v. United States,* 30 CIT 736, 757, 435 F.Supp.2d 1295, 1313–14 (2006)(emphasis added).

The court cannot now determine, however, whether Commerce has conducted the required analysis because, as noted above, one aspect of Commerce's evaluation of proposed surrogate values is that the agency "normally will value all factors in a single surrogate country." 19 C.F.R. § 351.408(c)(2). While the word "normally" leaves the agency some flexibility, the "single country" aspect of the agency's regulation still has the potential to affect its data choices. Thus, if on remand Commerce chooses another surrogate country, it will need to revisit its analysis of its data choices for valuing raw shrimp. The court, therefore, will defer further consideration of this issue until the remand determination is complete.

III. Separate Rate Determination

As noted above, in order for the court to uphold, as supported by substantial evidence on the record, Commerce's application of a dumping margin as reasonable for the Plaintiffs, the margin must be based on "such relevant evidence as a reasonable mind might accept as adequate to support a conclusion." *Matsushita,* 750 F.2d at 933 (quoting *Universal Camera,* 340 U.S. at 477, 71 S.Ct. 456). To allow the court to so conclude, Commerce must articulate a "rational connection between the facts found and the choice made," *Burlington Truck Lines,* 371 U.S. at 168, 83 S.Ct. 239, explaining why the rate chosen "is based on the best available information and establishes antidumping margins 'as accurately as possible." *Shakeproof Assembly Components, Div. of Ill. Tool Works, Inc. v. United States,* 268 F.3d 1376, 1382 (Fed.Cir.2001). For the reasons given below, based on the record here, Commerce's decision to assign dumping margins to Plaintiffs based only on the rates they were assigned in prior proceedings does not meet this standard.

To determine the dumping margin for non-mandatory respondents in NME cases (that is, to determine the "separate rates" margin), Commerce normally relies on the "all others rate" provision of 19 U.S.C. § 1673d(c)(5). *See Issues & Decision Mem.* 18–19. This subsection provides a general rule and an exception for determining such rates. The general rule states that "the estimated all-others rate shall be an amount equal to the weighted average of the estimated weighted average dumping margins established for exporters and producers individually investigated, excluding any zero and de minimis margins, and any margins determined entirely under section 1677e [determinations on the basis of facts available]." 19 U.S.C. § 1673d(c)(5)(A).

The exception found in 19 U.S.C. § 1673d(c)(5)(B) applies in cases where, as here, the dumping margins established for all individually investigated exporters or producers are zero or *de minimis.* In such cases, the agency "may use any reasonable method to establish the estimated all-others rate for exporters and producers not individually investigated, *including* averaging the estimated weighted average dumping margins determined for the exporters and producers individually investigated." 19 U.S.C. § 1673d(c)(5)(B)(emphasis added). Commerce therefore is not precluded from following the method that it used in the *Preliminary Results,* where it assigned the weighted average of the mandatory respondents' rates to the Plaintiffs, resulting in their being assessed a *de minimis* rate. *See Preliminary Results,* 73 Fed.Reg. at 12,135. Rather, as a legal matter, Commerce may choose to include or to exclude the mandatory respondents' zero or *de minimis* margins in calculating a separate rate. *See* 19 U.S.C. § 1673d(c)(5)(B).

All parties agree that the mandatory respondents are presumed to be representative of the respondents as a whole; consequently, the average of the mandatory respondents' rates may be relevant to the determination of a reasonable rate for the separate rate respondents. More particularly, that the mandatory respondents in the current review were found not to be engaged in dumping was evidence indicating that the responding separate rate Plaintiffs may also no longer be engaged in dumping.

This conclusion is bolstered by other recent investigations of shrimp producers and exporters from Vietnam. In the First Administrative Review of the underlying dumping order, for example, respondents Fish One and Grobest each received zero rates. *Certain Frozen Warmwater Shrimp from the Socialist Republic of Vietnam,* 72 Fed.Reg. 52,052, 52,054 (Dep't Commerce Sept. 12, 2007) (final results of first antidumping duty administrative review and first new shipper review). Thus there is at least some evidence to suggest that Vietnamese shrimp producers changed their pricing behavior so as to comply with the antidumping order, as is the intention of such orders. Whether or not this evidence alone is sufficient to compel a conclusion that only a *de minimis* rate could reasonably be applied to the separate rate Plaintiffs, it is evidence on the record in support of the reasonableness of such application.

That Commerce has, in the past, awarded separate rate respondents the weighted average of the mandatory respondent rates, even when all of the mandatory respondent rates are *de minimis,* supports this conclusion. *See Brake Rotors From the People's Republic of China,* 73 Fed. Reg. 32,678 (Dep't Commerce June 10, 2008) (final results of 2006–2007 administrative and new shipper review and partial rescission of 2006–2007 administrative review), and accompanying Issues and Decision Memorandum, A-570-846, AR & NSR 04/01/06-03/31/07 (June 10, 2008), *available at* http://ia.ita.doc.gov/frn/summary/PRC/E8-13001-1.pdf (last visited Sept. 23, 2009); *Honey from Argentina,* 72 Fed. Reg. 73,763 (Dep't Commerce Dec. 28, 2007) (preliminary results of antidumping duty administrative review and intent not to revoke in part) & 73 Fed.Reg. 24,220, 24, 221 (Dep't Commerce May 2, 2008) (final results of antidumping duty administrative review and determination not to revoke in part) (leaving separate rate determination unchanged).[15]

Nonetheless, when the weighted average of *all* exporters and producers individually investigated is zero or *de minimis,* Commerce is not required to use such weighted average as the separate or all-others rate, provided that it uses another "reasonable method to establish the estimated all-others rate." 19 U.S.C. § 1673d(c)(5)(B). The question before the court, therefore, is whether there is substantial evidence to support Commerce's choice to assign to Plaintiffs a rate from the original underlying investigation, or from the First Review—i.e., whether that determination was reasonable based on the record before us.[16] Because Commerce's

15 Commerce seeks to distinguish these decisions, arguing that the companies concerned therein were "fairly homogenous" and that no rates in those cases were determined on the basis of total or adverse facts available. (Def.'s Resp. to Pls.' Mots. for J. Upon Admin. R. 26 ("Def.'s Resp.").) But Commerce ignores its own decision here, as in these prior decisions, to select mandatory respondents to represent the practice in the industry.

16 In its briefing of this issue, Commerce relies on the decision of the court in *Longkou Haimeng Mach. Co. v. United States,* ___ CIT ___, 581 F.Supp.2d 1344 (2008). (Def.'s Resp. 18.) In *Longkou,* the court affirmed Commerce's choice to exclude from the separate rate determination any zero or *de minimis* rates, in light of the statute's clear grant of permission for such a choice. *Longkou,* ___ CIT at ___, 581 F.Supp.2d at 1357–60. The issue here, however, is not the exclusion of zero or *de minimis* rates, but whether there is evidence to support Commerce's selected rate as reasonable considering the record as a whole. Importantly, in *Longkou,* in

choice must be reasonable given the record as a whole, *Nippon Steel,* 458 F.3d at 1351, such choice requires evidence which a reasonable mind could find sufficient to offset the evidence supporting Commerce's assignment of *de minimis* rates to the cooperative uninvestigated respondents in the preliminary investigation results.

Commerce, however, has not provided us with sufficient evidence on the record which could justify ignoring the evidence in favor of assigning a *de minimis* rate to Plaintiffs and which would support as reasonable the alternative rate chosen. Nor has Commerce articulated a clear justification for choosing the dumping margins that it assigned. While relying on 19 U.S.C. § 1673d(c)(5)(B), *see Issues & Decision Mem.* at 19, "Commerce abandoned the methodology [involving] weight-averaging the estimated dumping margins of the Fully-Investigated Respondents[] even though that method is specifically provided for in . . . 19 U.S.C. § 1673d(c)(5)(B)[]." *Yantai Oriental Juice Co. v. United States,* 27 CIT 477, 487 (2003) (citation omitted). The sole reasoning that the Department provided for this decision was that thirty-five companies received margins based on AFA and that "the circumstances of this review are similar to those of the preceding review," *Final Results,* 73 Fed.Reg. at 52,275; *Issues & Decision Mem.* at 19, thereby explaining the use of margins established during the First Review for Fish One and Grobest and those established during the initial investigation for all other respondents.

But the Department's reference to the existence of thirty-five additional, non-cooperating companies named in the Second Review—who did not submit separate rate applications or file any other papers and were therefore assigned rates based on adverse facts available[17]—fails to justify its choice of dumping margin for the cooperative uninvestigated respondents. As this court indicated in *Yantai,* there is no basis in the statute for penalizing cooperative uninvestigated respondents due solely to the presence of non-cooperative uninvestigated respondents who receive a margin based on AFA. *See Yantai,* 27 CIT at 487. While under the "facts available" section of the antidumping statute, 19 U.S.C. § 1677e(b)(2),(3), Commerce may assign, to non-cooperating companies, dumping margins that are based on prior investigations, this section is only applicable when a party, "(A) withholds information that has been requested by the administering authority," "(B) fails to provide such information by the deadlines for submission

---

determining the rate to be applied to the non-selected respondents, Commerce assigned the non-selected, cooperative respondents a weighted-average percentage margin based on the calculated margins of the other mandatory respondents. *Longkou,* 581 F.Supp.2d at 1354, 1358.

17 *See* 19 U.S.C. § 1677e (b) ("If the [agency] finds that an interested party has failed to cooperate . . . [the agency] may use an inference that is adverse to the interests of that party in selecting from among the facts otherwise available."). As noted by Plaintiffs, there is some reason to doubt that these non-cooperating companies, if they exist at all, export to the United States to any substantial degree. We may leave that aside for now.

of the information or in the form and manner requested", or "(C) significantly impedes a proceeding under this title." 19 U.S.C. § 1677e(a). None of these factors apply in this case, and Commerce has not stated that any of the Plaintiffs were non-cooperative. *See Final Results,* 73 Fed. Reg. at 52,274. Therefore, 19 U.S.C. § 1677e does not provide a basis for the Department's use of results from a prior determination with respect to the cooperating companies in the present case.

With respect to the second ground offered in support of Commerce's chosen methodology—that "the circumstances of this review are similar to those of the preceding review," *Final Results,* 73 Fed. Reg. at 52,275; *Issues & Decision Mem.* at 19—the court notes that at oral argument, the Government observed that there were two mandatory respondents in the First Review who chose not to participate and who received AFA rates as a result. *See also Certain Frozen Warmwater Shrimp from the Socialist Republic of Vietnam,* 72 Fed. Reg. 10,689, 10,691–93 (Dep't Commerce Mar. 9, 2007) (preliminary results of first antidumping duty administrative review and new shipper review). While the court takes no position as to the weight of this evidence, we note that, as mandatory respondents are selected to be representative of the industry, there is thus some evidence in the record that, at least during the POR in the First Review, could support an inference that dumping of the subject merchandise from Vietnam was continuing.

Nevertheless, nowhere in the record does Commerce provide sufficient reasoning linking the evidence to its conclusion that margins established for past periods of review, and especially those established during the period of investigation, prior to the imposition of the antidumping duty order, are "based on the best available information and establish[] [the relevant] antidumping margins as accurately as possible." *Shakeproof,* 268 F.3d at 1382. As noted above, in *Chenery,* 332 U.S. at 196, 67 S.Ct. 1575, 91 L.Ed. 1995, the Supreme Court stressed the "simple but fundamental rule of administrative law" that:

> [A] reviewing court, in dealing with a determination or judgment which an administrative agency alone is authorized to make, must judge the propriety of such action solely by the grounds invoked by the agency. If those grounds are inadequate or improper, the court is powerless to affirm the administrative action by substituting what it considers to be a more adequate or proper basis.

Id. Further, "[i]f the administrative action is to be tested by the basis upon which it purports to rest, that basis must be set forth with such clarity as to be understandable[;][i]t will not do for a court to be compelled to guess at the theory underlying the agency's action." *Id.* at 196–97, 67 S.Ct. 1575. On the record before us, no adequate explanation is presented and, accordingly, the court declines to read into the record a justification which Commerce itself did not provide.

On remand, therefore, Commerce must either assign to Plaintiffs the weighted average rate of the mandatory respondents, or else must provide justification, based on substantial evidence on the record, for using another rate.

CONCLUSION

Accordingly, this matter is remanded to the agency for further consideration in accordance with this opinion. Commerce shall have until December 29, 2009 to complete and file its remand redetermination. Plaintiffs shall have until January 29, 2010 to file comments. Defendant and Defendant-Intervenors shall have until February 15, 2010 to file any reply.

It is SO ORDERED.

CANADIAN WHEAT BOARD
v.
UNITED STATES

637 F. Supp. 2d 1329 (C.I.T. 2009)
Decided September 1, 2009

Steptoe & Johnson LLP, Washington, DC (Mark A. Moran, Jamie B. Beaber, and Matthew S. Yeo), for plaintiff Canadian Wheat Board.

Weil, Gotshal & Manges LLP (M. Jean Anderson, John M. Ryan, and Peter J.S. Kaldes), and Wilmer Cutler Pickering Hale and Dorr LLP (Seth P. Waxman, Randolph D. Moss, Mark C. Fleming, and Danielle G. Spinelli), for plaintiff Government of Canada.

Arnold & Porter LLP, Washington, DC (Lawrence A. Schneider), for plaintiff-intervenor Government of Alberta.

Hogan & Hartson LLP, Washington, DC (Mark S. McConnell, H. Deen Kaplan, and Jonathon T. Stoel), for plaintiff-intervenor Government of Ontario.

Cameron & Hornbostel LLP, Washington, DC (Michele Sherman Davenport), for plaintiff-intervenor Government of Saskatchewan.

Tony West, Assistant Attorney General; Jeanne E. Davidson, Director, Patricia M. McCarthy, Assistant Director, Commercial Litigation Branch, Civil Division, United States Department of Justice (Stephen C. Tosini); Office of the Chief Counsel for Import Administration, United States Department of Commerce (Scott D. McBride), of counsel, for defendants.

OPINION

EATON, Judge.

This matter is before the court on the motion of defendants, the United States and the United States Department of Commerce ("Commerce" or "the Department"), for reconsideration, and the joint motion of plaintiffs, Canadian Wheat Board

("CWB") and the Governments of Canada[1] (collectively, "plaintiffs") for clarification. *See* Defs.' Mot. Reconsideration ("Defs.' Mot."); Mot. Clarification ("Pls.' Mot."). These motions follow the court's decision in *Canadian Wheat Board v. United States,* 32 CIT ___, 580 F.Supp.2d 1350 (2008) ("*Wheat Board II*"),[2] which held: (1) that Commerce must liquidate all of CWB's pre-*Timken* notice entries, whose liquidation has been suspended, without regard to duties; and (2) that the Governments of Canada lacked standing to sue under Article III of the Constitution.

As set forth at length in *Wheat Board II,* jurisdiction lies under 28 U.S.C. § 1581(i)(4). *See* 32 CIT at ___, 580 F.Supp.2d at 1357–64; *see also Canadian Wheat Bd. v. United States,* 31 CIT ___, 491 F.Supp.2d 1234 (2007) ("*Wheat Board I*"). Because the motions ask the court to consider important questions not previously addressed, it will treat them both as motions for reconsideration.[3] For the following reasons, defendants' motion for reconsideration is denied, and plaintiffs' motion for reconsideration is granted.

STANDARD OF REVIEW

The granting of a motion for reconsideration is within the court's sound discretion. *See Yuba Natural Res., Inc. v. United States,* 904 F.2d 1577, 1583 (Fed. Cir.1990); *Kerr-McGee Chem. Corp. v. United States,* 14 CIT 582, 583 (1990) (not reported in the Federal Supplement).

DISCUSSION

I. Defendants' Motion

In *Wheat Board II* the court considered questions relating to the liquidation of CWB's entries of hard red spring [HRS] wheat from Canada. By its motion the United States, on behalf of Commerce, makes a new argument that the court was statutorily barred from hearing plaintiffs' claims. In making its argument, defendants assert that "the statute upon which the Court concluded that Commerce had suspended liquidation

---

1 Plaintiff the Federal Government of Canada originally filed a suit under Court No. 07-00059. That action was consolidated with this action under Consol. Court No. 07-00058. Prior to consolidation, the Federal Government of Canada filed a consent motion to intervene in Court No. 07-00058, as did the governments of the provinces of Saskatchewan, Alberta, and Ontario. Each was granted plaintiff-intervenor status in Consol. Court No. 07-00058. In this opinion, and in *Canadian Wheat Board v. United States,* 32 CIT ___, 580 F.Supp.2d 1350 (2008), the Federal Government of Canada together with the governments of Saskatchewan, Alberta, and Ontario are referred to as the "Governments of Canada."

2 Familiarity with the court's October 20, 2008 opinion is presumed.

3 *See* Pls.' Mot. 3 n.1 ("Should this Court conclude that this issue is more properly addressed by means of a motion for modification or reconsideration, we respectfully request that the Court treat this submission as such a motion.").

of entries of hard red spring wheat from Canada . . . [19 U.S.C. § 1516a(g)(5)(C)[4]], expressly prohibits any judicial action with respect to Commerce's actions concerning the statutory suspension of liquidation." Defs.' Mot. 4 (citing 19 U.S.C. § 1516a (g)(5)(C)(iv)[5]) (internal citation omitted). Central to defendants' claim are their assertions that liquidation of CWB's merchandise was suspended pursuant to the provisions of 19 U.S.C. § 1516a(g)(5)(C) and that the court in *Wheat Board II* unlawfully reviewed Commerce's "actions" taken pursuant to that subsection. Thus, defendants' motion is dependent upon two sets of alleged facts: (1) that the court in *Wheat Board II* found that liquidation of CWB's merchandise had been suspended under § 1516a (g)(5)(C); and (2) that, in its *Wheat Board II* decision, the court was reviewing actions taken by Commerce pursuant to § 1516a (g)(5)(C).

Plaintiffs dispute both of these assertions. First, plaintiffs insist:

> [A]s the United States is well aware, the CWB entries at issue in this action were never suspended pursuant to section 1516a(g)(5)(C). That section provides for "continued suspension of liquidation" of entries during an appeal to a NAFTA panel of the results of an administrative review or scope determination. The hard red spring wheat entries at issue here were never the subject of an administrative review or scope determination. Rather, the entries were suspended pursuant to 19 U.S.C. § 1675 when the CWB requested an administrative review and, subsequently, by this Court's injunction when the request for administrative review was withdrawn. Because the entries at issue were not suspended under section 1516a(g)(5)(C), the limitation on judicial review of continued suspensions in subparagraph (C)(iv) does not apply.

---

4 This provision states:

> (C) Suspension of Liquidation
>
> (i) Notwithstanding the provisions of subparagraph (B), in the case of a determination described in clause (iii) or (vi) of subsection (a)(2)(B) of this section for which binational panel review is requested pursuant to article 1904 of the NAFTA or of the Agreement, the administering authority, upon request of an interested party who was a party to the proceeding in connection with which the matter arises and who is a participant in the binational panel review, shall order the continued suspension of liquidation of those entries of merchandise covered by the determination that are involved in the review pending the final disposition of the review.

19 U.S.C. § 1516a(g)(5)(C)(i). As set out in *Tembec, Inc. v. United States,* 30 CIT 1519, 1524–25, 461 F.Supp.2d 1355, 1360–61 (2006), *judgment vacated by Tembec, Inc. v. United States,* 31 CIT ___, 475 F.Supp.2d 1393 (2007), this subsection was designed to provide an injunction-like suspension of liquidation upon an appeal to a NAFTA binational panel of two types of final determinations made by Commerce so that liquidation results, in a NAFTA context, would parallel those that would result had an appeal been taken to this Court, i.e., liquidation would be made in accordance with the final NAFTA panel results.

5 Title 19 U.S.C. § 1516a(g)(5)(C)(iv) provides that:

> Any action taken by the administering authority or the United States Customs Service under this subparagraph shall not be subject to judicial review, and no court of the United States shall have power or jurisdiction to review such action on any question of law or fact by an action in the nature of mandamus or otherwise.

Pls.' Resp. Defs.' Mot. Reconsideration ("Pls.' Resp.") 2 (citations omitted). Thus, plaintiffs argue that defendants are factually incorrect in claiming that liquidation of CWB's merchandise was suspended pursuant to § 1516a(g)(5)(C).

As to defendants' contention that *Wheat Board II* purported to review actions of Commerce made pursuant to 19 U.S.C. § 1516a(g)(5)(C), plaintiffs maintain:

> [T]he United States' argument fails even on its own (counterfactual) terms. Section 1516a(g)(5)(C)(iv) operates only to bar judicial review of action taken by Commerce under 1516a(g)(5)(C), *i.e.,* action taken to continue suspension of liquidation. It would not oust this Court of jurisdiction over actions under 28 U.S.C. § 1581(i) like this one, which do not challenge the continued suspension of liquidation, but rather Commerce's failure to liquidate entries in accordance with the final NAFTA panel decision in the case.

Pls.' Resp. 2–3. Put another way, plaintiffs claim that § 1516a(g)(5)(C)(iv) prohibits judicial review only of specified actions taken by Commerce pursuant to § 1516a (g)(5)(C)(i). According to plaintiffs, in this case no such actions were taken and hence the court was not reviewing any action taken under § 1516a(g)(5)(C)(i).

The court finds that plaintiffs are correct in both of their contentions. First, despite defendants' claims to the contrary, in *Wheat Board II* liquidation of CWB's merchandise was not suspended pursuant to 19 U.S.C. § 1516a(g)(5)(C). Rather, liquidation was suspended or enjoined pursuant to other provisions of law. *See Wheat Board II,* 32 CIT at ___, 580 F.Supp.2d at 1355–56 ("Plaintiff CWB's entries were made in September 2004. . . . Liquidation of these entries was suspended on October 31, 2005[6], when CWB filed a request for administrative review of the AD/CVD Orders. . . . Thereafter, on February 26, 2007, CWB withdrew its request for administrative review. That same day, CWB moved to restrain temporarily and enjoin preliminarily the liquidation of its merchandise to allow it to litigate the merits of its case. . . .") (citations omitted). That liquidation of CWB's entries was never suspended pursuant to § 1516a(g)(5)(C) is apparent since that subsection provides for an injunction-like suspension of liquidation following a final determination of an administrative review or scope determination. Here, there was no scope determination and there was also no administrative review because the request for such review was withdrawn. *See Wheat Board II,* 32 CIT at ___, 580 F.Supp.2d at 1356.

Next, defendants argue that the court was barred from reviewing the effect of its notice of revocation, (Antidumping Duty Investigation and Countervailing Duty Investigation of HRS Wheat from Canada, 71 Fed.Reg. 8,275 (Dep't of Commerce Feb. 16, 2006) ("Notice of Revocation")),[7] because 19 U.S.C. § 1516(a)(g)(5)(C)(iv)).

---

6 A request for an administrative review results in the continuation of the suspension of liquidation. *See Tembec, Inc. v. United States,* 30 CIT 1519, 461 F.Supp.2d 1355, 1361 (2006), *judgment vacated by Tembec, Inc. v. United States,* 31 CIT ___, 475 F.Supp.2d 1393 (2007).

7 On February 16, 2006, the Department published the Notice of Revocation, which "revok[ed] the countervailing duty order and antidumping duty order on [HRS] wheat from Canada. . . ." Notice of Revocation, 71 Fed. Reg. at 8,275.

Expressly precludes judicial review of "any action" taken by Commerce "under this subparagraph." For the court, the operative word is "action." *See* Defs.' Mot. 6 (citing 19 U.S.C. § 1516(a)(g)(5)(C)(iv)). An examination of the subparagraph reveals that the "action" that Commerce is authorized to undertake under § 1516(a)(g)(5)(C)(i) is to "order the continued suspension of liquidation of those entries of merchandise" that are the subject of a completed administrative review or scope determination. *See* 19 U.S.C. § 1516(a)(g)(5)(C)(i). It is clear that the purpose of this subsection is to bar this Court from reviewing decisions of Commerce in a precise set of circumstances relating to the continuation of a suspension of liquidation following the completion of two specific administrative procedures. These continuations of the suspension of liquidation are the only actions authorized by the subsection. *See* 19 U.S.C. § 1516a(g)(5)(C)(i); 19 U.S.C. §§ 1516a(2)(B)(iii) and (vi). In this case, no party has challenged any action relating to the continued suspension of liquidation under § 1516a(g)(5)(C), nor could they, simply because there was no suspension of liquidation under that subsection.

Defendants endeavor to bolster their position by, for the first time, recharacterizing the Notice of Revocation as a "decision not to grant the benefit of section 1516a(g)(5)(C) suspensions to certain entries of subject merchandise." Defs.' Mot. 6. This recharacterization does not save defendants' argument. First, as noted, under the facts of this case there was no suspension of liquidation under 19 U.S.C. § 1516a(g)(5)(C). Second, this "decision," if in fact there ever was one, is simply not an action authorized by § 1516a(g)(5)(C).

Finally, the court notes language in *Wheat Board II* that may have led to a misunderstanding of the role played by 19 U.S.C. § 1516a(g)(5)(C) in that decision. First, the court's assertion that, "[f]or CWB, the exception found in § 1516a(g)(5)(C) applies," (*Wheat Board II,* 32 CIT at ___, 580 F.Supp.2d at 1367), is a misstatement to the extent it suggests that CWB relied on the suspension of liquidation found in § 1516a(g)(5)(C) in its arguments. As noted, the liquidation of CWB's merchandise was the result of other provisions of law.

In addition, in reaching its conclusions in *Wheat Board II,* the court relied on the reasoning found in *Tembec, Inc. v. United States,* 30 CIT 1519, 461 F.Supp.2d 1355 (2006) ("*Tembec II*"), *judgment vacated by Tembec, Inc. v. United States,* 31 CIT ___, 475 F.Supp.2d 1393 (2007) ("*Tembec III*").[8] In that case, suspension of liquidation of some of the entries at issue was accomplished pursuant to § 1516a(g)(5)(C). As has been noted, however, liquidation of none of CWB's entries was suspended pursuant to § 1516a(g)(5)(C), and plaintiffs have never asserted otherwise. Rather, the reason that 19 U.S.C. § 1516a(g)(5)(C) had such a prominent place in both *Tembec II* and *Wheat Board II* is that its language and

---

8 The *Tembec III* Court vacated as moot its prior judgment in *Tembec II,* but, having found "that the issues in *Tembec II* were decided within the context of a live controversy," kept the *Tembec II* decision in place. *Tembec III,* 31 CIT at ___, 475 F.Supp.2d at 1402–03.

legislative history demonstrate Congress's intent that a suspension of liquidation preserves entries for liquidation in accordance with a NAFTA panel's final determination. In order to make this point, the court in *Wheat Board II* referred to *Tembec II* by stating that (1) the court "expressly adopts the *Tembec II* panel's analysis," and (2) the court adopted *Tembec II's* observation "that the 'continued' suspension of liquidation provided for in § 1516a(g)(5)(C) 'acts as the equivalent of an injunction against liquidation and thus halts liquidation until the suspension expires.'" *Wheat Board II,* 32 CIT at ___ 580 F.Supp.2d at 1368–70 (citation omitted); *see also Tembec II,* 30 CIT at 1530, 461 F.Supp.2d at 1365–66 ("Congress, having intended parallel remedies, intended that the suspension of liquidation provided for in § 1516a(g)(5)(C) would provide the same result following a NAFTA panel decision, as would an injunction issued by this Court.").

The purpose of citing to these portions of *Tembec II* was to make the point that a suspension of liquidation under § 1516a(g)(5)(C) would preserve entries for liquidation in accordance with a final NAFTA panel ruling. It is, however, the fact of suspension that commands this result, not the means. In other words, suspension for any reason would have the same effect as suspension under § 1516a(g)(5)(C). As a result, even though none of the entries that were the subject of *Wheat Board II* were suspended in accordance with § 1516a(g)(5)(C), because liquidation was suspended under other provisions, they must be liquidated in accordance with the NAFTA panel's final ruling.

With this further explanation, the court finds that the holding and reasoning of *Wheat Board II* remain intact, i.e., "Commerce is obligated to liquidate all of CWB's pre-*Timken* Notice entries, whose liquidation has been suspended, without regard to duties." *See Wheat Board II,* 32 CIT at ___, 580 F.Supp.2d at 1370. Further, "[t]his result is demanded by both logic as well as the statute. That is, because the subject imports caused no injury during any time relevant to this inquiry, CWB should owe no duties." *Id.* at ___, 580 F.Supp.2d at 1370. Accordingly, defendants' motion is denied.

II. Plaintiffs' Motion

Plaintiffs ask the court to address that portion of *Wheat Board II* that dismissed the claims of the Governments of Canada for lack of Article III standing. *See* Pls.' Mot. 2; *see also Wheat Board II,* 32 CIT at ___, 580 F.Supp.2d at 1364–1366. The Canadian government plaintiffs do not dispute their dismissal as plaintiffs for lack of Article III standing, however, they seek to remain in this case as plaintiff-intervenors. Pls.' Mot. 2. Plaintiffs argue that when "an intervenor brings the same claims and seeks the same relief as the original plaintiff, the intervenor need not independently have Article III standing." Pls.' Mot. 5. In other words, plaintiffs argue that although any independent legal action brought by the Governments of Canada might be dismissed for lack of Article III standing, they should not be dismissed from CWB's case because they are properly plaintiff-intervenors. For the reasons that follow, the court finds that the Governments of Canada may take part in this case as permissive plaintiff-intervenors.

A. Background

In *Wheat Board II* the court dismissed the Federal Government of Canada's complaint for lack of standing. *See Wheat Board II,* 32 CIT at ___, 580 F.Supp.2d at 1366. In doing so the court held that none of the Governments of Canada had demonstrated "injury-in-fact" independent of CWB's claimed injury. *Wheat Board II,* 32 CIT at ___, 580 F.Supp.2d at 1366. As plaintiffs point out, however, *Wheat Board II* examined Article III standing to bring separate actions, but not in the context of participating in the case as intervenors. *See* Pls.' Mot. 2

B. Statutory Authorization and Intervention

Intervention before this Court is authorized by statute. *See* 28 U.S.C. § 2631(j)(1) ("Any person who would be adversely affected or aggrieved by a decision in a civil action pending in the Court of International Trade may, by leave of court, intervene in such action. . . ."). As noted in *Ontario Forest Industr. Assoc. v. United States,* 30 CIT 1117, 1130, 444 F.Supp.2d 1309, 1322 (2006), this statute has been given a broad construction: "The phrase 'adversely affected or aggrieved,' which mirrors the language in numerous statutes, including of Administrative Procedure Act, 5 U.S.C. § 702, represents a 'congressional intent to cast the [intervention net] broadly—beyond the common-law interests and substantive statutory rights' traditionally known to law. *Fed. Election Comm'n v. Akins,* 524 U.S. 11, 19, 118 S.Ct. 1777, 141 L.Ed.2d 10 (1998)."

Each Canadian entity has alleged an interest sufficient to demonstrate that it has been "affected" or "aggrieved" by Commerce's action within the meaning of 28 U.S.C. § 2631(j)(1). Cf. Mot. Intervene of Gov't of Canada 3 (". . . as a NAFTA Party and frequent party to U.S. AD/CVD actions against Canadian products, the [Federal] Government of Canada has broad concerns with the policy and practice of the United States of continuing to apply an AD or CVD order, to unliquidated pre-*Timken* Notice entries despite the invalidation through NAFTA binational panel review of an agency determination that was an essential underpinning of the order."). Although not NAFTA parties, the complaints of the governments of Saskatchewan, Ontario and Alberta make allegations similar to those of the Federal Government of Canada.

C. Intervention Under Rule 24

USCIT Rule 24 ("Rule 24"), governs the right to intervene in actions brought before this Court. *See* USCIT Rule 24. Rule 24 applies to intervention as a matter of right and to permissive intervention.[9] *Id.* Here, the Governments of Canada move in the alternative for intervention as of right or by permission. *See* Pls.'

---

9 USCIT Rule 24(b) states in pertinent part:

> (b) Permissive Intervention
>
> Upon timely application anyone may be permitted to intervene in an action . . . when an applicant's claim or defense and the main action have a question of law or fact in common. . . .

Reply Supp. Mot. Clarification ("Pls.' Reply") 7, 7 n.3. Because it finds that the Governments of Canada may proceed by permission, the court will address permissive intervention only.

In March of 2007 the Federal Government of Canada and the provinces of Alberta, Ontario and Saskatchewan each filed motions to intervene in the case brought by CWB. *See* Consent Mot. Intervene as Plaintiff-Intervenor by Gov't of Canada; Consent Mot. Intervene by Gov't of Alberta; Consent Mot. Intervene by Gov't of Ontario; Consent Mot. Intervene as Plaintiff-Intervenor by Gov't of Saskatchewan. Each of these motions was accompanied by a complaint. *Id.* Each motion was consented to by defendants, although this consent stated that it was for "procedural convenience . . ., without waiving any argument concerning standing or any other issue." *See, e.g.,* Consent Mot. Intervene as Plaintiff-Intervenor by Gov't of Canada 4. While defendants claim that the Governments of Canada may not proceed in this case as intervenors because they lack Article III standing, defendants have made no argument that they have not satisfied the requirements of USCIT Rule 24. The granting of permissive intervention is discretionary with the Court. *Manuli Autoadesivi, S.p.A. v. United States,* 9 CIT 24, 26, 602 F.Supp. 96, 98 (1985).

Permissive intervention under USCIT Rule 24(b) requires that an applicant's claim and that of the main action share a common question of law or fact. USCIT Rule 24(b). Here, the facts of the case are necessarily shared by all entities interested in the case. In addition, the respective complaints of the Governments of Canada are, in every material respect, the same as that of CWB. That being the case, the requirements of USCIT Rule 24(b) are satisfied.

As noted, defendants made no argument that the Governments of Canada failed to qualify as permissive intervenors at the time they consented to their intervention. Even now, defendants' only claim is that intervenors must have Article III standing in order to intervene. In other words, defendants appear to concede that the Governments of Canada have met the requirements of 28 U.S.C. § 2631(j)(1) and of USCIT Rule 24(b).

D. Article III Standing

As far as can be determined, the question of whether independent Article III standing is required for permissive intervenor status under USCIT Rule 24 or for that matter under Fed.R.Civ.P. 24[10] is a question of first impression for the Federal Circuit. *See Landmark Land Co. v. FDIC,* 256 F.3d 1365, 1382 (Fed.Cir.2001) ("*Landmark*"). As will be seen, the other Circuits are split on this question.

---

10 Because both the Federal Rules of Civil Procedure and the rules of this Court are undergoing drafting revisions, the text of Fed. R.Civ.P. 24 has newly revised language while USCIT Rule 24 retains the old wording. At the time the Governments of Canada made their motions to intervene the rules were, in all material respects, the same.

For its part, the United States Supreme Court appears to favor a finding that Article III standing is not required for an intervenor to participate in an action. While no case is directly on point, the Court has addressed questions related to the issue. *See Diamond v. Charles,* 476 U.S. 54, 68, 106 S.Ct. 1697, 90 L.Ed.2d 48 (1986) ("*Diamond*"). In *Diamond,* several physicians challenged the constitutionality of an Illinois abortion statute. *Id.* at 56–57, 106 S.Ct. 1697. The State of Illinois defended the statute's constitutionality, and a pediatrician who supported the law filed a motion to intervene on the side of the State. *Id.* at 57, 106 S.Ct. 1697. Thereafter, the district court enjoined certain provisions of the Illinois statute and the Court of Appeals for the Seventh Circuit affirmed. *Id.* at 61, 106 S.Ct. 1697. The state of Illinois did not file a petition for a writ of certiorari, but the intervening pediatrician did seek to appeal to the Supreme Court. *Id.*

The Court held that, because the State of Illinois did not appeal the circuit court's decision, there was no longer an Article III "case" or "controversy" to be heard. *Id.* at 63–64, 106 S.Ct. 1697. In reaching its conclusion, the Court found that intervention, whether permissive or as of right, does not confer a status sufficient to keep a case alive absent an independent showing of Article III standing. *Id.* at 68, 106 S.Ct. 1697 ("Although intervenors are considered parties entitled, among other things, to seek review by this Court, an intervenor's right to continue a suit in the absence of the party on whose side intervention was permitted is contingent upon a showing by the intervenor that he fulfills the requirements of Art. III.") (citations omitted); *see also id.* at 68, n. 21, 106 S.Ct. 1697 (noting the split of authority among circuit courts on this issue).

In deciding *Diamond,* the Court explicitly stated that it was not deciding whether those seeking to intervene on the side of a party that has demonstrated Article III standing must show that they too satisfy the case or controversy requirement.

> We need not decide today whether a party seeking to intervene before a District Court must satisfy not only the requirements of Rule 24(a)(2)[11], but also the requirements of Art. III. To continue this suit in the absence of Illinois, Diamond himself must satisfy the requirements of Art. III. The interests Diamond asserted before the District Court in seeking to intervene plainly are insufficient to confer standing on him to continue this suit now.

See Diamond, 476 U.S. at 68–69, 106 S.Ct. 1697. Nonetheless, the Court stated that: "[h]ad the State sought review, . . . [the pediatrician], as an intervening defendant below, also would be entitled to seek review, enabling him to file a brief on the merits, and to seek leave to argue orally." *Id.* at 64, 106 S.Ct. 1697. In addition, the Court observed that the "ability to ride 'piggyback' on the State's undoubted standing exists only if the State is in fact an appellant before the Court; in the absence of the State in that capacity, there is no case for Diamond to join." *Id.* at 64, 106 S.Ct. 1697. In other words, the Supreme Court appears to accept the idea

11 This subsection is "Intervention of Right."

that, if the party with which it is aligned has demonstrated Article III standing, an intervenor, despite the inability to demonstrate independent Article III standing, may participate in the case.

Likewise, in *Trbovich v. United Mine Workers of America,* 404 U.S. 528, 92 S. Ct. 630, 30 L.Ed.2d 686 (1972) ("*Trbovich*"), the Supreme Court allowed a plaintiff-intervenor to remain in a case even though his participation as a plaintiff was barred by statute.[12] Thus, while the intervenor could not independently satisfy the case or controversy requirement, the Court found that he too could "piggyback" on the standing of another so long as the intervention was limited to the claims presented by that party.

i. Federal Circuit Authority

As noted, the only Federal Circuit case that touches on this issue is *Landmark,* 256 F.3d at 1365. In *Landmark,* the Federal Deposit Insurance Corporation ("FDIC") sought to intervene in an action brought against the United States. *Id.* at 1379–80. The trial court granted FDIC's motion to intervene. *Id.* at 1380. On appeal, the Federal Circuit dismissed the FDIC as an intervenor because its claims were unrelated to those of the party on whose side it sought to intervene. *Id.* at 1382.

As to Article III standing, the Court found a lack of a justiciable controversy between the FDIC and defendant the United States because "[H]ere at no time were the FDIC and the United States truly adverse parties." *Landmark,* 256 F.3d at 1380. As a result, the FDIC could not demonstrate that it had standing under Article III. The Federal Circuit, however, went on to observe:

> The FDIC intervened in this case. Whether an intervening party must satisfy the case-or-controversy requirement independently of the claims brought by the other plaintiffs is an open question. We conclude, however, that because the FDIC's claims are unrelated to those brought by [the plaintiff], it would be improper to permit the FDIC to proceed given the lack of a justiciable controversy with respect to the claims.

Id. (citations omitted). Thus, the Federal Circuit in *Landmark* has left open the possibility that an intervenor need not satisfy the Article III case or controversy requirement so long as its claims are the same as those of a party that has satisfied the test.

ii. Circuits Holding That An Intervening Party Does Not Need To Have Independent Article III Standing

Unlike the Federal Circuit, other Circuits have taken a definitive position on this issue. In *United States Postal Service v. Brennan,* ("*Brennan*"), 579 F.2d 188, 190

12 The Secretary of Labor had instituted the action under 29 U.S.C. § 402(b) of the Labor Management Reporting and Disclosure Act ("LMRDA"). *Trbovich,* 404 U.S. 528 at 529, 531, 92 S.Ct. 630. ("This Court has held that § 403 [of LMRDA] prohibits union members from initiating a private suit to set aside an election."). Thus, the intervenor had no independent standing to sue.

(2d Cir.1978), the Second Circuit stated that intervening parties need not establish independent standing, so long as there is a case or controversy within the meaning of Article III between the plaintiff and defendant. *Brennan* involved a challenge to the constitutionality of the Private Express Statutes[13] and applicable Postal Service Regulations. The dispute arose when the United States Postal Service filed an action to permanently enjoin the Brennans from running a mail delivery business. *Id.* The National Association of Letter Carriers ("NALC"), a union representing Postal Service employees, filed a motion to intervene. The district court denied the motion because NALC could not demonstrate Article III standing. *Id.*

On appeal, the Second Circuit affirmed the denial[14] of NALC's motion to intervene but disagreed with the district court on the significance of standing. *Id.* The Court stated that the question of standing was to be considered in the framework of Article III, which restricts judicial power to "cases" and "controversies." *Id.* The Court went on to observe: "[t]he existence of a case or controversy having been established as between the Postal Service and the Brennans, there was no need to impose the standing requirement upon the proposed intervenor." *Id.* (citations omitted).

In *Ruiz v. Estelle,* 161 F.3d 814, 830 (5th Cir.1998) ("Ruiz"), the Fifth Circuit similarly held that Article III does not require intervenors to possess independent standing "where the intervention is into a subsisting and continuing Article III case or controversy. . . ." The *Ruiz* Court reasoned that, once a valid Article III case or controversy is present, a court's jurisdiction vests and the presence of additional parties, although they alone could not independently satisfy the Article III requirements, does not affect the jurisdiction that is already established. *Id.* at 832 (footnote omitted).

Recently, the Tenth Circuit also held that parties seeking to intervene under Rule 24 need not establish Article III standing, "so long as another party with constitutional standing on the same side as the intervenor remains in the case." *San Juan County, Utah v. United States,* 503 F.3d 1163, 1172 (10th Cir.2007) (en banc) (quotation and citation omitted).

The Sixth and Eleventh Circuits have echoed the view that an intervening party need not establish standing under Article III. *See Purnell v. City of Akron,* 925 F.2d 941, 948 (6th Cir.1991); *Dillard v. Chilton County Comm'n,* 495 F.3d 1324, 1336 (11th Cir.2007).

---

13 The statutes limited the ability of private parties to compete with the United States mail. *See Air Courier Conference v. Am. Postal Workers Union,* 498 U.S. 517, 519, 111 S.Ct. 913, 112 L.Ed.2d 1125 (1991).

14 The Court of Appeals found that NALC, having intervened as a matter of right under Fed.R.Civ.P. 24(a)(2) failed to demonstrate "any inadequacy of representation." *Brennan,* 579 F.2d at 191.

iii. Circuits Holding That An Intervening Party Must Establish Independent Article III Standing In Order To Intervene In An Action

By way of contrast, the Seventh, Eighth and D.C. Circuits have held that an intervening party must establish Article III standing in addition to meeting Rule 24's intervention requirements. *See Jones v. Prince George's County, Maryland,* 348 F.3d 1014, 1017 (D.C.Cir.2003) (per curiam) ("*Jones*"); *Fund for Animals, Inc., v. Norton,* 322 F.3d 728, 731–32 (D.C.Cir. 2003) ("*Fund for Animals*"); *Mausolf v. Babbitt,* 85 F.3d 1295, 1300 (8th Cir.1996) ("*Mausolf*"); *Solid Waste Agency v. United States Army Corps of Eng'rs,* 101 F.3d 503, 507 (7th Cir.1996) ("*Solid Waste Agency*"). In articulating their reasoning, these Circuits have found that intervenors must establish Article III standing because they seek to participate on an equal footing with the original parties to the action. *See, e.g., Mausolf,* 85 F.3d at 1300 ("An Article III case or controversy is one where all parties have standing, and a would-be intervenor, because he seeks to participate as a party, must have standing as well."); *see also Fund for Animals,* 322 F.3d at 731–732; *Jones,* 348 F.3d at 1017; *Solid Waste Agency,* 101 F.3d at 507.

E. The Governments of Canada Have Standing as Plaintiff-Intervenors

Plaintiffs' motion asks the court to permit the Governments of Canada to remain in this action as plaintiff-intervenors. *See* Pls.' Reply Mem. 7, 7 n.3. As noted, plaintiffs contend that because they are bringing "precisely the same claims and seek precisely the same relief" as CWB, they need not establish independent Article III standing, and should be allowed to continue in the ongoing litigation as plaintiff-intervenors. Pls,' Mot. 7.

The court finds that the Governments of Canada may participate in the ongoing litigation as permissive plaintiff-intervenors. This conclusion results from the clear indication of the Supreme Court in *Diamond* that this would be the outcome should it address the issue, and from the Federal Circuit decision in *Landmark,* suggesting this as a possible result. In reaching its conclusion the court relies, in particular, on the discussion in *Ruiz*:

> We find the better reasoning in those cases which hold that Article III does not require intervenors to possess standing. These cases recognize that the Article III standing doctrine serves primarily to guarantee the existence of a "case" or "controversy" appropriate for judicial determination. . . .
>
> Once a valid Article III case-or-controversy is present, the court's jurisdiction vests. The presence of additional parties, although they alone could independently not satisfy Article III's requirements, does not of itself destroy jurisdiction already established.

161 F.3d at 832 (citations and footnote omitted).

In other words, Article III establishes the jurisdictional requirement that the court address cases or controversies. Once that jurisdictional requirement is met, so long as the parties with standing remain in the case, the court's jurisdiction continues regardless of the presence of intervenors. Here, the court has a case or controversy before it brought by CWB against the United States and Commerce. The Governments of Canada have met the requirements of USCIT Rule 24(b) and their claims and prayers for relief are identical to those of CWB on whose side they seek to intervene. No party would be burdened by granting the Governments of Canada plaintiff-intervenor status, nor would the court. Therefore, the Governments of Canada may remain in this case as permissive plaintiff-intervenors despite being unable to demonstrate independent Article III standing.

F. Remedies

Finally, in *Wheat Board II* the court directed the parties to "consult and jointly submit to the court the form of a judgment comporting with this opinion. . . ." *Wheat Board II,* 32 CIT at ___, 580 F.Supp.2d at 1371. While this instruction has since been modified by a subsequent court order,[15] a dispute has arisen concerning the relief the order should grant. CWB and the Governments of Canada insist that the judgment should "award all of the injunctive and declaratory relief requested by CWB and the Canadian federal and provincial governments as plaintiff-intervenors." Pls.' Mot. 8. Plaintiffs argue that this relief should include a declaration that:

> The Tariff Act of 1930, as amended, requires unliquidated entries to be liquidated in accordance with the final and conclusive results of binational panel review, and 19 U.S.C. § 1516a(g)(5)(B) does not require or permit such entries to be liquidated in accordance with an ITC or Commerce determination finally and conclusively invalidated pursuant to binational panel review.

Pls.' Mot. 8, App. A at 4.

Plaintiffs insist that this remedy is appropriate because "If the judgment does not clearly grant declaratory relief, Defendants may contend that the judgment has no bearing on their conduct in future proceedings, resulting in future attempts to liquidate entries in accordance with AD or CVD determinations invalidated by binational panels." Pls.' Mot. 8. In other words, plaintiffs would have the court grant declaratory relief for use in future disputes in the event a situation arises with facts that are substantially the same as those presented here. The defendants oppose declaratory relief.[16]

---

15 *Canadian Wheat Board v. United States,* Consol. Ct. No. 07-00058 (Nov. 21, 2008) (order granting defendants' motion for relief from filing a judgment).

16 The defendants assert that: "The Declaratory Judgment Act prohibits the issuance of declaratory judgments 'in any civil action involving an antidumping or countervailing duty proceeding regarding a class or kind of merchandise of a free trade area country.'" Defs.' Resp. Pls.' Mot. Clarification 8 (quoting 28 U.S.C. § 2201(a)). Because the court declines to issue a declaratory judgment it does not address this argument.

The authority to grant a declaratory judgment is found in the Declaratory Judgment Act, (28 U.S.C. § 2201(a)), and the rules of this Court. *See* 28 U.S.C. § 2201(a) ("[A]ny court of the United States, upon the finding of an appropriate pleading, may declare the rights and other legal relations of any interested party seeking such declaration, whether or not further relief is or could be sought."); USCIT Rule 57.

The Supreme Court has explained that "[w]hile the courts should not be reluctant" to grant relief in appropriate cases, the declaratory judgment statute "is an enabling Act, which confers a discretion on the courts rather than an absolute right upon the litigant." *Pub. Serv. Comm'n v. Wycoff Co.,* 344 U.S. 237, 241, 243, 73 S.Ct. 236, 97 L.Ed. 291 (1952); *see also Wilton v. Seven Falls Co.,* 515 U.S. 277, 288, 115 S.Ct. 2137, 132 L.Ed.2d 214 (1995) ("By the Declaratory Judgment Act, Congress sought to place a remedial arrow in the district court's quiver; it created an opportunity, rather than a duty, to grant a new form of relief to qualifying litigants."); *Green v. Mansour,* 474 U.S. 64, 72, 106 S.Ct. 423, 88 L.Ed.2d 371 (1985).

The court will not exercise its discretion to enter a declaratory judgment. This case concerns the return of deposits now held by the United States government. Plaintiffs will ultimately have a judgment directing the return of their deposits. Plaintiffs have presented nothing to indicate that they have any reasonable belief that they will not receive their money or that they will be injured in the future in the same way by defendants' conduct. In this respect, the facts here can be contrasted with those in *Canadian Lumber Trade Alliance v. United States,* 30 CIT 892, 895, 441 F.Supp.2d 1259, 1263 (2006), where the Court found "that future injury to Plaintiffs from Defendant's conduct is certain." Thus, the court is unable to find that declaratory judgment, having prospective effect, is appropriate here.

Finally, plaintiffs seek injunctive relief, although they make no argument for this remedy in their moving papers. In addition, in their complaints none of the parties ask for mandatory injunctive relief. Because plaintiffs fail to make any argument with respect to their request for an injunction their application for this relief is denied. *See eBay Inc. v. MercExchange, L.L.C.,* 547 U.S. 388, 391, 126 S.Ct. 1837, 164 L.Ed.2d 641 (2006) ("According to well-established principles of equity, a plaintiff seeking a permanent injunction must satisfy a four-factor test before a court may grant such relief.").

CONCLUSION

For the foregoing reasons, the court denies defendants' motion for reconsideration and grants plaintiffs' motion for reconsideration. The parties are hereby ordered to contact Casey Ann Cheevers, Case Manager, United States Court of International Trade, One Federal Plaza, New York, New York, 10278, within five days of the issuance of this opinion to set the date for a hearing as to the form of judgment.

HUVIS CORPORATION
v.
UNITED STATES

570 F.3d 1347 (Fed. Cir. 2009)
Decided June 25, 2009

Michael P. House, McDermott Will & Emery LLP, of Washington, DC, argued for plaintiff-appellant. With him on the brief was Raymond Paretzky.

Stephen C. Tosini, Attorney, Commercial Litigation Branch, Civil Division, United States Department of Justice, of Washington, DC, argued for defendant-appellee. With him on the brief were Michael F. Hertz, Acting Assistant Attorney General, Jeanne E. Davidson, Director, and Patricia M. McCarthy, Assistant Director.

Before LOURIE, DYK, and PROST, Circuit Judges.

LOURIE, *Circuit Judge*.

Huvis Corporation ("Huvis") appeals from the judgment of the United States Court of International Trade affirming the United States Department of Commerce's ("Commerce's") valuation of Huvis's imports. *See Huvis Corp. v. United States*, 525 F. Supp. 2d 1370 (Ct. Int'l Trade 2007) ("*Huvis I*"); *Huvis Corp. v. United States*, No. 06-00380, 2008 Ct. Int'l. Trade Lexis 82 (Aug. 5, 2008) ("*Huvis II*"). Because Commerce's decision to use a constructed market price in valuing Huvis's imports was supported by substantial evidence and not contrary to law, we affirm.

BACKGROUND

Huvis is a Korean producer and exporter of polyester staple fiber, a synthetic fiber that is used for stuffing products such as clothing and pillows. It is subject to an antidumping duty order, under which a dumping margin is applied to all of Huvis's imports. Polyester staple fiber is made from terephthalic acid. Huvis uses three grades of terephthalic acid in manufacturing its fiber: qualified-grade, middle-grade, and purified. Huvis's importation of polyester staple fiber into the United States had been reviewed by Commerce four times in periodic administrative reviews, prior to the administrative review it now appeals. During the fifth period of review, which is the subject of the present appeal, Huvis purchased all of the terephthalic acid it used from affiliated companies.

Commerce assigns a "value" to an import to determine the dumping margin applied to it. When an importer purchases a "major input" from an affiliated party, instead of assuming the input was purchased at arm's length, Commerce applies the "major input rule" to determine the value of the input. 19 U.S.C. § 1677b(f)(2), (3). The parties agree that terephthalic acid constitutes a major input to polyester staple fiber. Commerce's interpretation of the major input rule requires Commerce normally to "determine the value of a major input purchased from an affiliated person based on the higher of: (1) [t]he price paid by the exporter or producer to the affiliated person for the major input; (2) [t]he amount usually reflected in sales of the major input in the market under consideration; or (3) [t]he cost to the affiliated person of producing the major input." 19 C.F.R. 351.407(b). Thus, for the fifth period of review, as with each of the previous review periods, Commerce requested that Huvis submit three measures for its purchases of each grade of terephthalic acid made during the period of review: (1) the price Huvis paid to its affiliated suppliers (the "transfer price"); (2) the price at which the affiliated producer made sales of the input to unaffiliated parties (the "market price"); and (3) the affiliated producer's cost of production for the input (the "cost of production"). For middle-grade terephthalic acid, Huvis submitted all three measures. For qualified-grade and purified terephthalic acids, Huvis submitted only the transfer price and cost of production measures because it did not have access to market price data, as its supplier for those two products, Samnam Petrochemical Company, Ltd. ("Samnam"), considered that data proprietary.

In each of its three previous reviews, Huvis had similarly submitted information that was missing certain market price data. Commerce had, in all cases but one, applied the major input rule for those products by comparing only the two measures Huvis had provided, transfer price and the cost of production,[1] but in the fifth administrative review, Commerce chose to include in the comparison a market price that was constructed from "facts available."

"If . . . necessary information is not available on the record," Commerce is required to "use the facts otherwise available in reaching the applicable determination under this title." 19 U.S.C. § 1677e(a). However, under 19 U.S.C. § 1677e(c), Commerce must corroborate such secondary information "from independent sources that are reasonably at [its] disposal." Commerce must also

> consider information that is submitted by an interested party and is necessary to the determination but does not meet all the applicable requirements . . . if
>
> (1) the information is submitted by the deadline established for its submission,
>
> (2) the information can be verified,

---

1 In the one counterexample, Commerce explained that the evidence suggested that the qualified-grade and middle-grade terephthalic acids were interchangeable, so it filled in the missing qualified-grade terephthalic acid market price with Huvis's submitted middle-grade terephthalic acid market price.

> (3) the information is not so incomplete that it cannot serve as a reliable basis for reaching the applicable determination,
>
> (4) the interested party has demonstrated that it acted to the best of its ability in providing the information and meeting the requirements established by the administering authority or the Commission with respect to the information, and
>
> (5) the information can be used without undue difficulties. 19 U.S.C. § 1677m(e). Commerce finally may not draw "adverse inferences" against an importer unless the importer fails to cooperate in the investigation.

19 U.S.C. § 1677e(b). The parties agree that Huvis cooperated with Commerce in the fifth review.

Commerce applied the major input rule by first constructing the missing market prices for Huvis's qualified-grade and purified terephthalic acids using facts available. It constructed the market prices by first calculating an average profit rate taken from the supplier's submitted financial statements. It then increased the costs of production by that profit rate to form constructed market prices for each of the qualified-grade and purified terephthalic acids. Applying the major input rule, Commerce found that the constructed market prices were the highest of the three measures for both the qualified- grade and purified terephthalic acids, so it determined that the value of each of those products was its market price, as constructed. For middle-grade terephthalic acid, the highest of the three measures was the transfer price, so Commerce determined that the value of the middle-grade terephthalic acid was its transfer price. The following chart demonstrates the relative values for each product. In the chart, "r" represents the profit rate that Commerce applied.

	Qualified-Grade Terephthalic Acid	*Middle-Grade Terephthalic Acid*	*Purified Terephthalic Acid*
Highest Measure Provided by Huvis	(QTA transfer price)	(MTA transfer price)	(PTA transfer price)
Value (Highest Measure After Constructing Missing Measures, the Result of Applying Major Input Rule)	(QTA constructed market price) = (QTA cost of production) x (1+r)	(MTA transfer price)	(PTA constructed market price) = (PTA cost of production) x (1+r)

Huvis challenged Commerce's application of the major input rule in the Court of International Trade, arguing that substantial evidence did not support the constructed market prices that Commerce had calculated to fill in the missing market prices for qualified-grade and purified terephthalic acids. The court held that the prices Commerce had constructed were consistent with the statutory requirements and supported by substantial evidence, as Commerce had used Huvis's own data in calculating the market prices and had not applied adverse inferences against Huvis. But the court held that Commerce's construction of the market prices was not consistent with Commerce's established practice, which had previously been, according to the court, to use the highest available measure rather than constructing a measure, *i.e.*, market price, that was otherwise unavailable. Thus, the court remanded for Commerce either to use only the available measures provided by Huvis, *i.e.*, transfer price and cost of production, in applying the major input rule, or to adequately explain its reason for treating Huvis differently in this administrative review than it had in prior administrative reviews.

On remand, Commerce explained its change in treatment, stating that it had recognized for the first time that it had evidence on the record that could be used to construct a market price, providing "a more complete analysis under the major input rule, and result[ing] in a more accurate calculation of Huvis's dumping margin." *Huvis II*, 2008 Ct. Intl. Trade Lexis 82, at *5. When Huvis returned to the Court of International Trade, the court found that the explanation was reasoned, explaining that Commerce is free to change its methodology to improve accuracy and that Huvis did not detrimentally rely on the prior practice. Thus, the court affirmed Commerce's application of the major input rule.

Huvis timely appealed the Court of International Trade's decision. We have jurisdiction pursuant to 28 U.S.C. § 1295(a)(5).

DISCUSSION

"We review the Court of International Trade's judgment, affirming or reversing the final results of an administrative review, *de novo*." *Fag Kugelfischer Georg Schafer AG v. United States*, 332 F.3d 1370, 1372 (Fed. Cir. 2003). In so doing, "[w]e apply anew the same standard used by the court, and will uphold Commerce's determination unless it is unsupported by substantial evidence on the record, or otherwise not in accordance with law." *Yancheng Baolong Biochem. Prods. Co. v. United States*, 337 F.3d 1332, 1333 (Fed. Cir. 2003) (citation and internal quotation marks omitted). However, "we give great weight to the informed opinion of the Court of International Trade . . . , [and] it is nearly always the starting point of our analysis." *Nippon Steel Corp. v. United States*, 458 F.3d 1345, 1351 (Fed. Cir. 2006) (quotation marks and citation omitted). Substantial evidence means "more than a mere scintilla" and "such relevant evidence as a reasonable mind might accept as adequate to support a conclusion." *Suramerica de Aleaciones Laminadas, C.A. v. United States*, 44 F.3d 978, 985 (Fed. Cir. 1994) (quoting *Consol. Edison Co. v. NLRB,* 305 U.S. 197, 229, 59 S. Ct. 206, 83 L. Ed. 126 (1938)). "[T]he substantiality of evidence must take into account whatever in the record fairly detracts from its weight," including "contradictory evidence or evidence from which conflicting inferences could be drawn." *Suramerica*, 44 F.3d at 985 (quotation marks omitted).

Huvis argues that Commerce's decision to use a constructed market price in applying the major input rule was both unsupported by substantial evidence and contrary to law. Huvis asserts that Commerce's standard practice was to use only the available measures, cost of production and transfer price, in applying the major input rule when market price data was unavailable. Thus, according to Huvis, this practice became "law of the proceeding," and Huvis reasonably expected Commerce to adhere to it. Huvis argues that such law of the proceeding does not require a showing of detrimental reliance on the standard practice, and, even if Huvis did have to show reliance, it never had a chance to present such evidence to the Court of International Trade. Huvis also argues that, in general, Commerce may not depart from a consistent past practice without explanation, and it did not explain what was different in this review from the four preceding reviews. Huvis argues that Commerce claims only to have recognized for the first time in this review that it could construct a market price based on existing evidence, so, according to Huvis, Commerce did not actually find any new evidence that would justify a departure from past practice.

Huvis also argues that Commerce's method of constructing a market price unlawfully violated Huvis's statutory rights. Huvis contends that Commerce unlawfully penalized Huvis for failing to provide information that it was unable to provide. According to Huvis, Commerce disregarded the cost of production, which was available information that Huvis provided and was necessary to its determination, violating 19 U.S.C. § 1677m(e). Huvis further asserts that Commerce's methodology for constructing a market price was both adverse to Huvis and demonstrably inaccurate, in violation of 19 U.S.C. § 1677e(b) and (c). According to Huvis, even though the record establishes that qualified-grade terephthalic acid is, on average, of lower quality and less expensive than middle-grade terephthalic acid, the relative values were switched after Commerce constructed the market price for qualified-grade terephthalic acid and applied the major input rule, resulting in a higher value for qualified-grade acid than middle-grade acid. Moreover, since Commerce constructed the market price by marking up the cost of production by an average profit margin, Huvis asserts that the resulting market price will always be higher than the cost of production. Thus, according to Huvis, Commerce's method effectively eliminates the cost of production from the comparison and will always be adverse to importers, contravening the statutory scheme.

The government responds that Commerce's decision to construct a market price was both supported by substantial evidence and not contrary to law. According to the government, Commerce had no consistent prior practice that it was required to continue to follow, and Huvis never submitted or identified evidence of detrimental reliance on any prior methodology. The government adds that Commerce had previously advised Huvis that it would use facts available to fill in missing measures, as long as there were reasonable, non-adverse data on the record to do so. Indeed, according to the government, Commerce had done the same thing in reviews of other imports. The government also argues that Commerce may deviate from its past practice when it reasonably explains its reasons for departure, and, according to the government, Commerce did so here. The government asserts that Commerce adequately explained why it treated Huvis differently in the fifth review than it did in earlier reviews, as it only then realized that record evidence would support a constructed market price and improve its accuracy.

The government also responds that its method for constructing market prices was consistent with Congress's statutory scheme. According to the government, market price data was necessary to apply the major input rule, as the rule requires a comparison of three measures, one of which is market price. Because market price data were not available, the government argues that Commerce permissibly relied upon the facts available to determine market prices for the major inputs. According to the government, Commerce did not ignore the submitted costs of production in violation of 19 U.S.C. § 1677m(e); indeed, it used cost of production as an element to construct a market price and it used cost of production for the ultimate comparison required by the major input rule. Thus, according to the government, Commerce complied with the statute. The government also asserts that the data upon which Commerce relied were reasonable, not adverse, and supported by substantial evidence, in compliance with 19 U.S.C. § 1677e(b) and (c). The government argues that, to construct market prices, Commerce used verified information submitted by Huvis, including its supplier's audited financial statements. Even though qualified-grade terephthalic acid is normally less expensive than middle-grade terephthalic acid, according to the government, Huvis acknowledges that sometimes the relationship between prices actually is reversed, with qualified-grade being more expensive than middle-grade. The government therefore asserts that Commerce was justified in producing an outcome wherein the qualified-grade value determined by applying the major input rule was greater than the middle-grade value determined by the rule. Thus, according to the government, Commerce applied a reasonable, statutorily based methodology.

We conclude that the Court of International Trade correctly found Commerce's methodology for applying the major input rule to be supported by substantial evidence and adequately explained, in accordance with the law. In general, an agency may deviate from a past practice when "the new policy is permissible under the statute, . . . there are good reasons for it, and . . . the agency *believes* it to be better, which the conscious change of course adequately indicates." *FCC v. Fox Television Stations, Inc.*, 129 S. Ct. 1800, 1811, 173 L. Ed. 2d 738 (2009). Thus, Commerce need only show that its methodology is permissible under the statute and that it had good reasons for the new methodology.

A. Commerce's Methodology Was Permissible Under the Statute

We agree with the government that Commerce's decision to construct a market price was in accordance with the governing statutes. We have found permissible Commerce's interpretation of the major input rule, which uses as the value the highest of the three measures, *viz.* transfer price, cost of production, and market price.

See NTN Bearing Corp. of Am. v. United States, 368 F.3d 1369, 1374–76 (Fed. Cir. 2004). Huvis argues that the constructed market price always consists of adding an amount to the cost of production, meaning the constructed market price will always be higher than the cost of production, and cost of production is therefore effectively ignored. That system, according to Huvis, violates 19 U.S.C. § 1677m(e) by ignoring available information that Huvis provided and was necessary to Commerce's determination. However, Commerce's decision to construct a market price did not ignore the cost of production data. In fact, cost of production was taken into account twice in Commerce's application of the major input rule. First, Commerce used the cost of production to construct the market price. Second, Commerce included the cost of production in the comparison of the three measures to calculate a value. Further, we agree with the government that the constructed market price will not always be higher than the cost of production, so even the comparison of the three measures does not ignore cost of production. If, for example, Huvis were to take a loss on a certain product, the profit rate would be negative, and the resulting market price would be lower than the cost of production; therefore, the value determined by applying the major input rule would be the cost of production. Thus, Commerce's methodology did not violate 19 U.S.C. § 1677m(e).

Huvis also asserts that Commerce's methodology for constructing a market price was adverse to Huvis and demonstrably inaccurate, in violation of 19 U.S.C. § 1677e(b) and (c). The parties agree that Huvis did not fail to cooperate in the investigation, so Commerce was not entitled to use adverse inferences against Huvis under § 1677e(b). Even when Commerce uses adverse inferences, it must use a "reasonably accurate estimate of the respondent's actual rate" when using "facts available." *F.Lii de Cecco di Filippo Fara S. Martino S.p.A. v. United States,* 216 F.3d 1027, 1032 (Fed. Cir. 2000).

We disagree with Huvis's argument that the constructed market price is demonstrably inaccurate or constitutes an adverse inference against Huvis. As evidence, Huvis points to the relative market prices of qualified-grade and middle-grade terephthalic acids. Qualified-grade has more impurities, making it presumably of lower quality, than middle-grade acid. However, the constructed market price of qualified-grade acid is higher than the verified market price of middle-grade acid. Thus, Huvis argues that Commerce's method of constructing market prices is clearly inaccurate. We disagree. As the government points out and the Court of International Trade found, the higher level of impurities in qualified-grade acid does not necessarily mean that it should have a lower market price. *See Huvis II, 2008 Ct. Intl. Trade Lexis* 82, at *7–9 n.2, *11–12. Other factors affect market price. Indeed, the month-by-month transfer prices reveal that Huvis paid more for qualified-grade acid than it did for middle-grade acid in certain months, even though the average transfer price of qualified-grade acid was lower.

Further, Commerce reasonably chose to construct the market price by adding the cost of production to the profit margin, since there is no suggestion here that product sales were unprofitable or that the profit margins were unusually low.[2] At oral argument, Huvis pointed out that the profit margin that Commerce used was the average profit margin for all of Samnam's products, rather than a more precise profit margin for the particular input, *e.g.*, qualified-grade terephthalic acid. Oral Arg. 11:17–11:44, May 4, 2009, *available at* http://oralarguments.cafc.uscourts.gov/mp3/2009-1021.mp3. However, Huvis never argued, and presented no evidence, that the overall average profit margin did not accurately reflect the profit margin for the particular input. Huvis instead argued that "the profit margin used, it's undisputed, was the profit margin for the supplier company as a whole. That *may or may not be accurate* in terms of reflecting correctly the profit on this particular input." *Id.* (emphasis added). Thus, rather than prove the inaccuracy of the profit margin directly, Huvis argued that it had proven the inaccuracy of the profit margin as reflected in the relative market prices of qualified-grade and middle-grade terephthalic acids. *Id.* at 9:20–9:39 ("The basis for our position that it was unreasonable to use it for this input is the verified information that the particular input here, this QTA, qualified terephthalic acid, is the least valuable, . . . the lowest quality of the three different terephthalic acids."). As we demonstrated above, the mere fact that the relative market prices of qualified-grade and middle-grade terephthalic acids were different than might have been expected, based on their average transfer prices, does not prove that Commerce's construction of market prices was either inaccurate or adverse to Huvis. We therefore agree with the government that Commerce's constructed market price is not demonstrably inaccurate and does not constitute an adverse inference against Huvis.

B. Commerce Had Good Reason for Its Change of Policy

We also agree with Commerce that it had good reason for changing its methodology. When it changes a past practice, an agency must also show that there are good reasons for its new policy. *See Fox Television*, 129 S. Ct. at 1811; *Nippon Steel Corp. v. U.S. Int'l Trade Comm'n,* 494 F.3d 1371, 1378 n.5 (Fed. Cir. 2007) ("[T]he Supreme Court requires us to give deference to agency decisions that embody policy changes. When an agency decides to change course, however, it must adequately explain the reason for a reversal of policy." (internal citations omitted)). Sometimes an agency must provide a more detailed justification than what would suffice for a new policy created on a blank slate, such as when "its new policy rests upon factual findings that contradict those which underlay its prior policy; or when its prior policy has engendered serious reliance interests that must be taken into account." *Fox Television*, 129 S. Ct. at 1811.

Here, Commerce stated that it changed its methodology to improve accuracy. Improving accuracy is generally a good reason for a change in methodology. *See SKF USA, Inc. v. United States*, 537 F.3d 1373, 1380 (Fed. Cir. 2008) (affirming

---

2 Indeed, the constructed market price could be too low under the Commerce methodology if it failed to take account of other costs.

a new methodology that was changed to improve accuracy and stating that, "[w]ith respect to Commerce's decision to revise [its] methodology after 14 annual reviews utilizing [a different] methodology, we have specifically affirmed changes to . . . methodologies by Commerce where reasonable"); *Fujian Mach. & Equip. Imp. & Exp. Corp. v. United States*, 178 F. Supp. 2d 1305, 1327, 25 Ct. Int'l Trade 1150 (Ct. Int'l Trade 2001) ("Commerce is free to discard one methodology in favor of another, the better to calculate more accurate dumping margins.").

Although Commerce need not show that its "reasons for the new policy are *better* than the reasons for the old one," *Fox Television*, 129 S. Ct. at 1811, here, Commerce stated its reasons for the new policy as *improving* accuracy. Thus, we address whether substantial evidence supported Commerce's belief that including a constructed market price in the major input rule would improve the accuracy of the value. We agree with the government that Commerce's belief was reasonable. For the same reasons that we discussed above with respect to 19 U.S.C. § 1677e(b) and (c), Commerce reasonably believed that its constructed market price would improve the accuracy of the value. As market price is reasonably defined in the circumstances of this case as the sum of the cost of production and a profit margin, Commerce reasonably believed that it could accurately estimate market price, given that Huvis provided both cost of production and profit margin. Commerce also reasonably believed the supplier's average profit margin adequately represented the profit margin for each specific product, as Huvis offered no evidence to the contrary. Commerce further reasonably believed that including a market price measure in the comparison would improve the accuracy of the value, given the statute's requirement of a comparison of all three measures. Finally, Huvis's argument concerning the relative market prices of qualified-grade and middle-grade acids is unavailing for the reasons discussed above, *viz.*, that the market prices of the two acids do not necessarily reflect their relative purities.

We also agree with the government that Huvis did not detrimentally rely on Commerce's old methodology used in multiple preceding reviews. *See Fox Television*, 129 S. Ct. at 1811; Fujian, 178 F. Supp. 2d at 1327 ("Commerce may not make minor but disruptive changes in methodology where a respondent demonstrates its specific reliance on the old methodology used in multiple preceding reviews."); *Shikoku Chems. Corp. v. United States*, 795 F. Supp. 417, 16 Ct. Int'l Trade 382 (Ct. Int'l Trade 1992) (overturning Commerce's use of a slightly improved methodology when the respondent demonstrated that it had set its prices in reliance on the old methodology). As the Court of International Trade found, Huvis did not and could not show that it had detrimentally relied on any consistent prior practice. Huvis did not report market price data to Commerce because "Huvis was powerless to force its affiliated supplier to provide such data, or at least Huvis represented as much to Commerce. Therefore, the absence of market price data from the record was not the result of Huvis's reliance on Commerce's prior practice; rather, it was due to its affiliated supplier's intransigence." *Huvis II,* 2008 Ct. Intl. Trade Lexis 82, at *14. We therefore agree with the government that

Commerce's change in methodology was reasonable and adequately explained and that no further explanation was required, such that Commerce was free to change its methodology.

Commerce has therefore shown that its new methodology of constructing a market price was permissible under the statute and that it had good reasons for the new methodology. We have considered Huvis's remaining arguments and find them unpersuasive.

CONCLUSION

Accordingly, the judgment of the Court of International Trade affirming Commerce's valuation of Huvis's imports is affirmed.

AFFIRMED

JTEKT CORPORATION
v.
UNITED STATES

675 F. Supp. 2d 1206 (C.I.T. 2009)
Decided December 18, 2009

Sidley Austin, LLP (Neil R. Ellis and Jill Caiazzo) for plaintiffs JTEKT Corporation and Koyo Corporation of U.S.A.

Baker & McKenzie, LLP (Washington, District of Columbia) (Kevin M. O'Brien, Kevin J. Sullivan, and Sonal Majmudar) for plaintiffs FYII Bearing Units USA, Inc. and Nippon Pillow Block Company Ltd.

Crowell & Moring, LLP (Matthew P. Jaffe, Alexander H. Schaefer, Nicole M. Jenkins, and Robert A. Lipstein) for plaintiffs NSK Corporation, NSK Ltd., and NSK Precision America, Inc.

Baker & McKenzie, LLP (Chicago, Illinois) (Donald J. Unger, Diane A. MacDonald, and Joseph W. LaFramboise) for plaintiffs American NTN Bearing Manufacturing Corp., NTN Bearing Corporation of America, NTN Bower Corporation, NTN Corporation, NTN Driveshaft, Inc., and NTN-BCA Corporation.

O'Melveny & Myers, LLP (Greyson L. Bryan) for plaintiffs Nachi Technology, Inc., Nachi-Fujikoshi Corporation, and Nachi America, Inc.

Tony West, Assistant Attorney General, Jeanne E. Davidson, Director, Patricia M. McCarthy, Assistant Director, Commercial Litigation Branch, Civil Division, United States Department of Justice (Claudia Burke); Jennifer I. Johnson, Hardeep Josan, Natasha Robinson, Sapna Sharma, Mykhaylo Gryzlov, Jonathan Zielinksi, and Deborah R. King, Office of Chief Counsel for Import Administration, United States Department of Commerce, of counsel, for defendant.

Stewart and Stewart (Geert M. De Prest, Terence P. Stewart, William A. Fennell, and Lane S. Hurewitz) for plaintiffs and defendant-intervenors The Timken Company.

Before: TIMOTHY C. STANCEU, Judge.

OPINION AND ORDER

STANCEU, Judge:

JTEKT Corporation, formerly Koyo Seiko Company, Ltd.,[1] and Koyo Corporation of U.S.A. (collectively, "JTEKT") brought an action pursuant to 28 U.S.C. § 1581(c) (2006) to contest the final determination of the United States Department of Commerce ("Commerce" or the "Department") in the sixteenth administrative reviews ("AFBs 16 reviews" or "AFBs 16") of antidumping duty orders on ball bearings and parts thereof ("subject merchandise") from France, Germany, Italy, Japan, and the United Kingdom. Summons 1; *Ball Bearings & Parts Thereof from France, Germany, Italy, Japan, & the United Kingdom: Final Results of Antidumping Duty Admin. Reviews,* 71 Fed. Reg. 40,064, 40,065 (July 14, 2006) ("*Final Results*"); *Issues & Decision Mem. for the Antidumping Duty Admin. Reviews of Ball Bearings & Parts Thereof from France, Germany, Italy, Japan, & the United Kingdom for the Period of Review May 1, 2004, through April 30, 2005,* at 2 (July 14, 2006) ("*Decision Mem.*"). The reviews applied to imports of subject merchandise made during the period of May 1, 2004 through April 30, 2005 ("period of review" or "POR"). *Final Results,* 71 Fed. Reg. at 40,065.

Upon defendant's consent motion, the court consolidated JTEKT's action with five other cases. Consent Mot. to Consolidate 1. The five other groups of plaintiffs in the consolidated cases (referred to in this Opinion and Order collectively with their affiliates) are FYH Bearing Units USA, Inc. and Nippon Pillow Block Company Ltd. (collectively, "NPB"); NSK Corporation, NSK Ltd., and NSK Precision America, Inc. (collectively, "NSK"); American NTN Bearing Manufacturing Corp., NTN Bearing Corporation of America, NTN Bower Corporation, NTN Corporation, NTN Driveshaft, Inc., and NTN-BCA Corporation (collectively, "NTN"); Nachi Technology, Inc., Nachi-Fujikoshi Corporation, and Nachi America, Inc. (collectively "Nachi"); and The Timken Company ("Timken").

JTEKT, NPB, NSK, NTN, and Nachi (collectively, "plaintiffs"), as well as Timken, which is both a plaintiff and the defendant-intervenor ("defendant-intervenor") in the consolidated cases, bring claims contesting various decisions and determinations that Commerce made in the Final Results. These claims are discussed in the respective sections of Part II of this Opinion and Order, as follows: (A) claims of JTEKT, NPB, NTN, and Nachi challenging the application of Commerce's "zeroing" methodology to non-dumped sales; (B) claims challenging the Department's revised model-match methodology, the adoption of which JTEKT, NPB, NSK, NTN, and Nachi oppose generally and the specific application of which JTEKT, NPB, NSK, and NTN challenge in certain respects; (C) JTEKT's claim objecting

---

1 *Notice of Final Results of Antidumping Duty Changed-Circumstances Review: Ball Bearings & Parts Thereof from Japan,* 71 Fed. Reg. 26,452, 26,452–53 (May 5, 2006) (finding that JTEKT is the successor-in-interest to Koyo Seiko Company, Ltd.) ("*JTEKT-Koyo Successor Notice*").

to Commerce's treating JTEKT and an affiliate as a single entity, (D) NSK's claim that Commerce unlawfully deducted certain benefits expenses when determining the constructed export price of NSK's subject merchandise, (E) NTN's claim opposing Commerce's reallocation of NTN's freight expense on the basis of weight, (F) NTN's claim opposing Commerce's recalculation of NTN's home market packing expenses, (G) NTN's claim challenging the Department's disallowance of NTN's downward price adjustments to reflect certain discounts to home market customers, (H) Nachi's claim challenging Commerce's use of facts otherwise available and adverse inferences in response to errors Nachi made in reporting physical characteristics of subject bearings, and (I) Timken's claim challenging Commerce's use of Japanese interest rates, rather than U.S. interest rates, for a portion of the adjustment for imputed interest carrying costs in the calculation of constructed export prices of subject merchandise of NTN and Nachi. As discussed in this Opinion and Order, the court grants relief on certain of these claims through an order of remand and, with respect to other claims, affirms Commerce's decisions and determinations in the Final Results.

I. Background

The court sets forth below the procedural history of the administrative and judicial proceedings in general terms common to all plaintiffs. Additional background information specific to the individual claims is presented in Part II of this Opinion and Order.

A. Administrative Proceedings

On May 15, 1989, Commerce issued antidumping duty orders on imports of ball bearings from France, Germany, Italy, Japan, and the United Kingdom.[2] On June 30, 2005, Commerce initiated the sixteenth set of administrative reviews of these orders. *Initiation of Antidumping & Countervailing Duty Admin. Reviews,* 70 Fed. Reg. 37,749, 37,756–57 (June 30, 2005); *Decision Mem.* 2. Commerce issued the preliminary results of the administrative reviews ("Preliminary Results") in March 2006, setting forth its analysis for certain of its initial determinations. *Ball Bearings & Parts Thereof from France, Germany, Italy, Japan, & the United Kingdom: Prelim. Results of Antidumping Duty Admin. Reviews,* 71 Fed. Reg. 12,170 (Mar. 9, 2006) ("*Prelim. Results*"). Later that year, Commerce issued the Final Results

2 *Antidumping Duty Orders: Ball Bearings, Cylindrical Roller Bearings, Spherical Plain Bearings, & Parts Thereof From France,* 54 Fed. Reg. 20,902 (May 15, 1989); *Antidumping Duty Orders: Ball Bearings, Cylindrical Roller Bearings, & Spherical Plain Bearings & Parts Thereof From the Federal Republic of Germany,* 54 Fed. Reg. 20,900 (May 15, 1989); *Antidumping Duty Orders: Ball Bearings & Cylindrical Roller Bearings, & Parts Thereof From Italy,* 54 Fed. Reg. 20,903 (May 15, 1989); *Antidumping Duty Orders: Ball Bearings, Cylindrical Roller Bearings, & Spherical Plain Bearings, & Parts Thereof From Japan,* 54 Fed. Reg. 20,904 (May 15, 1989); *Antidumping Duty Orders & Amendments to the Final Determinations of Sales at Less Than Fair Value: Ball Bearings, & Cylindrical Roller Bearings & Parts Thereof From the United Kingdom,* 54 Fed. Reg. 20,910 (May 15, 1989).

and incorporated by reference therein an internal Issues and Decision Memorandum ("Decision Memorandum") containing the Department's analysis of issues raised by interested parties subsequent to the Preliminary Results. *Final Results,* 71 Fed. Reg. at 40,065; *see Decision Mem.*

B. Judicial Review in the Consolidated Actions

On September 13, 2006, the court granted the consent motion of Timken to intervene on behalf of defendant. Upon defendant's consent motion, the court ordered consolidation under Consolidated Court No. 06-00250 of *JTEKT Corporation v. United States,* No. 06-00250, *Nippon Pillow Block Company Ltd. v. United States,* No. 06-00258, *Timken U.S. Corporation v. United States,* No. 06-00271, *NSK Ltd. v. United States,* No. 06-00272, *NTN Corporation v. United States,* No. 06-00274, and *Nachi-Fujikoshi Corporation v. United States,* No. 06-00275. Order 1, Nov. 15, 2006; Consent Mot. to Consolidate 1. Each plaintiff and Timken filed a motion for judgment upon the agency record on February 8, 2007, which motions defendant opposes in the entirety and Timken, as defendant-intervenor, opposes with respect to certain claims.[3]

Oral argument was held in camera on October 30, 2007. On June 18, 2008, the court requested additional briefing regarding certain matters, to which JTEKT, NPB, NSK, NTN, defendant, and Timken responded. *See* Letter from Timothy C. Stanceu, Judge, Ct. of Int'l Trade, to Counsel for Pls., Def., & Def.-Intervenor in Consol. Ct. No. 06-250 (June 18, 2008). In addition, defendant and Timken made five additional submissions, and defendant made one additional submission, to notify the court of supplemental authority.

II. Discussion

The court exercises jurisdiction pursuant to 28 U.S.C. § 1581(c), under which the Court of International Trade is granted exclusive jurisdiction of any civil action commenced under 19 U.S.C. § 1516a. 28 U.S.C. § 1581(c). The court reviews the Final Results on the basis of the agency record. *See* 28 U.S.C. § 2640(b) (2006); 19 U.S.C. § 1516a(b)(1)(B)(i) (2006). Upon such review, the court must "hold unlawful any determination, finding, or conclusion found," 19 U.S.C. § 1516a(b)(1),

---

3 Mem. of P. & A. in Support of Mot. of Pls. JTEKT Corp. & Koyo Corp. of U.S.A. for J. on the Agency R. ("JTEKT Mem."); Mem. in Support of the Mot. for J. upon the Agency R. Submitted by Pls. Nippon Pillow Block Co. Ltd. & FYH Bearing Units USA, Inc. ("NPB Mem."); Mem. of P. & A. in Support of NSK's Mot. for J. on the Agency R. ("NSK Mem."); Rule 56.2 Mot. & Mem. for J. on the Agency R. Submitted on behalf of Pls. NTN Corp., NTN Bearing Corp. of Am., Am. NTN Bearing Mfg. Corp., NTN-BCA Corp., NTN-Bower Corp., & NTN Driveshaft, Inc. ("NTN Mem."); Br. of Pls. Nachi-Fujikoshi Corp., Nachi Am., Inc. & Nachi Technology, Inc. in Support of Rule 56.2 Mot. for J. on the Agency R. ("Nachi Mem."); Timken U.S. Corporation's Mem. in Supp. of its Rule 56.2 Mot. for J. on the Agency R. ("Timken Mem."); Def.'s Resp. in Opp'n to Pls.' Mots. for J. upon the Agency R. ("Def. Resp."); Resp. of Timken U.S. Corp. to the Rule 56.2 Mots. of JTEKT Corp., et al. ("Def.-Intervenor Resp.").

"to be unsupported by substantial evidence on the record, or otherwise not in accordance with law." *Id.* § 1516a(b)(1)(B)(i). "Substantial evidence is more than a mere scintilla. It means such relevant evidence as a reasonable mind might accept as adequate to support a conclusion." *Consol. Edison Co. v. NLRB,* 305 U.S. 197, 229, 59 S.Ct. 206, 83 L.Ed. 126 (1938).

A. The Claims of JTEKT, NPB, NTN, and Nachi Challenging the Department's Zeroing Procedure Are Inconsistent with Controlling Judicial Precedent

Plaintiffs claim that the Department's policy of zeroing in administrative reviews violates U.S. antidumping laws and is inconsistent with international obligations of the United States. Citing 19 U.S.C. §§ 1673, 1677(35), 1677b(a), and 1677f–l, NTN and Nachi argue that zeroing precludes a fair comparison of normal value and export price, distorts margins by failing to account for all transactions, and does not merit deference under *Chevron U.S.A. Inc. v. Natural Resources Defense Council, Inc.,* 467 U.S. 837, 842–43, n. 9, 104 S.Ct. 2778, 81 L.Ed.2d 694 (1984), because Commerce is inconsistently applying zeroing under the statute. Rule 56.2 Mot. & Mem. for J. on the Agency R. Submitted on behalf of Pls. NTN Corp., NTN Bearing Corp. of Am., Am. NTN Bearing Mfg. Corp., NTN-BCA Corp., NTN-Bower Corp., & NTN Driveshaft, Inc. 8–10 ("NTN Mem."); Br. of Pls. Nachi-Fujikoshi Corp., Nachi Am., Inc. & Nachi Technology, Inc. in Support of Rule 56.2 Mot. for J. on the Agency R. 9–10, 13–15, 18 ("Nachi Mem."). JTEKT, NPB, and Nachi also argue that it is unreasonable for Commerce to continue to apply the zeroing practice under the *Charming Betsy* doctrine, under which the laws of the United States should be interpreted so as not to conflict with U.S. international obligations. Mem. of P. & A. in Support of Mot. of Pls. JTEKT Corp. & Koyo Corp. of U.S.A. for J. on the Agency R. 44–47 ("JTEKT Mem."); Mem. in Support of the Mot. for J. upon the Agency R. Submitted by Pls. Nippon Pillow Block Co. Ltd. & FYH Bearing Units USA, Inc. 29–30 ("NPB Mem."); Nachi Mem. 15; *see Murray v. Schooner Charming Betsy,* 6 U.S. (2 Cranch) 64, 118, 2 L.Ed. 208 (1804). In support of this argument, these plaintiffs point to recent reports from panels and the Appellate Body of the World Trade Organization ("WTO") concluding that the Department's zeroing practice is inconsistent with the WTO obligations of the United States. JTEKT Mem. 45–47; NPB Mem. 29–30; NTN Mem. 5–8; Nachi Mem. 15–16. Finally, JTEKT, NPB, and NTN claim that the Court of International Trade should remand the determination to permit Commerce to implement, or consider implementing, adverse reports of the WTO on the application of zeroing in administrative reviews. *See* JTEKT Mem. 47; NPB Mem. 30–31; NTN Mem. 10–11. Defendant rejects plaintiffs' various arguments, arguing that the Court of Appeals for the Federal Circuit ("Court of Appeals") repeatedly has sustained the Department's treatment of nondumped sales under the statute despite findings set forth in adverse reports from the WTO's Dispute Settlement Body ("DSB"). Def.'s Resp. in Opp'n to Pls.' Mots. for J. upon the Agency R. 72 ("Def. Resp.") (citing *Timken Co. v. United States,* 354 F.3d 1334

(Fed.Cir.2004), *cert. denied* 543 U.S. 976, 125 S.Ct. 412, 160 L.Ed.2d 352 (2004), and *Corus Staal BV v. Dep't of Commerce,* 395 F.3d 1343 (Fed.Cir.2005), *cert. denied* 546 U.S. 1089, 126 S.Ct. 1023, 163 L.Ed.2d 853 (2006) ("*Corus I")); see also* Resp. of Timken U.S. Corp. to the Rule 56.2 Mots. of JTEKT Corp., et al. 28–30 ("Def.-Intervenor Resp.").

The court concludes that plaintiffs' arguments challenging zeroing fail to raise new issues not already settled by binding precedent of the Court of Appeals. In *Timken,* the Court of Appeals held that Commerce "reasonably interpreted § 1677(35)(A) to allow for zeroing" in the context of administrative reviews and also explained that the "fair comparison" requirement, which applies to the calculation of normal value under § 1677b(a), which was incorporated by the Uruguay Round Agreements Act ("URAA"), did not affect its holding. *Timken,* 354 F.3d at 1343. The Court of Appeals also rejected the argument that Commerce must adhere to a single practice on zeroing for both investigations and administrative reviews. *Id.* at 1344–45. In *NSK,* the Court of Appeals emphasized that it repeatedly has upheld the practice of zeroing and again affirmed the Department's determination to apply zeroing to administrative reviews despite the Department's determination to cease doing so in investigations. *NSK Ltd. v. United States,* 510 F.3d 1375, 1379–80 (Fed.Cir.2007) ("*NSK III*") (citing *Timken,* 354 F.3d 1334; *Corus I,* 395 F.3d 1343; and *Corus Staal BV v. United States,* 502 F.3d 1370 (Fed.Cir.2007) ("*Corus II*")).

Regarding the application of the *Charming Betsy* doctrine, the Court of Appeals in *Timken* rejected the "fair comparison" argument that had been raised thereunder. *Timken,* 354 F.3d at 1343–44. The Court of Appeals rejected a plaintiff's argument that it was required "to interpret the 'fair comparison' language in the U.S. anti-dumping statute in a manner consistent with U.S. international obligations, thereby adopting the holding in *EC—Bed Linen* and finding Commerce's zeroing practice an unreasonable statutory interpretation." *Id.* at 1343. Observing that "[t]he crux of [respondent's] argument hinges on the *Charming Betsy* canon of claim construction," *id.,* the Court of Appeals rejected the respondent's position, explaining that "[w]hile [respondent] relies on *EC—Bed Linen* for its persuasive value in an effort to convince us of the unreasonableness of Commerce's zeroing practice, we do not find it sufficiently persuasive to find Commerce's practice unreasonable." *Id.* at 1344.

Finally, JTEKT and NPB argue that Commerce must comply with the findings set forth in adverse reports from the WTO DSB. JTEKT Mem. 45–47; NPB Mem. 29–30. JTEKT requests that the court remand the determination to Commerce so that Commerce may determine whether and how to comply with the decision of the Appellate Body of the WTO holding that zeroing in administrative reviews is impermissible. JTEKT Mem. 47 & n. 16. JTEKT asserts that its position is consistent with the holding of the Court of Appeals in *Corus I,* 395 F.3d at 1349, because JTEKT does not ask the court to act but rather to remand the matter to Commerce for reconsideration in light of recent legal developments in the WTO. *Id.* at 47, n. 16.

NTN argues, similarly, that the principles articulated in recent DSB decisions on the use of zeroing in administrative reviews should persuade the court to hold that the Department's zeroing practice is unlawful and points to the U.S. decision, reached under Section 123 of the URAA,[4] to comply with the DSB ruling that zeroing is impermissible in investigations ("Section 123 Determination"). NTN Mem. 5–8, 10–11. Defendant responds that the Section 123 Determination applies only to new and continuing investigations and therefore has no effect upon this administrative review. Def. Resp. 77; *see* Def.-Intervenor Resp. 33–34.

Section 123 delineates specific procedures for determining whether and how the United States will comply with decisions of the WTO. *See* 19 U.S.C. § 3533(g) (2006). The Section 123 Determination states that it will apply to current and future investigations as of the effective date. *Antidumping Proceedings: Calculation of the Weighted-Average Dumping Margin During an Antidumping Investigation; Final Modification,* 71 Fed. Reg. 77,722, 77,725 (Dec. 27, 2006) ("*Section 123 Determination*"). With respect to timing in this matter, the Final Results were issued on July 14, 2006 and the Section 123 Determination was issued on December 27, 2006, with an original effective date of January 16, 2007, and a final amended effective date of February 22, 2007. *Final Results,* 71 Fed. Reg.40,064; *Antidumping Proceedings: Calculation of the Weighted-Average Dumping Margins in Antidumping Investigations; Change in Effective Date of Final Modification,* 72 Fed. Reg. 3783 (Jan. 26, 2007) ("*Section 123 Determination Am. Effective Date*"); *Section 123 Determination,* 71 Fed. Reg. 77, 722. Because the effective date of the Section 123 determination occurred after the issuance of the Final Results, there is no basis for the court to consider whether the legal principles adopted therein should apply to this administrative review. The court, therefore, need not reach plaintiffs' other arguments on this issue.

Even if the court concluded that the timing of the Final Results did not preclude application of the Section 123 determination, the court could not hold in favor of plaintiffs on this issue. The Court of Appeals repeatedly and consistently has upheld as reasonable the Department's statutory interpretation that zeroing is permissible in administrative reviews. The Court of Appeals in *Corus II,* 502 F.3d at 1375, upheld the use of zeroing in an administrative review of an antidumping duty order and in *NSK III,* 510 F.3d at 1380, expressly rejected the argument that

---

4 The Uruguay Round Agreements Act ("URAA"), in Section 123, established a procedure for implementing adverse reports of the World Trade Organization ("WTO") in U.S. law. *See* 19 U.S.C. § 3533(g) (2006); *Corus Staal BV v. Dep't of Commerce,* 395 F.3d 1343, 1349 (Fed.Cir.2005) ("*Corus I*"). To implement a change of agency regulation or practice due to an adverse WTO ruling, § 3533(g)(1) provides a lengthy process of consultation between the United States Trade Representative, Congress, the agency, private sector advisory committees, and the public, a process that may culminate in a final rule. 19 U.S.C. § 3533(g)(1). The URAA also established a procedure in Section 129 of the URAA that provides for a more limited procedure for the implementation of an adverse WTO panel or Appellate Body report that addresses, *inter alia,* a particular antidumping determination by Commerce. *See id.* § 3538 (2006).

use of zeroing should be held unlawful based on a decision of the DSB and on statements by the United States indicating that the United States would comply with that decision.[5] With respect to a remand to allow Commerce time to consider implementation of a new practice, the Court of Appeals has stated explicitly that it is not for the courts to implement WTO decisions without explicit instructions from the Executive Branch:

> until Commerce abandons zeroing in administrative reviews such as this one, a remand in this case would be unavailing. Therefore, because Commerce's zeroing practice is in accordance with our well-established precedent, *until Commerce officially abandons the practice pursuant to the specified statutory scheme, we affirm its continued use in this case.*

NSK III, 510 F.3d at 1380 (emphasis added). Subsequently, the Court of Appeals reiterated its position:

> The determination whether, when, and how to comply with the WTO's decision on "zeroing," involves delicate and subtle political judgments that are within the authority of the Executive and not the Judicial Branch. Neither Commerce nor the Department of Justice has requested, or even suggested, such a remand. It would be most inappropriate for this court on its own to direct Commerce to reopen the Final Results of the 15th review to consider the impact on its decision of the subsequent WTO ruling, and we decline to do so.

Koyo Seiko Co. v. United States, 551 F.3d 1286, 1291 (Fed.Cir.2008) ("*Koyo II*"); *see Corus I,* 395 F.3d at 1349 (directing the application of current U.S. law until the law changes to prohibit zeroing in administrative reviews). In summary, Court of Appeals precedent entirely precludes the court from requiring Commerce to change its zeroing practice in administrative reviews based on the Section 123 determination, and it forecloses a remand under which Commerce would be directed or authorized to reconsider its practice in light of WTO decisions declaring unlawful the practice of zeroing in the context of administrative reviews.

B. The Court Rejects Plaintiffs' Various Claims Related to the Model-Match Methodology Except for NPB's Claim Relating to Sampling Months and NTN's Claim Relating to Commerce's Rejection of NTN's Proposed Bearing Design-Type Categories

In determining a dumping margin, Commerce compares the U.S. price of the subject merchandise with the price of comparable merchandise (the "foreign like product") in the home market. 19 U.S.C. § 1677b (2006). To do so, Commerce first attempts to match sales of the subject merchandise with sales of identical

---

5 The Court of International Trade recently discussed in detail the reasons why the developments related to decisions by the Dispute Settlement Body of the World Trade Organization do not provide the court a basis to depart from binding precedent of the Court of Appeals. *See SKF USA Inc. v. United States,* 33 CIT___, ___, 659 F.Supp.2d 1338, 1346–47 (2009) ("*SKF II*"); *Union Steel v. United States,* 33 CIT ___, ___, 645 F.Supp.2d 1298, 1308–09 (2009).

merchandise in the home market. 19 U.S.C. § 1677(16)(A) (2006). In the absence of identical merchandise, Commerce attempts to match a sale of subject merchandise in the United States with a sale of similar merchandise in the home market. *See id.* § 1677(16)(B)–(C). If Commerce finds there are no sales of similar merchandise in the home market, Commerce will calculate a constructed value. *Id.* § 1677b(a)(4).

The model-match methodology is the means by which Commerce identifies similar merchandise. For the initial fourteen administrative reviews of the subject merchandise, Commerce applied a model-match methodology in which it compared bearings on the basis of eight characteristics (the "family model-match methodology"). *Issues & Decision Mem. for the Antidumping Duty Admin. Reviews of Ball Bearings & Parts Thereof from France, Germany, Italy, Japan, Singapore, & the United Kingdom for the Period of Review May 1, 2003, through April 30, 2004*, at 19–26 (Sept. 16, 2005) ("*AFBs 15 Decision Mem.*"). The bearings that matched according to those eight characteristics were grouped in the same "family" for purposes of determining a foreign like product. *Id.* In the fifteenth administrative reviews of the bearings orders ("AFBs 15"), Commerce adopted a different methodology ("new model-match methodology") in which Commerce applies a multi-step process. *Id.; see Ball Bearings & Parts Thereof from France, Germany, Italy, Japan, Singapore, & the United Kingdom: Final Results of Antidumping Duty Admin. Reviews,* 70 Fed. Reg. 54,711, 54,712 (Sept. 16, 2005) ("*AFBs 15 Final Results*"). Commerce applied this new model-match methodology in the AFBs 16 reviews. *Decision Mem.* 12–27.

In the new model-match methodology, Commerce first matches a ball bearing model sold in the United States to one sold in the home market according to the following four physical characteristics: load direction, bearing design, number of rows of rolling elements, and precision rating. *AFBs 15 Decision Mem.* 19. For bearing design, in AFBs 16 reviews, Commerce recognized the following eight design types: angular contact, self-aligning, deep groove, integral shaft, thrust ball, housed, insert, and hub units. *Decision Mem.* 77. A match requires consistency with respect to all four of these physical characteristics. *AFBs 15 Decision Mem.* 19. If there is such consistency, Commerce then identifies the most appropriate home market ball bearing model according to four additional, quantitative characteristics: load rating, outer diameter, inner diameter, and width. *Id.* Commerce excludes any potential matches in which the sum of the deviations in the four quantitative characteristics exceeds 40%. *Id.* Finally, Commerce excludes matches for which the Department's difference-in-merchandise adjustment ("DIFMER") exceeds 20%. *See Decision Mem.* 19 ("Because we applied our normal methodology of disregarding potential matches with a difference-in-merchandise adjustment of greater than 20 percent, we regard all the matches we actually made to be approximately equal in commercial value."); *Imp. Admin. Policy Bulletin* 92.2 (July 29, 1992), http://ia.ita. doc.gov/policy/index.html (last visited Dec. 18, 2009).

Plaintiffs challenge the new model-match methodology on various grounds. Certain of the plaintiffs challenge specifics of the application of the methodology in the AFBs 16 reviews, including the Department's decision to consider only eight physical characteristics, the refusal by Commerce to increase the number of months in which it searched for matches, the Department's rejection of all but one of the proposed additional bearing design types, and the alleged unlawfulness of certain matches. For the reasons discussed below, the court rejects these various claims except for two claims, as discussed below, and affirms, in other respects, the model-match methodology as applied in the AFBs 16 reviews.

1. Contrary to the Claims of JTEKT, NPB, NSK, NTN, and Nachi, the Court Concludes that Commerce Acted Lawfully in Deciding to Change its Model-Match Methodology

Plaintiffs raise various arguments relating to the standard Commerce must meet to change its model-match methodology. JTEKT and NTN claim that Commerce failed to give compelling reasons to change the methodology and that Commerce must use the prior methodology as a matter of fairness due to respondents' reliance, NPB contends that Commerce failed to provide a reasoned explanation for its departure from past practice, and NSK claims that the Department's determination to change methodologies was not reasonable because Commerce failed to show that the new methodology would yield a more accurate dumping margin. JTEKT Mem. 26–28; NTN Mem. 20–26; NPB Mem. 9; Mem. of P. & A. in Support of NSK's Mot. for J. on the Agency R. 11–12 ("NSK Mem."). Defendant argues that Commerce need only have acted reasonably in changing the methodology and that Commerce has done so. Def. Resp. 15.

JTEKT, NPB, and NTN argue, further, that substantial record evidence does not support the claim of greater accuracy, that the new methodology actually yields less accurate dumping margins than the predecessor, that it is not possible to select a single most similar model for a ball bearing, and that Commerce, in deciding that price-to-price comparisons are more accurate than constructed values, contradicted the position it took in earlier reviews. JTEKT Mem. 24–25, 29–38; NPB Mem. 13–18; NSK Mem. 11–15. JTEKT, NPB, and NTN also reject as unsupported by substantial record evidence the Department's rationale that technology improvements enable Commerce to implement the new model-match methodology. JTEKT Mem. 39–40; NPB Mem. 11–13; NTN Mem. 22–23. Defendant and defendant-intervenor urge the court to reject these arguments and uphold the new methodology as reasonable and, as applied in this case, supported by the record evidence. *See* Def. Resp. 15–21; *see* Def.-Intervenor Resp. 12–22.

The court will review a change in methodology for reasonableness. *SKF USA, Inc. v. United States,* 537 F.3d 1373, 1377–78 (Fed.Cir.2008) ("*SKF I*"). The more demanding standards that plaintiffs advocate, *i.e.,* that Commerce must set forth compelling reasons for the change or that the change must be demonstrated to produce a more accurate dumping margin, are not correct statements of the law.

Id. at 1378 (stating that a review for reasonableness does not conflict with the substantial evidence standard). Further, the Court of Appeals previously has rejected arguments identical or similar to those advanced by plaintiffs, noting that "this statute 'is silent with respect to the methodology that Commerce must use to match a U.S. product with a suitable home-market product.'" *Id.* at 1379 (quoting *Koyo Seiko Co. v. United States,* 66 F.3d 1204, 1209 (Fed.Cir.1995) ("*Koyo I*")). Concluding that "Congress has granted Commerce considerable discretion to fashion the methodology used to determine what constitutes 'foreign like product' under the statute," the Court of Appeals deferred to the Department's choice of methodology as a reasonable construction of the antidumping statute. *Id.* (citing *Pesquera Mares Australes Ltda. v. United States,* 266 F.3d 1372, 1384 (Fed. Cir.2001), which cites, in turn, *Koyo I,* 66 F.3d at 1209). The Court of Appeals explained that Commerce was reasonable in seeking to improve accuracy, to select a model that would yield more price-to-price comparisons, and to capitalize on technological advances that enable implementation of a more accurate methodology. *Id.* at 1380.

JTEKT, NPB, and NSK argue that the change in methodology impermissibly was applied retroactively despite plaintiffs' reliance on the previous methodology. JTEKT Mem. 25, 41–43; NPB Mem. 18–22; NSK Mem. 17–22. NPB argues specifically that it relied upon the prior methodology for fourteen years and that principles of fairness preclude Commerce from changing the methodology. NPB Mem. 18–22. NSK contends that the longstanding agency practice carries the weight of law, explaining that the old methodology was well-established, confirmed as lawful by the courts, and unaffected by any intervening statute that would require modification of the methodology. NSK Mem. 19 (citing *Nat'l Corn Growers Ass'n v. Baker,* 840 F.2d 1547, 1555 (Fed.Cir.1988)). NSK further contends that it relied on this longstanding practice of applying the family model-match methodology and that it was not put on notice that the new methodology would apply in the review at issue. NSK Mem. 20–22. Defendant argues that the reliance arguments lack merit because Commerce had announced in earlier reviews that it was considering a revision of the methodology, provided respondents notice early in the proceedings of the determination to apply the revised methodology, and also provided an opportunity to comment on the determination. Def. Resp. 21–22; *see* Def.-Intervenor Resp. 23–27.

The Court of Appeals previously has rejected an argument that retroactivity and respondents' reliance on the old methodology preclude Commerce from modifying its methodology in a current administrative review. *SKF I,* 537 F.3d at 1381. The Court of Appeals reasoned that there is an inherent retroactivity to antidumping review determinations and that a change in methodology, like any application of a methodology in an antidumping review, permissibly involves a retroactive effect. *Id.* The Court of Appeals also rejected the assertion of plaintiff SKF of detrimental reliance, explaining that "SKF does not dispute that Commerce has consistently found that SKF continues to sell at dumped prices" and that "SKF cannot properly analogize its situation to that in *Shikoku,* where '[t]he record contain[ed] evidence that plaintiffs adjusted their prices in accordance with methodology consistently applied by Commerce in an attempt to comply with United States antidumping law.'" *Id.* (quoting *Shikoku Chemicals Corp. v. United States,* 16 CIT 382, 386, 795 F.Supp. 417, 420 (1992)). As in *SKF,* plaintiffs do not dispute that Commerce consistently has found that JTEKT, NPB, NSK, and NTN continue to sell at dumped prices.

In *SKF,* the Court of Appeals noted that Commerce had found that plaintiffs were selling at dumped prices for the periods of review prior to the one at issue, May 1, 2003 to April 30, 2004. *Id.* at 1377, 1381 (addressing the period of review from May 1, 2003 to April 30, 2004). Commerce had determined the following margins for SKF entities for the three periods of review preceding the one at issue in *SKF:* for the POR beginning May 1, 2002, SKF entities had margins of 1.38%, 2.49%, and 5.25%; for the POR beginning May 1, 2001, SKF entities had margins of 3.38%, 5.08%, and 6.70%; and for the POR beginning May 1, 2000, SKF entities had margins of 3.70% and 8.51%. *Antifriction Bearings & Parts Thereof From France, Germany, Italy, Japan, Singapore, & the United Kingdom: Final Results of Antidumping Duty Admin. Reviews, Rescission of Admin. Reviews in Part, & Determination To Revoke Order in Part,* 69 Fed. Reg. 55,574, 55,578–80 (Sept. 15, 2004) ("*Final Results POR 2002–03*"); *Ball Bearings & Parts Thereof From France & Japan; Am. Final Results of Antidumping Duty Admin. Reviews,* 68 Fed. Reg. 43,712, 43,712 (July 24, 2003) ("*Am. Final Results POR 2001–02*"); *Ball Bearings & Parts Thereof From France, Germany, Italy, Japan, & Singapore: Final Results of Antidumping Duty Admin. Reviews, Rescission of Admin. Review in Part, & Determination Not To Revoke Order in Part,* 68 Fed. Reg. 35,623, 35,625 (June 16, 2003) ("*Final Results POR 2001–02*"); *Ball Bearings & Parts Thereof From France, Germany, Italy, Japan, & the United Kingdom; Final Results of Antidumping Duty Admin. Reviews,* 67 Fed. Reg. 55,780, 55,781 (Aug. 30, 2002) ("*Final Results POR 2000–01*").

The period of review for the AFBs 16 reviews is May 1, 2004 through April 30, 2005. The court notes that Commerce determined in prior reviews that plaintiffs JTEKT, NPB, NSK, and NTN sold at dumped prices. For example, Commerce determined the following margins for plaintiffs for the three periods of review preceding the one at issue in this action: for the POR beginning May 1, 2003, 12.78% for Koyo (JTEKT), 15.51% for NPB, 8.25% for NSK, and 5.93% for NTN; for the POR beginning May 1, 2002, 5.56% for Koyo (JTEKT), 3.37% for NPB, 2.46% for NSK, and 2.74% for NTN; and for the POR beginning May 1, 2001, 4.98% for Koyo (JTEKT), 4.82% for NPB, 2.68% for NSK, and 4.51% for NTN. *Notice of Correction to Am. Final Results of Antidumping Duty Admin. Review: Ball Bearings & Parts Thereof from Japan,* 70 Fed. Reg. 69,316, 69,316 (Nov. 15, 2005) ("*Corrected Am. Japan Final Results POR 2003–04*"); *Notice of Am. Final Results of Antidumping Duty Admin. Reviews: Ball Bearings & Parts Thereof from Japan,* 70 Fed. Reg. 61,252, 61,252 (Oct. 21, 2005) ("*Am. Japan*

Final Results POR 2003–04"); *Ball Bearings & Parts Thereof from France, Germany, Italy, Japan, Singapore, & the United Kingdom: Final Results of Antidumping Duty Admin. Reviews,* 70 Fed. Reg. 54,711, 54,713 (Sept. 16, 2005) ("*Final Results POR 2003–04*"); *Final Results POR 2002–03,* 69 Fed. Reg. at 55,580; *Am. Final Results POR 2001–02,* 68 Fed. Reg. at 43,712; *Final Results POR 2001–02,* 68 Fed. Reg. at 35,625. In the AFBs 16 reviews, none of the plaintiffs actually has demonstrated detrimental reliance on the old methodology.

For the reasons stated above, the court will affirm the Final Results with respect to the Department's decision to depart from the previous model-match methodology.

2. The Court Rejects NPB's Claim that Commerce Must Include Additional Physical Characteristics in its Model-Match Methodology

While contesting the adoption of the new model match methodology, NPB argues in the alternative that Commerce should have included additional physical characteristics in the methodology to account for certain specialty bearings. NPB Mem. 22. NPB explains that its specialty bearings should not be considered to be foreign like products of standard bearings sold in the United States and identifies seven additional characteristics that it submits Commerce, at a minimum, should have applied when determining matches. *Id.* at 23–24. Specifically, NPB argues that Commerce should have incorporated the following additional physical characteristics into its methodology: "types of seals," "*greased v. ungreased,*" "*ceramic v. nonceramic,*" "diameter of second inner dimension," "diameter of second outer dimension," "diameter of second width dimension," and "diameter of third width dimension." *Id.* at 24. NPB argues that Commerce impermissibly rejected NPB's request to include these additional characteristics, challenging the Department's finding that NPB submitted the request too late in the proceedings and the finding by Commerce that NPB did not explain how Commerce could implement the proposed additional physical characteristics in the methodology. *Id.* at 25–26.

In their oppositions to NPB's motion for judgment upon the agency record, neither defendant nor defendant-intervenor addressed the issue of NPB's proposal for additional physical characteristics. *See* Def. Resp.; Def.-Intervenor Resp. NPB urges the court to enter judgment against defendant, relying on USCIT Rule 56(e)(2). Reply Br. in Supp. of the Rule 56.2 Mot. for J. upon the Agency R. Submitted by Pls. Nippon Pillow Block Co., Ltd. and FYH Bearing Units USA, Inc. 2–3 ("NPB Reply") (citing, *inter alia, Taylor v. City of N.Y.,* 269 F.Supp.2d 68, 75 (E.D.N.Y.2003), and *Precision Specialty Metals, Inc. v. United States,* 24 CIT 1016, 1016, 116 F.Supp.2d 1350, 1353 (2000)). However, USCIT Rule 56(e)(2) is inapposite in a case where the motion for judgment upon the agency record is made pursuant to USCIT Rule 56.2. Under USCIT Rule 56.2, defendant is deemed to have opposed the issue whether or not the opposition was specifically pled. Therefore, the court rejects NPB's argument under USCIT Rule 56(e)(2) that the court should enter judgment against defendant on this issue.

Regarding the timing of NPB's proposal to incorporate additional physical characteristics in the model-match methodology, Commerce stated in its Decision Memorandum that NPB was the only respondent to suggest additional physical characteristics and did not do so until its case brief, which NPB submitted on April 25, 2006, less than three months before the issuance of the Final Results. *Decision Mem.* 18; *Final Results,* 71 Fed. Reg. 40,064. Commerce explained that respondents must submit their arguments regarding physical characteristics earlier in the review, rather than after the Preliminary Results, in order for Commerce to have a reasonable opportunity to consider them and to allow interested parties to comment. *Decision Mem.* 23. NPB concedes that in the subject reviews, it first proposed the use of additional physical characteristics in its case brief.[6] NPB Mem. 25. Instead, NPB relies on 19 C.F.R. § 351.309(c)(2), which requires a party to submit all of its arguments in its case brief, including arguments presented before the publication of the preliminary results. NPB Mem. 26. NPB adds that it raised the same arguments in the prior review. *Id.* Finally, NPB rejects the Department's argument that interested parties would not have an opportunity to comment and argues instead that parties wishing to comment could have done so in their rebuttal briefs. *Id.*

NPB's reliance on 19 C.F.R. § 351.309(c)(2) is misplaced. In this regulatory provision, Commerce requires parties to submit all arguments in the case brief, including those already before the agency. *See* 19 C.F.R. § 351.309(c)(2) (2009). The regulation ensures that Commerce has before it all of a party's arguments for consideration prior to the Final Results. It does not guarantee that Commerce will adopt the positions suggested therein, nor does it preclude Commerce from deciding, according to specific circumstances, that a change in methodology advocated at that time would not be practicable.

The Court of Appeals has held that "Commerce has considerable discretion in defining 'identical in physical characteristics.'" *Pesquera Mares,* 266 F.3d at 1384 (quoting 19 U.S.C. § 1677(16)(A)). Commerce exercised that discretion in requiring NPB and other respondents to submit questionnaire responses according to the physical characteristics Commerce had identified. *Letter from Baker & McKenzie, LLP to Dep't of Commerce* 570–72 (Sept. 27, 2005) (Admin.R.Doc. No. 92) ("*NPB Questionnaire Resp.*") (stating, at B-2 through B-4 of the submission, that NPB reported its bearings according to the eight product characteristics indicated by Commerce and also added several fields). NPB was aware of those physical

6 Based on the court's examination of NPB's questionnaire responses, the court finds that NPB alluded to its desire for inclusion of certain additional physical characteristics in the way that it responded to the Department's request for information on physical characteristics. However, the responses do not constitute an actual proposal. *See Letter from Baker & McKenzie, LLP to Dep't of Commerce* 570–72 (Sept. 27, 2005) (Admin.R.Doc. No. 92) (stating, at B-2 through B-4 of the submission, that NPB reported its bearings according to the eight product characteristics indicated by Commerce, and that NPB added several fields because, according to NPB, the eight characteristics Commerce listed do not fully describe NPB's product).

characteristics at the time of submitting its questionnaire responses and could have advocated in a questionnaire response that Commerce adopt its detailed proposal. *See id.* It would have been preferable had Commerce notified parties that proposals for use of additional physical characteristics in the model-match methodology would not be considered if submitted after a specified date. Nevertheless, the Department's apparent failure to do so in this case does not compel the court to conclude that Commerce acted contrary to law in rejecting NPB's proposal for reasons of impracticability due to time constraints and the desirability of allowing meaningful comment by other parties. At or about the time NPB submitted its questionnaire response, NPB reasonably should have expected that Commerce, absent an objection lodged at this earlier stage of the reviews, would proceed with its analysis according to the physical characteristics that Commerce had identified. Commerce explained that there were practical issues with the additional characteristics proposed by NPB that Commerce could not resolve at a point so late in the review, *i.e.,* after Commerce had issued the Preliminary Results. *Decision Mem.* 23. Commerce also explained that it had an insufficient time period in which to determine how to amend its methodology to incorporate the suggested additional physical characteristics and to allow interested parties the opportunity to comment. *Id.* at 23–24.

NPB having failed to raise its proposal sooner, the court cannot conclude that Commerce erred in determining that it did not have enough time to review, and possibly implement, the proposal of NPB to use additional physical characteristics in the model matching process. Due to the statutory time constraints under which Commerce must conduct its administrative reviews, Commerce must be considered to have a measure of discretion in deciding whether a modification of its model-match methodology is practicable. That NPB had raised the same issue in a prior review does not alter the court's conclusion. Commerce could not know whether NPB intended to submit its proposal in the subject reviews until NPB actually did so, which NPB first did in its case brief.

For these reasons, the court concludes that the Department's decision in the Final Results to decline to consider NPB's proposal for additional physical characteristics was supported by substantial record evidence and adequate reasoning and was within the Department's discretion over procedural questions relevant to the conduct of its administrative reviews. The court, therefore, affirms that decision.

3. The Department's Decision Rejecting NPB's Proposal to Expand the Choice of Sample Months Misconstrues the Department's Regulation

NPB claims that Commerce, when searching for a ball bearing model to match with a particular subject ball bearing that a respondent sold in the United States, should have expanded the time period surrounding the date of the U.S. sale during which Commerce searched that respondent's home market sales data. NPB Mem. 27. NPB argues that Commerce, by confining its search for possible matches to the "sampled months" immediately preceding and following the month in which the target U.S. sale occurred, unnecessarily reduced the number of identical matches and increased the number of matches for which only similar, but not identical, merchandise was involved. *Id.* NPB argues that the Department's regulations do not require such a limited time period for the choice of sampled months and that the regulations allow Commerce to use a longer time period, such as a five-month time period, as NPB advocated. *Id.* at 28.

In the AFBs 16 reviews, the "sampled months" Commerce selected were February, June, August, September, and November of 2004, and February, March, and May of 2005. *Prelim. Results,* 71 Fed. Reg. at 12,174. According to the Department's explanation of its method of sampling transactions in the Preliminary Results, *see* 19 U.S.C. § 1677f-1(a), Commerce resorted to sampling of transactions for respondents who made more than 10,000 constructed export price ("CEP") sales transactions in the United States, or more than 10,000 home market sales transactions, during the period of review. *Prelim. Results,* 71 Fed. Reg. at 12,172–74. Commerce explained that for a respondent who engaged in more than 10,000 CEP sales of merchandise subject to a particular order, Commerce selected "sample weeks"—one week from each two-month period during the period of review, for a total of six weeks—and then reviewed the individual U.S. CEP sales transactions that occurred during those sample weeks. *Id.* at 12,172. Commerce further explained that for home market sales, Commerce selected as sampled months the months corresponding to the sample weeks selected for CEP sales in addition to a sampled month prior to the period of review and a sampled month following the period of review. *Id.* at 12,173–74. For NPB, Commerce "analyzed CEP sales of ball bearings in sample weeks because NPB had more than 10,000 CEP transactions of BBs [*i.e.,* ball bearings] during the POR" and "analyzed HM [*i.e.,* home market] sales using sample months because NPB made over 10,000 POR home-market transactions." *Mem. from Int'l Trade Compliance Analyst, AD/CVD Operations 5, to The File* 2 (Mar. 2, 2006) (Admin.R.Doc. No. 220). Commerce stated that for model match purposes it first searches the home market sales during the sampled month corresponding to the sampled week in which the U.S. sale occurred. *Decision Mem.* 86. Next, Commerce searches the preceding home-market sampled month, which, because not all months are sampled months, could result in a total span of several months. *Id.* Finally, Commerce searches the home market sampled month subsequent to the target sampled month, which, in these administrative reviews, also could result in a span of several months. *Id.* (stating that Commerce "matched each bearing model sold in the United States in one of the sampled weeks to the corresponding home-market month, then to the immediately preceding sampled home-market month, and then to the immediately following sampled home-market month"); see *Prelim. Results,* 71 Fed. Reg. at 12, 172–74.

In the Decision Memorandum, Commerce reported its decision not to include additional sampled months as proposed by NPB. *Decision Mem.* 86. Commerce based its decision on 19 C.F.R. § 351.414(e)(2), which addresses the selection of the "contemporaneous months," *i.e.,* the months to which Commerce limits the weighted averaging of prices in home market sales for use in making a comparison with an individual U.S. sale.[7] *See Decision Mem.* 86. Commerce stated in the Decision Memorandum its position that "[t]he contemporaneous months should not pass beyond the most recent of the three months prior or the two months subsequent to the month of the U.S. sale in which there was a sale of a foreign like product." *Id.* (citing 19 C.F.R. § 351.414(e)(2)). "Given the fact that sample home-market months are separated by a month or more between each other in either direction, extending the window period by a month in each direction often results in extending the window period beyond the time period our regulation allows." *Id.* If, for example, Commerce were to match a bearing sold in the United States with sales of a matching foreign like product that occurred in August 2004,[8] Commerce first would search home market sales in the target sampled month, August 2004; second, in the preceding sampled month, June 2004; and third, in the following sampled month, September 2004. As a result, subject bearings sold during a sample week in August 2004 potentially could be matched to home market sales in a sampled month that could only have occurred during the four-month period of June through September 2004. Were Commerce also to search for matching sales in the additional preceding and following sampled months, in this case February and November of 2004, that time period would be ten months long.

Neither defendant nor defendant-intervenor addressed NPB's "sampled month" issue in their oppositions to plaintiffs' motion for judgment upon the agency record. *See* Def. Resp.; Def.-Intervenor Resp. The court will not rule in favor of NPB on that basis. As discussed previously, the United States is deemed to have opposed summary judgment on an issue raised in a Rule 56.2 motion for judgment upon the agency record. *See* USCIT Rule 56.2.

---

7 The regulation addresses the selection of the "contemporaneous month," providing as follows:

> (2) Contemporaneous month. Normally, the Secretary will select as the contemporaneous month the first of the following which applies:
>
> (i) The month during which the particular U.S. sale under consideration was made;
>
> (ii) If there are no sales of the foreign like product during this month, the most recent of the three months prior to the month of the U.S. sale in which there was a sale of the foreign like product.
>
> (iii) If there are no sales of the foreign like product during any of these months, the earlier of the two months following the month of the U.S. sale in which there was a sale of the foreign like product.

19 C.F.R. § 351.414(e)(2) (2009). This regulation applies in the "average-to-transaction method" that Commerce normally employs in an administrative review. *See id.* § 351.414(c)(2).

8 As stated previously, in these reviews, the "sample months" Commerce selected were February, June, August, September, and November of 2004, and February, March, and May of 2005. *Ball Bearings & Parts Thereof from France, Germany, Italy, Japan, & the United Kingdom: Prelim. Results of Antidumping Duty Admin. Reviews,* 71 Fed. Reg. 12,170, 12,174 (Mar. 9, 2006) ("*Prelim. Results*"). Hence, for this example, the relevant sample months are June, August, and September of 2004.

In considering the sampling month issue on the merits, the court concludes that the premise underlying the Department's analysis, as stated in the Decision Memorandum, was in error. Commerce erroneously concluded that its regulation *required* it to reject NPB's proposal. *Decision Mem.* 86 (finding that "[g]iven the fact that sample home-market months are separated by a month or more between each other in either direction, extending the window period by a month in each direction often results in extending the window period beyond the time period our regulation allows"). But that was not the case. The regulation in question, § 351.414(e)(2), provides that "[*n*]*ormally,* the Secretary will select as the contemporaneous month the first of the following which applies." 19 C.F.R. § 351.414(e)(2) (emphasis added). Under the plain meaning of the regulation, Commerce is not precluded entirely from choosing as the "contemporaneous month" a sampled month outside of the total time span contemplated by § 351.414(e)(2). Instead, Commerce is free to exercise its discretion not to follow the normal procedure set forth in that provision. The regulation allows for an atypical circumstance under which it may be reasonable or appropriate to depart from the normal procedure.[9] The court notes that § 351.414(e)(2) is a general provision that does not address specifically the special circumstances in which Commerce resorts to sampling under 19 U.S.C. § 1677f–1(a).

In identifying the error in the Department's analysis, the court does not hold or imply that Commerce, on the administrative record before it, was required to accept NPB's proposal to expand the choice of sampling months. NPB may be correct that the proposal it advanced would have increased the accuracy of the model-match methodology; the review of a larger data base presumably would lead to more identical matches. Nevertheless, Commerce has considerable discretion in choosing the timing for conducting the comparison called for in the average-to-transaction method that normally applies during administrative reviews. *See* 19 C.F.R. § 351.414(c), (e). NPB's proposal may or may not have been practicable in the context of the subject reviews and in this case may have caused Commerce to exceed the time period recommended by its regulation. But in this case, Commerce did not reject NPB's proposal for considerations of practicability. Instead, it erroneously treated the method set forth in that regulatory provision as an ironclad requirement. The court, therefore, must remand for reconsideration the Department's decision to reject NPB's proposal to expand the choice of sampled months. The court must review the Department's decision on the basis of the reasoning that Commerce put forth. *See Bowman Transp., Inc. v. Arkansas-Best Freight Sys., Inc.,* 419 U.S. 281, 285–86, 95 S.Ct. 438, 42 L.Ed.2d 447 (1974)

9 Moreover, it appears that the situation Commerce said it wanted to avoid could have occurred even if no additional sampled months were added. For example, if Commerce selected a U.S. sale in June 2004, sampled transactions in June 2004 with no match, then sampled transactions in February 2004 with no match, and finally, sampled transactions in August 2004, the total time period would span seven months, which exceeds the total of six months envisioned by the regulation. *See* 19 C.F.R. § 351.414(e)(2).

(stating that the court "may not supply a reasoned basis for the agency's action that the agency itself has not given"). In this circumstance, the reasoning Commerce set forth in the Decision Memorandum cannot be reconciled with the plain meaning of 19 C.F.R. § 351.414(e) and the discretion Commerce is granted thereunder.

4. Commerce Failed to Provide an Adequate Explanation for its Rejection of NTN's Proposal for Additional Ball Bearing Design Types

NTN claims that Commerce erred in refusing to recognize and apply the additional ball bearing design types that NTN proposed for use in the model matching process. *See* NTN Mem. 26–30. NTN proposed designation of additional design types, all but one of which Commerce rejected. *Decision Mem.* 76–80. NTN argues that the ball bearing design types that Commerce identified, *i.e.,* angular contact, self-aligning, deep groove, integral shaft, thrust ball, housed, and insert, are overly broad and fail to account for significant physical characteristics. NTN Mem. 27. In the AFBs 16 reviews, Commerce adopted, in response to NTN's objection, only one additional design type, "hub units incorporating angular contact bearings." *Decision Mem.* 77 ("We do find, however, that NTN provided evidence. . . that demonstrates that NTN's hub units incorporating angular contact bearings are significantly different from standard angular contact bearings as well as housed bearings to warrant a bearing-design designation distinct and separate from the seven bearing-design types we identified in our questionnaire."). Commerce took the position that to include an additional design type in its model matching process, it had "to be satisfied that the classification is substantially different from each of the design types" already included. *Id.* Commerce concluded that NTN had not demonstrated the need for separate classifications for the other design types NTN proposed. *Id.* (stating that "NTN did not provide compelling evidence that each of its reported bearing-design types was so significantly different that it merited its own classification, distinct and separate from the seven bearing-design types we identified in our questionnaire"). Commerce also "found that, on many occasions, NTN's numerous bearing-design designations were distinguishable due to a single element of difference or an element of difference that is not pertinent, such as a different width of inner race or the type of bore, . . . etc.," *id.,* and that many of the differences correlate directly with load ratings, physical dimensions, and occasionally, the precision rating of bearings, which are characteristics that Commerce already uses to distinguish dissimilar products in its methodology. *Id.* at 77–78. In response to NTN's arguments in the reviews that the function or application of different bearings warrant a separate design designation, Commerce stated that

> it is the rolling element that is dispositive as to whether a bearing can be considered similar with respect to the purposes for which bearings are used (*e.g.,* a ball bearing cannot be considered similar to a cylindrical roller bearing under any circumstance), not whether a specific application for one bearing differs from the specific application of another.

Id. at 78 (internal quotation marks and citation omitted). Commerce explained that "[b]ecause all bearing models designated by NTN as different design types have a ball as a rolling element and fall within one of our seven bearing-design designations," Commerce "consider[s] them equally similar in component material or materials for model-match purposes, as instructed by section 771(16)(B)(ii) of the Act [i.e., 19 U.S.C. § 1677(16)(B)(ii)]." *Id.* at 77.

NTN maintains that its proposed additional design types, as presented and discussed in NTN's questionnaire response and case brief, were required to avoid unreasonable comparisons of dissimilar products. NTN Mem. 28. NTN further argues that it set forth detailed information in its questionnaire response demonstrating the need for these design types. *Id.* at 28–29. Finally, NTN argues that it relied on the Department's longstanding practice of using NTN's design types in the previous methodology and that it was improper for Commerce to change its methodology. *Id.* at 29–30.

Defendant responds that NTN, in response to the design-type portion of the questionnaire, provided general descriptions of its design types, technical drawings, and brochures but did not explain the submissions or explain why each of the design types merited designation separate from the general design types that Commerce included in the questionnaire. Def. Resp. 25. Defendant argues that Commerce has broad discretion to develop a methodology for determining "like" or "similar" merchandise under 19 U.S.C. § 1677(16)(B). *Id.* at 26. According to defendant, NTN also failed to show that the claimed differences in design type were so substantial that the DIFMER adjustment would not account for the differences. *Id.* at 27–29; *see* Def.-Intervenor Resp. 52–53. Pointing to its questionnaire responses, NTN disputes defendant's statement that NTN failed to provide the information, explanation, and analysis necessary to substantiate its request. Reply Br. of Pls. NTN Corp., NTN Bearing Corp. of Am., Am. NTN Bearing Mfg. Corp., NTN-BCA Corp., NTN-Bower Corp., & NTN Driveshaft, Inc. 3–4 ("NTN Reply").

The Court of Appeals in *Koyo II,* 551 F.3d 1286, confronted an issue similar to that posed by NTN's proposal for additional design types. In *Koyo II,* the plaintiff—which was NTN in that case as well-argued that its design types were significantly different from each other and that it had relied reasonably on the Department's acceptance of additional design types because Commerce had accepted its design types in prior reviews. *Id.* at 1292. The Court of Appeals held that "NTN has not demonstrated that Commerce's choice of design types, including its adjustments, was unreasonable" and that "even if Commerce had accepted NTN's proposals in the past, it was not required to do so in future reviews." *Id.* The Court of Appeals explained that "NTN's claim that its design types are superior does not show that Commerce's use of its own types was unreasonable." *Id.*

The court observes that some of the additional design-type categories proposed by NTN appear to describe ball bearings that fall within one, and only one, of

Commerce's accepted design-type categories. However, the court also observes that some of the bearings described in NTN's proposal for additional design types appear to fall within more than one of the Department's design-type categories. NTN raises this specific objection in support of its claim that Commerce should not have rejected its proposal. *See* NTN Mem. 28 ("Commerce's design codes do not take into account bearings, which fall into more than one category, such as bearings that are both 'angular contact' and 'deep groove' . . .."). Defendant does not respond to this issue in its briefs, nor is this issue addressed in the Decision Memorandum. Without a suitable explanation, the court is not able to discern how Commerce applied its model matching methodology to those of NTN's bearings that appear to fall within more than one accepted design type. The answer to this question is relevant to the court's consideration, in the entirety, of Commerce's decision to reject all of NTN's proposed design types other than the design-type category for hub units incorporating angular contact bearings. The court, therefore, will remand for reconsideration Commerce's decision in the Final Results to reject NTN's additional design types.

5. JTEKT, NPB, and NSK Failed to Demonstrate that Certain Identified Ball Bearing Matches Were Unlawful

At the invitation of the court, several plaintiffs filed supplemental briefs that set out, *inter alia,* certain matches they considered to be unreasonable. Supplemental Br. of Pls. JTEKT Corp. & Koyo Corp. of U.S.A. 2–3, Exs. I-K ("JTEKT Supplemental"); Pls. Nippon Pillow Block Co. Ltd. & FYH Bearing Units USA, Inc. Supplemental Br. 5–8 ("NPB Supplemental"); NSK's Supplemental Mem. in Supp. of Mot. for J. on the Agency R. 4–5 ("NSK Supplemental"); NTN Corp., NTN Bearing Corp. of Am., Am. NTN Bearing Mfg. Corp., NTN-BCA Corp., NTN-Bower Corp., & NTN Driveshaft, Inc.'s Supplemental Br. Pursuant to the Ct.'s Letter of June 18, 2008, at 3–7 ("NTN Supplemental"). JTEKT, NPB, NSK, and NTN assert that the methodology implemented by Commerce in the AFBs 16 reviews resulted in unlawful matches.

JTEKT identified three matches that it views are unreasonable. JTEKT Supplemental 2–3. The exhibits attached to its brief set forth a chart comparing physical or commercial characteristics of the U.S. model to one or two home market models. *Id.* at Exs. I-K. With respect to the first match, JTEKT states that "[b]ecause the purpose and applications of these models are quite different, there are remarkable differences between the U.S. model and the two home market models in terms of appearance and specifications." *Id.* at Ex. I, at 2. JTEKT asserts that "the home market models require higher specifications to ensure their performance than the U.S. model." *Id.* JTEKT further asserts that "[d]espite these differences, the Department matched the U.S. model with these home market models based on their coincidentally similar costs of production." *Id.* The second and third matches identified by JTEKT as unreasonable rely on substantively similar allegations. *See id.* at Exs. J-K. JTEKT's arguments essentially identify physical characteristics that were not separately recognized within the Department's new model-match methodology. JTEKT, however, has not demonstrated generally that the Department's matches were unreasonable according to the physical characteristics applied by the Department's methodology, or why that methodology, through the application of the DIFMER, failed to address the asserted "remarkable differences between the U.S. model and the two home market models in terms of appearance and specifications." *See id.* at Ex. I, at 2.

NPB also failed to demonstrate that Commerce applied an unreasonable methodology or exceeded its discretion in matching certain bearings. NPB states that "any number of unlawful comparisons with inappropriate foreign like products" occurred, NPB Mem. 26, and explains that Commerce "compared high temperature bearings NPB sold in the Japanese market to standard bearings that it sold in the U.S. market." *Id.* NPB explained that its "high temperature bearings contain heat-proof grease, special heat-proof seals, and may contain ceramic bearings" while its standard bearings "have standard grease, standard seals and stainless steel bearings." NPB Supplemental 5. NPB provides two examples of matches it considers unreasonable. First, NPB contends that Commerce "incorrectly compared the sales of NPB's U.S. model UC 211–32 G5 made in November 2004, to sales of Japanese model NA 211–32, also made in November 2004," arguing that Commerce "should have used the alternative model UC 211, a highly similar model to the UC 211–32 G5," which "has the same set screw design" and "differs only in that its inner diameter is slightly larger (55 mm. for the UC 211 versus 50.8 mm. for the UC 211–32 G5)." *Id.* at 6. NPB states that the "appropriate comparison model" was used in other sample months but that "the NA 211–32 was preferred in November only because it had the same inner diameter as the U.S. model." *Id.* NPB acknowledges, however, that "[t]he fundamentally different design of the NA 211–32 is reflected in the adjustment for the difference in merchandise vis-à-vis the UC 211–32 G5," which "adjustment is 18% of the total cost of production of the UC 211–32 G5, just short of the 20% that the Department uses as the maximum level for permissible comparisons." *Id.* at 6–7. Nonetheless, NPB asserts that Commerce should have used the other match, which yielded "a difference in merchandise [*i.e.,* DIFMER] of only 1%" and a percentage margin of 9%, as opposed to 84%. *Id.* at 7. NPB alleges, with respect to the first match, that the "single incorrect comparison by the Department contributes about one-tenth of the overall dumping margin." *Id.* at 6. NPB advances another match it considers unreasonable, asserting that the two models had fundamentally different designs, differed in inner diameter, and were sold in different months. *Id.* at 7. According to NPB, this match "contributes several percent to the dumping margin." *Id.*

NPB did not explain why the court must conclude that the matches to which it objects were unlawful. The existence of matches that NPB considers best do not compel the court to conclude that Commerce erred. As NPB acknowledged, "[t]hese specific model match comparisons highlight the larger issue . . . that is, additional physical characteristics are necessary to select the single most similar model matches." *Id.* at 8. As the court concluded above, however, Commerce was reasonable in limiting its methodology to the physical characteristics upon which it relied in conducting the administrative review at issue. The existence of isolated examples of matches that NPB asserts are preferable than the matches Commerce made pursuant to its methodology does not require the conclusion that the Department's methodology is unreasonable or that Commerce exceeded its discretion in making those matches. NPB fails to allege that the model-match methodology was misapplied by Commerce, and as applied to the specific matches to which NPB objects, the court cannot conclude that the results of the methodology were unreasonable.

NSK argues that "gross dissimilar matches infect much of the database used to calculate NSK's antidumping duty margin." NSK Mem. 13. NSK identified "two matches of dissimilar merchandise that the family methodology would have deemed unacceptable." NSK Supplemental 2. NSK highlights differences in load rates, inner diameters, and outer diameters, which are physical characteristics for which the new model-match methodology permits a 40% sum-of-the-deviations limit. *Id.* at 2–3. NSK also highlights the different uses of the matched bearings. *Id.* at 2. NSK's discussion of these examples does not present a reason for the court to conclude that Commerce exceeded its discretion or otherwise acted contrary to law in applying its new model-match methodology. Rather, the matches are offered only to illustrate, in nonspecific terms, the alleged superiority of the prior family model-match methodology. As the court stated above, however, the Court of Appeals has affirmed the Department's methodology as reasonable. *SKF II,* 537 F.3d at 1379–80. As affirmed by the Court of Appeals, the model-match methodology incorporated the 40% sum-of-the-deviations feature that NSK finds specifically objectionable. *Id.* at 1379. NSK's argument that it has presented "an extensive list of dissimilar bearing matches" in an affidavit it submitted with its motion for judgment upon the agency record is similarly unconvincing. NSK Supplemental 3 (citing NSK Mem., Ex. 12).

NTN also contests several matches: a specialized, farm implement bearing to a differently specialized set screw type bearing; a bearing with a pillow block housing to a bearing with square or round flange housing; a bearing with a dust cover to one without a dust cover; a bearing with a pillow-type housing to a bearing with a cartridge-type housing; and an eccentric locking collar bearing that has a spherical outer diameter to a set screw bearing that has a straight outer diameter. NTN Supplemental 3–9. In highlighting certain matches as unreasonable, NTN is challenging implicitly the reasonableness of the methodology itself. The variations that NTN highlights among the matched bearings result from differing physical characteristics or design types that are not recognized by the Department's model-matching methodology as applied in the AFBs 16 reviews. Thus, NTN's basic objection is to Commerce's choice of physical characteristics and design types. NTN argues that "[t]he sum-of-the-deviations may only be taken into consideration, however, *after* the bearing design has been correctly considered by the

Department" and "the [DIFMER] adjustment is only relevant for comparison between *similar* bearings, that is, once the bearings have been determined to be of the same design type, appropriately defined." *Id.* at 4–5. Stating its argument in general terms, NTN submits that "the first decision in the Department's model match methodology must be whether the paired bearings are alike in physical characteristics and function." *Id.* at 5. As discussed above, the court is remanding the Final Results for reconsideration of the decision to reject NTN's proposed additional design types. The Department's redetermination may affect specific matches.

The court again recalls that "Congress has granted Commerce considerable discretion to fashion the methodology used to determine what constitutes 'foreign like product' under the statute," *id.* at 1379 (citing *Pesquera Mares,* 266 F.3d at 1384), and that "Commerce's interpretation of the statute [with respect to the new model match methodology] merits deference. . .." *Id.* In alleging that certain matches were unreasonable, plaintiffs make a number of general arguments: they elevate the importance of certain physical characteristics beyond that which Commerce concluded was appropriate in its methodology, *see, e.g.,* JTEKT Supplemental 2–3, Exs. I-K; they set forth alternative matches that they contend would have been better matches, *see, e.g.,* NPB Supplemental 5–8; and they argue that the matches yielded by the family model-match methodology were more accurate, *see, e.g.,* NSK Mem. 13, Ex. 12 and NSK Supplemental 2–3. However, because the Department's methodology has been found to be reasonable and because Commerce has a significant degree of discretion when deciding which additional design types it will apply in its model-match methodology, the court will not deem particular matches unreasonable on the basis of physical characteristics unless Commerce abused its discretion or otherwise acted unreasonably. Overall, the Department's model matching decisions must be based on findings supported by substantial record evidence, and they must be reasonable determinations of foreign like products. Commerce is not required to refrain from making matches of bearings that are not identical, so long as it is reasonable to conclude that a home market bearing is sufficiently similar to the subject bearing to satisfy the reasonableness requirement of 19 U.S.C. § 1677(16)(B)–(C).

As discussed above, the Court of Appeals held that the Department's new methodology is lawful. *SKF II,* 537 F.3d at 1379–80. A respondent's showing that a particular match resulting from the new methodology would not have sufficed under the old methodology is not a sufficient basis upon which the court can conclude that Commerce acted unlawfully. With the possible exception of a problem posed by overlapping bearing design types, as discussed in the prior section with respect to NTN's merchandise, plaintiffs have not demonstrated that the new methodology yielded unreasonable matches. Commerce applied a general methodology affirmed by the Court of Appeals as reasonable. *Id.* The methodology affirmed by the Court of Appeals was highly similar to that used in the AFBs 16 reviews in physical characteristics, the 40% sum-of-the-deviations limit, and the 20% DIFMER limit. *See Decision Mem.* 16–27, 76–80; *AFBs 15 Decision Mem.* 19, 24–25.

In summary, the court will order that Commerce, upon remand, reconsider its rejection of NPB's proposal to expand the sample months in which Commerce searches for home market matches and its rejection of NTN's proposal for additional design-type categories for ball bearings but will affirm the use of the new model-match methodology in the AFBs 16 reviews in other respects.

C. Commerce Lawfully Decided to Treat JTEKT and Its Affiliate as a Single Entity

Commerce determined it appropriate to treat as a single entity (*i.e.,* "collapse") JTEKT and another producer of subject merchandise with which JTEKT is affiliated. *Decision Mem.* 61–63; *Final Results,* 71 Fed. Reg. at 40,065 (incorporating the Decision Memorandum). JTEKT claims a lack of substantial evidence to support this determination. JTEKT Mem. 11. To the contrary, the court concludes that the record contains substantial evidence to support the findings underlying Commerce's determination to treat JTEKT and its affiliate as a single entity in the AFBs 16 reviews.

Under its regulations, Commerce will treat two or more affiliated producers as a single entity when two conditions are satisfied. The first condition is that the producers at issue "have production facilities for similar or identical products that would not require substantial retooling of either facility in order to restructure manufacturing priorities. . .." 19 C.F.R. § 351.401(f)(1) (2009). The second condition is met if Commerce concludes that "there is a significant potential for the manipulation of price or production." *Id.*

JTEKT does not contest that it is affiliated with the other producer for purposes of 19 U.S.C. § 1677(33) (which defines the term "affiliated persons") and 19 C.F.R. § 351.401(f)(1), nor does it take issue with the finding of fact by Commerce, *see Decision Mem.* 58, that JTEKT and its affiliated producer "produce similar or identical merchandise." JTEKT Mem. 13. JTEKT argues, instead, that the second criterion in 19 C.F.R. § 351.401(f)(1)—*i.e.,* a significant potential for the manipulation of price or production between the two companies—is not satisfied by the record evidence when considered according to the totality of the circumstances. JTEKT Mem. 13–14.

The Department's regulations set forth three factors that the Secretary of Commerce "may consider" in identifying a significant potential for manipulation of price or production under § 351.401(f)(1). *See* 19 C.F.R. § 351.401(f)(2). The three factors are "[t]he level of common ownership," *id.* § 351.401(f)(2)(i), "[t]he extent to which managerial employees or board members of one firm sit on the board of directors of an affiliated firm," *id.* § 351.401(f)(2)(ii), and "[w]hether operations are intertwined, such as through the sharing of sales information, involvement in production and pricing decisions, the sharing of facilities or employees, or significant transactions between the affiliated producers," *id.* § 351.401(f)(2)(iii).

Commerce concluded in the Decision Memorandum that "facts here meet each of the factors listed under 19 CFR 351.401(f)(2) as indicative of . . . a potential" for the manipulation of price or production, stating that "[w]e found common ownership between the companies due to JTEKT's holdings in the affiliate, shared board members, and intertwined operations of the two companies." *Decision Mem.* 61. Commerce added that it "found that Koyo's standing as the largest shareholder of the affiliate to be indicative of the intertwined nature of the companies."

Id. The Decision Memorandum explained that the finding regarding intertwined operations of the two companies "was based on a sharing of sales information, which Commerce found to be implicit in the sharing of board members, and significant sales transactions between the two companies." *Id.* Commerce stated further that "[a]n analysis of Koyo's sales data, including its acquisition costs of products from the affiliate, led us to conclude that the shared transactions were significant and the potential existed for Koyo to be involved in the production and pricing decisions of the affiliate." *Id.* The decision cited for support an internal Commerce memorandum, the "Koyo Collapsing Memorandum."[10] *Id.; Mem. from Int'l Trade Compliance Analyst to Office Dir., AD/CVD Operations 5* (Mar. 2, 2006) (Admin.R.Doc. No. 218) ("*Collapsing Mem.*").

JTEKT does not dispute that it is the largest shareholder in the affiliate but points to record evidence indicating that its level of ownership is a minority share, not a controlling share. JTEKT Mem. 14. JTEKT argues that under Japanese law, a minority shareholder of a company cannot compel the company to disclose its sales and cost data. *Id.* at 14–15. With respect to shared board members, JTEKT asserts that these members "serve on a very limited basis as part-time ('non-stationed') auditors" on the board of directors of the affiliate, *id.* at 15, "are not permitted to vote, and have no control over the board's decisions as to corporate business matters—such as prices or production." *Id.* at 16. JTEKT argues that these directors, whose role is limited to conducting internal business audits, would have been acting *ultra vires,* and in breach of their fiduciary duty, were they to have shared with JTEKT pricing and cost information of the affiliate to which they had access. *Id.* JTEKT argues that the third reason Commerce gave for its decision to collapse the two entities, a significant level of sales transactions in which JTEKT purchased subject merchandise from the affiliate, does not provide a basis for that decision because these purchases were conducted at arm's length and, on average, prices were higher than the affiliate's cost of production. *Id.* at 17–18.

The court concludes that Commerce's finding that "there is a significant potential for the manipulation of price or production" is supported by substantial record evidence. 19 C.F.R. § 351.401(f)(1). It is uncontested that JTEKT is the largest shareholder of the affiliate (although not holding a majority share) and that JTEKT and its affiliate share board members. JTEKT Mem. 14. JTEKT disputes the level

10 The memorandum referred to JTEKT as "Koyo" based on the former name of the company, Koyo Seiko Company, Ltd. *See JTEKT-Koyo Successor Notice,* 71 Fed. Reg. at 26,452–53 (finding that JTEKT is the successor-in-interest to Koyo Seiko Company, Ltd.).

of control it may exercise over its affiliate via its minority share and also contests the Department's conclusion that the shared board members would have access to, or use, price and cost information for the affiliate upon attending board meetings. *Id.* at 14–16; *Collapsing Mem.* 4. However, under 19 C.F.R. § 351.401(f)(2), Commerce, in considering the level of common ownership and the extent to which there are shared board members, may exercise a significant degree of discretion. *See Decision Mem.* 61 (stating that "facts here meet each of the factors listed under 19 CFR 351.401(f)(2) as indicative of . . . *a potential*" for the manipulation of price or production (emphasis added)). The regulation does not require Commerce to find that a respondent exercises absolute control over its affiliate or that a board member may obtain and use price or cost information. The second factor in § 351.401(f)(2) is, therefore, satisfied. Commerce also satisfied the third factor, *i.e.,* "[w]hether operations are intertwined, such as through the sharing of sales information, involvement in production and pricing decisions, the sharing of facilities or employees, or significant transactions between the affiliated producers," 19 C.F.R. § 351.401(f)(2)(iii), in finding that JTEKT made a certain number of sales to its affiliate and of those sales a certain percentage were sold at or below the cost of production. *Collapsing Mem.* 4. Even if the court assumes that the shared board members are not permitted to share pricing information, and did not do so, and takes at face value JTEKT's statement that under Japanese law, a minority shareholder of a company cannot compel the company to disclose its sales and cost data, the court still must conclude that the record contains substantial evidence to support the findings underlying the Department's determination, in particular the level of ownership and the substantial volume of transactions between the companies, some of which were found to be below-cost sales. On the basis of findings supported by substantial evidence, Commerce permissibly reached the ultimate finding of a significant potential for manipulation of prices according to the factors in the Department's regulation, which regulation JTEKT does not challenge. The court therefore sustains the Department's determination to treat JTEKT and its affiliate as a single entity in the AFBs 16 reviews.

D. Commerce Lawfully Deducted Certain "Additional Benefit Expenses" when Determining the Constructed Export Price of NSK's Subject Merchandise

When determining constructed export price ("CEP") according to 19 U.S.C. § 1677a(b), Commerce is required to make a deduction from the price at which subject merchandise is first sold in the United States to an unaffiliated purchaser, to account for expenses of that sale, if those expenses are incurred by, or for the account of, the producer or exporter or the affiliated seller in the United States. 19 U.S.C. § 1677a(d)(1) (2006). Commerce has provided in its regulations that in establishing constructed export price, "the Secretary will make adjustments for expenses associated with commercial activities in the United States that relate to the sale to an unaffiliated purchaser, no matter where or when paid." 19 C.F.R. § 351.402(b) (2009).

NSK claims that Commerce, when calculating the constructed export price of NSK's subject ball bearings that were sold in the United States, erred in deducting certain expenses from the price at which the merchandise was sold to an unaffiliated purchaser. NSK Mem. 22–24. The expenses in question were additional benefits expenses that were paid to Japanese nationals located in the United States, who also were paid base salaries for certain activities that Commerce determined to relate to the sale of subject merchandise to unaffiliated customers in the United States. *Decision Mem.* 74–75. NSK does not dispute that "[t]he base wage for these workers is an expense that is associated with commercial actions in the United States that relate to sales activity, and thus should be deducted by Commerce from the CEP." NSK's Reply Mem. of P. & A. in Supp. of NSK's Mot. for J. on the Agency R. 11–12 ("NSK Reply"). NSK maintains, however, that the additional benefits expenses "are general and administrative ("G & A") in nature and otherwise are not associated with commercial actions in the United States, let alone sales activity." *Id.* at 12. According to NSK, the additional benefits expenses "are completely unrelated to the activities of these employees outside Japan." NSK Mem. 23.

NSK, in presenting its argument, refers to certain information about the additional benefit expenses for which it claims confidential treatment. Commerce, in the Decision Memorandum, characterized that information generally as follows: "According to NSK, the expenses associated with certain additional benefits for these Japanese workers are designed to mimic the parent company's compensation structure while the workers are residing outside Japan, regardless of whether the worker is in the United States or some other country." *Decision Mem.* 74. Based on its review of the confidential record information, the court finds accurate the general characterization that Commerce included in the Decision Memorandum to provide a description of the confidential information for purposes of public disclosure.

The court concludes that substantial record evidence, including specifically NSK's December 5, 2005 supplemental questionnaire response, is sufficient to establish that the employees in question were engaged in economic activity in the United States related to the sale of the subject merchandise. *Letter from Crowell & Moring, LLP to Dep't of Commerce* 51–52 (Dec. 5, 2005) (Admin.R.Doc. No. 160) ("*NSK Supplemental Resp.*") (setting forth pages S-34 to S-35 of NSK's response). It is also undisputed that the base salaries and the additional benefits expenses at issue were paid to these same employees. NSK's claim raises the question of whether or not the additional benefits expenses were paid as part of the total compensation that the Japanese nationals received for the activities they conducted in the United States associated with the sale of subject merchandise to unaffiliated producers, as opposed to activities conducted elsewhere or for some other purpose. Commerce expressly found in the Decision Memorandum that "[a]lthough the [additional benefit] expense[] may mimic the parent company's compensation structure it still represents full compensation associated with economic activity occurring in the United States." *Decision Mem.* 75. NSK's argument might have some merit were it supported by record evidence establishing that the additional benefits expenses pertained on the whole, or at least in part, to specifically-described economic activity *other than* the commercial activity in the United States that related to the sale of NSK's subject merchandise to unaffiliated purchasers. But NSK points to no such record evidence, nor is the court able to locate such evidence on the record. Such evidence as is present on the record is sufficient, under the standard of review, to support a finding that the additional benefits expenses related to the same activities for which the base salaries were paid to the Japanese nationals in the United States. Accordingly, the court concludes that NSK has not met its burden on this claim and affirms the Department's deduction of the additional benefits expenses from the prices paid to the unaffiliated purchasers for purposes of the determination of constructed export price.

E. The Department's Reallocation of NTN's Freight Expense Using Weight Instead of Value Arbitrarily Treated NTN Less Fairly than Other Respondents

Commerce makes deductions for freight expenses when determining export price and normal value. *See* 19 U.S.C. §§ 1677a(c)(2)(A), 1677b(a)(6)(B)(ii). In the AFBs 16 reviews, as it had in reviews for prior periods, Commerce made the freight deductions based on allocated freight costs rather than actual costs for freight in specific transactions. *See Decision Mem.* 47–56. Under the Department's regulations, "[a]ny party seeking to report an expense or a price adjustment on an allocated basis must demonstrate to the Secretary's satisfaction that the allocation is calculated on as specific a basis as is feasible, and must explain why the allocation methodology used does not cause inaccuracies or distortions." 19 C.F.R. § 351.401(g)(2). In the AFBs 16 reviews, NTN allocated its freight costs to its sales according to the value of the subject merchandise. *Decision Mem.* 48. Commerce concluded that NTN had failed to demonstrate that its value-based freight expense allocation did not cause distortions. *Id.* at 48–49. Noting that NTN did not incur the freight expenses on the basis of value but instead incurred them on various other bases (such as volume, distance, or hours of truck usage), Commerce expressed a concern that allocation based on value shifts freight expense from dumped to nondumped sales. *Id.* at 48–50. Upon rejecting NTN's allocation method, Commerce reallocated NTN's freight costs according to weight by using record data that NTN provided on the shipping weight for certain of its models, and, for other models for which actual weight data were not available on the record, by calculating estimates of weight based on size, using NTN's product data. *See id.* at 52–56.

NTN challenges on various grounds the Department's reallocation of its freight expense, which it maintains was reasonable and did not distort the margin calculations. *See* NTN Mem. 11–17. NTN argues that Commerce should not have departed from its long-standing practice of using value to allocate NTN's freight expense, which practice, according to NTN, Commerce followed "in *every* final determination it has issued regarding NTN since 1989." NTN Mem. 11. According to NTN's argument, "Commerce . . . is required to follow its past administrative practices in cases where the underlying facts presented to the agency have not changed," *id.* at 11–12, and that "none of the facts relating to how NTN ships merchandise and incurs freight expense have changed in this review from previous reviews." *Id.* at 12. The court finds this argument unpersuasive. First, NTN overstates the burden confronting an agency seeking to change an established practice or methodology. Commerce ordinarily may change a methodology provided it states its rationale for doing so and provided the stated rationale is reasonable. *NMB Singapore Ltd. v. United States,* 557 F.3d 1316, 1328 (Fed.Cir.2009). The reasonableness of the Department's previous practice of approving a value-based freight cost allocation for NTN does not itself preclude Commerce from discontinuing the practice. Second, contrary to NTN's contention that Commerce consistently has followed its long-standing practice of using value to allocate NTN's freight expense, and its claimed reliance on that practice, Commerce rejected NTN's reporting of freight expense according to a value-based allocation in at least one prior review, the twelfth administrative reviews of the orders ("AFBs 12"). *Issues & Decision Mem. for the Admin. Reviews of Ball Bearings (other than tapered roller bearings) & Parts Thereof from France, Germany, Italy, Japan, & the United Kingdom—May 1, 2000, through April 30, 2001,* at 75–79 (Aug 30, 2002). The issue of allocation of NTN's freight expense resulted in litigation in which the Court of International Trade and the Court of Appeals affirmed the Department's determination that NTN had failed to demonstrate that the value-based allocation method it sought to use in AFBs 12 was not distortive or inaccurate. *See NSK Ltd. v. United States,* 28 CIT 1535, 346 F.Supp.2d 1312 (2004) ("*NSK I*"); *NSK Ltd. v. United States,* 481 F.3d 1355, 1359–61 (Fed.Cir. 2007) ("*NSK II*"). Having been placed on notice in AFBs 12 that Commerce determined NTN's earlier allocation of freight expenses based on value to be unacceptable, a determination that the courts later upheld, NTN cannot plausibly contend that it reasonably relied on an expectation that it would be permitted to allocate freight expense based on value in AFBs 16.

Nevertheless, the court concludes that Commerce did not act lawfully in resolving the freight expense allocation issue that was presented by the sales of NTN and those of similarly situated respondents in AFBs 16. The administrative record includes an internal Commerce memorandum disclosing that other respondents in AFBs 16, like NTN, did not incur freight expense on a weight basis but submitted freight expense allocations that were based on the value of the merchandise. *See Mem. from Senior Int'l Trade Compliance Analyst, AD/CVD Operations, Office 5, and Int'l Trade Compliance Analyst, AD/ CVD Operations, Office 5, to Office Dir., AD/CVD Operations, Office 5,* at 5 (Mar. 2, 2006) (Admin.R.Doc. No. 217). The memorandum also discloses that Commerce declined to reject any of these other value-based allocations. Citing this internal memorandum, Commerce stated as follows in the Preliminary Results:

> With respect to other respondents in these administrative reviews that used a value-based methodology to allocate freight expenses, we recognize that no longer accepting

> value-based freight-expense allocation methodologies is a significant change in practice. Moreover, we do not have all of the data (*e.g.,* the per-unit weight of the bearings) we would need to reallocate these respondents' freight expenses. Therefore, we have not reallocated other respondents' freight expenses in the current reviews. For future reviews of these orders, we will not accept value-based methodologies for the allocation of inland freight or international freight expenses except in situations where the freight charges are, in fact, incurred on a value, not weight or volume, basis (*e.g.,* marine insurance).

Prelim. Results, 71 Fed. Reg. at 12,173. Commerce did not change its position on the freight allocation issue in the Final Results. As demonstrated by the internal memorandum and the Preliminary Results, Commerce reached a determination (which it described as "a significant change in practice") in the AFBs 16 reviews under which all value-based allocation of freight costs that were not charged according to value are distortive *per se. Id.*

NTN challenges the Department's "distinct treatment that was applied only to NTN." NTN Mem. 13. NTN takes issue with the Department's conclusion that it could reallocate NTN's freight cost from a value basis to a weight basis because the record contained data from NTN that allowed Commerce do so. *Id.* at 12 (stating that Commerce "used data that is [*sic*] incomplete and, in many cases, based on estimates not supported by the record.").

With respect to the allocation of freight, "the governing regulations require that a party seeking a particular expense adjustment or allocation must demonstrate its correctness to the Secretary of Commerce's 'satisfaction.' Under this standard, the decision whether to accept a proposed allocation lies primarily within Commerce's discretion." *Koyo II,* 551 F.3d at 1292. The Department had discretion to decline to apply its new position until a subsequent review, so long as it exercised that discretion in a way that was evenhanded and not arbitrary. The issue presented by Commerce's decision in this case is "whether Commerce abused its discretion. . ., that is, whether Commerce's decision was 'based on a consideration of the relevant factors and whether there has been a clear error of judgment.'" *Torrington Co. v. United States,* 68 F.3d 1347, 1351 (Fed.Cir.1995) (quoting *Citizens to Preserve Overton Park, Inc. v. Volpe,* 401 U.S. 402, 416, 91 S.Ct. 814, 28 L.Ed.2d 136 (1971), and addressing the issue of whether Commerce abused its discretion in the context of determining whether to conduct a verification). However, in the AFBs 16 reviews, Commerce acted arbitrarily. It adopted a blanket policy of deferring the application of its change in position, which it considered "a significant change in practice," *Prelim. Results,* 71 Fed. Reg. at 12, 173, under which all value-based allocations, except those where freight cost is actually incurred according to value, are deemed distortive *per se. Id.* New practice aside, Commerce selectively applied 19 C.F.R. § 351.401(g) to disallow NTN's freight expense allocation but not those of the other respondents, without a rational basis for the distinction. In the Final Results, according to the Decision Memorandum, Commerce rejected NTN's value-based allocation because it concluded that NTN had failed to demonstrate that NTN's allocation was non-distortive (which, under Commerce's new practice, no respondent could do), even though the other respondents also failed to make this demonstration. *See Decision Mem.* 48, 51–52.

"A long line of precedent has established that an agency action is arbitrary when the agency offer[s] insufficient reasons for treating similar situations differently." *Transactive Corp. v. United States,* 91 F.3d 232, 237 (D.C.Cir.1996); *SKF USA Inc. v. United States,* 263 F.3d 1369, 1382 (Fed.Cir.2001) ("*SKF I*") (quoting *Transactive Corp.*, 91 F.3d at 237). "Deference to agency authority or expertise . . . 'is not a license to . . . treat like cases differently.'" *Airmark Corp. v. FAA,* 758 F.2d 685, 691 (D.C.Cir.1985) (quoting *United States v. Diapulse Corp.*, 748 F.2d 56, 62 (2d Cir.1984)) (describing the Federal Aviation Administration's application of five criteria, in considering petitions for exemption from regulations imposing noise standards, as "grossly inconsistent and patently arbitrary" and stating that "[e]lementary even-handedness requires that if all five factors must be met by one petitioner, then all five factors must be met by the next." *Airmark,* 758 F.2d at 692.).

Defendant attempts to defend the Department's decision to accept the value-based freight allocations of the other respondents, but not that of NTN, by arguing that "Commerce reasonably determined that it would not reject value-based allocations when the record lacked all of the necessary data (the per-unit weights of bearings), necessary to reallocate certain respondents' freight expenses." Def. Resp. 48. This argument does not overcome the problem posed by the arbitrary and disparate treatment. Once Commerce had determined that all the value-based freight expense allocations at issue in the AFBs 16 reviews, including that of NTN, were distortive and therefore impermissible under 19 C.F.R. § 351.401(g), Commerce was faced with the task of effectuating that determination on a basis that was fair to all respondents. It failed in this task.

Referring to the Department's new position of deeming distortive all value-based allocations of freight charges that were not actually paid according to value, defendant argues, further, that "[i]t was not necessary for Commerce to postpone applying this determination to NTN because Commerce verified that NTN possessed the necessary weight information to reallocate NTN's freight expenses." Def. Resp. 48–49; *see also Decision Mem.* 52 ("Furthermore, our decision to not re-calculate other respondents' freight expenses in this review does not invalidate, in any way, our decision to implement such a change for NTN where we had readily available and verified data submitted by NTN that allowed us to calculate NTN's freight expenses on the basis of weight reasonably."). This argument also fails. It clearly *was* necessary for Commerce to postpone applying its new position to NTN because, under that new position, every respondent in the AFBs 16 reviews that used a value-based freight expense valuation failed the test of compliance with 19 C.F.R. § 351.401(g)(1). The Department's reliance on its conclusion that NTN failed to demonstrate that its value-based allocation was not distortive for purposes of § 351.401(g)(1), *see Decision Mem.* 48, was pretextual in light of the agency's announcing its new position, under which neither NTN nor anyone else could make such a demonstration. *See Prelim. Results,* 71 Fed. Reg. at 12,173. Commerce treated as inconsequential its own decision, apparent from the record, not to require the other respondents in the AFBs 16 reviews to make that demonstration. *See id.* Commerce attempted to justify its selective enforcement on a distinction as to whether it considered a party's data adequate to enable Commerce to perform a reallocation, finding only NTN's data suitable for this purpose, rather than on a distinction grounded in each party's compliance with § 351.401(g). *See id.* This was an insufficient reason "for treating similar situations differently." *See Transactive Corp.,* 91 F.3d at 237; *SKF I,* 263 F.3d at 1382. Commerce never determined that the allocations of the other respondents satisfied the requirement of 19 C.F.R. § 351.401(g)(1) and instead announced a new position under which these respondents, like NTN, necessarily would have failed to do so. The obligation to treat all respondents equally and fairly did not permit Commerce to overlook this failure and to reallocate NTN's freight expenses.

As an incidental matter, the court observes that the Department's justification for its arbitrary decision ignores the record fact that Commerce had weight data for only some of NTN's models and resorted to its own methodology of estimating shipping weights for others of NTN's models. *Mem. from Financial Analyst, AD/ CVD Operations, Office 5, to The File* 7–9 (Mar. 2, 2006) (Admin.R.Doc. No. 222) ("*NTN Prelim. Analysis Mem.*"). Thus, Commerce did not have on the record a complete set of product weight data with which to reallocate the value-based freight expense calculations of any respondent in the reviews. *See id.; Decision Mem.* 53–54; *Prelim. Results,* 71 Fed. Reg. at 12,173 ("With respect to other respondents in these administrative reviews that used a value-based methodology to allocate freight expenses, . . . we do not have all of the data (*e.g.,* the per-unit weight of the bearings) we would need to reallocate these respondents' freight expenses.").

In summary, Commerce's regulatory decision to postpone implementing its new position on value-based freight cost allocations was impermissibly arbitrary because it was applied selectively to all respondents other than NTN. The decision to reallocate only NTN's freight expense was also impermissibly arbitrary because, under the Department's new position, none of the other respondents in the AFBs 16 reviews who used a value-based freight allocation could have satisfied the test of compliance with 19 C.F.R. § 351.401(g)(1), and none were required even to attempt to make such a demonstration. Therefore, the Department's decision to reallocate NTN's freight cost must be set aside as contrary to law. *See* 19 U.S.C. § 1516a(b)(1)(B)(i).

F. Commerce Permissibly Recalculated NTN's Home Market Packing Materials Expenses

NTN claims that Commerce unlawfully decided to recalculate NTN's home market packing materials expenses and failed to support with substantial record evidence its redetermination of that expense. *See* NTN Mem. 30–35. Defendant responds that Commerce correctly determined that NTN's home market packing expenses, as reported by NTN, was affected by distortions and supported that determination with substantial record evidence. Def. Resp. 38–43.

Commerce determined that NTN's method of reporting data on expenses incurred for packing materials on home market sales was unsatisfactory in failing to account for differences in the packing materials expenses that were incurred in sales of foreign like products to different "customer categories," *i.e.,* original equipment manufacturers ("OEMs"), distributors, and after-market purchasers. *Decision Mem.* 81–82. Commerce concluded that NTN had reported its home market packing materials expenses according to "a single packing expense factor" rather than according to separate packing expense factors for these different customer categories. *Id.* at 82. Commerce considered the use of a single factor to cause distortions by failing to capture differences in expenses for packing materials inherent in packing requirements associated with the different customer categories. *Id.* Commerce noted that NTN indicated in its questionnaire responses that sales to OEMs are packed in bulk while sales to distributors and after-market purchasers are packed individually in boxes. *Id.* at 80. In response to its finding that NTN's single packing expense factor caused distortions, Commerce recalculated NTN's home-market packing materials expenses by using "as a proxy" customer-category-specific data that NTN submitted on the cost of repacking materials for its U.S. sales. *Id.* at 80. NTN claims that this recalculation was unlawful for various reasons. *Id.*

NTN first argues that in these reviews, NTN used the same method to report its home market packing expenses that it has used for many years, which method was based on previous decisions by Commerce that NTN should not allocate expenses for packing materials to account for differences among customer categories. NTN Mem. 31–32. NTN asserts that it has relied on the Department's "established methodology," *id.* at 31, and that Commerce should not be allowed to change that established methodology "without a reasoned explanation of its departure from previous, long-standing methods." *Id.* at 32. NTN also implies that Commerce must provide "a compelling reason to use a ratio for packing material that varies by customer category. . .." *Id.* Defendant responds that NTN was on notice regarding the Department's concerns and states that "Commerce raised concerns about NTN's packing expense calculation methodology as early as the fourteenth administrative review when NTN calculated its home market packing expenses using a sales value allocation methodology, without keeping records of packing costs on a unit-by-unit basis."[11] Def. Resp. 41 (citing *Final Results POR 2003–04,*

---

11 Defendant refers to the fourteenth administrative reviews but then cites to the final results for the fifteenth administrative reviews, which were the reviews preceding the administrative reviews at issue in this case. *See* Def. Resp. 41 (citing *Ball Bearings & Parts Thereof from France, Germany, Italy, Japan, Singapore, & the United Kingdom: Final Results of*

70 Fed. Reg. at 54,714); *see AFBs 15 Decision Mem.* 64–65 (finding that "it is appropriate to reallocate NTN's packing expenses . . . because packing in bulk costs less on a per-bearing basis than individual packing" and setting forth a methodology under which Commerce assigned sales of bulk-packaged merchandise a factor of one and sales of individually-packed merchandise a factor based on the number of bearings packed individually).

The court reviews a change in methodology for reasonableness. *SKF II,* 537 F.3d at 1377–78. As a general matter, Commerce is free to change its method of calculating home market packing expenses if it states its rationale for doing so and if that stated rationale is reasonable. *NMB Singapore,* 557 F.3d at 1328. In the Decision Memorandum, Commerce acknowledged that it "directed NTN not to report customer-specific packing expenses in an early administrative review of this order," but explained that in the prior administrative review, as well as the instant review, "it ha[d] become apparent that such reporting is necessary because [Commerce] designate[s] NTN's levels of trade based on its reported customer categories." *Decision Mem.* 82. Commerce further explained:

> When we calculate the level-of-trade adjustment factors for NTN's export-price sales, we compare weighted-average home-market prices for each level of trade, net of adjustments and expenses, including packing expenses. See 19 CFR 351.412(e). NTN derived and reported sale-specific packing expenses by multiplying the reported single packing-expense factor by gross unit prices. This results in distorted net prices among levels of trade because the average single packing-expense factor minimizes the disparity between packing costs for different customer categories. This in turn results in distorted level-of-trade adjustment factors which, in turn, results in distorted normal values after application of level-of-trade-adjustments for distributor, after-market, and OEM sales when we make comparisons at different levels of trade for NTN's export-price sales.
>
> In sum, the use of separate packing-expense factors by customer category is warranted because it captures differences in expenses for packing materials inherent in packing requirements with respect to different customer categories which, in turn, eliminates foreseeable distortions in our margin calculations.

Id.

Commerce is required to determine home market packing expenses and make level-of-trade adjustments when determining normal value and comparing it to export price. *See* 19 U.S.C. § 1677b(a)(1)(6), (7)(A). The court concludes that the Department's objective of seeking to allocate packing expenses by a more accurate methodology, for purposes of the level-of-trade adjustments Commerce makes when comparing U.S. and home market sales, was reasonable. A single packing-expense ratio that applies to different customer categories must be considered less accurate than separate ratios where packing expense variances exist with respect to

---

Antidumping Duty Admin. Reviews, 70 Fed. Reg. 54,711, 54,714 (Sept. 16, 2005) ("*Final Results POR 2003–04*")).

customer category. Additionally, although NTN claims that it relied on the Department's previous methodology, NTN has not shown how any reliance it may have had was reasonable, given that Commerce made a similar adjustment in AFBs 15. Moreover, NTN has not shown specifically why any reliance it may have had on the previous methodology was detrimental reliance.

Next, NTN objects that "Commerce did not ask NTN to explain or comment on why it did not report its packing material ratios by customer category." NTN Mem. 33. The court is unconvinced by this argument. At issue was not the question of *why* NTN did not report its packing material ratios by customer category—that much was clear from the record. Rather, the court must decide, first, whether the Department's findings were supported by substantial record evidence, including the ultimate finding that NTN's allocation of packing expenses according to sales value caused distortions. If so, the second question is whether it was reasonable for Commerce, in response to this finding, to recalculate the expenses based on packing materials factors derived from data on NTN's sales in the U.S. market, which factors were customer-category-specific.

The administrative record, considered as a whole, supports the findings that NTN sold subject ball bearings in the United States and foreign like products in its home market in different customer categories, did not maintain data on the home market packing materials expenses according to those various categories and, as a result, allocated its home market packing materials expenses based on the sales value of the merchandise. Specifically, the administrative record demonstrates that NTN sold subject merchandise in the United States through three channels of distribution—through its affiliated U.S. sales company, to unaffiliated OEM customers directly, and to a U.S. manufacturing affiliate that incorporates subject merchandise as a subject component—and that the packing expenses vary according to the channel of distribution and customer type. *Letter from Barnes, Richardson & Colburn to Dep't of Commerce* 26–27, 31 (Sept. 26, 2005) (Admin.R.Doc. No. 89) ("*NTN Questionnaire Resp.*") (at A-11, A-12, and A-16 of the response). NTN itself set forth the example of repacking merchandise in individual boxes when sold to distributor and aftermarket customers compared with the bulk packing for sales to OEMs. *Id.* NTN's questionnaire responses also show that NTN's home market sales involved different customer categories. *Id.* at 29 (at A-14 of the response).

The record indicates that in a supplemental questionnaire, Commerce made the following request:

> based on the information you provided in your response to section A of the Department's questionnaire, it is apparent that NTN packs merchandise for sale to OEMs in bulk and individually for sales to distributors and after-market purchasers. Please demonstrate that an allocation of packing expenses based on sales value does not cause distortion especially in light of the fact that margin calculation may result in the comparisons of same models at different levels of trade designated by customer category.

Letter from Dep't of Commerce to Barnes, Richardson & Colburn 19 (Oct. 20, 2005) (Admin.R.Doc. No. 105) ("*NTN Supplemental Questionnaire*") (at page 17, ¶ 82 of the questionnaire). NTN responded that

> The ITA has recognized on many previous occasions that NTN does not track individual packing expenses. Therefore, NTN has adopted the only available methodology: to report packing expense based on relative sales value. Additionally, individual distributor and aftermarket prices are generally higher than OEM prices and, under NTN's methodology, a greater proportion of the packing expenses will be allocated to these purchasers. We believe, therefore, that the methodology is not distortive; rather, it accurately reflects packing expenses in general.

Letter from Barnes, Richardson & Colburn to Dep't of Commerce 67–68 (Nov. 17, 2005) (Admin.R.Doc. No. 139) ("*NTN Supplemental Resp.*") (at B-14 to B-15 of the response). Commerce followed up on the issue with NTN in the notice prior to verification:

> Demonstrate how you allocated packing expenses. Provide all source documentation. Show how the packed form reported for the preselected sales relates to customers' packing requirements and to the per-unit expenses. Provide documentation supporting your calculation of packing labor for domestic sales. Contrast HM [*i.e.*, home market] packing costs with export packing costs.

Letter from Dep't of Commerce to NTN Corp. 12 (Nov. 23, 2005) (Admin.R.Doc. No. 145) ("*NTN Verification Notice*") (at page 10 of the notice). In its report on the verification of NTN's home-market and export-price sales, Commerce "found that NTN's calculation of packing expenses results in essentially the same packing ratios for distributors and OEMs." *Letter from Senior Int'l Trade Specialist, AD/CVD Operations, Office 5, to File* 11 (Jan. 4, 2006) (Admin.R.Doc. No. 184) ("*NTN Verification Report of Home-Market & Export-Price Sales*"). This finding, adopted by the Final Results, clearly was supported by substantial record evidence, which NTN itself provided in its questionnaire responses. *See NTN Supplemental Resp.* 67–68 (at B-14 to B-15 of the response). The finding was the basis for the conclusion by Commerce that NTN's reporting of its home market packing expenses causes distortions. That finding, also, is supported by the record evidence showing that NTN's packing methods were not uniform across the different customer categories. Although NTN points out that its method allocated more packing materials expenses to the distributor and aftermarket sales, which generally were of higher value than the OEM sales, *see* NTN Mem. 32–33 (citing *NTN Supplemental Resp.* 67–68 (at B-14 to B-15 of the response)), this argument fails to account for the distortion that necessarily would result upon the Department's making a level-of-trade adjustment.

The remaining question is whether the recalculation Commerce performed was reasonable. NTN argues that Commerce must use the actual home market data because it is accurate and the best evidence available, particularly when compared to the information related to U.S. packing expenses upon which Commerce relied.

NTN Mem. 33–35. NTN contends that the Department's adjustment is unrelated to the costs incurred, ignores evidence on the record, and distorts NTN's packing expenses. *Id.* at 35.

In the Decision Memorandum, Commerce explained that "the record does not have the necessary data to calculate home-market packing-expense factors for each customer category" and that Commerce "made that statement because, although NTN provided home-market packing-expense factors by customer category, [Commerce] found that [NTN] had derived such factors by allocating the total cost center-specific packing-materials and packing-labor expenses based on the ratio of customer category-specific sales value to the total sales value of each cost center." *Decision Mem.* 82–83. Commerce found that "each of [NTN's] cost centers is dedicated to capturing sales information applicable to the various customer categories" but that "these cost centers do not capture the expense information in the same manner." *Id.* at 83. Commerce explained that "the packing-expense factor for distributors for a particular cost center, as reported by NTN, does not capture actual packing expenses incurred by this cost center even though it does capture information concerning the value of sales to distributors." *Id.* Commerce restated its finding that "the home-market customer category-specific factors NTN reported are virtually identical in values on a cost center-specific level or on a company-wide level. . . ." *Id.*

Despite the shortcomings that Commerce found to exist in NTN's allocation method, NTN frames the issue as a choice between its home market packing cost data and its packing cost data pertaining to its U.S. sales. This formulation overlooks the problem that resulted for level-of-trade adjustments from NTN's having reported its home market packing materials expenses according to a single packing expense factor rather than actual packing cost data specific to the different customer categories. It was reasonable for Commerce to attempt to address this problem through a recalculation. Although NTN objects to the Department's use of U.S. packing data to accomplish the recalculation, the mere fact that the data used to perform the adjustment pertained to U.S. packing costs, not home market packing costs, does not support a conclusion that the Department's recalculation was impermissible. It is not apparent how use of any other data on the record would have solved the distortion problem that Commerce identified.

For these various reasons, the court affirms the Department's recalculation of NTN's home market packing materials expenses in the Final Results.

G. Commerce Lawfully Disallowed Certain Downward Price Adjustments that Resulted from NTN's Allocation of Discounts to Home Market Customers

NTN, when reporting its home market sales to Commerce, made downward adjustments to the original prices in sales of foreign like products to certain customers to account for discounts that it granted retroactively to those customers. At verification,

Commerce found a discrepancy between the adjusted prices as reported to Commerce and the actual method by which NTN granted the discounts, concluding that the downward adjustments were made to all sales of a particular customer during the fiscal year even though the discounts actually applied only to certain models for certain time periods.[12] Commerce disallowed NTN's downward adjustments, concluding that "NTN's allocation of the discounts in question results in the assignment of price adjustments to sales which cannotbe [*sic*] said to have been reasonably affected by such adjustments," *Decision Mem.* 67, and "results in a price adjustment that is not reasonably attributable to sales of the foreign like product, as required by 19 CFR 351.401(c)." *Id.* at 67–68. NTN contends, on several grounds, that "Commerce erroneously disallowed NTN's home market discounts because NTN provided sufficient evidence to support its allocation."[13] NTN Mem. 35; *see* NTN Reply 13–15. Defendant responds that "Commerce correctly rejected NTN's price adjustment methodology because the methodology inaccurately allocates price adjustments from sales that were actually adjusted to sales that did not receive adjustments." Def. Resp. 29. Defendant further argues that "[a]dditionally, NTN has not adequately explained why its methodology is not distortive." *Id.* (relying on 19 C.F.R. § 351.401(g)).

As a preliminary matter, NTN raises a procedural issue, arguing that because Commerce accepted NTN's allocation for the tenth through fifteenth administrative reviews and verified the data used in the methodology in the tenth and thirteenth reviews, Commerce should have explained its reasons for changing its policy. NTN Mem. 35, 39. As the Court of Appeals has held, "Commerce's acceptance of an allocation methodology in a previous review does not relieve a party of its burden of demonstrating the methodology is non-distortive in the current review." *NSK III,* 510 F.3d at 1381. Nonetheless, if Commerce changes a methodology to which it adhered in previous proceedings, Commerce must "provide[] a sufficient, reasoned analysis explaining why a change is necessary." *NMB Singapore,* 557 F.3d at 1328 ("Commerce, like any agency, is due deference from the courts in

---

12 Commerce concluded that:

> With respect to the customers we examined, we found that, although NTN sold other models to the customer for which NTN did not incur any adjustments and although NTN sold bearings to these customers during other periods in which NTN granted no adjustments, NTN allocated the total value of granted billing adjustments and other discounts over all sales of BBs [*i.e.,* ball bearings] during the entire fiscal year to the customer and applied the allocated ratios to all reported sales of all products to the customer during the POR.

Letter from Senior Int'l Trade Specialist, AD/CVD Operations, Office 5, to File 2 (Jan. 4, 2006) (Admin.R.Doc. No. 184) ("*NTN Verification Report of Home-Market & Export-Price Sales*").

13 NTN, in the underlying proceeding, also raised the issue of whether Commerce acted lawfully in maintaining certain upward adjustments while rejecting the downward adjustments at issue here. *Decision Mem.* 66, 68. However, in their complaint and their motion for judgment upon the agency record, NTN has not raised the issue of the lawfulness of the Department's determination to maintain the upward adjustments although disallowing the downward adjustments. *See* Compl. ¶¶ 37–40; NTN Mem. 35–39.

certain matters entrusted to it by Congress. Once Commerce establishes a course of action, however, Commerce is obliged to follow it until Commerce provides a sufficient, reasoned analysis explaining why a change is necessary." (citation omitted)); *NSK III,* 510 F.3d at 1381.

In these reviews, the Department's finding at verification that NTN's allocation method allocated price adjustments to sales that were not actually subject to these adjustments was the basis for the decision NTN challenges. The Court of Appeals addressed an analogous situation in *NSK III,* concluding that although Commerce had accepted a respondent's method of allocating lump-sum billing adjustments in previous reviews, the Department's observation of clear evidence of a substantial distortion was a sufficient basis for Commerce to change its position and reject the respondent's allocation methodology. *NSK III,* 510 F.3d at 1381–82. Here also, the Department's finding that an allocation method caused distortions and the explanation of the Department's reasoning in the Decision Memorandum provide adequate support for the Department's determination to change its position on the acceptability of NSK's allocation methodology.

NTN disputes the Department's statement in the Decision Memorandum that price adjustments must be product-specific and time-specific. NTN Mem. 36–37; *see Decision Mem.* 67 (in which Commerce stated that in determining an antidumping duty margin "we do not use customer-specific aggregate prices" and that "[w]e use product-specific and time-specific prices in our margin calculation"). NTN contends that "[a]ny product-specific or time-specific reporting must, necessarily, be based on a customer-specific buildup" and states, as an example, that "NTN does not simply grant a discount for a certain product for any and all sales of such product made in Japan during the period of review. On the contrary, the discount is granted based on sales of that product *to a particular customer.*" NTN Mem. 37. NTN further states that "the discount policy is a post hoc adjustment that is related to the *total* sales of a certain product that were made to a certain customer during the fiscal year," *id.* at 38, and concludes that "[o]nly when sales to a particular customer are aggregated can a product-specific, or time-specific, attribution be accomplished." *Id.* at 37.

To be recognized by Commerce, a price adjustment must be reasonably attributed to the subject merchandise or the foreign like product. 19 C.F.R. § 351.401(c). Under 19 C.F.R. § 351.401(g)(1), Commerce "may consider allocated . . . price adjustments when transaction-specific reporting is not feasible." 19 C.F.R. § 351.401(g)(1). A respondent, however, must satisfy Commerce that "the allocation method used does not cause inaccuracies or distortions." *Id.* Specifically, the requesting party "must demonstrate to the Secretary's satisfaction that the allocation is calculated on as specific a basis as is feasible, and must explain why the allocation methodology used does not cause inaccuracies or distortions." *Id.* at § 351.401(g)(2).

In the Decision Memorandum, Commerce "determined that NTN reported the discounts differently than how it granted such adjustments." *Decision Mem.* 67.

Commerce explained that it "determined that, in its attempt to derive a factor for reporting the discounts in question, NTN divided the total value of discounts granted (*i.e.,* the numerator) by the total value of certain sales (*i.e.,* the denominator)" and found, at verification, "that the total value of sales NTN used in the denominator contained sales . . . [that] did not bear any relationship to the discounts NTN had captured in the numerator." *Id.* Commerce concluded that "the numerator and denominator were not stated on a rational basis. In other words, NTN's methodology is distortive because NTN allocates adjustments from sales that actually had an adjustment to sales that did not have an adjustment." *Id.* Substantial record evidence supports the Department's finding that the allocation methodology was distortive. NTN does not refute the factual finding that was central to the Department's rejection of NTN's allocation method—that NTN applied the aggregate discounts to sales of all models from a specific customer for the fiscal year when the discounts were afforded only on certain models or for specific time periods.

NTN alleges that its allocation method was based on the most specific way that NTN could collect data due to the determination of, and distribution of, such discounts. NTN Mem. 38–39. However, this allegation does not find adequate support in the record of the administrative reviews. In the Final Results, Commerce rejected NTN's assertion that it was not feasible for NTN to report its discounts any more specifically, *Decision Mem.* 68, and NTN did not supply a convincing reason, either to Commerce or in its later submissions to the court, why records kept in the ordinary course of business and establishing the actual discounts could not have been used, manually if necessary, to make more accurate adjustments than those resulting from NTN's broad allocation method. As the regulations provide, the burden was on NTN to demonstrate that the allocation method does not cause inaccuracies or distortions. *See* 19 C.F.R. § 351.401(g). In determining whether the burden has been met, Commerce looks at "the records maintained by the party in question in the ordinary course of its business, as well as such factors as the normal accounting practices in the country and industry in question and the number of sales made by the party during the period of . . . review." 19 C.F.R. § 351.401(g)(3). Although Commerce "recognize[d] the potential existence of limitations associated with NTN's electronic record-keeping" it also observed that "NTN did not make an argument as to whether it could have accomplished the proper reporting of discounts in question from its records manually." *Decision Mem.* 68. Commerce explained:

> NTN granted the discounts in question to specific customers for purchases of specific products during specific periods of time. Surely NTN maintains the records in the ordinary course of its business, such as invoices, that are necessary to supplement its reporting. In addition, the number of sales for which the discounts were granted is insignificant in relation to NTN's universe of reported home-market sales. Furthermore, NTN is silent as to why it applied its allocated-discounts factor to reported home-market sales which were not eligible for such discounts (*i.e.,* sales to the same customer of products for which NTN did not grant the discounts and sales

> to the same customer of products for which NTN did grant the discounts but outside the period for which it granted the discounts).

Id. The Department's determination that NTN did not meet the burden imposed by 19 C.F.R. § 351.401(g) was supported by substantial evidence on the record.

In summary, the record evidence supports Commerce's overall finding that NTN's allocation method allocated discounts to sales ineligible to receive such discounts. The discrepancies that Commerce found at verification to exist between the home market prices reported by NTN and the prices that would have resulted from prices adjusted to reflect the actual discounts necessarily would have distorted the determination of normal value for specific like products and, accordingly, the dumping margins on sales of subject merchandise. The Department's regulations specifically allow the Secretary to reject price adjustments that cannot be shown to be reasonably attributable to the foreign like product, 19 C.F.R. § 351.401(c), because they have been allocated by a method that has not been shown not to cause inaccuracies or distortions, *id.* § 351.401(g). The court, therefore, concludes that Commerce acted within its authority under the applicable regulations to disallow NTN's downward price adjustments in the AFBs 16 reviews.

H. The Department's Use of Facts Otherwise Available and Adverse Inferences in Response to Discovering Nachi's Errors in Reporting Physical Bearing Characteristics Was Contrary to Law

To implement its model-match methodology, Commerce requested that respondents report individual physical characteristics for each bearing model in their U.S. and home market sales databases. Nachi Mem. 5. In response, Nachi reported physical characteristics for 2,084 individual models of bearings. *Id.* at 6. During verification, Commerce reviewed a sample of the data that Nachi reported on the physical characteristics of its bearings, examining information corresponding to forty of the 2,084 models reported. *Id.; Mem. from Senior Case Analyst, AD/CVD Enforcement & Case Analyst, AD/CVD Enforcement, to The File* 3–5 (Feb. 9, 2006) (Admin.R.Doc. No. 208) ("*Nachi Verification Mem.*"). Upon verification, Commerce found nineteen errors in Nachi's reporting of physical characteristics, which nineteen errors affected sixteen of the forty models reviewed. *Nachi Verification Mem.* 4. Based on the verification, Commerce reached a finding that "Nachi reported incorrect physical characteristics for 16 of the 40 models we examined at verification." *Final Results,* 71 Fed. Reg. at 40,066. Citing "the significant number of errors and the pervasive nature of those errors," Commerce characterized Nachi's reporting errors as "systemic in nature." *Decision Mem.* 34. Commerce concluded that "[b]ecause the errors in the reported physical characteristics were systemic in nature and can distort the model match. . . we cannot be sure that the similar matches we find using Nachi's reported physical characteristics are actually matches of the most similar models." *Id.* at 36. "Moreover, we cannot be sure, where we find no similar matches using Nachi's reported physical characteristics, that no similar matches actually exist because Nachi reported the characteristics of those potential matches incorrectly." *Id.*

Based on its finding of systemic reporting errors, Commerce, pursuant to 19 U.S.C. § 1677e(a), reached a general conclusion that it must use facts otherwise available in calculating the antidumping duty margin for *all* of Nachi's U.S. sales that lacked an identical match. *See Decision Mem.* 36 (stating that "we determine that we must use the facts available for any of Nachi's U.S. sales for which we did not find a contemporaneous identical match."). In response to Nachi's comments on the Department's intention to proceed in this way, Commerce determined that it was appropriate to make three exceptions. *Id.* at 38–39. First, Commerce did not use facts otherwise available where the Department's model-matching methodology resulted in a match to a model in the same bearing series as the U.S. model, reasoning that models in the same bearing series are essentially the same bearing with minor modifications and that, as a result, the model selected is in fact the most similar model. *Id.* at 38. Second, Commerce did not invoke facts otherwise available for U.S. sales of ball bearing parts that were further manufactured in the United States because, for parts sales, the Department's methodology does not attempt to find a similar match if it finds no identical match. *Id.* Finally, Commerce did not use facts otherwise available for Nachi's U.S. sales of models that did not have the same bearing design, load direction, number of rows, and precision grade as any models sold in the home market. *Id.* at 39. Commerce reasoned that because Nachi did not make substantial errors in reporting these particular four characteristics, the errors affecting these characteristics were not systemic in nature. *Id.* For Nachi's U.S. sales of models that did not have the same bearing design, load direction, number of rows, and precision grade as any models sold in the home market, Commerce based normal value on constructed value. *Id.*

Overall, Commerce resorted to facts otherwise available for 203 comparisons between constructed export price and normal value, out of a total of 7,385 such comparisons. Nachi Mem. 22. The result was that Commerce resorted to facts otherwise available for 2.7% of Nachi's U.S. sales. *Id.*

In the Final Results, Commerce further found that "Nachi did not act to the best of its ability in reporting its physical characteristics because Nachi had the correct data available to it." *Final Results,* 71 Fed. Reg. at 40,066. Based on the latter finding, Commerce determined under 19 U.S.C. § 1677e(b) that "it is appropriate to use adverse inferences in addressing the errors in the characteristics Nachi reported." *Id.* Commerce selected as "adverse facts available" the highest margin determined for Nachi in any previous proceeding, *i.e.,* the 48.69% rate Commerce determined for Nachi in *Final Determinations of Sales at Less Than Fair Value; Antifriction Bearings (Other Than Tapered Roller Bearings) & Parts Thereof From Japan,* 54 Fed. Reg. 19,101 (May 3, 1989) ("*Japan Final Determination 1987–1998*"). *See Final Results,* 71 Fed. Reg. at 40,066. As an adverse inference under § 1677e(b), Commerce applied that rate to all of Nachi's U.S. sales for which Commerce found no identical match, and to which none of the three exceptions discussed above applied. *Id.; see also Decision Mem.* 38–39. In the Final Results, Commerce assigned Nachi a weighted average dumping margin of 16.02%. *Final Results,* 71 Fed. Reg. at 40,066.

Nachi argues that "[t]he Department's choice to use adverse facts available as a result of several errors in Nachi's reporting was improper." Reply Br. of Pls. Nachi-Fujikoshi Corp., Nachi Am., Inc. & Nachi Tech., Inc. in Supp. of Rule 56.2 Mot. for J. on the Agency R. 7 ("Nachi Reply"). Nachi acknowledges that Commerce was justified in invoking the "facts otherwise available" provision of 19 U.S.C. § 1677e(a) with respect to the matching of "similar" bearing models when the dumping calculation was affected by Nachi's errors. Nachi Mem. 11. Nachi submits, however, that Commerce acted contrary to law, and without support in record evidence, when it used "adverse inferences," pursuant to 19 U.S.C. § 1677e(b), in selecting from among the "facts otherwise available." *Id.* Nachi further argues that the 48.69% rate Commerce selected by Commerce as "adverse facts available" is contrary to law because it is unduly punitive and bears no relationship to Nachi's pricing and cost structure in this current review. *Id.* at 12.

1. The Department's Use of Facts Otherwise Available Was Impermissibly Broad

Under subsection (a)(1) of § 1677e, Commerce uses facts otherwise available when "necessary information is not available on the record." 19 U.S.C. § 1677e(a)(1). In addition, the statute directs Commerce generally to use facts otherwise available in the circumstances identified in any of the four subparagraphs of subsection (a)(2) of the section, which circumstances include, as provided in subparagraph (B), where the requested information is not submitted within the applicable time period, and the circumstances in subparagraph (D), where the requested information is provided but cannot be verified.[14] 19 U.S.C. § 1677e(a)(2). If one of the four conditions is met, Commerce shall, subject to § 1677m(d) (which addresses deficient submissions), "use the facts otherwise available in reaching the applicable determination." 19 U.S.C. § 1677e(a). In the Decision Memorandum, Commerce invoked subparagraphs (B) and (D) in support of its decision to use "facts otherwise available." *Decision Mem.* 33; *Final Results,* 71 Fed. Reg. at 40,066.

Subparagraph (B) of § 1677e(a)(2) does not apply to the incorrect data that Nachi reported, for which Commerce did not make a finding of untimeliness, although

14 Under § 1677e(a)(2), use of facts otherwise available is required generally when an interested party or any other person:

> (A) withholds information that has been requested by the administering authority. . . under this subtitle,
>
> (B) fails to provide such information by the deadlines for submission of the information or in the form and manner requested, subject to subsections (c)(1) and (e) of section 1677m of this title,
>
> (C) significantly impedes a proceeding under this subtitle, or
>
> (D) provides such information but the information cannot be verified as provided in section 1677m(i) of this title.

19 U.S.C. § 1677e(a)(2)(A)–(D) (2006). Under § 1677e(a), use of facts otherwise available is made subject to § 1677m(d).

subparagraph (B) would have applied to corrected information, had Nachi later attempted to submit any, because the deadline for submission of questionnaire responses had already passed. Subparagraph (D) calls for the use of facts otherwise available as a substitute for information that "cannot be verified as provided in section 1677m(i) of this title."[15] Commerce found that certain of the reported information on physical bearing characteristics was incorrect because it was inconsistent with information in Nachi's technical drawings and catalogs, *Decision Mem.* 34, a finding that Nachi does not contest in this litigation.

Commerce did not explain in the Final Results why it considered it reasonable to construe subparagraph (D) of 19 U.S.C. § 1677e(a)(2) to allow it to proceed as it did in the subject review. Nevertheless, the court discerns in the Final Results an implied construction of the statute, which it reviews according to the deference required by *Chevron,* 467 U.S. at 842–44, 104 S.Ct. 2778. *See Pesquera Mares,* 266 F.3d at 1379–82. Under Chevron, the court first considers "whether Congress has directly spoken to the precise question at issue. If the intent of Congress is clear, that is the end of the matter; for the court, as well as the agency, must give effect to the unambiguously expressed intent of Congress." *Chevron,* 467 U.S. at 842–43, 104 S.Ct. 2778. If, however, "the statute is silent or ambiguous with respect to the specific issue, the question for the court is whether the agency's answer is based on a permissible construction of the statute." *Id.* at 843, 104 S.Ct. 2778.

Read according to plain meaning, subparagraph (D) allows Commerce to substitute facts otherwise available for specific record information *provided that* the information "cannot be verified." 19 U.S.C. § 1677e(a)(2)(D). According to this plain meaning, the provision obviously would be satisfied if a party refuses to allow verification of information it has reported to Commerce or fails to maintain or produce the records that are needed to verify that information. Because the word "verify" is generally understood to mean "to prove to be true" or "to confirm or establish the authenticity or existence of," the court concludes that the provision, when read according to its plain meaning, also encompasses situations in which specific reported information, when examined according to the supporting records, is shown to be incorrect. Webster's Third New International Dictionary 2543 (1993) (defs. 2 & 5); 19 Oxford English Dictionary 540 (2d ed.1989) (defining "verify," in the fourth definition, as "[t]o ascertain or test the accuracy of (something), esp. by examination or by comparison with known data, an original, or some standard. . . ."). In invoking § 1677e(a)(2)(D), however, Commerce went much further. First, it treated all the reported information on physical bearing characteristics that Nachi reported, and that Commerce actually examined (except to the extent one of the three aforementioned exceptions applied), as information that

15 Under 19 U.S.C. § 1677m(i), Commerce is required to "verify all information relied upon in making—. . . a final determination in a review under section 1675(a) of this title" if certain conditions are met. 19 U.S.C. § 1677m(i) (2006).

could not be verified, including the information that Commerce actually found to be correct. *See Decision Mem.* 33–35. Second, Commerce treated as unverifiable all of Nachi's reported information on physical bearing characteristics that it did *not* examine during verification (again, other than in instances in which one of the three exceptions applied). Therefore, for purposes of *Chevron,* 467 U.S. at 843, 104 S.Ct. 2778, the "precise question at issue" is whether it was permissible for Commerce impliedly to construe 19 U.S.C. § 1677e(a)(2)(D) so broadly as to encompass specific information that Commerce determined upon examination to be correct. A second question is whether Commerce could treat as unverifiable a second body of reported information that Commerce did *not* examine but that, based on findings stemming from its examination of the first body of information, assumed to contain errors.

As to the first question, the court concludes that the Department's statutory construction is contrary to the clearly expressed intent of Congress. In § 1677e(a)(2), Congress referred to specific information that "has been requested by the administering authority" and that "*cannot* be verified." 19 U.S.C. § 1677e(a)(2)(A),(D) (emphasis added). Specific reported information that Commerce did examine, and find to be correct, is the opposite of information that "cannot" be verified; it is information that *was* verified. Although Commerce found some physical characteristics information that Nachi reported at the same time to be unverifiable, that finding did not apply to the same "information." This inherent contradiction is sufficient to demonstrate that the Department's implied construction of subparagraph (D) and, specifically, of the term "cannot be verified," contravenes the congressional intent. Even though it is not necessary to consider the question further, the court observes that other provisions in the statute confirm Congress's intent. In 19 U.S.C. § 1677m(e), Congress addressed the situation in which reported information "can be verified" but nevertheless "does not meet all the applicable requirements established by the administering authority," directing that Commerce use the information if certain requirements are met. *See* 19 U.S.C. § 1677m(e)(2). The specific information on physical bearing characteristics that Nachi reported and that Commerce confirmed as correct must be considered to meet all applicable requirements, as Commerce did not find to the contrary. Because Commerce, according to § 1677m(e)(2), would have been required to use this information even if the information were found not to meet all applicable requirements, it would be nonsensical to construe the statute to allow Commerce to reject it, in favor of facts otherwise available, even though it was information that could be, and was, verified, and that otherwise met all applicable requirements. The court concludes, therefore, that Congress explicitly conditioned the application of § 1677e(a)(2)(D) on a finding of fact that the particular information at issue be found to be unverifiable. In summary, Commerce acted unlawfully in impliedly construing § 1677e(a)(2)(D) to allow it to reject as unverifiable specific information that it actually verified.

With respect to the second question, the issue presented is whether Commerce may treat as information that "cannot be verified" information that a party made available for examination but that Commerce, for reasons of its own, made no attempt to examine. The court does not find in the statute an expression of congressional intent on this precise question. Congress gave no indication of foreclosing an application of § 1677e(a)(2)(B) simply because Commerce chose not to conduct an actual verification procedure with respect to the specific information involved. Nor does the court, under the second step of the analysis required in *Chevron,* find unreasonable an implied construction under which the mere fact that no examination was conducted does not necessarily foreclose an application of subparagraph (D). Instead, the general terms in which the provision is stated indicates that Congress did not attempt to anticipate the myriad circumstances in which information may be found to be unverifiable and instead left it to Commerce to decide what those factual circumstances might be. There may be circumstances in which Commerce conceivably could reach a legitimate finding that information cannot be verified, even though no actual verification procedure ensued. The answer in any specific circumstance may depend partly on the reasons for the Department's decision not to conduct the examination. The question is properly analyzed as a question of substantial evidence for the factual finding of unverifiability. Here, Commerce made an express or implied finding, or inference, that all of Nachi's reported information on physical bearing characteristics that Commerce chose not to examine, except where one of the three exceptions applied, could not be verified. The issue presented in this case is whether substantial evidence on the record supported that finding or inference. The court concludes that it does not.

There is no evidence of record that could support an actual finding of fact that errors exist in the unexamined information on physical characteristics that Nachi reported to Commerce. Although the unexamined reported information is on the administrative record, the business records of Nachi that would be needed to verify that information are not on the record. The record discloses that the examined information contained errors at a significant level. The fact that these errors occurred is undisputed. Commerce could draw an inference from this evidence that the unexamined information is likely to contain errors as well. Commerce drew just such an inference. *See Decision Mem.* 35 ("Given that we found additional errors for individual models within each additional 10 models we selected, however, we do not have any reason to believe that we would not have continued to find errors had we enlarged the sample size."). But the record evidence is not sufficient under the substantial evidence standard to support a finding or an inference under 19 U.S.C. § 1677e(a)(2)(D) that *all* of the unexamined information (except where one of the three exceptions applied) was incorrect and therefore unverifiable. Because the Department's decision to substitute facts otherwise available for all of this information necessarily required such a finding of fact, the Department's decision to make the substitution under § 1677e(a)(2)(D) was contrary to law and must be set aside.[16]

---

16 The court does not reach the question of whether Commerce lawfully could have substituted facts otherwise available for some portion of the unexamined information, based on the inference discussed above, because that is not what Commerce did in this case. *See Decision*

Nor is there record evidence indicating that Nachi did anything that would have prevented Commerce from subjecting the unexamined information to verification, had Commerce chosen to do so. The only evidence is to the contrary. In the Decision Memorandum, Commerce cited time constraints, not Nachi's failure to cooperate, as the reason for its not conducting further examination of Nachi's data. *Decision Mem.* 35 ("We allotted one week to verify Nachi's home-market sales. . . . [I]t would not be possible for us to examine the characteristics for all of the models a respondent reports in its sales database during the limited time for conducting verification of the data.").[17]

In summary, subparagraph (D) of § 1677e(a)(2) was applicable on this administrative record to the specific information that Commerce had found to be unverifiable because it was inconsistent with Nachi's technical drawings and catalogs. The procedure of subparagraph (D) was not available as to the body of reported information that Commerce actually verified. The Department's finding or inference of unverifiability for the larger body of information (except where one of the exceptions applied) that Commerce made no attempt to verify was not supported by substantial evidence on the record. Commerce also erred in concluding that subparagraph (B) of § 1677e(a)(2) was applicable to any of these two categories of information, for which Commerce never made a finding of untimely submission.

In the Decision Memorandum, Commerce cited *Micron Tech. v. United States,* 117 F.3d 1386, 1396 (Fed.Cir.1997), for the principle that its methodology of conducting a spot check is reasonable. *Micron* did not involve an application by Commerce of 19 U.S.C. § 1677e(a)(2) in its present form but instead was concerned with a claim by the petitioner, the plaintiff in that case, that Commerce had conducted an inadequate verification of the cost of production data of two respondents that Commerce used in determining constructed value. *Micron,* 117 F.3d at 1388–89. The Court of Appeals, applying an abuse of discretion standard to verification procedures employed by Commerce, held that Commerce acted reasonably in conducting a spot check of the respondents' financial data and did not thereby violate 19 U.S.C. § 1677e(b), which is now superseded but then required Commerce to use "best information available" if it was unable to verify the accuracy of submitted information. *Micron,* 117 F.3d at 1394–97. The case does not stand for the principle that Commerce, under the current statute, is empowered to substitute facts otherwise available for information it actually verified or unexamined information

---

Mem. 33–36. Had Commerce adopted such an approach, the court would have been faced with a question as to the extent of the Department's authority under 19 U.S.C. § 1677e(a)(2)(D). In that instance, the inference that some proportion of the reported information is unverifiable would not have been associated with any *specific* reported information.

17 The time constraints cited by Commerce obviously do not constitute evidence that the unexamined data "cannot be verified," within the intended meaning of that term as used in 19 U.S.C. § 1677e(a)(2)(D). Under such an absurd construction of the statute, Commerce could reject any submitted information solely on the ground that verifying the information would have been impracticable, albeit not impossible.

for which the record contains insufficient evidence to support a finding of unverifiability.

On remand, Commerce must revise its analysis under 19 U.S.C. § 1677e(a)(2)(D) and redetermine Nachi's dumping margin accordingly. As required by this statutory provision, Commerce may substitute facts otherwise available only for the portion of Nachi's reported information on physical characteristics that is the subject of a valid finding of unverifiability, *i.e.,* a finding that is supported by substantial evidence on the record.

2. The Department's Finding that Nachi Failed to Cooperate by Not Acting to the Best of Its Ability to Comply with the Information Request Is Supported by Substantial Record Evidence

Nachi also contests the finding Commerce made in support of the determination to use "adverse inferences" in selecting substitute data for unverifiable data, *i.e.,* the finding that Nachi failed to cooperate by not acting the best of its ability to fulfill the Department's information request. Nachi Mem. 19. According to Nachi, this finding is unreasonable and lacks a stated connection between the facts found and the choice made. *Id.* at 20. While acknowledging that some of the information submitted to Commerce was incorrect, Nachi argues that Commerce properly cannot make a finding that Nachi failed to cooperate to the best of its abilities simply because the correct information existed on Nachi's books. *Id.* "Because such a justification would exist in every instance in which any error was made, it would be tantamount to requiring a perfect submission in order to avoid adverse facts available. . . ." *Id.* at 11. Relying upon the Court of International Trade's decision in *Fujian Machinery and Equipment Import & Export Corp. v. United States,* 25 CIT 1150, 1177, 178 F.Supp.2d 1305, 1334 (2001), and upon 19 U.S.C. §§ 1677e and 1677m, Nachi contends that it is unreasonable for Commerce to expect that no reporting errors would occur and that a review could be "'completely errorless.'" Nachi Mem. 20–22 (quoting *Fujian,* 25 CIT at 1177, 178 F.Supp.2d at 1334). According to Nachi, Commerce must instead look at the "the totality of a respondent's cooperation in an antidumping proceeding." *Id.* at 11. Nachi argues that the application of adverse inferences is not warranted with respect to its entries because Nachi's reporting errors were inadvertent and only affected 2.7% of constructed export price comparisons, because the proceeding was especially complex, because this is the first review in which Nachi has been required to report its information pursuant to the Department's new model-match methodology, and because Nachi fully cooperated with the Department's requests for information. *Id.* at 12, 19, 24–26. Nachi requests that the court instruct Commerce, "for the 2.7 percent of CEP comparisons affected by Nachi's reporting errors," to "use as facts available the weighted-average of all possible normal values, including the normal value calculated based upon constructed value." *Id.* at 26.

Defendant responds that Commerce properly drew an adverse inference because Nachi failed to cooperate to the best of its ability in providing accurate physical characteristics. Def. Resp. 53. Defendant sets forth the principle that the standard of cooperation imposed by 19 U.S.C. § 1677e(b) assumes that respondents are familiar with the process and will "'take reasonable steps to keep and maintain full and complete records.'" *Id.* (quoting *Nippon Steel Corp. v. United States,* 337 F.3d 1373, 1382 (Fed.Cir.2003)). In defendant's view,

> [b]ecause Commerce discovered errors each time it attempted to examine the reported physical characteristics, and because Commerce discovered that Nachi could have used its own drawings and catalogs to provide the correct information, Commerce correctly determined that the incorrect reporting was not an isolated mistake but rather a systemic occurrence resulting from Nachi's failure to act to the best of its ability.

Id. Defendant further argues that the revised model-match methodology did not change the actual product characteristics that must be reported, and that Nachi's alleged difficulties with the additional reporting requirements of the new methodology are not adequately explained. *Id.* at 54.

Under 19 U.S.C. § 1677e(b), if Commerce "finds that an interested party has failed to cooperate by not acting to the best of its ability to comply with a request for information," Commerce, "in reaching the applicable determination . . . may use an inference that is adverse to the interests of that party in selecting from among the facts otherwise available." 19 U.S.C. § 1677e(b). The statutory obligation to act to the best of one's ability in complying with an agency's request for information requires the respondent to do the "maximum" it is able to do, which includes putting forth its maximum efforts to obtain the requested information from its records. *Nippon Steel Corp.,* 337 F.3d at 1382–83.

Commerce found, and Nachi does not dispute, that specific data describing the physical characteristics of some of Nachi's models were not reported correctly. *Decision Mem.* 36; Nachi Mem. 11, 19. Still, Nachi argues, and argues correctly, that the statute does not require a completely errorless review. *See Nippon Steel Corp.,* 337 F.3d at 1382 (stating that "the standard does not require perfection and recognizes that mistakes sometimes occur"). Nevertheless, the evidence of record in the review demonstrates that Nachi provided Commerce incorrect information on physical bearing characteristics at a frequency (nineteen errors affecting sixteen out of forty models reviewed) that cannot be described as negligible or inconsequential. The record evidence consists of the documentation Commerce produced to report on the verification process, in which documentation it is reported that information in Nachi's technical drawings and catalogs was inconsistent with Nachi's questionnaire responses. *Decision Mem.* 36. Commerce found that Nachi "had the correct data available to it in the technical-specification sheets it maintains in its normal course of business and in its catalog," *id.,* and used the "technical specifications and catalog descriptions provided by Nachi at verification to compare them for accuracy against the reported physical characteristics." *Id.* at 37. Commerce further found that "Nachi has not proffered an adequate or reasonable justification for why it could not have reported the correct characteristics." *Id.* at 36. Nachi's argument that this was the first review in which Nachi was required to report its information pursuant to the Department's new model-match methodology is unavailing. As Commerce pointed out, Commerce has required "Nachi, and all respondents, to provide such information in every review since the first review." *Decision Mem.* at 36–37 (citing *Ball Bearings & Parts Thereof From France, Germany, Italy, & Singapore: Prelim. Results of Antidumping Duty Admin. Reviews, Partial Rescission of Admin. Reviews, & Notice of Intent To Revoke Order In Part,* 68 Fed. Reg. 6404, 6408 (Feb. 7, 2003)). The correct reporting of information on physical characteristics of bearings was also important under the Department's prior model-match methodology. For these various reasons, the court is unable to agree with Nachi that the record lacks substantial evidence to support the Department's finding that Nachi failed to cooperate by not acting to the best of its ability to comply with the Department's request for information on the physical characteristics of Nachi's bearings. The court concludes that Nachi's reporting of these data fell short of the standard established by 19 U.S.C. § 1677e(b) as interpreted by the Court of Appeals in *Nippon Steel Corp.,* 337 F.3d at 1382.

3. The Court Affirms the Department's Choice of the 48.69% Rate

Nachi claims that Commerce erred in applying the 48.69% rate as an adverse inference. Nachi Mem. 12. Nachi argues that this seventeen-year-old rate bears no relationship to Nachi's pricing and cost structure in the current review and objects that the rate chosen is "*five* times the rate found for Nachi in the most recent review in which Nachi participated prior to the 2004–2005 review." *Id.* at 13.

In explaining the choice of the 48.69% rate, the Final Results state that "[a]s adverse facts available, we have selected the highest margin we have determined for Nachi in any previous segment of this proceeding. . . ." *Final Results,* 71 Fed. Reg. at 40,066. In the Decision Memorandum, Commerce expressed a finding that this rate is corroborated by the fact that a substantial number of Nachi's transactions for which Commerce determined positive margins in the subject review had margins higher than the 48.69% rate. *Decision Mem.* 37.

The Court of Appeals has stated that "[i]t is clear from Congress's imposition of the corroboration requirement in 19 U.S.C. § 1677e(c) that it intended for an adverse facts available rate to be a reasonably accurate estimate of the respondent's actual rate, albeit with some built-in increase intended as a deterrent to non-compliance." *F.lli De Cecco Di Filippo Fara S. Martino S.p.A. v. United States,* 216 F.3d 1027, 1032 (Fed.Cir.2000) ("*De Cecco*"). Congress imposed the corroboration requirement "to prevent the petition rate (or other adverse inference rate), when unreasonable, from prevailing and to block any temptation by Commerce to overreach reality in seeking to maximize deterrence." *Id.* The Court of Appeals, while recognizing the breadth of the Department's discretion under 19 U.S.C. § 1677e(b), also cautioned that "Commerce's discretion in these matters, however, is not unbounded." *Id.* As the Court of Appeals reiterated,

> "Congress could not have intended for Commerce's discretion to include the ability to select unreasonably high rates with no relationship to the respondent's actual dumping margin. Obviously a higher adverse margin creates a stronger deterrent, but Congress tempered deterrent value with the corroboration requirement. It could only have done so to prevent the petition rate (or other adverse inference rate), when unreasonable, from prevailing and to block any temptation by Commerce to overreach reality in seeking to maximize deterrence."

Ta Chen Stainless Steel Pipe, Inc. v. United States, 298 F.3d 1330, 1340 (Fed.Cir. 2002) (quoting *De Cecco,* 216 F.3d at 1032).

The 48.69% rate was a rate Commerce actually assigned to Nachi, but it occurred in 1989 in the final less-than-fair-value determination resulting from the antidumping duty investigation. *Japan Final Determination 1987–1998,* 54 Fed. Reg. at 19,108. Because it is so remote in time, the rate might be seen as having only an attenuated relationship to Nachi's actual dumping margin in the subject reviews. Nevertheless, Commerce's reliance on record evidence of the number of transactions in the current reviews that had individual margins exceeding the 48.69% rate must be considered sufficient to satisfy the corroboration requirement of 19 U.S.C. § 1677e(c).

Timken directs the court's attention to *PAM, S.p.A. v. United States,* 582 F.3d 1336 (Fed.Cir.2009), in which the Court of Appeals recently held to be corroborated a rate of 45.49% that Commerce chose as an adverse inference for a respondent that had failed to report all of its home market sales in the sixth administrative review of an antidumping duty order. *PAM, S.p.A. v. United States,* 582 F.3d 1336, 1340–41 (Fed.Cir.2009). In support of a finding of corroboration in *PAM,* Commerce relied on 29 sales by the same respondent in the fourth review of the order (*i.e.,* two reviews prior to the review under consideration) with margins above 45.49%, which sales represented only 0.5% of the respondent's total sales of subject merchandise during the period of the fourth administrative review. *Id.* at 1340. The Court of Appeals in *PAM* rejected the respondent's argument that these sales constituted "outlier data," concluding that the respondent's position was rejected in *Ta Chen,* 298 F.3d at 1339. *Id.*

PAM does not hold that corroboration of a specific rate chosen as an adverse inference necessarily is established in *any* case in which 0.5% or more of individual sales of the non-cooperating respondent have dumping margins above that rate. To the contrary, the Court of Appeals implicitly recognized that the question of whether the record evidence relied on for corroboration meets the substantial evidence standard must be considered according to the record as a whole. *See PAM,* 582 F.3d at 1340 ("The burden imposed by substantial evidence review may not be heavy, but it is not ephemeral. There must be at least enough evidence to allow reasonable minds to differ."). Additionally, a finding of corroboration is not dispositive of the question of whether Commerce has discretion to apply a particular rate as an adverse inference; that question, too, must be decided according to the relevant factual circumstances as shown by the entire record. Once Commerce satisfies the statutory corroboration requirement that the statute imposes on the use of secondary information, Commerce is entitled to exercise a significant, albeit still not unlimited, measure of discretion in selecting, from among the facts otherwise available, those facts that will provide "a proper deterrent to non-cooperation." *De Cecco,* 216 F.3d at 1032.

In *PAM,* the Court of Appeals was confronted with a circumstance in which PAM, the party against whom the adverse inference was used, was found to have withheld requested information on sales that "combined amounted to about two-thirds of PAM's total domestic sales." *PAM,* 582 F.3d at 1338. The Court of Appeals reasoned that "Commerce's discretion in applying an AFA margin is particularly great when a respondent is uncooperative by failing to provide or withholding information." *Id.* at 1340. In this case, Nachi did not withhold information. The finding of non-cooperation instead was based on a failure to exercise due care in reporting the information contained in the business records.

With respect to support for the corroboration finding in this case, the court's examination of the record evidence supports the finding in the Decision Memorandum that a "substantial number" of Nachi's sales in the AFBs 16 reviews had margins exceeding 48.69%. *Decision Mem.* 37; *see* Nachi Mem. 8–9. The court concludes, therefore, that substantial record evidence supports the Department's finding of corroboration for its chosen adverse inference rate of 48.69%.

Based on the entire record in this case, the court concludes, further, that the use of the 48.69% rate does not exceed the scope of Commerce's discretion under 19 U.S.C. § 1677e(b). Commerce discovered that Nachi's reporting errors were present in a significant percentage of the transactions that Commerce examined at verification. It is essential to the proper administration of the statute that respondents participating in an antidumping proceeding endeavor to provide Commerce correct information about the sales of their merchandise. *See PAM,* 582 F.3d at 1339 ("Congress has made very clear the importance of accurate and complete reporting of home market sales."). In reviewing the exercise of Commerce's discretion under § 1677e(b), a court must be mindful that Commerce "is in the best position, based on its expert knowledge of the market and the individual respondent, to select adverse facts that will create a proper deterrent to non-cooperation with its investigations and assure a reasonable margin." *De Cecco,* 216 F.3d at 1032. The rate Commerce selected was, as Nachi points out, five times the rate Commerce assigned to Nachi in its most recent review. Nachi Mem. 13. Nevertheless, the court cannot conclude that the choice of rate was unreasonable or an abuse of discretion under all the circumstances present here, including the circumstance that the party's efforts to report the physical data correctly did not even come close to satisfying the standard for cooperation that 19 U.S.C. § 1677e(b) establishes.

I. Commerce Did Not Provide a Full and Adequate Rationale for its Decision to Use Japanese Interest Rates to Calculate a Portion of the Adjustment for Imputed Interest Carrying Costs when Determining Constructed Export Prices for NTN and Nachi

In determining constructed export price, Commerce deducts from the price paid in the first unaffiliated resale (the "starting price"), as a selling expense under 19 U.S.C. § 1677a(d)(1), an amount representing inventory carrying cost of the subject merchandise in the United States, to the extent the inventory carrying cost relates to that resale. *See* 19 U.S.C. § 1677a(d)(1). To quantify the deduction, Commerce determines an applicable interest rate. In the administrative review, Commerce used Japanese interest rates when calculating certain U.S. inventory carrying costs with respect to two respondents, Nachi and NTN. *Decision Mem.* 40–41. Commerce found as a fact that in both instances, the Japanese foreign parent, by extending credit terms to the U.S. affiliate, assumed the burden of the U.S. inventory carrying costs for the portion of time that the merchandise was held in the inventory of the U.S. affiliate and concluded that "it is that party's short-term interest rate that we should use in calculating inventory carrying costs" for that time period. *Id.* Timken claims that Commerce acted contrary to law, and, specifically, contrary to its own regulations, in using Japanese interest rates to calculate the inventory carrying costs. Timken U.S. Corporation's Mem. in Supp. of its Rule 56.2 Mot. for J. on the Agency R. 7 ("Timken Mem."). Timken maintains that Commerce instead should have used interest rates prevailing in the United States. *Id.* at 24. NTN and Nachi urge the court to reject Timken's claim. Resp. of Pls.' NTN Corp., NTN Bearing Corp. of Am., Am. NTN Bearing Mfg. Corp., NTN-BCA Corp., NTN-Bower Corp., & NTN Driveshaft, Inc. to the Rule 56.2 Mot. of Def.-Intervenor Timken U.S. Corp. 2 ("NTN Resp."); Resp. Br. of Pls. Nachi-Fujikoshi Corp., Nachi Am., Inc., & Nachi Technology, Inc. in Opp'n to Def.-Intervenor Timken U.S. Corp.'s Mot. for J. on the Agency R. 4 ("Nachi Resp."). NTN argues that Commerce correctly determined in the Final Results that "the party that extends the payment terms to its U.S. affiliate carries the financial burden of financing the inventory." NTN Resp. 7; *see* Nachi Resp. 4. NTN and Nachi also argue that the Department's determination to apply the Japanese interest rate rather than the U.S. interest rate reflected the commercial and financial reality of NTN Japan's financing of the inventory cost. NTN Resp. 10; *see* Nachi Resp. 4.

Timken's first argument is that the Department's choice of Japanese interest rates improperly relied on the payment terms between the producer and the affiliated reseller in calculating constructed export price using the sales between the affiliated reseller and the unaffiliated purchaser. Timken Mem. 9–11. Timken construes 19 U.S.C. § 1677a(d) to prohibit Commerce from relying on "affiliated party data" for this purpose, arguing that

> to the extent the Japanese interest rates are lower, and to the extent the payment terms extend beyond the date of importation—thus reducing the period calculated at U.S.

> interest rates, Commerce has permitted the affiliated parties to reduce the adjustment and inflate the U.S. price, and, to that extent, has failed in its duty to prevent those parties from competing unfairly in the U.S. market.

Id. at 11. According to Timken, this result is contrary to the intent of the statute and to the decision of the Court of Appeals in *AK Steel Corp. v. United States,* 226 F.3d 1361, 1367 (Fed.Cir.2000). Timken Mem. 11.

The court finds nothing in § 1677a(d) that prohibits Commerce, expressly or impliedly, from using credit terms existing between the foreign parents and the U.S. affiliates in reaching its findings that, in the case of both Nachi and NTN, the foreign parent bore the burden of inventory carrying costs subsequent to importation of the subject merchandise. *See Decision Mem.* 40–41. Commerce concluded that, in calculating the inventory carrying cost, it was reasonable to use the short term interest rates to which the parties actually bearing the inventory costs—*i.e.,* the foreign affiliates—were subject. *See* 19 U.S.C. § 1677a(d). Timken fails to point to any specific language in § 1677a(d) that the court could construe as posing a barrier to the Department's reaching this conclusion. The subsection requires Commerce to reduce the starting price by "the amount of" the selling expense without specifying how Commerce is to determine that amount. *Id.* The Department's quantifying of the inventory carrying cost according to the interest rate to which the party bearing the cost was subject appears to the court to be reasonable.

The credit terms constituted substantial record evidence that supported the Department's findings. *See Decision Mem.* 41 (stating that "payment terms demonstrate that NTN bears the cost of carrying the merchandise for a portion of the time that the merchandise is in inventory"). The court is aware of no rule or principle that would prohibit Commerce from using, as evidence in support of those findings, credit terms that were negotiated between the related parties and that are disclosed by record evidence. In arguing to the contrary, Timken advocates as a general rule or principle that "[t]he cost to be measured to determine an adjustment to U.S. price for inventory carrying cost is the cost of holding inventory, not the cost of extending credit, and so the proper credit rate is that of the company holding the inventory." Timken U.S. Corp.'s Reply Br. 2 ("Timken Reply"). The court is not convinced by this argument that it must adopt the general rule or principle that Timken advocates. Moreover, the distinction Timken attempts to draw would disregard the significance of the factual findings that the foreign parents, not their U.S. affiliates, bore the actual inventory carrying costs at issue. *See Decision Mem.* 41. According to those findings, the "cost of holding inventory" *was* "the cost of extending credit," *i.e.,* it was the credit cost as borne by the foreign parents. Timken Reply 2.

The Court of Appeals in *AK Steel Corp.,* 226 F.3d 1361, does not establish a rule or principle that prohibits Commerce from using credit terms existing between the foreign parents and the U.S. affiliates in reaching its findings that, in the case of both Nachi and NTN, the foreign parent bore the burden of inventory carrying costs subsequent to importation of the subject merchandise. Timken cites to general language in the case explaining that the purpose of the statutory distinction between constructed export price transactions and export price transactions is to isolate an arm's-length transaction, and that the purpose of making deductions from the starting price to arrive at a constructed export price "'is to prevent foreign producers from competing unfairly in the United States market by inflating the U.S. Price with amounts spent by the U.S. affiliate on marketing and selling the products in the United States.'" Timken Mem. 10 (quoting *AK Steel Corp.,* 226 F.3d at 1367). Nothing in the decision of the Court of Appeals establishes that Commerce acted contrary to law in relying on the credit terms for its findings.

NTN, Nachi, and the defendant United States rely on certain cases in which courts previously have affirmed the Department's use of foreign interest rates to quantify the cost of carrying U.S. inventory where that cost is borne by the foreign affiliate. NTN Resp. 6 (citing *LMI-La Metalli Industriale, S.p.A. v. United States,* 912 F.2d 455, 461 (Fed.Cir.1990); *Thai Pineapple Pub. Co. v. United States,* 20 CIT 1312, 1329–30, 946 F.Supp. 11, 26–27 (1996); *Timken Co. v. United States,* 18 CIT 619, 625–26, 858 F.Supp. 206, 212–13 (1994)); Nachi Resp. 5 (citing *Timken Co. v. United States,* 18 CIT 942, 948–49, 865 F.Supp. 881, 886–87 (1994)); *see* Def. Resp. 60–62. Timken argues that the prior cases are distinguishable in arising before the enactment of the Uruguay Round Agreements Act ("URAA") and specifically before Commerce promulgated the current 19 C.F.R. § 351.402(b) (1997) as an implementing regulation. Timken Mem. 12–17, 20–21. Timken argues, further, that the Department's use of Japanese interest rates is inconsistent with the amended statute and the regulation. *Id.* However, the enactment of 19 U.S.C. § 1677a(d) by the URAA does not lend support to Timken's argument. As discussed above, nothing in § 1677a(d) expressly or impliedly disallows the methodology Commerce employed here to quantify the inventory carrying cost.

The court is unable to agree with Timken's argument that the use of Japanese interest rates violates 19 C.F.R. § 351.402(b). The regulation provides that "'[i]n establishing constructed export price under section 772(d) of the Act [19 U.S.C. § 1677a(d)], the Secretary will make adjustments for expenses associated with commercial activities in the United States that *relate to the sale to an unaffiliated purchaser, no matter where or when paid*'" and further provides that "'[t]he Secretary *will not make an adjustment for any expense that is related solely to the sale to an affiliated importer in United States,* although the Secretary may make an adjustment to normal value for such expenses under section 773(a)(6)(C)(iii) of the Act [19 U.S.C. § 1677b(a)(6)(C)(iii)].'" Timken Mem. 13 (quoting 19 C.F.R. § 351.402(b)). In taking issue with the Department's relying on the payment terms between the foreign sellers and their U.S. affiliates in support of the decision to use the Japanese interest rates, Timken argues that "[h]ere, the payment terms which the affiliate (reseller) and its parent (producer) agreed on incontrovertibly relate 'solely' to the Japanese parent's sale of bearing products to its affiliated importer in the United States." *Id.* This characterization of the payment terms is inconsistent with the Department's finding that the Japanese foreign parents, by extending credit terms to the U.S. affiliates, assumed the burden of the U.S. inventory carrying costs for the portion of time that the merchandise was held in the inventory of the U.S. affiliate. With respect to Timken's argument based on 19 C.F.R. § 351.402(b), the regulatory provision at issue is addressed to whether a particular expense is related to the sale of the subject merchandise from the foreign seller to the unaffiliated U.S. importer or, alternatively, to the resale to an unaffiliated purchaser. 19 C.F.R. § 351.402(b). Under the regulation, only if the expense relates to the sale to the unaffiliated purchaser will Commerce make a deduction from the starting price when determining constructed export price. *Id.* In providing that the Secretary "will make certain of the adjustments" for expenses associated with commercial activities in the United States that relate to the sale to an unaffiliated purchaser, the regulation governs *whether* the Secretary will make the adjustment, not *how* the Secretary will make it. *Id.* In this case, the expense involved is the carrying cost of subject merchandise from the time of importation until the time payment is due to the affiliated foreign seller. *See Decision Mem.* 40–41, 43. Commerce found, according to substantial record evidence, that the expenses were associated with commercial activities in the United States that related to the sales to the unaffiliated purchasers.

Timken also argues that the Department's reliance on the payment terms as record evidence contradicts the logic and purpose of calculating the carrying costs. Timken Mem. 17. Timken submits that the issue of whether the parent or the affiliate bears the actual expense associated with the carrying costs is not material to the determination of those carrying costs because Commerce does not use actual costs but instead estimates cost according to objective factors such as the period of time that credit is extended, the period of time merchandise remains in inventory, and the cost of borrowing money in the market. *Id.* at 17–18. Timken quotes the Department's explanation set forth in the final results of the first administrative review, in which Commerce explains its reasons for calculating an estimated cost based on objective criteria rather than using actual costs. *Id.* at 18 (quoting *Antifriction Bearings (Other Than Tapered Roller Bearings) & Parts Thereof From the Federal Republic of Germany; Final Results of Antidumping Duty Admin. Review,* 56 Fed. Reg. 31,692, 31,727 (July 11, 1991)). The Department's explanation, which occurred in the context of the Department's rejection of the petitioner's argument that it is appropriate to apply adjustments for inventory carrying cost only for the United States price, not the foreign market value, concerned the issue of whether it is appropriate to impute a cost where it is not possible to identify actual cost. It did not speak directly to the question of which interest rate is appropriate in this case.

Finally, Timken argues that in using payment terms to determine the period for which the Japanese interest rates apply, Commerce departed from the evidentiary standard it applied in previous proceedings. In support of this argument, Timken relies on the Department's decisions in *Certain Welded Stainless Steel Pipe From Taiwan: Final Results of Antidumping Duty Admin. Review & Determination To Revoke Order In Part,* 65 Fed. Reg. 39,367 (June 26, 2000) ("*Welded Steel Pipe from Taiwan Final Results*") (incorporating *Issues & Decision Mem. for the Admin. Review of Certain Welded Stainless Steel Pipe from Taiwan: Dec. 1, 1997 through Nov. 30, 1998,* at Comment 1 (June 19, 2000) ("*Welded Steel Pipe from Taiwan Decision Mem.*")), and *Notice of Final Results of Antidumping Duty Admin. Review & Notice of Final Results of Antidumping Duty Changed Circumstances Review: Certain Softwood Lumber Products From Canada,* 69 Fed. Reg. 75,921 (Dec. 20, 2004) ("*Softwood Lumber from Canada Final Results*") (incorporating *Issues & Decision Mem. for the Final Results of the Antidumping Duty Admin. Review of Certain Softwood Lumber Products From Canada* 141–42 (Dec. 13, 2004) (at Comment 39) ("*Softwood Lumber from Canada Decision Mem.*")). Timken Mem. 21–24; Timken Reply 5–6. Timken submits that payment terms requiring payment by a specific date do not establish that payment occurred on that date, and that Commerce therefore should have applied U.S. interest rates for part of the period in question due to an alleged lack of proof of actual payments by the U.S. affiliate to the foreign parent on, and not before, the due dates. Timken Reply 5–6. Defendant responds that payment terms constitute sufficient record evidence to support the determination that the U.S. affiliates benefitted from the Japanese parents' ability to borrow money in Japan. Def. Resp. 61 (citing *Thai Pineapple,* 20 CIT at 1329–30, 946 F.Supp. at 26–27).

In *Welded Steel Pipe from Taiwan Decision Mem.,* Commerce stated that:

> It is the Department's practice to use the short-term borrowing rate in the currency in which the cost of the inventory is incurred by the entity that bears the cost of producing or acquiring such inventory. The Department deviates from this practice only in instances where there is clear evidence that an entity other than the one holding the merchandise in inventory absorbs the full cost of financing the cost of the merchandise during the time that the merchandise is held in inventory. In this case, Ta Chen [the foreign producer] provided no clear record evidence that it, and not TCI [the U.S. affiliate], incurs the cost of the merchandise in inventory during the entire period of credit days given to TCI. Since there is no record evidence of when payment is made by TCI, the Department cannot assume that TCI does not pay Ta Chen until the last day of the payment period.

Welded Steel Pipe from Taiwan Decision Mem., at Comment 2; *Welded Steel Pipe from Taiwan Final Results,* 65 Fed. Reg. 39,367–68. In *Certain Softwood Lumber Products from Canada,* Commerce stated that it agreed with the position of respondent Weyerhaeuser, who commented that the correct rate for use in calculating inventory carrying costs "is the short-term borrowing rate of the company that holds title to the subject merchandise and invoices the ultimate customer." *Softwood Lumber from Canada Decision Mem.* 141. In light of the language of these two administrative decisions, the court cannot rule out the possibility that Commerce, subsequent to the decisions in *LMI,* 912 F.2d at 461, *Thai Pineapple,* 20 CIT at

1329–30, 946 F.Supp. at 26–27, and *Timken,* 18 CIT at 625–26, 858 F.Supp. at 212–13 (on which Commerce relies in the Decision Memorandum, *Decision Mem.* 41), has adopted a practice or established methodology from which it departed in some way in reaching the decision to use Japanese interest rates in the AFBs 16 reviews. This specific issue is not addressed in the Decision Memorandum. Although citing *LMI* and *Thai Pineapple* for the principle that courts have affirmed the use of foreign interest rates to value carrying costs for inventory in the United States, defendant does not address in its response to Timken's motion for judgment upon the agency record the specific issue of whether the decision to use Japanese interest rates in the reviews was a departure from a practice or established methodology, and if so, whether Commerce knowingly departed from that practice or methodology and provided adequate reasoning for doing so. *See* Def. Resp. 60–61. Accordingly, the court is directing that Commerce include in its remand redetermination an analysis responding to Timken's argument concerning a departure from an alleged practice or methodology and reconsider accordingly its decision to use Japanese interest rates when calculating the subject U.S. inventory carrying costs with respect to Nachi and NTN.

III. Conclusion

For the reasons discussed in the foregoing, the court will affirm in part, and remand in part, the Final Results, and will set aside as unlawful certain decisions and determinations in the Final Results.

ORDER

Upon consideration of all papers and proceedings herein, it is hereby

ORDERED that the Rule 56.2 motions for judgment upon the agency record of JTEKT and NSK, be, and hereby are, denied; it is further

ORDERED that the Rule 56.2 motions for judgment upon the agency record of NBP, NTN, Nachi be, and hereby are, granted in part and denied in part; it is further

ORDERED that the Rule 56.2 motion of Timken be, and hereby is, granted to the extent that the Department is directed on remand to reconsider its decision to allow use of Japanese interest rates to calculate a portion of the adjustment for imputed interest carrying costs when calculating constructed export prices for NTN and Nachi and to include in its remand redetermination an analysis responding to the issue Timken raised concerning departure from a practice or established methodology concerning choice of interest rate, as provided herein; it is further

ORDERED that the final determination of the International Trade Administration, United States Department of Commerce ("Commerce" or the "Department"), published as *Ball Bearings & Parts Thereof from France, Germany, Italy, Japan, & the United Kingdom: Final Results of Antidumping Duty Administrative Reviews,* 71 Fed. Reg. 40,064, 40,065 (July 14, 2006) (the "Final Results"), be, and hereby is, affirmed in part and set aside in part as contrary to law, and remanded to the Department as provided herein; it is further

ORDERED that the following decisions and determinations by Commerce in the *Final Results,* for the reasons that are set forth in the following respective subparts of Part II of this Opinion and Order, be, and hereby are, affirmed: (A) the decision to apply the Department's zeroing procedure; (B) the decision to discontinue the use of the previous model-match methodology and the decisions Commerce reached in applying the Department's revised model-match methodology, except the decision to reject NPB's proposal to expand the choice of sampling months and the decision to reject NTN's proposal to incorporate into the model-match methodology additional design-type categories for specific types of ball bearings; (C) the decision to treat JTEKT and its affiliate as a single entity; (D) the decision to deduct certain additional benefits expenses when determining the constructed export price of NSK's subject merchandise; (F) the recalculated determination of NTN's home market packing materials expenses; (G) the decision to disallow certain downward price adjustments resulting from NTN's allocation of discounts to home market customers; and (H) the factual determination that Nachi failed to cooperate by not acting to the best of its ability to comply with the Department's request for certain information on physical bearing characteristics and the Department's selection of the 48.69% rate; it is further

ORDERED that the following decisions and determinations by Commerce in the *Final Results,* for the reasons that are set forth in the respective sections of Part II of this Opinion and Order, be, and hereby are, set aside as contrary to law: (E) the Department's redetermination of NTN's freight expense; and (H) the Department's decision to substitute facts otherwise available for information that Nachi submitted on physical bearing characteristics, except for the specific information that Commerce determined during its verification procedure to be incorrect; it is further

ORDERED that Commerce, on remand, shall reconsider its decision to reject NPB's proposal to expand the choice of sampling months and NTN's proposal to incorporate into the model-match methodology additional design-type categories, as reviewed in subparts (B.3) and (B.4), respectively, of Part II of this Opinion and Order; shall redetermine NTN's freight expense using a method that is consistent with the Department's treatment of the freight expense of other respondents in the administrative reviews that are the subject of this action, as set forth in subpart (E) of Part II of this Opinion and Order; shall redetermine the application of facts otherwise available for information that Nachi submitted on physical bearing characteristics as discussed in subpart (H) of Part II of this Opinion and Order; and shall reconsider its decision to allow use of Japanese interest rates to calculate a portion of the adjustment for imputed interest carrying costs when calculating constructed export prices for NTN and Nachi as discussed in subpart (I) of Part II of this Opinion and Order, and in doing so, shall provide an analysis responding to

Timken's argument concerning a departure from an alleged practice or methodology; it is further

ORDERED that Commerce shall redetermine the weighted-average dumping margins of plaintiffs, as appropriate, in complying with this Opinion and Order; it is further

ORDERED that Commerce shall have ninety (90) days from the date of this Opinion and Order in which to file its redetermination upon remand, which shall comply with all directives in this Opinion and Order; it is further

ORDERED that plaintiffs and defendant-intervenor shall have thirty (30) days from the filing of the remand redetermination in which to file comments thereon.

MILLENIUM LUMBER DISTRIBUTION LTD.
v.
UNITED STATES

558 F.3d 1326 (Fed. Cir. 2009)
Decided March 5, 2009

Joel R. Junker, Joel R. Junker & Associates, of Seattle, Washington, argued for plaintiff-appellant. With him on the brief was William N. Baldwin.

Aimee Lee, Trial Attorney, Commercial Litigation Branch, Civil Division, International Trade Office, United States Department of Justice, of New York, New York, argued for defendant-appellee. With her on the brief were Jeanne E. Davidson, Director, and Barbara S. Williams, Attorney in Charge, International Trade Field Office. Of counsel was Chi S. Choy, Attorney, Office of Assistant Chief Counsel, International Trade Litigation, United States Customs and Border Protection, of New York, New York.

Before MAYER, CLEVENGER, and RADER, Circuit Judges.

CLEVENGER, *Circuit Judge.*

This case involves the tariff classification of Canadian lumber imported into the United States by Millenium Lumber Distribution, Ltd. ("Millenium"). Millenium appeals the decision of the United States Court of International Trade granting summary judgment in favor of the United States ("the government") that the United States Bureau of Customs and Border Protection ("Customs") correctly classified Millenium's imported lumber under heading 4407 of the Harmonized Tariff Schedule of the United States ("HTSUS"). *Millenium Lumber Distrib. Ltd. v. United States*, No. 02-595, 2007 Ct. Intl. Trade LEXIS 56, 2007 WL 1116148 (Ct. Int'l Trade April 16, 2007). HTSUS heading ("heading") 4407 covers certain "[w]ood sawn or chipped lengthwise, sliced or peeled, whether or not planed, sanded or finger-jointed, of a thickness exceeding 6 mm." In granting the government's motion, the court denied Millenium's cross-motion for summary judgment to classify the subject lumber under heading 4418, which covers "[b]uilders' joinery and carpentry of wood" or alternatively under heading 4421 which covers certain [o]ther articles of wood." *Millenium*, 2007 Ct. Intl. Trade LEXIS 56, 2007 WL 1116148, at *1, *7. We affirm.

I.

Millenium imported approximately 215 entries of cut lumber between October 1999 and January 2001 under HTSUS subheading 4418.90.40. The imported merchandise included 2x3, 2x4, and 2x6 spruce/pine/fir lumber of various grades, cut to various even-foot lengths ranging from 5 to 20 feet. Each board had a 90 [degrees] square-cut end, and an angle cut between 67.4 [degrees] and 80.5 [degrees] on the board's opposite end. *Millenium*, 2007 Ct. Intl. Trade LEXIS 56, 2007 WL 1116148, at *1. According to Millenium, it sold all of the subject lumber to truss manufacturers, either directly or through wholesalers.[1]

In December 2000, Customs notified Millenium that it was classifying the subject merchandise under HTSUS subheading 4407.10.0015 rather than under Millenium's entered HTSUS subheading 4418.90.40. Customs liquidated the merchandise accordingly. Millenium filed two protests, which were both denied, and then commenced this action in the Court of International Trade pursuant to 28 U.S.C. § 1581(a). *Millenium*, 2007 Ct. Intl. Trade LEXIS 56, 2007 WL 1116148, at *1

The parties filed cross motions for summary judgment. Millenium asserted that the imported merchandise was classifiable under heading 4418 as "[b]uilders' joinery and carpentry of wood" or alternatively under heading 4421 as "[o]ther articles of wood." The government maintained that Millenium's imported merchandise was standard dimensional lumber, classifiable under heading 4407 as "[w]ood sawn or chipped lengthwise . . . of a thickness exceeding 6 mm." The court agreed with the government and granted summary judgment accordingly. *Millenium*, 2007 Ct. Intl. Trade LEXIS 56, 2007 WL 1116148, at *1, *7.

II.

Millenium appeals the grant of summary judgment upholding Customs' classification of the imported lumber under heading 4407. Millenium asserts that the court should have instead granted Millenium's summary judgment motion and classified the lumber under heading 4418 or, in the alternative, under heading 4421. We have jurisdiction over Millenium's appeal pursuant to 28 U.S.C. § 1295(a)(5).

We review a grant of summary judgment by the Court of International Trade for correctness as a matter of law and decide *de novo* the proper interpretation of the tariff provisions as well as whether there are genuine issues of material fact to preclude summary judgment. *Rollerblade, Inc. v. United States*, 282 F.3d 1349, 1351 (Fed. Cir. 2002). In reviewing summary judgment decisions, we must bear in mind the parties' burdens as well as the evidentiary standards under the applicable law. *See Anderson v. Liberty Lobby, Inc.*, 477 U.S. 242, 254, 106 S. Ct. 2505, 91 L. Ed. 2d 202 (1986).

---

1 A truss is a wood assembly that forms a rigid triangulated framework of wood used to support the roof or other parts of a building.

Proper classification of goods under the HTSUS entails first ascertaining the meaning of specific terms in the tariff provisions and then determining whether the subject merchandise comes within the description of those terms. *Rollerblade*, 282 F.3d at 1351. The proper meaning of the tariff provisions is a question of law, whereas the determination of whether the subject imports properly fall within the scope of the possible headings is a question of fact. *Universal Elecs. Inc. v. United States*, 112 F.3d 488, 491 (Fed. Cir. 1997). Because Customs' classification decisions are presumed correct, Millenium bears the burden of proving otherwise. *See Rollerblade*, 282 F.3d at 1351.

The General Rules of Interpretation ("GRIs") govern classification of merchandise under the HTSUS. *N. Am. Processing Co. v. United States*, 236 F.3d 695, 698 (Fed. Cir. 2001). Under GRI 1, the court must determine the appropriate classification "according to the terms of the headings and any relative section or chapter notes." The terms of the HTSUS are construed according to their common commercial meanings. *Len-Ron Mfg. Co. v. United States,* 334 F.3d 1304, 1309 (Fed. Cir. 2003). "Although the Explanatory Notes are not legally binding or dispositive, they may be consulted for guidance and are generally indicative of the proper interpretation of the various HTSUS provisions." *N. Am. Processing*, 236 F.3d at 698.

III.

Heading 4407 provides for "[w]ood sawn or chipped lengthwise, sliced or peeled, whether or not planed, sanded, or finger-jointed, of a thickness exceeding 6 mm." The explanatory note to heading 4407 provides that "[w]ith few exceptions, this heading covers all wood and timber, of any length but of a thickness exceeding 6 mm." Note 44.07, Vol. 2, Explanatory Notes, World Customs Organization (2d ed. 1996) [hereinafter Explanatory Note]. Despite its breadth, heading 4407 excludes merchandise that meets heading 4418's more specific terms. *Id.* While the parties agree that Millenium's imported lumber falls within heading 4407's broad terms, they dispute whether the merchandise also falls under the more specific heading 4418.

Heading 4418 covers "[b]uilders' joinery and carpentry of wood." The explanatory note to heading 4418 provides that "[t]his heading applies to woodwork, including that of wood marquetry or inlaid wood, used in the construction of any kind of building, etc., in the form of assembled goods or as recognizable unassembled pieces." 44.18 Explanatory Note. Carpentry includes woodwork "used for structural purposes or in scaffoldings, arch supports, etc." *Id.* To qualify as "recognizable unassembled pieces" of particular articles, the subject merchandise must be "dedicated solely or principally for use in those articles." *Baxter Healthcare Corp. of P.R. v. United States*, 182 F.3d 1333, 1339 (Fed. Cir. 1999). In addition, unassembled pieces must be more than just basic material generally suitable for use in the finished article. Rather, "if the item as imported can be made into *multiple* parts of articles, the item must identify and fix with certainty the individual parts that are to be made from it." *Id.*

In granting the government's motion for summary judgment, the court explained that the subject merchandise was not identifiable or fixed with certainty as unassembled truss pieces because "the evidence on the record demonstrates that there is no genuine issue as to the fact that some or all of the imported lumber would require significant additional processing in order to be assembled into completed wood trusses." *Millenium*, 2007 Ct. Intl. Trade LEXIS 56, 2007 WL 1116148, at *4. In particular, the court explained that the even-foot-length boards would not generally be suitable for use without recutting because building plans seldom call for nothing but even-foot-length trusses. *Millenium*, 2007 Ct. Intl. Trade LEXIS 56, 2007 WL 1116148, at *5. The court further explained that the subject merchandise was also not sufficiently advanced to be dedicated solely or principally for use in completed wood trusses because the lumber maintained its identity and usefulness as general sawn lumber for potentially numerous purposes, notwithstanding the angle cuts on one end. *Millenium*, 2007 Ct. Intl. Trade LEXIS 56, 2007 WL 1116148, at *6. Last, the court added that Millenium's imported lumber was not identifiable as particular pieces of any specific finished truss—as opposed to the general makings of trusses in the abstract—and therefore could not qualify as unassembled truss components under heading 4418. *Id.*

On appeal, Millenium asserts that summary judgment was inappropriate because it sees a factual dispute as to whether its imported lumber required recutting to be used in a final truss. Millenium points to testimony indicating that builders often splice two boards together to form a longer truss, thereby eliminating the need for angle cuts at both ends. Millenium also cites testimony from Customs' expert witness, Dr. Woeste, who, when asked if the lumber could be used in its exact length and with its existing precut angles by splicing two boards together at their square ends, responded that it was "possible." Millenium also submitted affidavit testimony from one of its customers who claimed that "[t]he angle cut truss components produced by Millenium Lumber Distribution Co. were used to manufacture trusses without re-cutting except for about 10% which was surplus to specific job needs or contained defects." In addition, Millenium proffered evidence that builders used the original angle cut without reshaping. Millenium asserts that together, this testimony created a material factual dispute, and that summary judgment was therefore inappropriate. We disagree.

The germane question is not whether Millenium's imported lumber can be used in a truss without recutting, but whether the subject lumber requires recutting before it is sufficiently "recognizable" as unassembled pieces of a finished truss to warrant classification under heading 4418. *See* 44.18 Explanatory Note. It may have been possible to use the subject merchandise in finished trusses without recutting, and some of Millenium's customers may have used nearly all of the lumber it imported from Millennium to manufacture trusses without recutting as the testimony above indicates. This does not mean, however, that the subject merchandise was "dedicated solely or principally for use in" a finished truss so that the merchandise could be fairly characterized as "in the form of. . . recognizable unassembled pieces" of a truss. *See Baxter Healthcare*, 182 F.3d at 1339; 44.18 Explanatory Note. Millenium's proffered testimony, even taken as true, does not establish that the merchandise, in its as-imported condition "identify[ies] and fix[es] with certainty the individual parts that are to be made from it." *Baxter Healthcare*, 182 F.3d at 1339.

Because Customs' classifications decisions are presumed correct, Millenium bears the burden of proving otherwise. *Rollerblade*, 282 F.3d 1349, 1351. Yet, Millenium has offered nothing to belie the Court of International Trade's conclusion that "[b]ecause the merchandise maintained its identity and usefulness as general sawn lumber for potentially numerous purposes, it was not sufficiently advanced at the time of importation to be classified under 4418." *Millenium*, 2007 Ct. Intl. Trade LEXIS 56, 2007 WL 1116148, at *6. Millenium does not dispute that the merchandise as imported was neither bundled as truss kits ready for assembly nor labeled as specific components of completed trusses. In its motion for summary judgment, Millenium acknowledged that each component "may be used either as a stand alone chord or attached to another truss component" and that "[t]russ manufacturers order and maintain an inventory of available truss components. . . [and] may not know which specific truss design a truss component will go into." These statements show that the imported components are more raw material for trusses or other purposes generally than they are identifiable parts of a specific finished truss.

Millenium also contends, in the alternative, that its imported merchandise is sufficiently advanced beyond simple dimensional lumber to be classified under heading 4421. Heading 4421 covers "other articles of wood" but excludes any that are "specified or included in the preceding headings." 44.21 Explanatory Note. Therefore, simple dimensional lumber subject to classification under heading 4407 cannot fall under heading 4421. Millenium argues that its imported merchandise is too far advanced to be classified as standard dimensional lumber under heading 4407 because the lumber has "specified dimensions, minimal grade, Machine Stress Rating, minimal moisture content, species, and precision cut[s] at one end to particular angles." These characteristics, however, do not preclude classification under heading 4407.

The explanatory note to heading 4407 specifies that "[w]ith a few exceptions, this heading covers all [sawn, chipped or cut] wood and timber, of any length but of a thickness exceeding 6 mm." 44.07 Explanatory Note. As to the angle cut at one end of the lumber, 44.07's explanatory note specifies that "the wood of this heading need not necessarily be of rectangular (including square) section nor of uniform section along the length." *Id.* Millenium offers no further objection to Customs' classification under heading 4407. The imported merchandise therefore cannot be classified under heading 4421.

CONCLUSION

For the foregoing reasons, we affirm the judgment of the United States Court of International Trade.

AFFIRMED

NINGBO DAFA CHEMICAL FIBER CO., LTD.
v.
UNITED STATES

580 F.3d 1247 (Fed. Cir. 2009)
Decided September 2, 2009

Gregory S. Menegaz, DeKieffer & Horgan, of Washington, DC, argued for plaintiffs-appellants, Ningbo Dafa Chemical Fiber Co., Ltd., et al. With him on the brief was James K. Horgan.

Stephen C. Tosini, Attorney, Commercial Litigation Branch, Civil Division, United States Department of Justice, of Washington, DC, argued for defendant-appellee, United States. With him on the brief were Michael F. Hertz, Acting Assistant Attorney General, Jeanne E. Davidson, Director, and Patricia M. McCarthy, Assistant Director.

David C. Smith, Kelley Drye & Warren LLP, of Washington, DC, argued for defendants-appellees, Dak Americas LLC, et al. With him on the brief was Paul C. Rosenthal.

Before MICHEL, Chief Judge, LINN, Circuit Judge, and ST. EVE,* District Judge.

* The Honorable Amy J. St. Eve, District Judge, United States District Court for the Northern District of Illinois, sitting by designation.

ST. EVE, *District Judge.*

This appeal concerns an antidumping investigation of recycled polyester staple fiber ("PSF") from China. In its Final Determination from that investigation, the United States Department of Commerce ("Commerce") imposed a 4.86% antidumping duty on Ningbo Dafa Chemical Fiber Company, Ltd. ("Ningbo"). *Certain Polyester Staple Fiber from the People's Republic of China*, 72 Fed. Reg. 19,690 (Dep't of Commerce Apr. 19, 2007) ("*Final Determination*"). Ningbo, along with Consolidated Fibers, Inc., Fibertex Corporation, and Stein Fibers, Ltd., (collectively "Appellants") appeal from the judgment of the United States Court of International Trade affirming Commerce's Final Determination. *See Ningbo Dafa Chem. Fiber Co. v. United States*, 577 F. Supp. 2d 1304 (Ct. Int'l Trade 2008).

Because Commerce's Final Determination was supported by substantial evidence and not contrary to law, we affirm.

I. Background

Ningbo is a Chinese manufacturer of PSF. Appellees DAK Americas LLC and Nan Ya Plastics Corporation America (collectively, the "Domestic Producers") are domestic PSF producers that petitioned Commerce to investigate whether imports of PSF from China had been "dumped"—sold at less than fair value—in the United States. Commerce is also an Appellee.

PSF is used as stuffing in consumer items such as sleeping bags, mattresses, pillows, comforters, and furniture. Ningbo manufactures PSF from recycled polyethylene terephthalate ("PET") bottle flake, often in the form of shredded used plastic bottles, such as soda bottles. PET flake constitutes nearly 100% by weight of the raw material used in Ningbo's production of recycled PSF. PET flake comes in a variety of colors, including white, green, and brown, and the color of PET flake used in production determines the PSF's ultimate color. Thus, white PSF is made primarily from white PET flake, green PSF from green PET flake, and brown PSF from brown PET flake. In general, white is the most expensive PET flake color, followed by green and then brown. Similarly, once PET flake is processed into PSF, white PSF commands the highest prices, followed by green and then brown. During the period of investigation here, Ningbo produced approximately 60% white PSF, 32% green PSF, and 8% brown PSF. At issue is whether Commerce properly relied on Ningbo's PET flake invoices in determining Ningbo's antidumping margin.

In 2006, Commerce commenced an investigation into whether Chinese-manufactured PSF was, or was likely to be, sold in violation of United States policy against the dumping of goods. "The statutory definition of 'dumping' is the 'sale or likely sale of goods at less than fair value.'" *SKF USA, Inc. v. U.S. Customs & Border Prot.*, 556 F.3d 1337, 1340 (Fed. Cir. 2009) (quoting 19 U.S.C. § 1677(34) (2006)). Commerce assesses antidumping duties on the basis of a "dumping margin"—the amount by which the calculated "normal value" of subject merchandise exceeds its export price. 19 U.S.C. § 1677(35)(A).

In antidumping investigations of merchandise produced in either market economy or nonmarket economy countries, § 1677b(a) prescribes Commerce's default methods for calculating normal value. *See id.* § 1677b(a). Very often, however, Commerce is unable to calculate normal value using the general framework of subsection (a). For nonmarket economy ("NME") countries, such as China, Commerce must then apply § 1677b(c)(1)—the "factors of production" methodology—to calculate the normal value of merchandise produced in such countries:

> (1) In general
>
> If—
>
> (A) the subject merchandise is exported from a nonmarket economy country, and

> (B) the administering authority finds that available information does not permit the normal value of the subject merchandise to be determined under subsection (a) of this section,
>
> the administering authority shall determine the normal value of the subject merchandise on the basis of the value of the factors of production utilized in producing the merchandise . . . . Except as provided in paragraph (2), the valuation of the factors of production shall be based on the best available information regarding the values of such factors in a market economy country or countries considered to be appropriate by the administering authority.

Id. § 1677b(c)(1).[1] Thus, pursuant to § 1677b(c)(1), Commerce bases its valuation of factors of production on the "best available information" of their values in a market economy country. In a "factors of production" analysis, Commerce considers purchases from market economy suppliers the most reliable evidence of an input's value. Consequently, "where a factor is purchased from a market economy supplier and paid for in a market economy currency, [Commerce] normally will use the price paid to the market economy supplier [to value that factor]." 19 C.F.R. § 351.408(c)(1) (2009).

Pursuant to that policy, Commerce requested the invoices from Ningbo's market economy PET flake purchases during the period of investigation. Commerce determined that color-specific PET flake values were needed to accurately calculate Ningbo's dumping margin because the cost of PET flake varies based on color and Ningbo's prices for finished PSF concomitantly vary based on the color of PET flake used during production. Commerce thus asked Ningbo to identify, by color, the quantities and values of its market economy purchases of PET flake.

Ningbo supplied Commerce with fifty-eight invoices from its qualified market economy purchases of PET flake from the period of investigation, but only a few of those invoices identified the specific color of PET flake purchased. Specifically, three of Ningbo's market economy invoices specified white PET flake purchases, and five specified green PET flake purchases. None of Ningbo's market economy invoices indicated a purchase of brown PET flakes. Thereafter, Commerce again requested that Ningbo provide information regarding the quantities and values of its market economy purchases of PET flake segregated by color. Despite Commerce's repeated requests, however, Ningbo did not supply Commerce with complete market economy PET flake purchase prices based on color or its usage ratios based on color because, according to Ningbo, it did not maintain such records

---

1 The exception in "paragraph (2)" to which § 1677b(c)(1) refers (i.e., § 1677b(c)(2)) provides that, if Commerce finds that the "available information is inadequate for purposes of determining the normal value of subject merchandise under paragraph (1)"—the factors of production methodology—Commerce shall determine normal value based on the price for which similar merchandise produced in comparable market economy countries is sold in other countries, including the United States. 19 U.S.C. § 1677b(c)(2); *Allied Pac. Food (Dalian) Co. v. United States*, 587 F. Supp. 2d 1330, 1353 n.11 (Ct. Int'l Trade 2008). Commerce did not apply that exception here.

in the ordinary course of business. Because Ningbo did not provide the complete requested information on its most significant raw material, Commerce invoked 19 U.S.C. § 1677e(a)(2)(B) in its Final Determination and applied neutral partial "facts available" to calculate color-specific values for Ningbo's PET flake. *Final Determination*, 72 Fed. Reg. at 19,691.

Section 1677e(a)—the "facts otherwise available" or "facts available" provision—provides in relevant part:

> If—
>
> (1) necessary information is not available on the record, or
>
> (2) an interested party or any other person—
>
> (A) withholds information that has been requested by the administering authority or the Commission under this subtitle, [or]
>
> (B) fails to provide such information by the deadlines for submission of the information or in the form and manner requested, subject to subsections (c)(1) and (e) of section 1677m of this title,
>
> . . .
>
> the administering authority and the Commission shall, subject to section 1677m(d)[2] of this title, use the facts otherwise available in reaching the applicable determination under this subtitle.

19 U.S.C. § 1677e(a). Subsection (c)(1) of § 1677m provides that, if an interested party promptly notifies Commerce that it is unable to submit the information in the requested form and manner, together with a full explanation and suggested alternative forms in which it is can submit the information, Commerce shall consider the party's ability to submit the information in the requested form and manner and may modify such requirements to the extent necessary to avoid imposing an unreasonable burden on the party. *Id.* § 1677m(c)(1).

---

2 Section 1677m(d) provides:

> If the administering authority. . . determines that a response to a request for information under this subtitle does not comply with the request, the administering authority . . . shall promptly inform the person submitting the response of the nature of the deficiency and shall, to the extent practicable, provide that person with an opportunity to remedy or explain the deficiency in light of the time limits established for the completion of investigations or reviews under this subtitle. If that person submits further information in response to such deficiency and either—
>
> (1) the administering authority . . . finds that such response is not satisfactory, or
>
> (2) such response is not submitted within the applicable time limits,
>
> then the administering authority . . . may, subject to subsection (e) of this section, disregard all or part of the original and subsequent responses.

19 U.S.C. § 1677m(d). Ningbo does not contest that Commerce complied with § 1677m(d) in this case.

When § 1677e(a) applies, Commerce may use as "facts available" any "information or inferences which are reasonable to use under the circumstances" to make the applicable determination or substitute for the missing information. *See* Statement of Administrative Action, H.R. Rep. No. 103-316, at 869 (1994), *reprinted in* 1994 U.S.C.C.A.N. 4040, 4198; *Nippon Steel Corp. v. United States*, 25 C.I.T. 1192, 1196 (Ct. Int'l Trade 2001). In addition, § 1677e(b) authorizes Commerce to draw adverse inferences from the facts available when it concludes that a party "failed to cooperate by not acting to the best of its ability" in supplying the requested information. 19 U.S.C. § 1677e(b).

As already discussed, Commerce requested color-specific PET flake prices because it determined they were important to accurately calculate the normal value of Ningbo's PSF products, and thus the applicable antidumping margin. When Ningbo did not provide color-specific PET flake values, Commerce concluded that Ningbo did not provide the requested information in the form and manner requested, thus justifying application of the "facts otherwise available" under 19 U.S.C. § 1677e(a): "For this final determination, in accordance with [§ 1677e(a)(2)(B) and § 1677m(c)(1)], we have determined that the use of neutral facts available is appropriate for Ningbo Dafa's PET flake." *Final Determination*, 72 Fed. Reg. at 19,691. Commerce applied neutral, rather than adverse, partial facts available. *Id.* Specifically, Commerce used those invoices that indicated white and green to extrapolate the value of Ningbo's white and green PET flake, respectively. Commerce then assigned the color brown to the remaining market economy purchases reflected in approximately fifty invoices—those which did not indicate a color—and used the average price from those invoices as the value of Ningbo's brown PET flake. Relying on the incomplete information contained in Ningbo's color-specific market economy invoices, Commerce assigned Ningbo an anti-dumping duty margin of 4.86%. Although imperfect, it was the only color-specific evidence Ningbo provided.

The Court of International Trade affirmed Commerce's final determination in all respects. *Ningbo Dafa*, 577 F. Supp. 2d 1304. This appeal followed. The Federal Circuit has jurisdiction over appeals from the Court of International Trade pursuant to 28 U.S.C. § 1295(a)(5).

II. Discussion

A. Standard of Review

"The Federal Circuit reviews Commerce's anti-dumping orders using the same standard of review used by the Court of International Trade." *NMB Singapore Ltd. v. United States*, 557 F.3d 1316, 1319 (Fed. Cir. 2009); *NSK Ltd. v. United States*, 481 F.3d 1355, 1359 (Fed. Cir. 2007). This court upholds Commerce's decisions unless they are "unsupported by substantial evidence on the record, or otherwise not in accordance with law." 19 U.S.C. § 1516a(b)(1)(B)(i); NMB Singapore, 557 F.3d at 1319; *Timken U.S. Corp. v. United States*, 434 F.3d 1345, 1350 (Fed. Cir. 2006).

"Substantial evidence means 'more than a mere scintilla' and 'such relevant evidence as a reasonable mind might accept as adequate to support a conclusion.'" *Huvis Corp. v. United States*, 570 F.3d 1347, 1351 (Fed. Cir. 2009) (quoting *Consol. Edison Co. v. NLRB*, 305 U.S. 197, 229, 59 S. Ct. 206, 83 L. Ed. 126 (1938)); *SKF USA, Inc. v. United States*, 537 F.3d 1373, 1378 (Fed. Cir. 2008); *Inland Steel Indus., Inc. v. United States*, 188 F.3d 1349, 1359 (Fed. Cir. 1999). The "substantiality of evidence must take into account whatever in the record fairly detracts from its weight, including contradictory evidence or evidence from which conflicting inferences could be drawn." *Huvis*, 570 F.3d at 1351 (internal quotation marks omitted). Though decisions of the Court of International Trade affirming or reversing final administrative determinations are reviewed de novo, "'we give great weight to the informed opinion of the Court of International Trade . . . , [and] it is nearly always the starting point of our analysis.'" *Id.* (alteration and omission in original) (quoting *Nippon Steel Corp. v. United States,* 458 F.3d 1345, 1351 (Fed. Cir. 2006)).

"We review de novo whether Commerce's interpretation of a governing statutory provision is in accordance with law, but we do so within the framework established by *Chevron* . . . ." *Agro Dutch Indus. Ltd. v. United States*, 508 F.3d 1024, 1029-30 (Fed. Cir. 2007); *see Elkem Metals Co. v. United States*, 468 F.3d 795, 800 (Fed. Cir. 2006). The first step of the *Chevron* analysis is to determine "whether Congress has directly spoken to the precise question at issue. If the intent of Congress is clear, that is the end of the matter; for the court, as well as the agency, must give effect to the unambiguously expressed intent of Congress." *Chevron, U.S.A., Inc. v. Natural Res. Def. Council, Inc.*, 467 U.S. 837, 842-43, 104 S. Ct. 2778, 81 L. Ed. 2d 694 (1984); FDA v. Brown & *Williamson Tobacco Corp.*, 529 U.S. 120, 132, 120 S. Ct. 1291, 146 L. Ed. 2d 121 (2000); *Agro Dutch,* 508 F.3d at 1030. "Under step two of *Chevron*, if an agency's statutory interpretation promulgated under the authority delegated it by Congress is 'reasonable' it is 'binding [o]n the courts unless procedurally defective, arbitrary or capricious in substance, or manifestly contrary to the statute.'" *Wheatland Tube Co. v. United States*, 495 F.3d 1355, 1360 (Fed. Cir. 2007) (alteration in original) (quoting *Chevron*, 467 U.S. at 844; Administrative Procedure Act, 5 U.S.C. § 706(2)(A), (D)).

B. Application of "Facts Available" in Nonmarket Economy Cases

As noted above, because complete color-specific PET flake information was not available, Commerce resorted to "facts otherwise available" under 19 U.S.C. § 1677e(a) to calculate color-specific values for Ningbo's PET flake. Ningbo argues that § 1677b(c)(1)'s "best available information" standard—on which Commerce "shall" base the valuation of the factors of production for merchandise exported from a NME country—bars Commerce from invoking facts available under § 1677e(a) when valuing factors of production. Thus, according to Ningbo, Commerce acted "contrary to law" by applying "facts available" in this NME case. The court disagrees.

1. Plain Language of 19 U.S.C. § 1677b(c)(1) and § 1677e(a)

This appeal revolves, in part, around the proper interpretation and interaction of 19 U.S.C. § 1677b(c)(1) and § 1677e(a). Both § 1677b and § 1677e are found in Subtitle IV of Title 19 of the United States Code. Section 1677b(c)(1) provides that in NME investigations, Commerce "shall" use the "best available information regarding the values of such factors [of production]." Section 1677e(a) specifically provides: "If . . . (1) necessary information is not available on the record, or (2) an interested party or any other person . . . fails to provide such information . . . in the form and manner requested," Commerce "shall . . . use the facts otherwise available in reaching the applicable determination *under this subtitle.*" 19 U.S.C. § 1677e(a) (emphasis added); Huvis, 570 F.3d at 1349. Accordingly, under § 1677e(a), where necessary information is unavailable on the record or a party fails to provide requested information, Commerce "shall" use the "facts otherwise available" to fill information gaps when determining the value of the factors of production under § 1677b(c)(1) using the "best available information." *See Nippon Steel Corp. v. United States*, 337 F.3d 1373, 1381 (Fed. Cir. 2003) ("Under subsection (a) [of 19 U.S.C. § 1677e], if a respondent 'fails to provide [requested] information by the deadlines for submission,' Commerce shall fill in the gaps with 'facts otherwise available.' The focus of subsection (a) is respondent's *failure to provide information*. The reason for the failure is of no moment. The mere failure of a respondent to furnish requested information—for any reason—requires Commerce to resort to other sources of information to complete the factual record on which it makes its determination." (second alteration in original)); M*erck & Co. v. Hi-Tech Pharmacal Co.*, 482 F.3d 1317, 1322 (Fed. Cir. 2007) ("Use of the word 'shall' in a statute generally denotes the imperative."); *Grav v. United States,* 886 F.2d 1305, 1307 (Fed. Cir. 1989) (noting that use of the word "shall" indicates the action is mandatory).

Nor does the plain language of § 1677b(c)(2) preclude application of § 1677e(a)'s "facts otherwise available" to valuations of NME merchandise. Section 1677b(c)(2) provides an "exception" in NME cases where information, though "available," is nevertheless "inadequate" to calculate the normal value of subject merchandise. 19 U.S.C. § 1677b(c)(2) ("available information is inadequate"). Section 1677e(a), in contrast, applies when necessary information is "not available on the record" or where a party withholds or fails to provide requested information. There is nothing in the statutory text to indicate that the "exception" in § 1677b(c)(2) was meant to serve as Commerce's exclusive recourse in situations where information is in some way deficient in a NME investigation. The court's plain language reading is further confirmed and strengthened by legislative history as well as the deference due to agency interpretations of their governing statutes.

2. Legislative History

Contrary to Ningbo's contentions, the plain language of these statutory provisions empowers Commerce to resort, in certain circumstances, to "facts available" in

NME cases. "If the statute is clear and unambiguous on its face, as is the case here, 'there is usually no need to resort to the legislative history underlying the statute.'" *Ortiz v. Principi*, 274 F.3d 1361, 1364 (Fed. Cir. 2001) (quoting *Munson v. Merit Sys. Prot. Bd.*, 216 F.3d 1037, 1040 (Fed. Cir. 2000)); *see* Garcia v. United States, 469 U.S. 70, 75, 105 S. Ct. 479, 83 L. Ed. 2d 472 (1984) ("[O]nly the most extraordinary showing of contrary intentions from [the legislative history] would justify a limitation on the 'plain meaning' of the statutory language."); *Mudge v. United States*, 308 F.3d 1220, 1230 (Fed. Cir. 2002). Nonetheless, the legislative history of the *Uruguay Round Agreements Act* ("URAA"), Pub. L. No. 103-465, 108 Stat. 4809 (1994), which codified the current version of § 1677e(a),[3] reinforces the court's reading of the plain language of these provisions. *See United States v. Wells*, 519 U.S. 482, 492, 117 S. Ct. 921, 137 L. Ed. 2d 107 (1997) (proceeding to note that the legislative history was consistent with the Court's interpretation of the statute's plain and unambiguous text); *Merck*, 482 F.3d at 1322. The Statement of Administrative Action ("SAA") accompanying the URAA is, by statute, "an authoritative expression by the United States concerning the interpretation and application of the Uruguay Round Agreements and this Act in any judicial proceeding in which a question arises concerning such interpretation or application." 19 U.S.C. § 3512(d); *see Timken U.S. Corp. v. United States*, 421 F.3d 1350, 1354 n.2 (Fed. Cir. 2005). The SAA provides that the "facts otherwise available" provision is intended to permit Commerce to "fill [] gaps in the record." *See* Statement of Administrative Action, H.R. Rep. No. 103-316, at 869, *reprinted in* 1994 U.S.C.C.A.N. at 4198–99 (explaining that 19 U.S.C. § 1677e(a) "generally will require Commerce to reach a determination by filling gaps in the record due to deficient submissions or other causes").

The legislative history of the URAA thus reveals that Congress intended § 1677e(a) to provide Commerce with gap-filling power to facilitate its implementation of the antidumping laws. Ningbo has not identified any support in the legislative history or case law, and the court has found none, for its position that, despite § 1677e(a)'s mandatory language and express applicability to Commerce's determinations under the same subtitle, Commerce cannot resort to facts available in NME cases.

3. Deference to Commerce's Interpretation of Governing Statutes

Because Congress's intent as to the interaction of § 1677b(c)(1) and § 1677e(a) is clear from the plain language of these statutes, the court need not determine whether Commerce's interpretation warrants *Chevron* deference. *See Chevron*, 467 U.S. at 842–43; *Wheatland Tube*, 495 F.3d at 1359. In the interest of completeness,

---

3 Prior to the URAA, § 1677e(a) "mandated the use of the 'best information [otherwise] available' if a respondent refused or was unable to produce information in a timely manner or in the form requested by Commerce." *Nippon Steel*, 337 F.3d at 1381. Apparently, the change to "facts otherwise available" was one in terminology only and was intended to incorporate prevailing practice. *See* Statement of Administrative Action, H.R. Rep. No. 103-316, at 869, *reprinted in* 1994 U.S.C.C.A.N. at 4198 ("The [Uruguay Round Agreements] largely track current law, but use different terminology.").

however, the court will address the *Chevron* analysis. If ambiguity existed, *Chevron* obligates the court to defer to Commerce's reasonable interpretations of its governing statutes, such as § 1677b and § 1677e. *See SKF USA*, 537 F.3d at 1379.

It is "well established that 'statutory interpretations articulated by Commerce during its antidumping proceedings are entitled to judicial deference under *Chevron*.'" *Agro Dutch*, 508 F.3d at 1029 n.4 (quoting *Pesquera Mares Australes Ltda. v. United States*, 266 F.3d 1372, 1382 (Fed. Cir. 2001)); *Thai Pineapple Canning Indus. Corp. v. United States*, 273 F.3d 1077, 1083 (Fed. Cir. 2001). Although not in an identical case, Commerce has invoked its § 1677e(a) "facts available" authority in other NME cases. *See, e.g., Polyethylene Retail Carrier Bag Comm. v. United States*, 232 F. App'x 965, 968-69 (Fed. Cir. 2007) (nonprecedential); *Shandong Huarong Gen. Group Corp. v. United States*, 27 C.I.T. 1568, 1596 (Ct. Int'l Trade 2003) ("Commerce has exercised this ability [to apply partial adverse facts available] in the context of NME investigations."). These cases, as well as its position in this case, confirm that Commerce interprets 19 U.S.C. § 1677e(a) to apply, where appropriate, to NME investigations.

Further, "this court gives Commerce's interpretation of antidumping laws significant deference because of its special expertise in administering antidumping duty law." *Wheatland Tube*, 495 F.3d at 1361. Indeed, "'[d]eference to an agency's interpretation is at its peak in the case of a court's review of Commerce's interpretation of the antidumping laws.'" *SKF USA*, 537 F.3d at 1379 (quoting *Koyo Seiko Co. v. United States*, 36 F.3d 1565, 1570 (Fed. Cir. 1994)). The court's conclusion that "facts available" can apply when valuing factors of production in NME cases is further strengthened by the "considerable deference" due to Commerce's interpretation of the antidumping statutes. *See Micron Tech., Inc. v. United States*, 243 F.3d 1301, 1312 (Fed. Cir. 2001); *cf. Chen v. Mukasey*, 524 F.3d 1028, 1032 (9th Cir. 2008) ("Because the statute is silent on the interaction between the two provisions at issue, we must defer to the agency as long as its interpretation is reasonable.").

In order to affirm Commerce's determination here, however, it is not enough that the law permits Commerce to apply "facts available" in valuing factors of production. Commerce's decision to do so also must be supported by substantial evidence. In addition, substantial evidence must support Commerce's color-specific PET flake valuations.

C. Substantial Evidence Supports Commerce's Resort to "Facts Available"

Ningbo's argument that Commerce should have relied on a single, non-color-specific PET flake value as the best available information is unavailing. In the supporting memorandum to its Final Determination, Commerce explained:

> [T]here is a direct relation between the sale price of PSF and the color of PET flake price used to produce PSF (i.e., generally, white PET flake is more expensive than green PET flake, and therefore, generally, the sale price of white PSF is greater than

> that of green PSF). . . . Therefore, in order to accurately calculate dumping margins in this case, it is important to make identical or similar comparisons between the sales of a specific color of finished PSF and the normal value based on the color of PET flake used to produce the PSF. Thus, the Department requested that Ningbo Dafa report its usage ratios of PET flake based on color and its market economy purchase prices of PET flake based on color.

Investigation of Certain Polyester Staple Fiber from the People's Republic of China: Issues & Decision Mem. at 61 (Dep't of Commerce Apr. 10, 2007). Thus, substantial evidence, including the color-based relationship between PET flake cost and PSF price, supports Commerce's conclusion that it required color-specific PET flake values to accurately calculate Ningbo's dumping margin. Ningbo did not provide complete color-specific PET flake information. Accordingly, Ningbo's failure "to provide information in the form and manner requested by [Commerce]" and failure to "suggest alternative forms in which it was able to submit the requested information," *id.*, forced Commerce to apply the "facts otherwise available" to determine color-specific PET flake values. Resorting to the "facts available"—namely, verified invoices from Ningbo's actual market economy purchases—Commerce properly relied on incomplete color-specific and non-color-specific invoices to calculate color-specific PET flake values.

"In determining the valuation of the factors of production, the critical question is whether the methodology used by Commerce is based on the best available information and establishes antidumping margins as accurately as possible." *Shakeproof Assembly Components v. United States*, 268 F.3d 1376, 1382 (Fed. Cir. 2001); *Parkdale Int'l v. United States*, 475 F.3d 1375, 1380 (Fed. Cir. 2007). "While § 1677b(c) provides guidelines to assist Commerce in this process, this section also accords Commerce wide discretion in the valuation of factors of production in the application of those guidelines." *Shakeproof*, 268 F.3d at 1381 (quoting *Nation Ford Chem. Co. v. United States*, 166 F.3d 1373, 1377 (Fed. Cir. 1999)); *see Lasko Metal Prods., Inc. v. United States*, 43 F.3d 1442, 1446 (Fed. Cir. 1994). In the context of § 1677b(c), where a party fails to provide requested information or certain necessary information is wholly absent from the record, such that no "best" information exists as to a particular factor of production, Commerce can resort to the general, gap-filling "facts available" authority conferred by § 1677e(a). *See Shandong Huarong Gen. Group Corp. v. United States*, 60 Fed. Appx. 797, 799–800 (Fed. Cir. 2003) (nonprecedential) (concluding that, although Commerce's determination must be based on "the best *available* information," where a respondent did not provide sufficient information, Commerce made a reasonable determination based on the available information). Commerce may be able to identify the "best" information among that available to it, but requiring Commerce to do so does not ensure that the available record information includes the information Commerce needs to fulfill its responsibility to calculate antidumping margins "as accurately as possible" under § 1677b(c). *Shakeproof*, 268 F.3d at 1382. Section 1677e(a) is secondary to, but nonetheless supplements, § 1677b(c)(1).

Here, no information was available as to the specific value of brown PET flake—none of Ningbo's market economy invoices indicated brown, and color-specific Indian surrogate values did not exist. Thus, having permissibly determined that color-specific PET flake values were important to an accurate margin calculation, Commerce followed its longstanding policy that market economy prices are the "best available information" under 19 U.S.C. § 1677b(c)(1) and relied on the prices from Ningbo's market economy invoices to value PET flake.[4] Commerce resorted to partial "facts available" under 19 U.S.C. § 1677e(a) for the necessary information that was missing from the record, but did so in accordance with the "best available information" mandate of § 1677b(c)(1). *See NSK Ltd. v. United States*, 358 F. Supp. 2d 1276, 1290, 29 Ct. Int'l Trade 1 (Ct. Int'l Trade 2005) ("By its nature, a 'facts available' analysis necessarily implies that Commerce used facts where the actual facts are an insufficient basis for a complete analysis.").

D. Commerce's Valuation of Ningbo's PET Flake Factor of Production

Having determined that Commerce properly relied on the "facts otherwise available" to value Ningbo's PET flake purchases by color, the court must next consider whether Commerce's *application* of the facts available was reasonable and supported by substantial evidence.[5] Indeed, the invocation of "facts available" does not alter the court's mandate to ensure that Commerce's determinations and

---

4 Pursuant to established policy, Commerce considers average ME purchase price the "best available information" to value a given input as long as the volume of the input purchased from ME suppliers as a share of total purchases of that input is "meaningful." *Antidumping Methodologies*, 71 Fed. Reg. 61,716, 61,716 (Dep't of Commerce Oct. 19, 2006) (request for comment). Ningbo argues that Commerce departed from its then-governing policy to rely on market economy invoices to value a factor of production only when such invoices represented at least 5% of a respondent's total volume of purchases during the period of investigation. Ningbo argues that, even under the 5% policy, the market economy invoices upon which Commerce relied here constituted only 1.6% of just the total market economy flake purchases during the POI. The government responds that Ningbo's market economy purchases were well over 5% of the total volume of PET flake purchased. Commerce's treatment of white and green PSF as distinct products must fairly extend to its treatment of each product's unique inputs. The record does not permit the necessary comparison, however, because Ningbo did not report the total amount of white or green PET flake it purchased from all sources during the POI. Nevertheless, Commerce is required to explain deviations from policy. *Huvis*, 570 F.3d at 1353. On the other hand, if Commerce's reliance on this small sample of ME invoices to value white and green PET flake was based not on the best available information, as its brief before this court suggests, but on partial "facts available," as the Final Determination implies, the 5% policy may not apply. The court need not decide this issue to resolve this appeal.

5 In an apparent attempt to lower the court's standard of review, the Domestic Producers note that the SAA provides that "facts available" need only be those "reasonable to use under the circumstances." Statement of Administrative Action, H.R. Rep. No. 103-316, at 869, *reprinted in* 1994 U.S.C.C.A.N. at 4198. Semantics aside, this court's review is governed by statute, pursuant to which the court will affirm Commerce's calculated color-specific PET flake values if they are supported by "substantial evidence on the record" and otherwise in accordance with law. 19 U.S.C. § 1516a(b)(1)(B)(i); *see SKF USA*, 537 F.3d at 1378 (concluding that the

methodology are supported by substantial evidence. *See NTN Bearing Corp. v. United States*, 368 F.3d 1369, 1377 (Fed. Cir. 2004) (evaluating Commerce's facts available methodology for substantial evidentiary support); *Ta Chen Stainless Steel Pipe, Inc. v. United States*, 298 F.3d 1330, 1335 (Fed. Cir. 2002) (applying substantial evidence standard to Commerce's imposition of adverse facts available); *Nippon Steel*, 25 C.I.T. at 1196 ("Commerce may thus employ record evidence to arrive at a margin calculation in the absence of complete data, even if the evidence does not necessarily replace the precise data missing, subject to the constraint that the facts and the manner in which they are employed are reasonable.").

Ningbo argues that Commerce's methodology for allocating the "facts available" market economy invoices to value its PET flake by color was not supported by substantial evidence because it did not match its actual production experience. Ningbo contends that "a reasonable investigator would have assigned the color white to the invoices (the top 60%) with the highest unit values; and would have assigned the color green to the unknown color invoices in the middle of the unit value range (the next 32%); and the remainder (approximately 8%) to brown." Appellant's Br. 47.

The government argues that, as a threshold matter, this court cannot consider Ningbo's argument that Commerce should have calculated color-specific PET flake values according to Ningbo's period-of-investigation production of finished PSF because Ningbo failed to exhaust its administrative remedies with respect to that argument. The government and the Domestic Producers further assert that Commerce's determinations, including its calculation of "facts available" color-specific PET flake values, are supported by substantial evidence and not contrary to law.

1. Exhaustion of Administrative Remedies

According to the government, prior to briefing before the Court of International Trade, Ningbo had never suggested allocating its non-color-specific market economy invoices based on its color-specific production ratios. Nor, the government adds, did Ningbo present the production-based invoice allocations and calculations to which it now points. The government concludes that the court cannot consider Ningbo's production-based arguments because Ningbo did not exhaust its administrative remedies by presenting them to Commerce during the investigation.

The Court of International Trade "shall, where appropriate, require the exhaustion of administrative remedies." 28 U.S.C. § 2637(d). This court has "held that applying exhaustion principles in trade cases is subject to the discretion of the judge of the Court of International Trade." *Corus Staal BV v. United States*, 502 F.3d 1370, 1381 (Fed. Cir. 2007). Here, the Court of International Trade concluded that

---

trade court's reasonableness-focused inquiry did not conflict with our controlling "substantial evidence" standard).

"the record does not indicate a clearly better method for valuation than the one used by Commerce." *Ningbo Dafa*, 577 F. Supp. 2d at 1312. Addressing Commerce's exhaustion argument, however, that court stated that it "d[id] not agree with Commerce's stance" that Commerce lacked an opportunity to consider Ningbo's production and sales numbers as an alternative methodology. *Id.* at 1311. Indeed, Commerce verified Ningbo's color-specific production quantities during the investigation, and the government confirmed at oral argument that Commerce was aware of Ningbo's actual production data. Moreover, the record before Commerce contained at least a suggestion, incorporated in Ningbo's internal cost allocation, of a production-based allocation methodology. Accordingly, the Court of International Trade did not abuse its discretion in finding that Commerce had the opportunity to consider a production-based methodology. *See Corus Staal*, 502 F.3d at 1381. The court, therefore, will consider Ningbo's arguments on the merits.

2. Substantial Evidence Supports Commerce's Determinations

"Commerce is the 'master of antidumping law,' and reviewing courts must accord deference to the agency in its selection and development of proper methodologies." *Thai Pineapple Pub. Co. v. United States*, 187 F.3d 1362, 1365 (Fed Cir. 1999). In fact, the "methodologies relied upon by Commerce in making its determinations are presumptively correct." *Id.; Fla. Citrus Mut. v. United States*, 550 F.3d 1105, 1110 (Fed. Cir. 2008). Even when Commerce makes "adverse inferences" in connection with its reliance on "facts otherwise available," however, Commerce cannot "overreach reality" in imposing a dumping margin in the name of maximizing deterrence. *See Ta Chen*, 298 F.3d at 1340; *Huvis*, 570 F.3d at 1353 ("Even when Commerce uses adverse inferences [which it did not in *Huvis*], it must use a reasonably accurate estimate of the respondent's actual rate when using 'facts available.'" (internal quotation marks omitted)). This limitation holds especially true where, as here, Commerce concluded that adverse inferences were not warranted.

a. Commerce's Color-Specific Valuation Methodology

The court disagrees with Ningbo's argument that Commerce's methodology for calculating color-specific PET flake values was demonstrably distortive and inaccurate. Ningbo asserts that Commerce made unrealistic assumptions about Ningbo's PET flake purchases, out of proportion to Ningbo's verified period-of-investigation production ratios contained in the record before Commerce. Ningbo argues that it would have been impossible for it to produce the amount of each color of PSF it actually produced if it had in fact purchased the amount of white and green PET flake assumed by Commerce. Ningbo further contends that any reasonable alternative values for its PET flake purchases, such as the values derived from allocating the non-color-specific invoices in rough proportion to the colors of its PSF production, would result in a *de minimis* or negative margin, for which no duty would be assessed.

In support of its position, Ningbo points out that Commerce relied on three invoices representing 0.41% by weight of Ningbo's total market economy flake purchases during the period of investigation to value Ningbo's white PET flake, even though finished PSF is almost entirely PET flake, the color of PET flake used in production dictates the color of the finished PSF, and 60% of Ningbo's flake consumption was for production of white PSF. Similarly, the five invoices which identified the flake color as green represented 1.2% of Ningbo's market economy flake purchases, yet the production of green PSF accounted for 32% of flake consumption. Commerce then assumed that the remaining 95% of market economy flake purchases during the period of investigation, for which the invoices did not identify a color, were purchases of brown flake. Only 8% of Ningbo's PSF production during the period of investigation, however, was brown. Thus, as Ningbo puts it, Commerce averaged the prices of 95% by weight of Ningbo's market economy PET flake purchases to value the input that constituted approximately 8% of the product. Moreover, the record reveals that although Ningbo purchased PET flake from a number of market economy suppliers, all the color-indicating invoices were from a single supplier. Pointing to this record evidence, Ningbo concludes that Commerce assumed unrealistic facts and, as a result of failing to allocate an appropriate proportion of purchases to white and green flake, unreasonably overstated the value of all three flake colors.

Despite some conflicting evidence, the following substantial record evidence supports Commerce's allocation methodology. To begin, as the Domestic Producers point out, the factors of production methodology focuses on input purchases, not production, and the record reveals that Ningbo purchased materially less PET flake during the period of investigation than it consumed during the period. Ningbo also had two to three months inventory of PET flake on hand. Moreover, according to Ningbo, the market economy invoices upon which Commerce relied represented only 40% of its total flake purchases during the period of investigation. That is, Ningbo's flake purchases from other countries—constituting 60% of its purchases during the period of investigation—were not reflected in Commerce's methodology. In sum, no exact correlation between Ningbo's market economy flake purchases and production was possible given the lack of information provided by Ningbo. As already discussed, although Commerce may have had the opportunity to consider Ningbo's production quantities, despite Commerce's clear requests, Ningbo did not provide its PET flake usage ratios based on color or an alternative means for determining the color of its market economy PET flake purchases. Accordingly, Commerce, working with the incomplete information before it, reasonably and realistically assigned a color to the market economy invoices without stated colors. In light of the broad discretion Commerce enjoys in valuing factors of production, see *Nation Ford*, 166 F.3d at 1377, Commerce's methodology for valuing white, green, and brown PET flake based on the invoices from Ningbo's market economy purchases is supported by substantial evidence and in accordance with law.

b. Commerce's Color-Specific Valuations of Ningbo's PET Flake

As indicated above, Ningbo also argues that Commerce diverted invoices fairly attributable to white and green PET flake and added them to the average for brown, the least expensive PET flake. In support, Ningbo points to the following verified facts suggesting that the actual cost of white flake was lower than Commerce's constructed value: (1) the invoices Commerce relied on to value white PET flake reflected the highest cost PET flake Ningbo purchased during the period of investigation; (2) Ningbo's PSF production is 60% white PSF; (3) white PSF is made almost entirely from white PET flake; and (4) the amount of white PET flake reflected by the white-indicating invoices was significantly less than required to produce the amount of white PSF Ningbo actually manufactured during the period of investigation. Consequently, non-color-specific invoices from purchases of relatively lower-priced white PET flake were necessarily excluded from Commerce's calculation. Ningbo reasons that Commerce's constructed color-specific PET flake valuations are thus clearly and demonstrably inaccurate. The court disagrees.

Despite some evidence detracting from its weight, substantial record evidence supports Commerce's valuations. To begin, for the reasons discussed above, no exact correlation between Ningbo's PET flake purchases and PSF production is possible based on the incomplete information on the record. Commerce's constructed prices for white, green, and brown PET flake (which are confidential) approximate the relative price differences between white and green and white and brown PET flake that Ningbo employees reported to Commerce during its verification visit. Moreover, Commerce's calculated values are identical to the prices derived from co-respondent Cixi Jiangnan's[6] color-specific market economy invoices and are comparable to the prices listed in Ningbo's internal inventory allocation chart from one month during the period of investigation. Although Cixi's prices were for *washed* PET flake, while Ningbo purchased only less expensive, *unwashed* flake, this evidence is nonetheless more than a mere scintilla supporting Commerce's valuations. Finally and most significantly, as the Court of International Trade found, Ningbo has not demonstrated that Commerce's constructed prices resulted in higher dumping margins than if Ningbo had provided actual PET flake purchases by color. *See Ningbo Dafa*, 577 F. Supp. 2d at 1311. In sum, Commerce's determination appears to reflect a reasonable approximation in light of Ningbo's actual record keeping.

Substantial evidence is a deferential standard of review, which requires only that a determination be supported by "'such relevant evidence as a reasonable mind might accept as adequate to support a conclusion.'" *SKF USA*, 537 F.3d at 1378 (quoting *Consol. Edison*, 305 U.S. at 229). Commerce's methodology and

6 Like Ningbo, its cross-town rival, Cixi Jiangnan is a Chinese producer of recycled PSF.

resulting color-specific PET flake valuations, while not perfect, are supported by substantial evidence.

III. Conclusion

For the aforementioned reasons, we affirm the judgment of the Court of International Trade affirming Commerce's determinations as to Ningbo.

AFFIRMED.

NMB SINGAPORE LTD.
v.
UNITED STATES

557 F.3d 1316 (Fed. Cir. 2009)
Decided February 18, 2009

Matthew P. Jaffe, Crowell & Moring, LLP, of Washington, DC for plaintiffs-appellees. With him on the brief was Robert A. Lipstein. Of counsel were Sobia Haque and Alexander H. Schaefer.

Jill Caiazzo Sidley Austin LLP, of Washington, DC, argued for plaintiff-appellant. With him on the brief was Neil R. Ellis. Of counsel was Lawrence R. Walders.

David F. D'Alessandris, Trial Attorney, Commercial Litigation Branch, Civil Division, United States Department of Justice, of Washington, DC, argued for defendant-appellee. With him on the brief were Gregory G. Katsas, Assistant Attorney General, Jeanne E. Davidson, Director, and Patricia M. McCarthy, Assistant Director. Of counsel on the brief was Deborah R. King, United States Department of Commerce, of Washington, DC.

Eric P. Salonen, Stewart and Stewart, of Washington, DC, argued for defendant/cross appellant. With him on the brief were Terence P. Stewart and Patrick J. McDonough. Of counsel was Philip A. Butler.

Before MICHEL, Chief Judge, SCHALL, and MOORE, Circuit Judges.

MICHEL, *Chief Judge*.

JTEKT Corporation and Koyo Corporation of U.S.A. (collectively, "JTEKT") and the Timken Company ("Timken") have cross-appealed different aspects of the Court of International Trade's judgment affirming a final decision of the Department of Commerce ("Commerce"). On appeal, JTEKT argues that Commerce ignored evidence and argument JTEKT presented, and that Commerce's finding that dumping was likely to continue (and the resulting continuation of the anti-dumping duty) should be vacated. In a cross-appeal, Timken argues that Commerce lacked substantial evidence to justify recalculating (and reducing) dumping margins for the Japanese parties and also impermissibly deviated in several respects from its established methodology when it decided to recalculate their dumping margins. Oral argument was held on December 5, 2008. We affirm the Court of International Trade's judgment in JTEKT's appeal, but vacate and remand in Timken's cross-appeal.

I. Background

NSK Corporation and NSK, Ltd. (collectively, "NSK"), NTN Corporation and NTN USA (collectively, "NTN"), JTEKT, and Timken all manufacture ball bearings. NTN, NSK, and JTEKT are Japanese manufacturers, while Timken is a domestic entity.[1]

In 1988, Commerce began an investigation into whether Japanese-made antifriction bearings were being dumped in the United States. In 1989, Commerce determined that Japanese manufacturers were dumping bearings and issued an anti-dumping order. *Antifriction Bearings (Other than Tapered Roller Bearings) & Parts Thereof from Japan*, 54 Fed. Reg. 19,101 (Dep't of Commerce May 3, 1989) (final determination). Commerce subjected the Japanese manufacturers to anti-dumping duties as follows: JTEKT, 73.55%; NSK, 42.99%; and NTN, 21.36%. *Id.* at 19,108.

Commerce must periodically reconsider such anti-dumping orders, 19 U.S.C. § 1675(c)(1), in what are termed "sunset reviews." *Agro Dutch Indus. v. United States*, 508 F.3d 1024, 1028 (Fed. Cir. 2007). On appeal are the results of the second sunset review of the anti-dumping order against Japanese antifriction bearing imports.

In late 2005, Commerce issued a preliminary second sunset review decision in which Commerce determined (1) that dumping was likely to continue, and (2) that the margins applicable to the Japanese companies should remain unchanged. *Ball Bearings & Parts Thereof from Japan & Sing.*, 70 Fed. Reg. 76,754 (Dep't of Commerce Dec. 28, 2005) (prelim. results); *Ball Bearings & Parts Thereof from Japan & Sing.*, 70 ITADOC 76,754, *available at* http://ia.ita.doc.gov/frn/summary/multiple/05-24510-1.pdf (Dep't of Commerce Dec. 28, 2005) (prelim. results memo.) ("Preliminary Memo").[2] Commerce based its preliminary decision to leave the anti-dumping order in place on its findings "that the total weight and value of complete Japanese ball bearings imported decreased substantially post-order and remain well below pre-order levels" and "that dumping continues at above de minimis levels." Preliminary Memo, slip op. at 10. Commerce based its preliminary decision to not recalculate the applicable margins on its finding that "above *de minimis*" dumping persisted with the order in place. *Id.* at 12.

1 NMB Singapore Ltd. is a Singaporean ball-bearing manufacturer that was involved in these proceedings before Commerce and the Court of International Trade, but is not a party to this appeal. Although Timken's cross-appeal challenging Commerce's recalculation of the anti-dumping duty applies to NTN, NTN did not participate in the appeal, either.

2 Commerce released a version of the Preliminary Memo to the parties on December 19, 2005.

Commerce thereafter received arguments from interested parties, including JTEKT and Timken. In a final decision released in the spring of 2006, Commerce reaffirmed—although with an altered rationale—that dumping was likely to continue (a finding JTEKT contests on appeal). *See Ball Bearings & Parts Thereof from Japan & Sing.*, 71 Fed. Reg. 26,321, 26,322 (Dep't of Commerce May 4, 2006) (final results) ("Final Results"); *Ball Bearings & Parts Thereof from Japan & Sing.*, http://ia.ita.doc.gov/frn/summary/MULTIPLE/E6-6763-1.pdf, slip op. at 5 (Dep't of Commerce May 4, 2006) (final results memo.) ("Final Memo").[3] Commerce mentioned only "above *de minimis*" levels of dumping in support of its final decision to leave the anti-dumping order in place, and did not discuss import volumes. Final Memo, slip op. at 5. Reversing course, Commerce also determined that the margins applicable to the Japanese respondents should be lower than before the anti-dumping order (a finding Timken contests). *See id.* at 7–10, 12. Commerce based this decision on its findings that the Japanese respondents' dumping margins had decreased during the order while their import volumes had increased or remained steady. *Id.* at 9–10.

The Court of International Trade affirmed Commerce's final decision in all respects. *NMB Singapore Ltd. v. United States*, 533 F. Supp. 2d 1244 (Ct. Int'l Trade 2007). We have jurisdiction over appeals from the Court of International Trade pursuant to 28 U.S.C. § 1295(a)(5).

II. Discussion

A. Standard of review

The Federal Circuit reviews Commerce's anti-dumping orders using the same standard of review used by the Court of International Trade. *NSK Ltd. v. United States*, 481 F.3d 1355, 1359 (Fed. Cir. 2007); *NTN Bearing Corp. of Am. v. United States*, 368 F.3d 1369, 1372 (Fed. Cir. 2004). This court will uphold Commerce's decisions unless they are "unsupported by substantial evidence on the record, or otherwise not in accordance with law." 19 U.S.C. § 1516a(b)(1)(B)(i); *see also Timken U.S. Corp. v. United States*, 434 F.3d 1345, 1350 (Fed. Cir. 2006).

Commerce must explain the basis for its decisions; while its explanations do not have to be perfect, the path of Commerce's decision must be reasonably discernable to a reviewing court. *Motor Vehicle Mfrs. Ass'n v. State Farm Mut. Auto. Ins. Co.*, 463 U.S. 29, 43, 103 S. Ct. 2856, 77 L. Ed. 2d 443 (1983) ("*State Farm*") ("We will . . . 'uphold a decision of less than ideal clarity if the agency's path may reasonably be discerned.'" (quoting *Bowman Transp. v. Ark.-Best Freight Sys.*, 419 U.S. 281, 286, 95 S. Ct. 438, 42 L. Ed. 2d 447 (1974))). Specifically in the anti-dumping context, a final determination by Commerce must include "an explanation of the basis for its determination that addresses relevant arguments[] made by interested parties who are parties to the investigation or review." 19 U.S.C.

3 Commerce released a version of the Final Memo to the parties on April 27, 2006.

§ 1677f(i)(3)(A). However, Congress did not intend for enactment of § 1677f(i) to alter the law; § 1677f(i) is instead a partial codification of the Supreme Court's standard for judicial review of administrative decisions from *State Farm. Timken U.S. Corp. v. United States*, 421 F.3d 1350, 1355 (Fed. Cir. 2005).

B. JTEKT's appeal

JTEKT makes two arguments against Commerce's decision to continue the anti-dumping order. First, JTEKT argues that Commerce did not consider—in violation of Commerce's statutory mandate—evidence JTEKT submitted, specifically, (1) JTEKT's evidence that its import levels did not decrease substantially and thus could be considered "steady" and (2) evidence that a U.S. recession caused decreases in JTEKT's import levels around 2001. Second, JTEKT argues that even if Commerce may disregard certain portions of JTEKT's evidence, Commerce's decision to continue the anti-dumping order is not supported by substantial evidence. However, these two arguments overlap and we address them simultaneously.[4] Both the United States and Timken oppose JTEKT on appeal.

In deciding whether lifting an anti-dumping order would be likely to lead to continued or resumed dumping, Commerce is required by statute to consider previous estimates of dumping margins and the volume of imports pre- and post-order. 19 U.S.C. § 1675a(c)(1). The statute does not explain how this comparison is to indicate to Commerce whether an anti-dumping order should be lifted, but a report by the House of Representatives on the Uruguay Round Agreements Act, H.R. Rep. No. 103-316 (1994), *as reprinted in* 1994 U.S.C.C.A.N. 4040, commonly known as the Statement of Administrative Action (or "SAA"), is, by statute, an "authoritative expression" of the interpretation of that act, including § 1675a. 19 U.S.C. § 3512(d); *see also Timken*, 421 F.3d at 1354 n.2. According to the SAA, "declining (or no) dumping margins accompanied by steady or increasing imports may indicate that foreign companies do not have to dump to maintain market share in the United States and that dumping is less likely to continue or recur if the order were revoked." 1994 U.S.C.C.A.N. at 4213–14.

A regulation provides that Commerce "will revoke" an anti-dumping order during a sunset review if Commerce "determines that revocation or termination is not likely to lead to continuation or recurrence of . . . dumping." 19 C.F.R. § 351.222(i)(1)(ii). The SAA provides:

> The Administration believes that *existence of dumping margins* after the order, or the cessation of imports after the order, *is highly probative of the likelihood of continuation or recurrence of dumping*. If companies continue to dump with the discipline of an

4 At oral argument, JTEKT asserted that Commerce's reasoning was "opaque" and clarified that JTEKT was not asking this court to hold outright that Commerce should have lifted the anti-dumping order, but that JTEKT was asking this court to vacate Commerce's decision to leave the anti-dumping order in place and remand the matter to Commerce with instructions to provide a sufficient explanation of whatever new decision Commerce reached.

> order in place, it is reasonable to assume that dumping would continue if the discipline were removed.

1994 U.S.C.C.A.N. at 4214 (emphasis added). A similar standard is set forth in Commerce's *Sunset Policy Bulletin*[5]:

> [T]he Department normally will determine that revocation of an antidumping order or termination of a suspended dumping investigation is likely to lead to continuation or recurrence of dumping where—
>
> (a) *dumping continued at any level above de minimis after the issuance of the order* or the suspension agreement, as applicable;
>
> . . .

63 Fed. Reg. at 18,872 (emphasis added).

JTEKT argues that it submitted comments and evidence regarding import levels to Commerce, but that Commerce ignored JTEKT's import levels in violation of § 1675a(c). Specifically, JTEKT points to the weight and dollar value of all ball bearings imported from Japan into the United States, and compares the average values for the two years before the anti-dumping order (1987 and 1988) with average values for the five years of the sunset review period (2000 through 2004). By weight, average annual Japanese ball bearing imports for 2000 through 2004 were 90 percent of the levels for 1987 and 1988; by dollar value, 126 percent.[6] JTEKT does not argue that this particular method of comparison is required; JTEKT does argue that these data show Commerce could not have reasonably determined that

---

5 *Policies Regarding the Conduct of Five-year ("Sunset") Reviews of Antidumping & Countervailing Duty Orders*, 63 Fed. Reg. 18,871 (Imp. Admin., Int'l Trade Admin., Dep't of Commerce Apr. 16, 1998).

6 Using 1988 as a baseline, the relative values for each year, considered individually, are as follows:

Year	*Weight*	*Dollar value*
1987	76%	72%
1988	100%	100%
2000	91%	135%
2001	75%	110%
2002	71%	98%
2003	76%	94%
2004	84%	105%

Although the parties have not requested confidential treatment of this particular set of data, the issues on appeal focus on relative trends rather than absolute numbers. For ease of comparison and to protect the confidentiality of data elsewhere in the opinion, we will use relative figures throughout. At oral argument, when asked by the court if using percentages in an opinion would be acceptable, counsel for JTEKT stated "I think that would be okay but I would want to take a look at the record and—and discuss internally." The court has not heard further from the parties regarding this issue in the more than two months since oral argument.

import levels decreased after the anti-dumping order issued, and JTEKT states that Commerce should have explained why it did not agree with JTEKT's analysis.[7]

Commerce did discuss import levels in the Preliminary Memo, slip op. at 10, but omitted any such analysis from the Final Memo, *see* slip op. at 4–5. While in the Final Memo Commerce acknowledged that it is to consider import levels, Commerce also stated, "Normally, the Department will determine that revocation of an antidumping duty order is likely to lead to continuation or recurrence of dumping where dumping continued at any level above *de minimis* after the issuance of the order." Final Memo, slip op. at 4. Commerce justified its finding of a likelihood of continued dumping with the following paragraph:

> The calculated margins in the investigation and fifteen subsequent antidumping administrative reviews for ball bearings from Japan have been above *de minimis* for NSK, NTN, and [JTEKT]. Given that dumping continued with the discipline of the orders in place, it is reasonable to assume dumping would continue if the orders were removed. Therefore, we find that revocation of the orders would likely lead to continuation of dumping.

Id. at 5.

When upholding Commerce's decision on this point, the Court of International Trade stated that Commerce had considered volume: "Here, Commerce determined that dumping continued above *de minimis* levels and identified a steady decrease in import volumes and therefore reasonably concluded that dumping was likely to recur." *NMB Singapore*, 533 F. Supp. 2d at 1255. The United States likewise indicates on appeal that Commerce did consider JTEKT's volume information when deciding whether to continue the anti-dumping order. Both the Court of International Trade and the United States cite to the Preliminary Memo to support their assertions that Commerce considered import levels; they do not address the absence of such analysis from the Final Memo. In contrast, JTEKT argues that the Preliminary Memo is only incorporated into the Final Memo where Commerce does so expressly, e.g., "For the reasons we discuss above in response to the comments of the Japanese respondents, we affirm our decision in the *Preliminary Sunset Results*." Final Memo, slip op. at 6 (discussing likelihood of continued dumping by Singaporean companies).

The parties have not made clear whether Commerce's final results should be considered a *replacement for* the preliminary results, or instead an *addition to* them;[8]

---

7 JTEKT appears to recognize that for it to ultimately prevail, Commerce must find, inter alia, that Japanese imports of ball bearings have been "steady or increasing" since the anti-dumping order took effect. *See* SAA, 1994 U.S.C.C.A.N. at 4213–14.

8 Commerce's regulations generally require Commerce to issue preliminary and final results when reviewing anti-dumping orders, 19 C.F.R. § 351.221(b)(4)–(5), although in certain circumstances, Commerce may issue only final results when conducting a sunset review, 19 C.F.R. § 351.221(c)(5)(ii). The *content* of these results, however, does not appear to be specified by regulation.

or, more narrowly, whether Commerce's discussion of import volumes only in its Preliminary Memo comports with the mandate of § 1675a(c)(1)(B). Even if we assume that—as JTEKT implies—only Commerce's Final Results and Final Memo are the proper subjects of our review, we may, as explained below, nonetheless affirm Commerce's decision to leave the anti-dumping order in place.

Timken points out that it is consistent with the SAA for Commerce to leave the anti-dumping order in place based solely on Commerce's finding that above de minimis levels of dumping persisted in spite of the anti-dumping order. JTEKT does not address the fact that Commerce's determination that dumping is likely to continue without an anti-dumping order based solely on above de minimis dumping during the review period is consistent with not only the SAA, but also the *Sunset Policy Bulletin* and Commerce's past practice.[9] Because JTEKT does not challenge the validity of the SAA or the *Sunset Policy Bulletin*, we assume they are valid. Thus, we reject JTEKT's contention that the absence of discussion of import levels from Commerce's Final Memo by itself constitutes reversible error.

Because we agree Commerce could permissibly decide to leave the anti-dumping order in place based solely on its finding of the persistence of dumping, we need not address JTEKT's argument that the conflict between Commerce's finding in the Preliminary Memo that imports had "decreased substantially" (in connection with its decision to leave the anti-dumping order in place) and Commerce's finding in the Final Memo that imports remained at a "steady level" (in connection with its decision to recalculate the likely margin of dumping) renders Commerce's decision to leave the anti-dumping order in place unsupported by substantial evidence. *Compare* Preliminary Memo, slip op. at 10, *with* Final Memo, slip op. at 10. Similarly, JTEKT's argument that Commerce did not consider "relevant arguments . . . made by interested parties" (including JTEKT's arguments that import volumes were affected by a recession) as required by § 1677f(i)(3)(A) fails because we agree the persistence of dumping alone was sufficient to justify Commerce's decision in these circumstances. We have previously held that § 1677f(i) does not require us to invalidate a decision of Commerce if Commerce failed to explicitly address a party's non-dispositive argument. *See Timken*, 421 F.3d at 1357. While a more substantial explanation from Commerce might have been helpful to us or preferable to JTEKT, its absence here is not grounds for us not to affirm because we can nonetheless reasonably discern the path of Commerce's decision. *See State Farm*, 463 U.S. at 43.

---

9 *See, e.g.*, *Ball Bearings from Sing.*, 64 Fed. Reg. 60,287, 60,295 (Dep't of Commerce Nov. 4, 1999) (final results) ("Regardless of the level of imports, dumping margins above de minimis levels continue as do imports of the subject merchandise; dumping continues to exist."); *Certain Iron Constr. Castings from Braz.*, Can. & P.R.C., 64 Fed. Reg. 30,310, 30,311 (Dep't of Commerce Jun. 7, 1999) (final results) (Commerce "indicated that normally it will determine that revocation of an antidumping order is likely to lead to continuation or recurrence of dumping when . . . dumping continued at any level above de minimis after the issuance of the order.").

C. Timken's cross-appeal

Although defending Commerce's determination to continue the anti-dumping order, Timken attacks a different facet of Commerce's decision, namely, Commerce's recalculation (and lowering) of the anti-dumping margins applicable to the Japanese parties. Timken argues that (1) substantial evidence does not support Commerce's finding that imports by the three Japanese parties had remained steady or increased, (2) Commerce's methodology for determining import levels was an unexplained—and therefore impermissible—departure from Commerce's established past practice, and (3) Commerce's method of determining market share was likewise an unexplained departure from established past practice. Timken's cross-appeal is opposed by the United States, JTEKT, and NSK.

1. Evidence of increasing imports

Commerce ordinarily assumes that if an anti-dumping order is lifted, exporters will resume dumping at the same margins that existed before the anti-dumping order was in place. SAA, 1994 U.S.C.C.A.N. at 4214 ("The Administration intends that Commerce normally will select the rate from the investigation, because that is the only calculated rate that reflects the behavior of exporters and foreign governments without the discipline of an order or suspension agreement in place."). The parties agree, however, that if an exporter's volume of goods has been steady or increasing and its margin of dumping has been steady or decreasing over the life of an anti-dumping order, Commerce may instead calculate a new margin based on more recent data and assume this would be the margin after an anti-dumping order was lifted. *See id.* ("For example, if dumping margins have declined over the life of an order and imports have remained steady or increased, Commerce may conclude that exporters are likely to continue dumping at the lower rates found in a more recent review.").

The Japanese respondents submitted confidential sales data to Commerce. Commerce summarized these data as follows:

> The Department also analyzed each respondent's submission that reported its relative market share of imports of subject merchandise from Japan to the United States for the five-year sunset review period. NSK's *import volumes* since the issuance of the order and *market share* of imports, *as measured in complete bearings*, have remained steady or increased during the sunset review period. Likewise, NTN has maintained the level of its *market share* of imports and *import volumes* since the issuance of the order over the past five years with *negligible fluctuations*. [JTEKT]'s *market share* of imports and *level of imports* since the issuance of the order also have remained steady over the same five-year period. The information provided by the parties reflects a steady level of exports of subject merchandise to the United States from Japan.

Final Memo, slip op. at 9–10 (footnotes omitted; emphasis added). We note that Commerce specified it relied upon data on "complete bearings" for NSK,[10] but did not specify the type of data it relied upon for JTEKT or NTN.

10 NSK also provided Commerce with data for the sunset review period on import volumes of bearing parts, as well as dollar values for finished bearing and bearing part imports,

The data for NSK's shipments of ball bearings to the United States, using 2000 as a baseline, are as follows:

Year	*Finished bearings (units)*	*Finished bearings (dollars)*	*Bearing parts (units)*	*Bearing parts (dollars)*	*Total bearings (units)*	*Total bearings (dollars)*	*Share of Japanese exports*
2000	100%	100%	100%	100%	100%	100%	100%
2001	54%	67%	91%	120%	88%	79%	105%
2002	55%	61%	96%	124%	93%	75%	114%
2003	48%	48%	79%	118%	77%	64%	95%
2004	61%	52%	108%	141%	105%	72%	134%

Aside from a downward drop from 2002 to 2003, NSK's share of the Japanese export market increased year to year during the sunset review period.[11]

NSK argues that, although its levels of finished bearings dropped significantly from 2000 to 2001, its levels from 2001 through 2004 were steady, and since these four years were the ones "closest to the time in which the order would be revoked" it would be reasonable to disregard 2000. It is not at all apparent that Commerce analyzed NSK's finished bearing data in this manner. Because, however, there are methodological flaws in Commerce's analysis (as discussed below in parts II.C.2 and 3), it is irrelevant whether Commerce's findings regarding NSK's import levels are supported by substantial evidence.

---

but Commerce did not discuss this data in the Final Memo. Since the anti-dumping order applies to ball bearings and ball bearing parts, *Antifriction Bearings (Other than Tapered Roller Bearings) & Parts Thereof from Japan*, 54 Fed. Reg. at 19,101, it seems unusual that Commerce would, without explanation, not consider total levels of finished bearings and bearing parts when determining whether imports of the subject merchandise have increased or remained steady. At oral argument, the United States indicated that data on imports of finished bearings and bearing parts was not available for all three Japanese respondents. NTN and JTEKT did provide such data. While NSK provided separate tables for finished bearings and bearing parts for the sunset review period, it is a matter of simple addition to calculate total levels from these two tables. What NSK did not provide was complete pre-order data; NSK stated that it only had available data from 1987 on finished ball bearings.

11 As noted in footnote 7, above, throughout this opinion we use relative figures. In the case of the above table and the seven other tables in the opinion, we have arrived at relative figures by extrapolating from the absolute numbers in the record. Those absolute numbers, the parties have informed us, are confidential. We present the relative figures in the opinion in an effort to demonstrate what the confidential absolute numbers clearly reflect. Our selection of baseline years used to calculate the percentages in the charts was done for ease of comparison and may not necessarily reflect the methodology Commerce used in drawing its conclusions. Unless explicitly addressed in this opinion, our selection of baseline years should be considered immaterial. For example, we do not mean to suggest merely by using a certain year as a baseline that Commerce should consider that year the starting point for its analysis.

The data for JTEKT's shipments of ball bearings to the United States, using 2000 as a baseline, are as follows:

Year	*Finished bearings (units)*	*Finished bearings (dollars)*	*Bearing parts (units)*	*Bearing parts (dollars)*	*Total bearings (units)*	*Total bearings (dollars)*	*Share of Japanese exports*
2000	100%	100%	100%	100%	100%	100%	100%
2001	106%	100%	48%	53%	73%	98%	87%
2002	113%	85%	11%	19%	54%	81%	66%
2003	87%	91%	9%	15%	42%	87%	53%
2004	96%	118%	9%	13%	46%	111%	59%

Aside from a slight uptick from 2003 to 2004, JTEKT's share of the Japanese export market declined for the entire sunset review period. JTEKT's share in 2004 was 59 percent of what it was in 2000. Commerce's finding that JTEKT's "market share of imports . . . have remained steady over the . . . five-year period," Final Memo, slip op. at 10, lacks substantial evidentiary support.

Commerce did not specify what data it was using to determine JTEKT's "level of imports," but Commerce did find JTEKT's imports "remained steady." *Id.* JTEKT's volume of finished bearings was not completely steady over the sunset review period (and drops noticeably from 2002 to 2003), but provides the most support for a finding that JTEKT's import levels were "steady." Other possible measures, such as the number of bearing parts or the total number of bearings and bearing parts sold, clearly do not support such a finding. As with NSK, it is irrelevant to the outcome whether we could affirm this particular finding in isolation for the reasons discussed below in parts II.C.2 and 3.

The data for NTN's shipments of ball bearings to the United States, using 2000[12] as a baseline, are as follows:

Year	*Finished bearings (units)*	*Finished bearings (dollars)*	*Bearing parts (units)*	*Bearing parts (dollars)*	*Total bearings (units)*	*Total bearings (dollars)*	*Share of Japanese exports*
2000	100%	100%	100%	100%	100%	100%	100%
2001	125%	97%	56%	111%	68%	98%	90%
2002	224%	89%	84%	264%	107%	99%	88%
2003	187%	93%	16%	246%	45%	101%	116%
2004	150%	107%	24%	238%	45%	115%	57%

12 NTN's data is reported for a fiscal year beginning with the fourth quarter of the listed year and running through the third quarter of the following year.

While NTN's share of the Japanese export market was relatively stable from 2000 through 2003, NTN's market share halved from 2003 to 2004. Commerce's finding that "NTN has maintained the level of its market share of imports . . . since the issuance of the order over the past five years with negligible fluctuations," Final Memo, slip op. at 9–10, lacks substantial evidentiary support.

As with JTEKT, Commerce did not specify what data it was using to determine NTN's import volumes. NTN's volume of finished bearings more than doubled from 2000 to 2002, and then fell back to 50 percent over the 2000 level—also hardly "negligible fluctuations." At oral argument, the United States indicated that an arrow drawn in the margin of the table of data NTN provided (and pointing to the line for total bearings and parts numbers) showed that Commerce had considered total numbers of bearings and parts for NTN. The United States also suggested that Commerce had considered for NTN just the "stabilization" of the levels of total bearings from 2003 to 2004. The least fluctuating figures NTN provided were for dollar values of total bearings sold. Commerce, however, said it was considering NTN's "import volumes," implying number of units sold, rather than total dollar value sold. Furthermore, it would seem incongruous for Commerce to consider numbers of finished bearings sold for JTEKT and NSK, but without explanation, dollar value of total bearings sold for NTN. We thus must hold that Commerce's finding on this point is not supported by substantial evidence.

Looking at Commerce's findings as a whole, it is difficult to square many of Commerce's statements that the Japanese importers' levels of imports were steady or increasing with the actual data before Commerce, even if we accepted the arguments that Commerce could permissibly consider different types of import data and different segments of the five-year review period for different importers while ignoring pre-order levels. This is a situation in which we cannot reasonably discern Commerce's path because there does not appear to be a reasonable way to consider the data as a whole and arrive at Commerce's conclusion that dumping margins should be recalculated. *See State Farm*, 463 U.S. at 43.

2. Consideration of pre-order levels

Timken also argues that Commerce should have considered not just 2000 through 2004 data in isolation, but should have compared data for these years to data from before the anti-dumping order to determine whether import volumes from Japan were steady or increasing. Or, to state Timken's argument more directly, just because imports were steady or increasing from 2000 to 2004 is not sufficient for Commerce to declare them steady or increasing for purposes of the second sunset review—imports must also have been steady or increasing during the review period compared to 1987 or 1988. According to Timken, Commerce has established a clear practice of comparing imports during a sunset review period to pre-order levels and has not explained why it did not in the instant matter.[13]

---

13 Although Timken argued in its opening brief that Commerce lacks the discretion not to consider pre-order export volumes when determining whether export volumes have increased or remained steady, Timken appears to have abandoned this argument in its reply.

As a threshold matter, NSK argues that Commerce indeed considered pre-order levels because pre-order data appear in the attachments to Commerce's memo and Commerce even rearranged some of the data submitted by the parties so that 2000 through 2004 data appeared on the same page as pre-order data. However, the actual discussion of import levels (the paragraph quoted above on page 13) is limited solely to 2000 to 2004.[14] In any event, as discussed below, merely looking at such data but not relying on them when determining how import levels are changing would be contrary to Commerce's established practice.[15]

The parties did not each provide exactly the same type of pre-order data. JTEKT and NSK provided data from 1987, while NTN provided data from 1988.[16] JTEKT's preorder data included units and dollar figures for finished bearings, bearing parts, and total bearings. NSK's pre-order data were only for finished bearings, and NTN's was only for total bearings. Using each company's pre-order data as a baseline, the Japanese respondents' import figures generally show declines in numbers of bearings imported but have mixed results for changes in dollar value of bearings imported:

JTEKT

Year	*Finished bearings (units)*	*Finished bearings (dollars)*	*Bearing parts (units)*	*Bearing parts (dollars)*	*Total bearings (units)*	*Total bearings (dollars)*
1987	100%	100%	100%	100%	100%	100%
2000	65%	130%	21%	200%	30%	133%
2001	70%	131%	10%	107%	22%	130%
2002	74%	111%	2%	38%	16%	108%
2003	57%	119%	2%	31%	12%	115%
2004	63%	153%	2%	26%	14%	148%

14 Additionally, for each of the Japanese respondents, Commerce stated it considered import volumes "since the issuance of the order." The language "since the issuance of the order" refers to the period of time during which an anti-dumping order is in effect, not the period before the order.

15 The United States argues—incorrectly—that the Court of International Trade addressed Timken's argument that Commerce had to consider pre-order volumes and rejected Timken's position, citing *NMB Singapore*, 533 F. Supp. 2d at 1258–59. The cited portion of the Court of International Trade's opinion, however, does not contain any analysis of this issue.

16 NTN and NSK indicated that their data were for fiscal years, while JTEKT indicated its data were for a calendar year.

NSK

Year	*Finished bearings (units)*	*Finished bearings (dollars)*
1987	100%	100%
2000	124%	180%
2001	67%	122%
2002	69%	110%
2003	60%	87%
2004	76%	94%

NTN

Year	*Total bearings (units)*	*Total bearings (dollars)*
1988	100%	100%
2000	208%	65%
2001	141%	63%
2002	222%	64%
2003	93%	65%
2004	93%	74%

Notably, JTEKT's imports of total bearings fell by over two-thirds from 1987 to 2000, and fell by over half from 2000 to 2004. The trends for NSK and NTN are less pronounced; both had increased numbers of units sold early in the sunset review period compared to before the anti-dumping order, but both finished the sunset review period importing fewer units than before the anti-dumping order.

Pursuant to 19 U.S.C. § 1675a(c)(1)(B), when determining whether dumping is likely to recur if an anti-dumping order is terminated, Commerce is required to consider, inter alia, "the volume of imports of the subject merchandise for the period before and the period after the issuance of the antidumping duty order or acceptance of the suspension agreement." Under 19 U.S.C. § 1675a(c)(3), Commerce is to determine what the margin of dumping is likely to be if an anti-dumping order is lifted. The margin is "normally" the one determined in the original, pre-order investigation, but Commerce is not directed by statute to consider any specific factors in determining the likely margin. *Id.*

The SAA explains that, "[f]or example, if dumping margins have declined over the life of an order and imports have remained steady or increased, Commerce may conclude that exporters are likely to continue dumping at the lower rates found in a more recent review." 1994 U.S.C.C.A.N. at 4214. The plain language of this report— "over the life of an order"—refers only to the period of time during which an anti-dumping order is in effect, not the period of time before the order.

Because, however, Commerce is not acting in the first instance, we need not decide whether Commerce would be required by statute or the SAA to consider preorder volumes when determining whether exports have remained steady or increased. Commerce, like any agency, is due deference from the courts in certain matters entrusted to it by Congress. *See Br. Steel PLC v. United States*, 127 F.3d 1471, 1475 (Fed. Cir. 1997). Once Commerce establishes a course of action, however, Commerce is obliged to follow it until Commerce provides a sufficient, reasoned analysis explaining why a change is necessary. *See id.; see also Save Domestic Oil, Inc. v. United States*, 357 F.3d 1278, 1283–84 (Fed. Cir. 2004) ("[I]f Commerce has a routine practice for addressing like situations, it must either apply that practice or provide a reasonable explanation as to why it departs therefrom.").

Timken points to a number of Commerce decisions that Timken claims support its course-of-action theory. Although many of the cases Timken cites do not address the issue clearly, those that do indicate that Timken is correct that Commerce ordinarily compares pre-order volumes to volumes during the life of an anti-dumping order, rather than just considers volumes during the life of an anti-dumping order in isolation.

For example, in *Antifriction Bearings from Romania*, Commerce issued an anti-dumping order in 1989. 64 Fed. Reg. 60,313, 60,314 (Nov. 4, 1999) (final results). Commerce noted that imports of ball bearings from Romania "declined significantly since 1988, dropping from 13.5 million units to 0.7 million units. Although imports increased to 2.5 million units in 1997, they remain significantly below pre-order volumes." *Id.* at 60,316–17. Thus, Commerce was faced with a situation where levels of imports were increasing during the life of the anti-dumping order, yet were still below pre-order levels. During the order, dumping margins were consistently "below de minimis levels." *Id.* at 60,317. Commerce nonetheless concluded that this did not present a situation warranting recalculation of the dumping margins because import levels were not steady or increasing. *Id.*

Similarly, in *Corrosion-Resistant Carbon Steel Flat Products from Japan*, Commerce rejected a party's contention that an increase just during the life of an order was sufficient to recalculate dumping margins; Commerce rejected this argument because the import levels were less during the order than they were pre-order.[17] In other decisions Timken cites, that import levels were lower during the anti-dumping order than before the order was a factor in Commerce's decision, although this was not the sole reason Commerce gave for leaving the anti-dumping

17 http://ia.ita.doc.gov/frn/summary/japan/00-19562-1.txt (Dep't of Commerce Aug. 2, 2000) (final results memo.).

orders in place.[18] Other decisions Timken cites were made after the decision Timken is appealing, so these cases do not prove that Commerce went against an established policy in the matter on appeal; however, in each of these cases, Commerce decided against recalculating dumping margins because import levels during the order were less than import levels pre-order.[19] No party cites any case in which Commerce has rejected the idea that import levels during an anti-dumping order should be compared to pre-order import levels.

Timken is therefore correct that Commerce's focus in this case on only import volumes during the life of the anti-dumping order—instead of a comparison of such volumes to pre-order volumes—is a deviation from an otherwise consistent practice of Commerce. The decision of the Court of International Trade affirming Commerce must be vacated so that Commerce can reconsider its analysis of this issue accordingly.

3. Share of Japanese exports

Timken also argues that Commerce, for the purpose of determining whether to recalculate dumping margins, has a clearly established policy of using measurements other than a company's share of exports to the United States from its home country as the measure of import levels.[20]

In connection with Commerce's determination whether to rely on an old margin or calculate a new one, 19 U.S.C. § 1675a(c)(3) does not direct Commerce to consider any particular factors. However, the SAA notes that "declining (or no) dumping margins accompanied by steady or increasing imports may indicate that foreign companies do not have to dump to maintain *market share in the United States*." 1994 U.S.C.C.A.N. at 4213–14 (emphasis added). The parties do not point to any

---

18 *Certain Stainless Steel Sheet & Strip in Coils from Mex.*, http://ia.ita.doc.gov/frn/summary/mexico/E5-514-1.pdf, at 4 (Dep't of Commerce Feb. 8, 2005) (final results memo.); *Fresh & Chilled Atlantic Salmon from Nor.*, http://ia.ita.doc.gov/frn/summary/norway/E5-8136-1.pdf, at 8 (Dep't of Commerce Dec. 30, 2005) (final results memo.).

19 *Canned Pineapple Fruit from Thail.*, http://ia.ita.doc.gov/frn/summary/THAILAND/E7-3891-1.pdf, at 4 (Dep't of Commerce Mar. 6, 2007) (final results memo.); *Honey from Arg. & P.R.C.*, http://ia.ita.doc.gov/frn/summary/MULTIPLE/E7-4052-1.pdf, at 11 (Dep't of Commerce Mar. 7, 2007) (final results memo.); *Carbon & Certain Alloy Steel Wire Rod from Braz., Can., Indon., Mex., Mold., Trin. & Tobago, & Ukr.*, http://ia.ita.doc.gov/frn/summary/MULTIPLE/E8-114-1.pdf, at 14 (Dep't of Commerce Dec. 31, 2007) (final results memo.).

20 Timken also argues that using market share of Japanese exports to the United States as a proxy for U.S. market share "makes no sense" and points out that it would be possible for total Japanese exports to the United States to decline significantly but for an individual manufacturer's share of Japanese exports to remain steady or even increase significantly. The other parties do not dispute that changes in a manufacturer's share of Japanese exports to the United States do not necessarily correspond to changes in its U.S. market share. It appears that export market share may be a poor proxy. However, because the path of Commerce's decision is unclear, we need not decide if or under what circumstances share of exports to the United States may be considered a reasonable proxy for share of the U.S. market.

controlling document that further explains the meaning of "market share" in this context. Timken, however, argues that "market share in the United States" makes it inappropriate for Commerce to use a measure from some foreign market, and furthermore that Commerce's prior decisions preclude it from using respondents' shares of Japanese ball bearing exports as a proxy for their shares of the U.S. ball bearing market.

The relative data for each Japanese respondent's share of the U.S. import market for the subject goods are—using 2000 as a baseline for each company—as follows:

Year	*JTEKT*	*NSK*	*NTN*
2000	100%	100%	100%
2001	87%	105%	90%
2002	66%	114%	88%
2003	53%	95%	116%
2004	59%	134%	57%

(As noted above, even assuming that such data are properly considered instead of the U.S. market share, the declines experienced by JTEKT and NTN during the sunset review period cannot reasonably be considered "steady or increasing.")

Commerce does recognize there is a difference between an importer's share of exports from its country and U.S. market share: "[A]lthough there would be a correlation between a company's share of total subject exports and its share of the U.S. market, we do not agree that a company's share of exports is the same as its relative market share."[21] Commerce has explained that

> in analyzing whether imports [sic] volumes remained steady or increased, the Department normally will consider the company's relative market share. The emphasis on the market share of an importer derives from the SAA, which states that declining (or no) dumping margins accompanied by steady or increasing imports may indicate that foreign companies do not have to dump to maintain *market share in the United States*.[22]

The other parties cite to only one case in which Commerce has clearly relied on relative export data as a proxy for U.S. market share, and this case post-dates the decision under appeal.[23]

---

21 *Tapered Roller Bearings from P.R.C.*, 65 ITADOC 11,550 (Dep't of Commerce Mar. 3, 2000) (final results memo.).

22 *Corrosion-Resistant Carbon Steel Flat Products from Can.*, 65 ITADOC 47,379 (Dep't of Commerce Aug. 2, 2000) (final results memo.) (emphasis added).

23 *Oil Country Tubular Goods from Mex.*, http://ia.ita.doc.gov/frn/summary/MEXICO/E6-22076-1.pdf (Dep't of Commerce Dec. 26, 2006) (prelim. results memo.). There, Commerce based its

Thus, if it is the case that the U.S. market share of the Japanese companies could be determined from the data before Commerce, then Commerce's determination went against the practice it had established as of the time of the decision under review.[24] Commerce, however, has noted that its analysis is driven by the information parties submit: "[I]n determining whether a more recently calculated margin is probative of an exporters's [sic] behavior absent the discipline of an order, we will normally consider the company's relative market share, *with such information to be provided by the parties*."[25] Commerce is, in some circumstances, able to determine U.S. market share from other data.[26]

Commerce did not state in this instance whether it was able to determine the U.S. market share of each of the Japanese respondents. However, the record contains a table entitled "BBs - Apparent Consumption and Imports from Japan as a Share Thereof," which lists dollar values of total imports of ball bearings from Japan for 1987 through 1990 and 2000 through 2004. While it appears to us that it may be possible to estimate each Japanese company's share of the U.S. market by combining these data with each company's percentage share of Japanese exports to the United States, Commerce did not discuss this, and we may not make such a factual determination in the first instance. *See Mittal Steel Point Lisas Ltd. v. United States*, 542 F.3d 867, 875 (Fed. Cir. 2008) ("Appellate courts do not make factual findings; they review them."). Because we cannot discern whether Commerce's finding on this issue is contrary to its past practice or supported by substantial

---

analysis on a manufacturer's relative share of its country's exports to the United States rather than the manufacturer's share of the U.S. market:

> In determining whether import volumes remained steady or increased, pursuant to the SAA, the Department will also normally consider a company's relative market share. During the investigation, Hylsa accounted for less than 40 percent of all shipments of OCTG from Mexico to the United States. In 2005, Hylsa accounted for more than 50 percent of all shipments of OCTG from Mexico to the United States. The dumping margins for sales by Hylsa during the Second Sunset Review period are substantially below those of the "all others" rate in the investigation, the rate applied to exports by Hylsa after the publication of the order. Thus, the lower dumping margins for Hylsa's sales in the Second Sunset Review period occurred while Hylsa increased shipments of OCTG from Mexico to the United States and captured larger market share of the Mexican OCTG market in the United States. Therefore, we find that a more recent rate obtained in an administrative review is a more appropriate rate for Hylsa in this sunset review.

Id. at 15–16 (citations and footnote omitted).

24 Additionally, if the Japanese respondents' shares of the U.S. market could be estimated from the available data and were shown to have decreased during the sunset review period, we would have concerns about whether Commerce's findings that their market shares were steady or increasing were supported by substantial evidence.

25 *Certain Circular Welded Non-Alloy Steel Pipe From Braz., S. Korea, Mex., Taiwan, & Venez.*, 64 Fed. Reg. 67,854, 67,858 (Dep't of Commerce Dec. 3, 1999) (final results) (emphasis added).

26 *See Aramid Fiber Formed of Poly Para-Phenylene Terephthalamide from Neth.*, 65 ITADOC 65,294 (Dep't of Commerce Nov. 1, 2000) (final results memo.).

evidence, we must vacate and remand. *Atchison, Topeka & Santa Fe Ry. Co. v. Wichita Bd. of Trade*, 412 U.S. 800, 808, 93 S. Ct. 2367, 37 L. Ed. 2d 350 (1973) ("Whatever the ground for the departure from prior norms, however, it must be clearly set forth so that the reviewing court may understand the basis of the agency's action and so may judge the consistency of that action with the agency's mandate.").

CONCLUSION

For the reasons provided above, we affirm the Court of International Trade's decision affirming Commerce's determination to leave the anti-dumping order in place, but vacate and remand the Court of International Trade's decision affirming Commerce's recalculation of the anti-dumping duties for to JTEKT, NTN, and NSK.

AFFIRMED-IN-PART and VACATED-AND-REMANDED-IN-PART

PAM, S.P.A.
v.
UNITED STATES

582 F.3d 1336 (Fed. Cir. 2009)
Decided September 24, 2009

David L. Simon, Law Office of David L. Simon, of Washington, DC, argued for plaintiff-appellant.

Jane C. Dempsey, Attorney, Commercial Litigation Branch, Civil Division, United States Department of Justice, of Washington, DC, argued for defendant-appellee United States. With her on the brief were Michael F. Hertz, Assistant Attorney General, Jeanne E. Davidson, Director, and Reginald T. Blades, Jr., Assistant Director.

Mary T. Staley, Kelley Drye & Warren LLP, of Washington, DC, argued for defendants-appellees American Italian Pasta Company, et al. With her on the brief were David C. Smith, Jr. and Paul C. Rosenthal.

Before MICHEL, Chief Judge, LOURIE, Circuit Judge, and CLARK, District Judge.*

* Honorable Ron Clark, District Judge, United States District Court for the Eastern District of Texas, sitting by designation.

CLARK, *District Judge*.

Appellant PAM, S.p.A. ("PAM") appeals from a final judgment of the United States Court of International Trade ("CIT") concerning pasta imported into the United States by PAM. The CIT affirmed a remand determination issued by the Department of Commerce ("Commerce") in compliance with the CIT's earlier order directing Commerce to explain and recalculate an adverse-facts-available ("AFA") antidumping margin, which had been corroborated in accordance with 19 U.S.C. § 1677e(c). Because the 45.49% AFA margin assessed against PAM is supported by substantial evidence, we *affirm*.

I. Background

PAM is an Italian producer and exporter of pasta. PAM's pasta is the subject of a 1996 Commerce antidumping order. *Notice of Antidumping Duty Order and Amended Final Determination of Sales at Less than Fair Value: Certain Pasta from Italy*, 61 Fed. Reg. 38,547-01 (Dep't of Commerce July 24, 1996). PAM participated in the sixth administrative review of this antidumping order between July 1, 2001 and June 30, 2002, during which it filed questionnaire responses and participated in verification of its sales databases.

PAM failed to report its sales to one customer, AGEA, a governmental entity that buys pasta for distribution to charitable causes rather than for commercial resale. PAM also neglected to include a set of invoices with the prefix "FP," which denote invoices for goods shipped from an external warehouse to the customer. The AGEA and FP sales combined amounted to about two-thirds of PAM's total domestic sales.

Commerce found that PAM had not fully cooperated in the sixth administrative review, and applied an AFA margin. *Notice of Preliminary Results: For the Sixth Administrative Review of the Antidumping Duty Order on Certain Pasta from Italy*, 68 Fed. Reg. 47,020-02 (Dep't of Commerce Aug. 7, 2003). Commerce assessed an AFA margin of 45.49%, the highest margin applied to any party that had been previously upheld in the proceeding.[1]

PAM appealed to the CIT, arguing that the 45.49% AFA margin was unlawful for a number of reasons. The CIT found that Commerce had not adequately corroborated the AFA margin applied to PAM and remanded. In doing so, it stated that Commerce must select a margin that is a reasonably accurate estimate of PAM's actual rate, not merely one that is related to the overall level of dumping during the period of review. Because Commerce did not explain how the other respondents' transaction-specific margins were related to PAM's dumping activity during the period of review, the CIT concluded that the 45.49% margin appeared punitive and aberrational. The CIT remanded for Commerce "to explain and recalculate an adverse facts available rate that is corroborated in accordance with 19 U.S.C. § 1677e(c)."

On remand, Commerce used PAM's databases from the fourth administrative review—in which PAM was also a respondent—and found the 45.49% AFA margin it had assessed in the sixth administrative review was corroborated by United States sales in the fourth review with margins in excess of 45.49%. On appeal to the CIT, PAM argued that these sales were unrepresentative outliers (i.e., statistical anomalies). The CIT disagreed, and affirmed Commerce's findings.

---

1 The rate was applied to Barilla, five years earlier in the first administrative review in 1995–97, and was affirmed on appeal by the CIT. *World Finer Foods, Inc. v. United States,* 120 F. Supp. 2d 1131, 1134, 24 Ct. Int'l Trade 1235 (Ct. Int'l Trade 2000). The same rate was also applied to Barilla in the fourth administrative review, in which Barilla declined to participate.

PAM moved for reconsideration in the CIT, which was denied. This appeal followed. We have jurisdiction pursuant to 28 U.S.C. § 1295(a)(5).

II. Discussion

A. Standard of Review

When reviewing Commerce's determinations, this Court will "apply anew the same standard of review used by the Court of International Trade." *Tung Mung Dev. Co. v. United States*, 354 F.3d 1371, 1378 (Fed. Cir. 2004). We will uphold Commerce's determinations unless it is "'unsupported by substantial evidence on the record, or otherwise not in accordance with law.'" *Alloy Piping Prods., Inc. v. Kanzen Tetsu Sdn. Bhd.,* 334 F.3d 1284, 1289 (Fed. Cir. 2003) (quoting 19 U.S.C. § 1516a(b)(1)(B)(i)).

"Substantial evidence" is defined as "more than a mere scintilla," or "such relevant evidence as a reasonable mind might accept as adequate to support a conclusion." *Micron Tech., Inc. v. United States*, 117 F.3d 1386, 1393 (Fed. Cir. 1997) (quoting *Consol. Edison Co. v. N.L.R.B.,* 305 U.S. 197, 229, 59 S. Ct. 206, 216, 83 L. Ed. 126 (1938)). The court will review the record as a whole—including any evidence that "fairly detracts from the substantiality of the evidence"—in determining whether substantial evidence exists. *Micron Tech.*, 117 F.3d at 1393 (internal quotation omitted).

B. Analysis

1. Duty to provide complete and accurate information

PAM attempts to describe its failure to provide information as merely two "errors," one of which was supposedly a computer error, and the other allegedly due to mistaken advice from an attorney. However, PAM had refused to answer an initial questionnaire requesting the information and failed to include the sales data in responses to two supplemental questionnaires that clearly requested the information.

Parties and attorneys filing documents with the Department of Commerce have an obligation to provide complete and correct information. The duty is not unlike that of an attorney appearing before the Court of International Trade or any federal district court *See U.S. Ct. Int'l Trade R. 11(b);* Fed. R. Civ. P. 11(b) (An attorney presenting to the court "a pleading, written motion, or other paper . . . certifies that to the best of the person's knowledge, information, and belief, formed *after an inquiry* reasonable under the circumstances" that, among other things, "factual contentions have evidentiary support[.]") (emphasis added).

Congress has made very clear the importance of accurate and complete reporting of home market sales to the Department of Commerce. If an interested party "withholds information that has been requested by the administering authority" or provides information that cannot be verified, the administering authority "shall . . . use the facts otherwise available in reaching" its decision on an antidumping issue.

19 U.S.C. § 1677e(a)(2)(A), (D). If the interested party fails to cooperate by not acting, to the best of its ability, to comply with a request for information from Commerce, Section 1677e(b) permits Commerce to "use an inference that is adverse to the interests of that party in selecting from among the facts otherwise available." Such adverse inferences may include reliance on information derived from previous administrative review or any other information placed on the record. *Id.* § 1677e(b)(3), (4).

2. Deferential review of adverse antidumping inference

Because of Commerce's special expertise in antidumping cases, the court applies the deferential "substantial evidence" standard when reviewing agency action in this field. *F.lii de Cecco di Filippo Fara S. Martino S.p.A. v. United States*, 216 F.3d 1027, 1032 (Fed. Cir. 2000). PAM argues that the 45.49% AFA margin applied to it is not supported by substantial evidence, because the sales with margins over 45.49% from the fourth administrative review that Commerce relied upon are aberrant outlier values.

Commerce's discretion in applying an AFA margin is particularly great when a respondent is uncooperative by failing to provide or withholding information. *See Id.* § 1677e. While the possibility of a high AFA margin creates a powerful incentive to avoid dumping and to cooperate in investigations, there is a limit to Commerce's discretion. "Congress tempered deterrent value with the corroboration requirement. It could only have done so to prevent the petition rate (or other adverse inference rate), when unreasonable, from prevailing and to block any temptation by Commerce to overreach reality in seeking to maximize deterrence." *de Cecco,* 216 F.3d at 1032.

Congressional foresight in this regard was highlighted at oral argument when both attorneys for the Appellees maintained that the price of a single box of pasta out of sales of thousands of cases would, in and of itself, corroborate an AFA margin based on that price. The burden imposed by substantial evidence review may not be heavy, but it is not ephemeral. There must be at least enough evidence to allow reasonable minds to differ. *See Consol. Edison*, 305 U.S. at 229, 59 S. Ct. at 217; *Heisig v. United States*, 719 F.2d 1153, 1156 (Fed. Cir. 1983). A single sale supported a 30.95% margin under the specific facts of *Ta Chen Stainless Steel Pipe, Inc. v. United States*, 298 F.3d 1330 (Fed. Cir. 2002). This does not mean that one sale by itself will always rise to the level of substantial evidence.

In the present case, Commerce's assessment of the 45.49% AFA margin is supported by substantial evidence. There were 29 sales with margins over 45.49%. PAM asserts that since these amounted to only 0.5% of PAM's total United States sales during the period of the fourth administrative review, they constitute outlier data that cannot be relied upon. This position was rejected by the *Ta Chen* court:

> Here, the 30.95% dumping margin is corroborated by actual sales data, and Ta Chen admits that it is reflective of some, albeit a small portion, of Ta Chen's actual sales.

> So long as the data is corroborated, Commerce acts within its discretion when choosing which sources and facts it will rely on to support an adverse inference.

Id., 298 F.3d at 1339.[2]

We reject PAM's suggestion that *Ta Chen* is called into question by *Exxon Shipping Co. v. Baker,* ______*U.S.*______, 128 S. Ct. 2605, 171 L. Ed. 2d 570 (2008). In *Exxon Shipping*, the Court reviewed a punitive damages award under maritime common law rendered against Exxon in connection with the 1989 oil spill of the Exxon Valdez off the Alaskan coast. The opinion noted the "stark unpredictability" of punitive damages awards when compared to compensatory awards, including the presence of "outlier" cases where the punitive damages dwarf the compensatory damages awarded. *Id.* at 2625. The Court ultimately settled on a rule where the appropriate upper limit ratio for punitive to compensatory damages in maritime cases was 1:1. *Id.* at 2633.

According to PAM, *Exxon Shipping*—a case involving punitive damages in the area of maritime common law—should be read "expansively" for the proposition that unpredictable outlier results are generally to be avoided. Nothing in *Exxon Shipping*, a case with a very different fact pattern and legal issues, requires us to impose new limits on the discretion Congress granted to the Department of Commerce.

III. Conclusion

The judgment of the Court of International Trade is affirmed.

AFFIRMED

---

2 PAM also argues that the data from the fourth administrative review is not actually representative of its sales during that period, because costs and home market sales are not included, and the sales consist mostly of specialty pasta (which make up a small portion of total United States sales). However, PAM never previously challenged the data from the fourth administrative review. Commerce is permitted to use the information available to it in choosing and supporting an AFA value. *See Ta Chen,* 298 F.3d at 1338–39 ("In the case of uncooperative respondents, the discretion granted by the statute appears to be particularly great, allowing Commerce to select among an enumeration of secondary sources as a basis for its adverse factual inferences. In cases in which the respondent fails to provide Commerce with the most recent pricing data, it is within Commerce's discretion to presume that the highest prior margin reflects the current margins." (internal citation omitted)).

SIDENOR INDUSTRIAL SL
v.
UNITED STATES

664 F. Supp. 2d 1349 (C.I.T. 2009)
Decided October 30, 2009

Riggle & Craven (David J. Craven and David A. Riggle), Washington, DC, for Plaintiff Sidenor Industrial SL.

Tony West, Assistant Attorney General; Jeanne E. Davidson, Director, Patricia M. McCarthy, Assistant Director, Commercial Litigation Branch, Civil Division, U.S. Department of Justice (L. Misha Preheim); and Deborah King, Office of Chief Counsel for Import Administration, U.S. Department of Commerce, of Counsel, for Defendant United States.

Kelley Drye & Warren LLP (Mary T. Staley and Grace W. Kim), Washington, DC, for Defendant-Intervenors Carpenter Technology Corporation, Electralloy Corporation, a Division of G.O. Carlson, Inc., and Valbruna Slater Stainless, Inc.

OPINION

WALLACH, Judge:

I. Introduction

This action arises out of the administrative review of an antidumping duty order conducted by the United States Department of Commerce ("Commerce"). Plaintiff Sidenor Industrial SL ("Sidenor") challenges Commerce's decision to apply adverse facts available ("AFA") to calculate Sidenor's dumping margin. Alternatively, Sidenor challenges the AFA dumping margin selected by Commerce. In addition, Sidenor argues that Commerce's denial of its request to report its cost data on a fiscal year basis, rather than for the period of review, was an abuse of discretion.

This court has jurisdiction pursuant to 28 U.S.C. § 1581(c). Because Commerce's decisions are supported by substantial evidence and otherwise in accordance with law, Commerce's determination in *Stainless Steel Bar from Spain: Final Results of Antidumping Duty Administrative Review,* 72 Fed. Reg. 42,395 (August 2, 2007) ("*Final Results*") is affirmed.

II. Background

Commerce imposed an antidumping duty order on stainless steel bar from Spain in 1995. *Amended Final Determination and Antidumping Duty Order: Stainless Steel Bar from Spain,* 60 Fed. Reg. 11,656 (March 2, 1995) ("*AD Order*"). In March 2006, Commerce published notice of the opportunity to request an administrative review of the *AD Order* for the period of review beginning March 1, 2005 and ending February 28, 2006. *Antidumping or Countervailing Duty Order, Finding, or Suspended Investigation; Opportunity to Request Administrative Review,* 71 Fed. Reg. 10,642 (March 2, 2006). In response to this notice, Sidenor requested that Commerce conduct an administrative review of its U.S. sales of stainless steel bar. Letter from David J. Craven, Riggle & Craven, to Carlos M. Gutierrez, Secretary of Commerce (March 28, 2006), Public Record ("P.R.") 1. Commerce thereafter initiated an administrative review of Sidenor's sales of stainless steel bar for the period of review. *Initiation of Antidumping and Countervailing Duty Administrative Reviews,* 71 Fed. Reg. 25,145 (April 28, 2006), P.R. 2.

Commerce sent Sections A, B, and C of its antidumping duty questionnaire to Sidenor on May 5, 2006.[1] Sidenor responded with a letter dated May 19, 2006; in the letter, Sidenor requested that Commerce clarify certain aspects of the questionnaire. Letter from David J. Craven, Riggle & Craven, to Carlos M. Gutierrez, Secretary of Commerce (May 19, 2006), P.R. 8. Sidenor also requested authorization from Commerce to report its cost of production and constructed value data for its 2005 fiscal year rather than for the period of review (March 1, 2005 through February 28, 2006). *Id.* In responding to Sidenor's requests, Commerce expressed its willingness to consider authorizing Sidenor to report its cost data on the basis of the 2005 fiscal year, provided that Sidenor demonstrate that such a shift in the cost reporting would not distort costs for the period of review. Letter from Laurie Parkhill, Office Director, Department of Commerce, to David J. Craven, Riggle & Craven (May 30, 2006), P.R. 12. Commerce requested that Sidenor answer four specific questions, the answers to which would assist Commerce in determining whether a shift in the cost reporting period would lead to distortion in the data. *Id.* Sidenor "did not provide the specific information" that Commerce requested.

---

1 The antidumping questionnaire is designed to elicit all information necessary to determine whether a respondent is dumping and, if so, to calculate the dumping margin. *See* Department of Commerce, Antidumping Manual (February 10, 1998) ("AD Manual"), Chap. 6 at 11. The antidumping questionnaire normally consists of five sections (A through E) and several appendices. *Id.,* Chap. 4 at 2–8. Section A is designed to elicit general information about a respondent's corporate structure and business practices as well as information concerning the allegedly dumped goods. *Id.,* Chap. 4 at 2. Section B is' designed to assist Commerce in determining the normal value of the goods; it requires respondents to list sales transactions of the subject goods in the home country market (or a third-country market, where appropriate). *Id.,* Chap. 4 at 3. Section C is designed to assist Commerce in determining the U.S. price against which normal value is compared. *Id.,* Chap. 4 at 5. Section D inquires about the costs of producing the goods. *Id.* Section E inquires about the value added in the U.S. to the goods prior to delivery to unaffiliated U.S. customers, if any. *Id.,* Chap. 4 at 6.

Memorandum from Stephen J. Claeys, Deputy Assistant Secretary for Import Administration, to David M. Spooner, Assistant Secretary for Import Administration, Re: Issues and Decision Memorandum for the Antidumping Duty Administrative Review of Stainless Steel Bar from Spain for the Period of Review March 1, 2005, through February 28, 2006 (July 26, 2007), P.R. 84 ("*Final Decision Memo*"), 2.

Subsequently, Commerce published the preliminary results of this administrative review. *Stainless Steel Bar from Spain: Preliminary Results of Antidumping Duty Administrative Review,* 72 Fed. Reg. 14,522 (March 28, 2007) ("*Preliminary Results*"). In the *Preliminary Results,* Commerce found that the statutory criteria for application of an AFA rate to Sidenor were met. *Id.* at 14,522–24. Commerce selected an AFA rate of 62.85%, the highest rate established by Commerce in the initial less-than-fair-value ("LTFV") investigation. Commerce determined that this rate remained both reliable and relevant. *Id.* at 14,524.

Sidenor filed a case brief challenging Commerce's conclusions with respect to its questionnaire responses and Commerce's application of total adverse facts available. Commerce rejected Sidenor's arguments. *See Final Decision Memo.* Sidenor was assigned a final AFA rate of 62.85%. *Final Results* at 42,395.

III. Standard of Review

The court will hold unlawful a determination by Commerce resulting from an administrative review of an antidumping duty order if that determination is "unsupported by substantial evidence on the record, or otherwise not in accordance with law." 19 U.S.C. § 1516a(b)(1)(B)(i); *see* 19 U.S.C. § 1516a(a)(2)(B)(iii).

A determination is supported by substantial evidence if the record contains "evidence that a reasonable mind might accept as adequate to support a conclusion." *Cleo Inc. v. United States,* 501 F.3d 1291, 1296 (Fed.Cir.2007) (citing *Universal Camera Corp. v. NLRB,* 340 U.S. 474, 477, 71 S. Ct. 456, 95 L.Ed. 456 (1951)). While the court must consider contradictory evidence, "the substantial evidence test does not require that there be an absence of evidence detracting from the agency's conclusion, nor is there an absence of substantial evidence simply because the reviewing court would have reached a different conclusion based on the same record." *Id.* (citing *Universal Camera Corp.,* 340 U.S. at 487–88, 71 S. Ct. 456); *see also Am. Silicon Techs. v. United States,* 261 F.3d 1371, 1375–76 (Fed. Cir.2001); *U.S. Steel Group v. United States,* 96 F.3d 1352, 1356–57 (Fed. Cir.1996).

To determine whether Commerce's interpretation and application of the antidumping statute at issue is otherwise "in accordance with law," the court must conduct the two-step analysis articulated by the Supreme Court in *Chevron U.S.A., Inc. v. Natural Resources Defense Council, Inc.,* 467 U.S. 837, 842–43, 104 S. Ct. 2778, 81 L.Ed.2d 694 (1984). Under the first step of the *Chevron* analysis, the court must ascertain "'whether Congress has directly spoken to the precise question at issue. If the intent of Congress is clear, that is the end of the matter; for the court, as well as the agency, must give effect to the unambiguously expressed intent of Congress.'" *Wheatland Tube Co. v. United States,* 495 F.3d 1355, 1359 (Fed. Cir.2007) (quoting *Chevron,* 467 U.S. at 842–43, 104 S. Ct. 2778).

The court reaches the second step of the *Chevron* analysis only "'if the statute is silent or ambiguous with respect to the specific issue.'" *Id.* (quoting *Chevron,* 467 U.S. at 843, 104 S. Ct. 2778). Under this second step, the court must evaluate whether Commerce's interpretation "is based on a permissible construction of the statute." *Chevron,* 467 U.S. at 843, 104 S. Ct. 2778. The agency's construction need not be the only reasonable interpretation or even the most reasonable interpretation. *See Zenith Radio Corp. v. United States,* 437 U.S. 443, 450, 98 S. Ct. 2441, 57 L.Ed.2d 337 (1978) (citations omitted). The court must defer to Commerce's reasonable interpretation of a statute even if it might have adopted another interpretation had the question first arisen in a judicial proceeding. *Id.* (citations omitted).

IV. Discussion

Sidenor challenges three decisions made by Commerce during the course of the administrative review. First, Sidenor argues that Commerce's denial of its request to report its cost data on a fiscal year basis, rather than for the period of review, was an abuse of discretion. Second, Sidenor contests Commerce's decision to apply adverse facts available to calculate its dumping margin. Third, Sidenor argues that even if Commerce's decision to calculate its dumping margin on the basis of adverse facts available is affirmed, the margin selected by Commerce should be lower. Each of Commerce's determinations survives these challenges. Commerce reasonably exercised its discretion to deny Sidenor's request to submit information in a form different than that originally requested. Commerce's decision to calculate Sidenor's dumping margin on the basis of adverse facts available is supported by substantial evidence and in accordance with law. The AFA rate selected by Commerce is supported by substantial evidence and in accordance with law.

A. Commerce Reasonably Exercised Its Discretion To Deny Sidenor's Request To Submit Information In A Form Different Than That Originally Requested

Sidenor argues that Commerce's denial of its request to report its cost data on a fiscal year basis, rather than for the period of review, was an abuse of discretion. *See* Motion for Judgment on the Agency Record Submitted Pursuant to Rule 56.2 of the Rules of the U.S. Court of International Trade ("Plaintiff's Motion") at 13. Commerce generally allows a respondent to shift its cost-reporting period if the respondent shows that such a shift will not distort the costs for the period of review. *Final Decision Memo* at 2. Sidenor did not make that showing. *Id.* at 3.

After receiving Sidenor's request for authorization to shift the cost-reporting period from the period of review to the fiscal year, Commerce responded that it "may agree to Sidenor's request . . . only if [Commerce] can establish that the shifted costs will not distort the costs for the period of review." Letter from Laurie Parkhill,

Office Director, Department of Commerce, to Sidenor Industrial Ltd. c/o Donald J. Craven (May 20, 2006), P.R. 12. To that end, Commerce asked that Sidenor respond to four specific questions. *Id.* Sidenor did not respond to these questions. *Final Decision Memo* at 2. Two months later, Commerce followed up with a second letter reiterating its request. *Id.* Although Sidenor responded, it failed to provide the information that Commerce requested. *Id.* Commerce thereafter concluded that "without Sidenor's response. . ., we could not determine whether a shift in the reporting period was reasonable." *Id.*

Accordingly, Commerce did not abuse its discretion in denying Sidenor's request.

B. Commerce's Decision To Calculate Sidenor's Dumping Margin On The Basis Of Adverse Facts Available Is Supported By Substantial Evidence And In Accordance With Law

When Commerce uses the phrase "adverse facts available," it is referring to a two-step procedure: (1) resort to "facts otherwise available" when information it has requested is unavailable or deficient, 19 U.S.C. § 1677e(a); and (2) use of "adverse inferences" in selecting from the "facts otherwise available" when "an interested party has failed to cooperate by not acting to the best of its ability," 19 U.S.C. § 1677e(b). *See Ad Hoc Shrimp Trade Action Committee v. United States,* 616 F. Supp. 2d 1354, 1368–69 (CIT 2009) (citing *Jinan Yipin Corp. v. United States,* 526 F. Supp. 2d 1347, 1353 n. 7 (CIT 2007)). Sidenor argues that Commerce erred with respect to both steps.

First, Sidenor contends that the requisite statutory criteria for determinations on the basis of "facts otherwise available" have not been met. Second, Sidenor contends that the application of adverse inferences is inappropriate because it acted to the best of its ability in responding to Commerce's requests for information. Lastly, Sidenor argues that Commerce is not authorized to calculate a respondent's dumping margin on the basis of adverse facts available unless it has conducted a verification of the information submitted during the course of the administrative review.

1. Commerce's Resort To "Facts Otherwise Available" Was Appropriate Because Sidenor Did Not Provide The Requested Information

Sidenor contends that the requisite statutory criteria for determinations on the basis of "facts otherwise available" have not been met. Plaintiffs Motion at 15. The relevant statute directs Commerce to use the facts otherwise available in making determinations in antidumping proceedings when any one of the following conditions is met:

> (1) necessary information is not available on the record; or (2) an interested party . . . (A) withholds information that has been requested by [Commerce] . . ., (B) fails to provide such information by the deadlines for submission or in the form and manner requested . . ., (C) significantly impedes a proceeding . . ., or (D) provides such information but the information cannot be verified . . . .

19 U.S.C. § 1677e(a). Before using the facts otherwise available, however, Commerce is required to notify the responding party of the deficiency and, to the extent practicable, permit that party to remedy or explain the deficiency. *Id.* § 1677m(d). Commerce must consider information submitted by an interested party if the following five criteria are met:

> (1) the information is submitted by the deadline established for its submission,
>
> (2) the information can be verified,
>
> (3) the information is not so incomplete that it cannot serve as a reliable basis for reaching the applicable determination,
>
> (4) the interested party has demonstrated that it acted to the best of its ability in providing the information and meeting the requirements established by [Commerce] . . . with respect to the information, and
>
> (5) the information can be used without undue difficulties.

Id. § 1677m(e). If, however, Commerce finds the party's explanation of the deficiency either untimely or insufficient, and one of the five criteria in 19 U.S.C. § 1677m(e) is not met, Commerce can disregard all or part of the original and subsequent responses. *Id.* § 1677m(d).

Here, Commerce determined that four of the conditions enumerated in 19 U.S.C. § 1677e were present; the existence of only one condition is sufficient for Commerce to make a determination on the basis of facts otherwise available. According to Commerce, "necessary information was not available on the record and Sidenor withheld critical information requested by Commerce, failed to provide information in the form and manner requested, and significantly impeded the proceeding." Defendant's Memorandum in Opposition to Plaintiff's Rule 56.2 Motion for Judgment Upon the Agency Record ("Defendant's Response") at 14. These findings are supported by substantial evidence.

When determining normal value, Commerce normally calculates costs "based on the records of the exporter . . ., if such records are kept in accordance with the generally accepted accounting principles of the exporting country . . . and reasonably reflect the costs associated with the production and sale of the merchandise." 19 U.S.C. § 1677b(f)(1)(A). In order to determine whether the cost data provided by an exporter is reasonably allocated to the subject merchandise, Commerce first "ensure[s] that the aggregate amount of the reported costs captures all costs incurred by the respondent in producing the merchandise under consideration." Memorandum from Mark Todd, Senior Accountant, Department of Commerce, to the file (March 22, 2007), Confidential Record ("C.R.") 29 ("*AFA Memo*"), 2. Commerce does so by reconciling the cost data submitted by the respondent to the respondent's audited financial statements. *Id.* This court has recognized that "Commerce must ensure that [a respondent's] reported costs capture all of the costs incurred by the respondent in producing the subject merchandise" before it can appropriately use that respondent's cost allocation methodology. *Myland Indus., Ltd. v. United States,*

2007 WL 3120293, 6 (CIT 2007). Sidenor's failure to furnish to Commerce (1) actual documentation from its normal books and records to support its reported direct materials cost and (2) a reconciliation between its sales and production figures made it impossible for Commerce to do so.

Sidenor claimed that it calculated its direct material costs by subtracting the non-material costs from the total production costs for the final products. Section D Antidumping Questionnaire, Response of Sidenor Industrial SL (September 19, 2006), C.R. 12, D-24 to D-25. Sidenor did not, however, provide Commerce with appropriate documentation to support this assertion.

Commerce provided Sidenor with the opportunity to remedy or explain the deficiencies in its response, as required by 19 U.S.C § 1677m(d), by issuing three supplemental questionnaires requesting a proper cost reconciliation and supporting information for the direct materials cost for the merchandise under consideration. *Final Decision Memo* at 10. Commerce explained that the purpose of its request "was to obtain support from Sidenor's normal books and records for the information included in [certain of Sidenor's] exhibits." *Id.* at 5. Yet, Sidenor "failed to provide . . . supporting documentation linking its reported direct material costs to its financial accounting records maintained in the normal course of business." *AFA Memo* at 2; *see also Final Decision Memo* at 7. Commerce found this failure particularly problematic because Sidenor's direct material costs account for [[a large]] percent of the merchandise under consideration and only [[a small]] percent of Sidenor's stainless steel bar was reported as merchandise under consideration (with [[a large]] percent reported as sold outside of the United States and the home market). *AFA Memo* at 6.

Sidenor maintains that it "is of no moment" that it did not reconcile its sales directly to the costs because, "[s]ince both [sales and costs] were reconciled to the audited financial statement, they necessarily reconcile to each other." Plaintiff's Motion at 15. This misses the point; the fact remains that Sidenor did not provide to Commerce the information necessary "to gain an understanding of Sidenor's reporting methodology." *AFA Memo* at 3; *see also Final Decision Memo* at 7. Commerce found that Sidenor's failure to provide the requested reconciliations left it "with no support or assurance that the quantity of [stainless steel bar] reported as merchandise under consideration is complete and accurate." *AFA Memo* at 6.

As a result of Sidenor's failure to furnish the requested documentation, necessary information was neither on the record (19 U.S.C. § 1677e(a)(1)) nor provided in the form and manner requested by Commerce (19 U.S.C. § 1677e(a)(2)(B)). Further, by failing to furnish the information, Sidenor withheld information (19 U.S.C. § 1677e(a)(2)(A)) and significantly impeded the conduct of the administrative review (19 U.S.C. § 1677e(a)(2)(C)). Accordingly, Commerce's decision to rely on facts otherwise available to calculate Sidenor's dumping margin was supported by substantial evidence and otherwise in accordance with law.

2. Commerce Properly Applied Adverse Inferences When Selecting Amongst The Facts Otherwise Available Because Sidenor Did Not Act To The Best Of Its Ability

Commerce is authorized to employ adverse inferences when selecting from the facts otherwise available if it finds that an interested party "has failed to cooperate by not acting to the best of its ability." 19 U.S.C. § 1677e(b); *see also* Statement of Administrative Action accompanying the Uruguay Round Agreements Act, H.R. Doc. No. 103-316 ("SAA")[2] at 870 (1994), *reprinted in* 1994 U.S.C.C.A.N. 4040, 4199. The Federal Circuit has interpreted this language to mean that a party must "do the maximum it is able to do" to comply with Commerce's request. *Nippon Steel Corporation v. United States,* 337 F.3d 1373, 1382 (Fed.Cir.2003).

"Whether a respondent has done the maximum it was able to do to comply with Commerce's requests involves both objective and subjective inquiries." *Fujian Lianfu Forestry Co. v. United States,* 638 F. Supp. 2d 1325, 1337–38 (CIT 2009). Under the objective inquiry, Commerce must demonstrate "'that a reasonable and responsible importer would have known that the requested information was required to be kept and maintained under the applicable statutes, rules, and regulations.'" *Id.* (quoting *Nippon Steel,* 337 F.3d at 1382–83). Under the subjective inquiry, Commerce must demonstrate that a respondent's failure to promptly produce the requested information "'is the result of the respondent's lack of cooperation in either: (a) failing to keep and maintain all required records, or (b) failing to put forth its maximum efforts to investigate and obtain the requested information from its records.'" *Id.* at 1337–38 (quoting *Nippon Steel,* 337 F.3d at 1382–83).

With respect to the objective component of the inquiry, "[p]arties and attorneys filing documents with the Department of Commerce have an obligation to provide complete and correct information." *PAM, S.p.A. v. United States,* 582 F.3d 1336, 1339 (Fed.Cir.2009). Moreover, a respondent has "'a statutory obligation to prepare an accurate and complete record in response to questions plainly asked by Commerce.'" *Fujian,* at 1340 (citing *Tung Mung Dev. v. United States,* 25 CIT 752, 758 (CIT 2001)). Here, Commerce did not request that Sidenor keep its books and records a certain way; it asked that Sidenor provide information that would assist Commerce in understanding how certain financial data related to the information contained in its normal books and records. Sidenor did not provide this information.

---

2 The Uruguay Round Agreements Act was signed into law on December 8, 1994. The Act approved the new WTO Agreement, and the agreements annexed thereto, "resulting from the Uruguay Round of multilateral trade negotiations [conducted] under the auspices of the General Agreement on Tariffs and Trade." 19 U.S.C. § 3511(a)(1). The Statement of Administrative Action approved by Congress to implement the Agreements is regarded as "an authoritative expression by the United States concerning the interpretation and application of the Uruguay Round Agreements and [the Uruguay Round Agreements] Act in any judicial proceeding in which a question arises concerning such interpretation or application." 19 U.S.C. § 3512(d).

With respect to the subjective component of the inquiry, Commerce afforded Sidenor several opportunities to provide the requested reconciliations and documentation.[3] Because the requested information was within Sidenor's control, Commerce found that Sidenor's failure to furnish the requested information was effectively a failure to act to the best of its ability. *Final Decision Memo* at 12.

Sidenor disputes this finding and claims that it did act to the best of its ability. Plaintiff's Motion at 19. In support of this claim, Sidenor focuses on "reporting methodologies, conversion costs, cost variances, and the overall cost reconciliation." *Final Decision Memo* at 4; *see* Plaintiff's Motion at 19–30. Sidenor ignores what Commerce characterizes as "the primary reason for [its] finding that Sidenor did not cooperate to the best of its ability, [namely] Sidenor's failure to provide adequate explanations and requested documentation linking its reported direct-materials cost to cost-accounting records it maintains in the normal course of business." *Final Decision Memo* at 4; *see also AFA Memo* at 2–5 (discussing Sidenor's failure to provide proper data for an overall cost reconciliation and for a quantity reconciliation between reported sales and production quantities).

Thus, Commerce's decision to apply adverse inferences when selecting from the facts otherwise available is supported by substantial evidence.

3. Commerce's Authority To Calculate A Respondent's Dumping Margin On The Basis Of Adverse Facts Available Does Not Depend On Whether It Has Conducted A Verification

Sidenor argues that Commerce cannot calculate its dumping margin on the basis of adverse facts available because it "was not subject to, and did not fail, a verification." Plaintiff's Motion at 10. Sidenor does not cite to any authority for this proposition.[4] *See id.* at 8–11.

---

3 For a more detailed discussion of these opportunities, *see* Section IV.B.1.

4 When asked at oral argument to provide citation to authority in support of this argument, Sidenor responded that "this case is a difficult case to cite specific legal authority [for]." In fact, Sidenor appears to have abandoned this argument. At oral argument, Sidenor clarified that "the argument is not that . . . AFA cannot be assigned in the absence of verification. Certainly it can be. . . . But the facts here are different." In any event, the court interprets Sidenor's failure to support its argument with citation to authority as tantamount to consent to denial of its argument. "'[I]ssues adverted to in a perfunctory manner, unaccompanied by some effort at developed argumentation, are deemed waived. It is not enough merely to mention a possible argument in the most skeletal way, leaving the court to do counsel's work, create the ossature for the argument, and put flesh on its bones.'" *Fujian Lianfu Forestry Co. v. United States,* 638 F. Supp. 2d 1325, 1349 (CIT 2009) (quoting *United States v. Zannino,* 895 F.2d 1, 17 (1st Cir.1990)); *see also Fagersta Stainless AB v. United States,* 577 F. Supp. 2d 1270, 1279 n. 6 (CIT 2008). "Briefs supporting motions for judgment on the agency record filed in actions arising under 28 U.S.C. § 1581(c) '*must* include the authorities relied on and the conclusions of law deemed warranted by the authorities.'" *MTZ Polyfilms, Ltd. v. United States,* 659 F. Supp. 2d 1303, 1308–09 (CIT 2009) (quoting USCIT Rule 56.2(c)(2)) (emphasis added in *MTZ*). "Failure to enforce [such requirements] will ultimately deprive [the appellate system]

The antidumping statute establishes the criteria that must be met in order to justify the use of adverse facts available to calculate a respondent's dumping margin; verification is not among the criteria listed. *See* 19 U.S.C. § 1677e(a) (use of "facts otherwise available") and 19 U.S.C. § 1677e(b) (use of adverse inferences in selecting from the facts otherwise available). The applicable statute requires verification in the context of an antidumping administrative review only if a domestic party makes a timely request for verification and either no verification has been performed in the prior two administrative reviews or good cause is shown. 19 U.S.C. § 1677m(i). The applicable regulation requires verification only if a domestic party makes a timely request for verification and no verification has been performed in the prior two administrative reviews or if good cause is shown. 19 C.F.R. § 351.307(b). These conditions are absent in the challenged review: Sidenor has not demonstrated that a domestic party requested verification of its information, and this is the first administrative review of the *AD Order*. Moreover, this court has found that a respondent's act of purposefully withholding or providing misleading information is, in itself, grounds for the application of adverse facts available. *See Shanghai Taoen Int'l Trading Co. v. United States,* 29 CIT 189, 195, 360 F. Supp. 2d 1339, 1345 (CIT 2005).

Accordingly, Sidenor's verification argument cannot succeed.

C. The AFA Rate Selected By Commerce Was Supported By Substantial Evidence And Otherwise In Accordance With Law

Sidenor contends that, even if Commerce were correct in calculating its dumping margin on the basis of adverse facts available, the rate selected by Commerce is inappropriate for two reasons. First, Sidenor contends that the AFA rate was not corroborated. Second, Sidenor argues that the AFA rate is "aberrational" and "punitive."

1. Commerce Properly Corroborated The AFA Rate

Sidenor asserts that Commerce did not corroborate the AFA rate. Plaintiff's Motion at 34. This portion of Plaintiffs Motion contains no citations to authority, statutory or otherwise.[5] *See id.* at 34–35. According to Sidenor, "the sole basis for selecting this rate is that it was an adverse rate that applied to a company related to Sidenor in the original investigation. However, this is not a reasonable basis for corroboration." *Id.* at 34. Sidenor further argues that "[t]he rate is also not corroborated for time. The selected rate is from a period many years prior to the [period of review] at issue. There is no showing that it still reflects the current rate. . . ." *Id.* at 35.

---

in substantial measure of that assistance of counsel which the system assumes." *Carducci v. Regan,* 714 F.2d 171, 230 U.S.App. D.C. 80 (D.C.Cir.1983).

5 Plaintiff's failure to cite authority for this argument is, in effect, a consent to denial of its argument. *See* note 4, *supra.*

Commerce properly corroborated the AFA rate within the applicable legal framework.

Commerce is explicitly authorized to rely on "information derived from [a] previous administrative review or any other information placed on the record," including information derived from the petition, in establishing an AFA rate. *PAM, S.p.A.,* at 1339 (citing 19 U.S.C. § 1677e(b)). Information from a prior segment of the proceeding (for example, the AFA rate established in the initial LTFV investigation) is characterized as "secondary information." SAA at 870, 1994 U.S.C.C.A.N. at 4199. When Commerce uses secondary information, it is required *"to the extent practicable . . .* [to] corroborate that information from independent sources that are reasonably at [its] disposal." 19 U.S.C. § 1677e(c) (emphasis added). The Federal Circuit has interpreted Congress's purpose in enacting the corroboration requirement as follows:

> It is clear from Congress's imposition of the corroboration requirement in 19 U.S.C. § 1677e(c) that it intended for an adverse facts available rate to be a reasonably accurate estimate of the respondent's actual rate, albeit with some built-in increase intended as a deterrent to non-compliance. Congress could not have intended for Commerce's discretion to include the ability to select unreasonably high rates with no relationship to the respondent's actual dumping margin.

F.lli De Cecco Di Filippo Fara S. Martino S.p.A. v. U.S., 216 F.3d 1027, 1032 (Fed. Cir.2000). To corroborate secondary information, Commerce must find that "the secondary information to be used has probative value." SAA at 870, 1994 U.S.C.C.A.N. at 4199. In addition, "Commerce needs to demonstrate how the selected proxy satisfies the *De Cecco* standard." *Fujian,* at 1336–37. If Commerce determines that it is not "practicable" to tie the selected AFA rate to the actual respondent, Commerce must explain why. *Id.* at 1337.

Commerce evaluates whether secondary information has probative value by assessing its reliability and relevance. *KYD, Inc. v. United States,* 613 F. Supp. 2d 1371, 1378 (CIT 2009); *Mittal Steel Galati S.A. v. United States,* 491 F. Supp. 2d 1273, 1278 (CIT 2007) (citing *Ball Bearings and Parts Thereof from France, Germany, Italy, Japan, Singapore, and the United Kingdom: Final Results of Antidumping Duty Administrative Reviews,* 70 Fed. Reg. 54,711, 54,712–13 (September 16, 2005)). The reliability of an AFA rate is assessed by determining whether the rate was reliable when first used. *See KYD,* 613 F. Supp. 2d at 1379 (citing *Tianjin Mach. Imp. & Exp. Corp. v. United States,* 2007 WL 2701368, 14, 2007 Ct. Int'l Trade LEXIS 137, 44 (CIT 2007)). The relevance of an AFA rate is measured against "'past practices in the industry in question.'" *Id.* at 1380 (quoting *D & L Supply Co. v. United States,* 113 F.3d 1220, 1223–24 (Fed.Cir.1997)) and *Shanghai Taoen,* 29 CIT at 197, 360 F. Supp. 2d at 1346.

In this case, Commerce stated that it "reviewed all potential rates in the history of the proceeding which could be applied to Sidenor as an [AFA] rate in this segment of the proceeding." *Final Decision Memo* at 15. The potential rates available for

Commerce were from the initial LTFV investigation; these included the 7.7% weighted-average margin calculated for a cooperative respondent, the 25.77% all-others rate, and the 62.85% rate calculated for a noncooperative respondent. *Id.* Commerce "found the rate of 62.85 percent to be reliable in the investigation" and, "[b]ecause the information was supported by source documents, . . . determine[d] that the information is still reliable." *Id.* at 17. Commerce found that the rate remained reliable because it has not been judicially discredited and because there was no new information that called into question its reliability. *Id.* at 18. With respect to relevance, Commerce evaluated whether there were any circumstances that would render the margin irrelevant. *Id.* According to Commerce, such circumstances might include judicial invalidation or a finding that the rate was based on another company's uncharacteristic business expense. *Id.* Commerce found "that [such] unusual circumstances . . . are absent in the instant review and, therefore, the selected rate retains its relevance." *Id.* With respect to the *De Cecco* standard, Commerce explained that "because Sidenor is a first-time participant in the current administrative review . . ., there are no prior weighted-average dumping margins that were ever calculated for Sidenor in prior segments of the proceeding." *Id.* at 19.

Thus, because Commerce found that the AFA rate applied in the initial LTFV investigation remained reliable and relevant, and because Commerce explained why it was not practicable to demonstrate that the rate was a reasonable approximation of Sidenor's actual rate, Commerce properly corroborated the rate for use in this administrative review.

2. The AFA Rate Is Neither "Aberrational" Nor "Punitive"

Sidenor also argues that the rate selected by Commerce cannot be "aberrational" or "punitive." Plaintiffs Motion at 35. Sidenor asserts that "if an [AFA] rate is selected, it should reasonably reflect the rate that would have applied had the data been able to be used with a reasonable additional amount to deter non-compliance." *Id.* (citing *Shandong Huarong Gen. Group Corp. v. United States,* 2007 WL 54067, 2007 Ct. Int'l Trade LEXIS 3 (CIT 2007)). In addition, Sidenor asserts that "the principles underlying" the 1:1 ratio for punitive damages established in *Exxon Shipping Co. v. Baker,* ___ U.S. ___, 128 S. Ct. 2605, 171 L.Ed.2d 570 (2008), "should have guided [Commerce] in its examination of the calculated AFA rate." Plaintiffs Motion at 37.

Like the argument proffered in Section IV. C.1 above with respect to relevance, these arguments have been addressed and rejected by the court on numerous occasions. *See, e.g., KYD,* 613 F. Supp. 2d 1371, 1381–82; *PAM, S.p.A. v. United States,* 577 F. Supp. 2d 1318, 1321 (CIT 2008). The court has already determined that *Shandong* does not provide a numerical limit and that Commerce "is unfettered by absolute numerical limitations" when selecting an AFA rate. *Universal Polybag Co. v. United States,* 577 F. Supp. 2d 1284, 1301 (CIT 2008). The Federal Circuit has unequivocally stated that "[n]othing in Exxon Shipping, a case with a very different fact pattern and legal issues, requires us to impose new limits on the discretion Congress granted to the Department of Commerce." *PAM, S.p.A.*, at 1340.

V Conclusion

For the above stated reasons, Plaintiffs Motion for Judgment on the Agency Record Submitted Pursuant to Rule 56.2 of the Rules of the U.S. Court of International Trade is DENIED and Commerce's determination in *Stainless Steel Bar from Spain: Final Results of Antidumping Duty Administrative Review,* 72 Fed. Reg. 42,395 (August 2, 2007) is AFFIRMED.

UNITED STATES STEEL CORPORATION
v.
UNITED STATES

627 F. Supp. 2d 1374 (C.I.T. 2009)
Decided May 18, 2009

Skadden Arps Slate Meagher & Flom, LLP (Robert E. Lighthizer, Jeffrey D. Gerrish, Ellen J. Schneider, and Luke A. Meisner), for Plaintiff United States Steel Corporation.

Stewart and Stewart, (Terence P. Stewart and William A. Fennell), for Plaintiff ArcelorMittal Steel USA, Inc.

Wiley Rein, (Timothy C. Brightbill), for Plaintiff-Intervenor Nucor Corporation.

Michael F. Hertz, Deputy Assistant Attorney General; Jeanne E. Davidson, Director; Patricia M. McCarthy, Assistant Director, Commercial Litigation Branch, Civil Division, United States Department of Justice (Claudia Burke) for Defendant United States.

Steptoe & Johnson LLP (Richard O. Cunningham, Joel D. Kaufman, Alice A. Kipel, and Jamie B. Beaber) for Defendant-Intervenor Corus Staal BV.

Before: Judith M. Barzilay, Judge Consol.

OPINION

BARZILAY, Judge.

Plaintiffs United States Steel Corporation ("U.S. Steel") and ArcelorMittal USA, Inc. ("ArcelorMittal") (collectively, the "Plaintiffs") challenge the U.S. Department of Commerce ("Commerce") decision to use offsetting to calculate the weighted-average dumping margins as such and as applied in certain antidumping duty proceedings, pursuant to 28 U.S.C. § 1581(i).[1] *Antidumping Proceedings: Calculation*

---

1 The "dumping margin" refers to the amount by which the normal value exceeds the export price or constructed export price, expressed functionally as DM = NV—(EP or CEP). 19 U.S.C. § 1677(35)(A). The "weighted-average dumping margin" expresses the dumping

of the Weighted-Average Dumping Margin During an Antidumping Investigation; Final Modification, 71 Fed. Reg. 77,722, 77,722 (Dep't Commerce Dec. 27, 2006) ("*Section 123 Determination*").[2] Specifically, Plaintiffs allege that Commerce's *Section 123 Determination*, and the application of that determination to a specific antidumping investigation, is not in accordance with law. U.S. Steel Compl. ¶¶ 20–22; AcelorMittal Compl. ¶¶ 18–21. Nucor Corporation ("Nucor") and Corus Staal BV ("Corus") join as a Plaintiff- and Defendant-Intervenor, respectively, pursuant to USCIT R. 24.[3] Here, Defendant United States requests that the court, under USCIT R. 12(b)(1) and (b)(5), dismiss the Plaintiffs' complaints, alleging that the Court lacks subject matter jurisdiction over the claims because (1) the challenge here essentially contests the final results of a Section 129 determination,[4]

---

margin as a percentage and is determined by dividing the aggregate dumping margins of a specific exporter or producer by the aggregate export or constructed export prices of such exporter or producer. § 1677(35)(B).

Offsetting is the practice whereby Commerce, when calculating the numerator in the weighted-average dumping equation, offsets sales made at less than fair value with fair value sales. Zeroing is a practice that is related to, but distinct from, offsetting, whereby Commerce gives the sales margins of merchandise sold at or above fair value prices an assumed value of zero. *See Corus Staal BV v. Dep't of Commerce*, 395 F.3d 1343, 1345–46 (Fed. Cir. 2005). With zeroing, Commerce uses only the sales margins of merchandise sold at less than fair value prices to calculate the final dumping margin. *See id.*

Finally, an "as such," or facial, challenge contests the general policy to use a law, regulation or practice, whereas an "as applied" challenge argues against its application in a particular proceeding.

2 Commerce twice delayed the implementation of the *Section 123 Determination*, with the change in policy ultimately taking effect on February 22, 2007. *Antidumping Proceedings: Calculation of the Weighted-Average Dumping Margins in Antidumping Investigations; Change in Effective Date of Final Modification*, 72 Fed. Reg. 1,704, 1,704 (Dep't Commerce Jan. 16, 2007); *Antidumping Proceedings: Calculation of the Weighted-Average Dumping Margins in Antidumping Investigations; Change in Effective Date of Final Modification*, 72 Fed. Reg. 3,783, 3,783 (Dep't Commerce Jan. 26, 2007).

3 Corus filed a Motion to Dismiss on February 22, 2008 in response to U.S. Steel's, complaint. U.S. Steel responded to Corus's motion, but the court stayed a decision on those proceedings pending a motion to consolidate Court Nos. 07-170, 07-201, 07-475, and 08-015. On September 4, 2008, the court consolidated Court Nos. 07-475 and 08-015 to form the current action. Defendant has since moved the court to dismiss the case here, with all other parties filing their respective response briefs. The court notes that while it addresses only Defendant's arguments by name below, it also considers Corus's contentions, which mirror those of the United States, in its analysis.

4 In Consol. Court No. 07-170, Plaintiffs contest Commerce's *Section 123 Determination* under an alternative jurisdictional provision, 28 U.S.C. § 1581(c), both as such and as applied to the specific investigation addressing the subject merchandise. U.S. Steel Br. 4. Additionally, Plaintiffs challenge the final results of the Section 129 determination that resulted in the revocation of the antidumping duty order on the subject merchandise. *Id.*; *Implementation of the Findings of the WTO Panel in US-Zeroing (EC): Notice of Determinations under Section 129 of the Uruguay Round Agreements Act and Revocations and Partial Revocations of Certain Antidumping Duty Orders*, 72 Fed. Reg. 25,261, 25,262 (Dep't Commerce May 4, 2007)

(2) no provision of the United States Code provides for the judicial review of a Section 123 determination, (3) the United States has not waived its sovereign immunity from being subject to such a claim, and (4) the *Section 123 Determination* is not an agency action under the Administrative Procedure Act ("APA"). Additionally, Defendants allege that Plaintiffs (5) lack standing and (6) have otherwise failed to state a claim upon which relief may be granted under USCIT R. 8(a). The court grants Defendant and Defendant-Intervenor's Motions to Dismiss for reasons explained herein.

I. Background

A. Sections 123 and 129 of the Uruguay Round Agreements Act

In enacting Sections 123 and 129 of the Uruguay Round Agreements Act ("URAA"), Congress established two procedures by which an adverse decision from the World Trade Organization ("WTO") Dispute Settlement Panel or Appellate Body may be implemented into domestic law. A Section 123 determination amends, rescinds, or modifies an agency regulation or practice that is found to be inconsistent with any of the Uruguay Round Agreements. 19 U.S.C. § 3533(g)(1). Under this scheme, the United States Trade Representative ("USTR") is required to consult with the appropriate congressional and private sector advisory committees, as well as to provide an opportunity for public comment, before determining whether and how to implement the agency regulation or practice at issue. *Id.* As part of the consultation process, the USTR is required to provide the relevant congressional committees with a report that describes "the proposed modification, the reasons for the modification, and a summary of the advice obtained" from the private sector advisory committees. *Id.* at § 3533(g)(1)(D). To take effect, the final modification must ultimately be published in the Federal Register. *Id.* at § 3533(g)(1)(F).

A Section 129 determination amends, rescinds, or modifies the application of an agency regulation or practice in a specific antidumping, countervailing duty, or safeguards proceeding. In particular, a Section 129 determination alters a specific agency determination that is found to be inconsistent with U.S. obligations under the WTO Antidumping Agreement ("*AD Agreement*"), the Agreement on Subsidies and Countervailing Measures, or the Safeguards Agreement. 19 U.S.C. § 3538(a)(1), (b)(1). Under this procedure, the USTR must consult with the relevant congressional committees and request in writing that the pertinent agency issue a new determination consistent with the findings set forth in the WTO Panel or Appellate Body Report. *Id.* at § 3538(a)(1), (a)(3)-(5), (b)(1)-(3). Interested parties may also submit written comments on the proposed modification and, where appropriate, ask for an administrative hearing on the matter. *Id.* at § 3538(d). A Section 129

("*Section 129 Determination*"). Plaintiffs filed their complaints here under § 1581(i) after Defendant and Defendant-Intervenor indicated they would challenge the Court's ability to hear Plaintiffs' claims concerning the *Section 123 Determination* under § 1581(c) in Consol. Court No. 07-170. U.S. Steel Br. 5.

determination takes effect on or after the date on which the USTR directs the agency to implement the determination, in whole or in part, and when Commerce publishes the determination in the Federal Register. *Id.* at § 3538(c)(1)-(2).

The Court has exclusive jurisdiction over all civil actions commenced under section 516A of the Tariff Act of 1930, as amended, 19 U.S.C. § 1516a, to contest a Section 129 determination. § 1516a(a)(2)(B)(vii); § 1581(c). In contrast, no provision of the United States Code, including § 1516a, expressly grants this or any federal court jurisdiction over challenges to a Section 123 determination.[5]

B. The Original Antidumping Duty Order & Subsequent Developments

On November 29, 2001, after receiving petitions from domestic producers to initiate an investigation on the subject merchandise and making a preliminary finding that such merchandise was dumped in the U.S., Commerce issued an antidumping duty order covering hot-rolled carbon steel flat products from the Netherlands. *Antidumping Duty Order: Certain Hot-Rolled Carbon Steel Flat Products From the Netherlands*, 66 Fed. Reg. 59,565, 59,566 (Dep't Commerce Nov. 29, 2001). Commerce used zeroing to calculate the final dumping margin for the subject merchandise. *Notice of Final Determination of Sales at Less Than Fair Value; Certain Hot-Rolled Carbon Steel Flat Products From The Netherlands*, 66 Fed. Reg. 50,408, 50,409 (Dep't Commerce Oct. 3, 2001); *Issues and Decision Memorandum for the Antidumping Investigation of Certain Hot-Rolled Carbon Steel Flat Products from the Netherlands; Notice of Final Determination of Sales at Less Than Fair Value* (A-421-807), A-421-807 (Oct. 3, 2001), available at 2001 WL 1168309, at 7–8.

The European Communities thereafter challenged Commerce's use of zeroing in several antidumping investigations and administrative reviews before the WTO, including the investigation that resulted in the imposition of an antidumping duty order on hot-rolled carbon steel flat products from the Netherlands. *See* Request for Consultations by the European Communities, *United States—Laws, Regulations and Methodologies for Calculating Dumping Margins ("Zeroing"),* WT/DS294/1, at 4 (June 19, 2003). On October 31, 2005, a WTO Panel found Commerce's use of zeroing in investigations involving comparisons of weighted-average normal values to weighted-average U.S. prices to be inconsistent with U.S. obligations under the *AD Agreement*. *See* Report of the Panel, *United States—Laws, Regulations and Methodology for Calculating Dumping Margins ("Zeroing")*, ¶¶ 8.2-8.4, WT/DS294/R (Oct. 31, 2005) ("Panel Report"). Specifically, the WTO Panel founds that zeroing violates the *AD Agreement* as such, and as applied in the specific

5 Defendant emphasizes that the absence of such a jurisdictional grant in the United States Code demonstrates that Congress declined to waive its sovereign immunity over challenges to Section 123 determinations, and as such, those agency proceedings are not reviewable agency actions under the APA. Def. Br. 10-11; Def. Reply Br. 3.

investigations at issue.[6] *Id.* The Appellate Body upheld the WTO Panel's determination on appeal and went further, stating that Commerce's use of zeroing in certain administrative reviews was also inconsistent with the AD Agreement. *See* Report of the Appellate Body, *United States—Laws, Regulations and Methodology for Calculating Dumping Margins ("Zeroing")*, ¶¶ 132-35, 263(a)(i), WT/DS294/AB/R (Apr. 18, 2006).

On December 27, 2006, in response to the *Panel Report*, Commerce announced that as a general policy it would use offsetting and no longer zero negative margins in antidumping investigations involving comparisons of "average-to-average" prices. *Section 123 Determination*, 71 Fed. Reg. at 77,722. Commerce noted that the department's new policy would specifically apply in (1) the recalculation of the dumping margins in the "specific antidumping investigations challenged by the EC in [the *Panel Report*]" and (2) all then current and future investigations involving comparisons of average-to-average prices. *Id.* at 77,725. Notably, the *Section 123 Determination* did not embrace all the findings of the WTO Appellate Body, stating that the change in policy applied only to investigations that use average-to-average comparisons and did not extend to any other kind of investigation or administrative review. *Id.* at 77,724.

On May 4, 2007, Commerce implemented its findings made under Section 129 of the URAA at the request of the USTR. *Section 129 Determination*, 72 Fed. Reg. at 25,261. In the Section 129 proceeding, Commerce recalculated the dumping margin on the subject merchandise with the use of offsetting, finding that it decreased from 2.59 % to zero. *Id.* at 25,262. The agency, therefore, revoked the antidumping order on hot-rolled carbon steel from the Netherlands, effective for entries of the subject merchandise made on or after April 23, 2007. *Id.* Importantly, Plaintiffs argued during the Section 129 proceeding that Commerce's *Section 123 Determination* was not in accordance with law because the statute prohibits the use of offsetting and requires zeroing. *Issues and Decision Memorandum for the Final Results of the Section 129 Determinations*, A-122-838, A-421-807, A-427-820, A-428-830, A-475-829, A-412-822, A-401-806, A-469-807, A-475-820, A-423-808, A-475-824, A-475-818 (Apr. 9, 2007), Def. Br. App. B at 5-7 *("Section 129 Determination Issues and Decision Memorandum")*. Defendant, however, rejected that notion, stating that the *Section 129 Determination* was concerned only with

6 A determination by the WTO Dispute Settlement Body that a law, regulation, or measure of a WTO Member violates a WTO agreement "as such" means that the "Member's conduct—not only in a particular instance that has occurred, but in future situations as well—will necessarily be inconsistent with that Member's WTO obligations." Report of the Appellate Body, *United States—Sunset Reviews of Anti-Dumping Measures on Oil Country Tubular Goods from Argentina*, WT/ DS268/AB/R, at ¶ 172 (Nov. 29, 2004), available at http://www.wto.org/english/tratop_e/ dispu_e/cases_e/ds268_e.htm. In contrast, an "as applied" determination means that the WTO Member's "application of a general rule to a specific set of facts" is inconsistent with that Member's WTO obligations. *See id.* at 3 n. 22.

bringing the specific investigations at issue in the *Panel Report* into conformity with U.S. obligations under the *AD Agreement. See id.* at 9–11.

II. Standard of Review

The Court assumes that all undisputed facts alleged in the complaint are true and must draw all reasonable inferences in the plaintiff's favor when deciding a motion to dismiss based upon either lack of subject matter jurisdiction or failure to state a claim for which relief may be granted. *See Henke v. United States*, 60 F.3d 795, 797 (Fed. Cir.1995); *Gould, Inc. v. United States*, 935 F.2d 1271, 1274 (Fed. Cir. 1991).

A fundamental question in any action before the Court is whether subject matter jurisdiction exists over the claims presented. *See Steel Co. v. Citizens for a Better Environment*, 523 U.S. 83, 94–95, 118 S. Ct. 1003, 140 L.Ed.2d 210 (1998). "Without jurisdiction the court cannot proceed at all in any cause. Jurisdiction is power to declare the law, and when it ceases to exist, the only function remaining to the court is that of announcing the fact and dismissing the cause." *Ex parte McCardle*, 7 Wall. 506, 74 U.S. 506, 514, 19 L.Ed.2d 264 (1868). The party invoking the Court's jurisdiction bears the burden of establishing it. *See Norsk Hydro Can., Inc. v. United States*, 472 F.3d 1347, 1355 (Fed. Cir. 2006).

The United States is immune from suit unless it consents to be sued, and "the terms of its consent to be sued in any court define that court's jurisdiction to entertain the suit." *Blueport Co., LLC v. United States*, 533 F.3d 1374, 1378 (Fed. Cir. 2008) (quotations & citations omitted). To determine whether there is a waiver of sovereign immunity, the Court must discern the expressed intent of Congress as it appears in the statute, with ambiguities resolved in favor of the sovereign. *See United States v. Williams*, 514 U.S. 527, 531, 115 S. Ct. 1611, 131 L.Ed.2d 608 (1995).

Finally, assuming that all the allegations in the complaint are true, a plaintiff states a claim upon which relief may be granted when it alleges facts that are "enough to raise a right to relief above the speculative level. . . ." *Bell Atl. Corp. v. Twombly*, 550 U.S. 544, 555, 127 S. Ct. 1955, 167 L.Ed.2d 929 (2007) (citations omitted). Though detailed factual allegations are not required, "more than labels and conclusions, and a formulaic recitation of the elements of a cause of action" are needed for the plaintiff's complaint to provide the defendant with fair notice of its claims and survive a motion to dismiss for failure to state a claim upon which relief may be granted. *See id.*

III. Discussion

A. Subject Matter Jurisdiction: The Section 123 Determination

For the first time the Court must decide whether a challenge to a Section 123 determination as such, and as applied in a particular proceeding, falls within its exclusive subject matter jurisdiction. Defendant asks the court to look to the true nature of the action, which allegedly is a challenge to Commerce's *Section 129 Determination*, and dismiss Plaintiffs' complaint because that kind of claim is properly brought only under § 1581(c). Def. Br. 6, 8-9. Alternatively, Defendant argues that a Section 123 determination is not subject to judicial review, given its absence from the list of reviewable agency determinations under § 1516a. Def. Br. 7, 9-10. Defendant also claims that the failure of Congress to provide for judicial review of such agency determinations, in contrast to its treatment of Section 129, demonstrates that the United States has not waived its sovereign immunity as to suits challenging a Section 123 determination. Def Br. 10-11. Finally, even if a challenge to the *Section 123 Determination* could conceivably fit within the confines of § 1581(i), Defendant argues that such determinations have no independent legal effect and that there is no agency action here under the APA because the determination does not aggrieve or affect Plaintiffs. Def. Br. 7, 9-10.

Chapter 95 of Title 28 of the United States Code contains Congress's jurisdictional grant to the Court. The first section, § 1581, is titled "Civil actions against the United States and agencies and officers thereof," consisting of subsections (a) through (j). Each subsection of § 1581 "delineates particular laws over which the Court of International Trade may assert jurisdiction." *Nat'l Corn Growers Ass'n v. Baker*, 840 F.2d 1547, 1555 (Fed. Cir. 1988). In § 1581(i), Congress provided the Court with broad residual jurisdiction over civil actions that arise out of import transactions. *See Conoco, Inc. v. United States Foreign-Trade Zones Bd.*, 18 F.3d 1581, 1588 (Fed. Cir. 1994). However, a caveat to subsection (i) prevents the Court from establishing jurisdiction over a challenge to an antidumping proceeding that is otherwise reviewable under § 1516a(a). § 1581(i). Thus, the subsections of § 1581 must be read in concert and a litigant may only invoke the Court's jurisdiction under § 1581(i) if (1) jurisdiction is unavailable under all other subsections of § 1581, or (2) jurisdiction is available under another subsection of § 1581, but the relief provided by that subsection is manifestly inadequate. § 1581(i); *see NEC Corp. v. United States*, 151 F.3d 1361, 1368 (Fed. Cir. 1998). Where there is doubt over the Court's ability to hear a particular claim, the Court must examine the true nature of the action to determine whether it has subject matter jurisdiction over the issue. *See Norsk Hydro Can., Inc.*, 472 F.3d at 1355.

The Court has recognized that a facial challenge to a statute or regulation is different from a claim that a law, as applied, is contrary to law, involving unique legal questions and distinct remedies. *See, e.g.*, *Impact Steel Can. Corp. v. United States*, 31 CIT ___, ___, 533 F. Supp. 2d 1298, 1302 (2007) ("Impact Steel"); *Parkdale Int'l, Ltd. v. United States*, 31 CIT ___, ___, 508 F. Supp. 2d 1338, 1347–48 (2007) ("Parkdale"). A facial challenge involves a claim that a practice or rule is per se illegal, and could not be statutorily valid under any circumstances. *See Parkdale*, 31 CIT at ___ n. 5, 508 F. Supp. 2d at 1347 n. 5. In contrast, an as applied challenge concerns a claim that the application of a law to a particular proceeding, and the factual determinations and legal conclusions reached as a result of the use of such rule or practice, is unlawful. *See* id., 31 CIT at ___, 508 F. Supp. 2d at 1347.

1. Availability of 28 U.S.C. § 1581(c) and Adequate Relief Thereunder

Under the facts of this case, the true nature of Plaintiffs' challenge to the application of the *Section 123 Determination* in a particular proceeding is nothing more than a mislabeling of the charge that the final results of the *Section 129 Determination* are contrary to law, a claim properly brought only under § 1581(c).[7] The purpose of a Section 123 determination is to amend, rescind, or modify an agency regulation or practice found to be inconsistent with any of the Uruguay Round Agreements, whereas a Section 129 determination affects the application of that regulation or practice in a specific proceeding. §§ 3533(g)(1), 3538(a)(1), 3538(b)(1). It is clear that these proceedings are indeed different in kind, and the Defendant admits as much. Def. Br. 8. However, it cannot be said in this case that the application of the *Section 123 Determination* is any different in substance from the existing *Section 129 Determination*. Here Commerce's decision to use offsetting in certain proceedings was applied to recalculate the weighted-average dumping margin for the subject merchandise. Additionally, the relief sought by the Plaintiffs in this claim is identical to that sought in the challenge to the final results of a Section 129 proceeding—that Commerce's decision to use offsetting in its calculation of the weighted-average dumping margin for the subject merchandise is contrary to law. U.S. Steel Compl. ¶¶ 20–21 in Consol. Court No. 07-170; ArcelorMittal Compl. ¶¶ 29–31 in Consol. Court No. 07-170. Thus, the court must dismiss Plaintiffs' challenge to the application of the *Section 123 Determination* because adequate relief for the claim is available under § 1581(c) and that subsection has not been shown to provide a manifestly inadequate remedy under the circumstances.

Moreover, adequate relief exists under § 1581(c) for Plaintiffs' facial challenge to the *Section 123 Determination*. It is true that a Section 123 determination is not one of the listed administrative proceedings that are subject to judicial review under § 1516a. Indeed, no other provision of the United States Code expressly states whether a Section 123 determination is subject to judicial review and, if so, which federal court has jurisdiction over such an action. However, a careful reading of the complaints and briefings in Consol. Court Nos. 07-170 and 07-475 forces the court to dismiss Plaintiffs' facial challenge to the *Section 123 Determination* here because the remedy sought in this case may be adequately provided under § 1581(c). In Consol. Court No. 07-170, Plaintiffs challenge both the *Section 123 Determination* as such, as well as the final results of the *Section 129 Determination* under § 1581(c). U.S. Steel Compl. ¶¶ 16–21 in Consol. Court No. 07-170;

---

7 Pursuant to § 1581(c), this Court has exclusive jurisdiction over any civil action commenced under section 516A of the Tariff Act of 1930, codified as amended at § 1516a, which provides for judicial review of, among other proceedings, a Section 129 determination. § 1516a(a)(2)(B)(vii).

ArcelorMittal Compl. ¶¶ 25–31 in Consol. Court No. 07-170. The Court, as it has done in other cases under § 1581(c), may address a facial challenge to a general agency practice employed by Commerce, as well as to the final results of an agency proceeding that is subject to judicial review under § 1516a. *See, e.g., Parkdale Int'l v. United States*, 30 CIT 551, 429 F. Supp. 2d 1324 (2006). Equally important is the fact that Plaintiffs raised a facial challenge to the *Section 123 Determination* during the Section 129 proceeding, a claim that Defendant disregarded as being outside the scope of the proceeding. *Section 129 Determination Issues and Decision Memorandum* at 5–7, 9–11. Plaintiffs may contest Defendant's determination on this issue when it asks the court to review the final results of the *Section 129 Determination*, and in fact has done so in Consol. Court No. 07-170 under § 1581(c). Thus, because adequate relief lies under another subsection of § 1581, the court may not exercise jurisdiction over Plaintiffs' claims here under § 1581(i).[8] *See NEC Corp.*, 151 F.3d at 1368.

Finally, because the court finds that it does not have jurisdiction over Plaintiffs' claims under the facts of this case as they have an adequate alternative remedy, there is nothing left for it to decide and therefore it must dismiss this action filed pursuant to § 1581(i). *See Ex parte McCardle*, 74 U.S. at 514, 19 L.Ed. 264. Accordingly, the court need not address Defendant's arguments of whether (1) the United States waived its sovereign immunity, (2) a Section 123 determination is agency action under the APA, (3) Plaintiffs have Article III constitutional and prudential standing, or (4) Plaintiffs stated a claim upon which relief may be granted.

IV. Conclusion

For the reasons discussed herein, Defendant and Defendant-Intervenor's Motions to Dismiss are granted as adequate relief lies for Plaintiffs' facial and as applied challenges to the *Section 123 Determination* under § 1581(c).

---

8 The court's decision here should not be read to suggest that an agency action under Section 123 of the URAA is free from judicial review. It may be the case that, under certain facts where none of the other subsections of § 1581 provides a plaintiff with adequate relief, § 1581(i) will be the most appropriate avenue to challenge a general change in agency practice as it is adopted by the United States in a Section 123 determination. However, because the remedy provided by § 1581(c) will address the relief sought by Plaintiffs, the facts of this case do not permit the court to assume jurisdiction under § 1581(i).

UNITED STATES
v.
EURODIF S. A.

129 S. Ct. 878 (2009)
Decided January 26, 2009

Malcolm L. Stewart for the petitioner in No. 07-1059.

H. Bartow Farr, Washington, DC, for the petitioners in No. 07-1078.

Caitlin J. Halligan, New York, NY, for the respondents.

Gregory G. Garre, Solicitor General, Counsel of Record, Department of Justice, Washington, D.C., for the United States.

Peter B. Saba, General Counsel, James A. Schoettler, Jr., Assistant General Counsel, USEC Inc., of Counsel, H. Bartow Farr III, Farr & Taranto, Washington, D.C. 20036, Sheldon E. Hochberg, Counsel of Record, Eric C. Emerson, Charles G. Cole, Michael A. Vatis, John P. Nolan, Steptoe & Johnson LLP, Washington, D.C., for Petitioners USEC Inc. and United States Enrichment Corporation.

Nancy A. Fischer, Counsel of Record, Stephan E. Becker, David J. Cynamon, Joshua D. Fitzhugh, Christine J. Sohar, Pillsbury Winthrop Shaw Pittman LLP, Washington, D.C., for Respondent the Ad Hoc Utilities Group.

Lisa R. Eskow, Arthur C. D'Andrea, Weil, Gotshal & Manges LLP, Austin, TX, Stuart M. Rosen, Caitlin J. Halligan, Counsel of Record, Gregory Silbert, W. Andrew Ryu, Weil, Gotshal & Manges LLP, New York, NY, for Respondents Eurodif S.A., Areva NC S.A., and Areva NC Inc.

John B. Bellinger, III, Legal Adviser, Department of State, Washington, D.C., Daniel J. Dell'Orto, Acting General Counsel, Department of Defense, Washington, D.C., Lily Fu Claffee, General Counsel, John D. McInerney, Chief Counsel for Import Administration, David R. Mason, Jr., Senior Counsel, Quentin M. Baird, Attorney, Department of Commerce, Washington, D.C., David R. Hill, General Counsel, Department of Energy, Washington, D.C.,

Gregory G. Garre, Acting Solicitor General, Counsel of Record, Gregory G. Katsas, Assistant Attorney General, Edwin S. Kneedler, Deputy Solicitor General, Leondra R. Kruger, Assistant to the Solicitor General, Jeanne E. Davidson, Patricia M. McCarthy, Stephen C. Tosini, Attorneys, Department of Justice, Washington, D.C., for the United States.

Justice SOUTER delivered the opinion of the Court.

Section 731 of the Tariff Act of 1930 calls for "antidumping" duties on "foreign merchandise" sold in the United States at "less than its fair value," 19 U.S.C. § 1673, but does not touch international sales of services. These cases test the application of this antidumping provision to imports of low enriched uranium (LEU), a highly processed derivative of natural uranium used as nuclear fuel, when domestic utilities contract to obtain LEU for cash plus unenriched uranium delivered to a foreign enricher. Although the parties' contracts call these transactions sales of uranium enrichment services, the Commerce Department treats them as sales of "foreign merchandise" subject to the antidumping provision. The issue is whether the Commerce Department's way of seeing the transactions as sales of goods rather than services reflects a permissible interpretation and application of § 1673. We hold that it does.

I.

There are five steps in transforming elemental uranium into fuel rods for nuclear powerplants. After uranium ore is mined, it is milled into uranium concentrate called "yellowcake," which is next converted into uranium hexafluoride gas or "feed uranium." The fissionable isotope in unenriched feed uranium is then concentrated, producing LEU in pellet form, which is in turn made into uranium fuel rods. These cases are about the fourth step: enriching uranium feedstock into LEU.

The uranium isotope needed for a nuclear reaction, U-235, amounts only to .711 percent by weight of natural uranium. Uranium whose concentration or "assay," of U-235 has been enhanced to 20 percent or more is weapons-grade, highly enriched uranium (HEU), whereas LEU has a U-235 assay of 3 to 5 percent, making it useful as nuclear fuel. One way to produce LEU, and the method at issue in these cases, is gaseous diffusion,[1] whereby gaseous feed uranium is pushed through a long series of filters, separating the gas into two streams. The stream passing through the filters (the "product stream") gains a higher concentration of the lighter U-235 isotope than the stream that is filtered out (the "tails"). Because the concentration reached at each individual filter is minor, the gas must be forced through hundreds or even thousands of filters, at great expenditure of electricity, before the product stream reaches the desired assay. The amount of energy required to enrich a quantity of feed uranium to a given assay is measured in terms of an industry standard called a "separative work unit" or SWU (pronounced "swoo"). In practice,

1 LEU can also be produced through a centrifuge method or by back-blending unenriched uranium with weapons-grade uranium.

however, a given degree of enrichment will depend on adjusting the quantities of two separate variables, feed uranium and electricity, in inverse proportions. Thus, if the electric rate is stable but the value of feed uranium falls, an enricher may produce LEU by "overfeeding," subjecting a greater quantity of feed uranium to fewer SWUs, and when the value of feed uranium goes up and electricity does not, "underfeeding" can use more SWUs to squeeze extra U-235 from the tails.

Nuclear utilities generally get LEU in one of two ways. Under an "enriched uranium product" or "EUP" contract, a utility simply buys a desired quantity and assay of LEU for cash. Under a "SWU contract," the utility provides a quantity of feed uranium and pays the enricher for the SWUs to produce the quantity and assay of LEU called for.[2] Despite their name, SWU contracts do not require that the contractual number of SWUs actually be applied to the quantity of uranium provided, Notice of Final Determination of Sales at Less Than Fair Value: Low Enriched Uranium From France, 66 Fed. Reg. 65877, 65884 (2001) (hereinafter LEU from France); rather, the enricher remains free to overfeed or underfeed so long as it delivers the specified LEU. Moreover, because feed uranium is fungible, and "for all intents and purposes, trades like a commodity," *ibid.,* and because profitable operation of an enrichment plant requires the constant processing of feed uranium from the enricher's undifferentiated stock, the LEU provided to a utility under a SWU contract cannot be traced to the particular unenriched uranium the utility provided.

Petitioners, USEC Inc. and its subsidiary, United States Enrichment Corporation, (USEC collectively) run the only uranium enrichment factory in the United States,[3] which was built by the United States Government in the 1950s and run by various federal agencies until it was leased to USEC in 1998. In December 2000, USEC petitioned the Commerce Department for relief under § 731 of the Tariff Act, alleging that LEU imported from France and other European countries under both EUP and SWU contracts was being sold in the United States at less than fair value and was materially harming domestic industry. Notice of Initiation of Antidumping Duty Investigations: Low Enriched Uranium From France, Germany, the Netherlands, and the United Kingdom, 66 Fed. Reg. 1080 (2001).

Section 731 of the Tariff Act of 1930, as added by § 101 of the Trade Agreements Act of 1979, 93 Stat. 144, as amended, 19 U.S.C. § 1673, provides a two-step process to address harm to domestic manufacturing from foreign goods sold at an unfair price:

> "If—
>
> "(1) the administering authority [the Secretary of Commerce] determines that a class or kind of foreign merchandise is being, or is likely to be, sold in the United States at less than its fair value, and

---

2 Many SWU contracts give the utility the option of providing a comparable quantity of uranium concentrate in lieu of the specified feed uranium. App. 13, 83, 268–69 (Sealed).

3 There are only five major uranium enrichers in the world, a scarcity that illustrates the "huge financial investment in facilities and a technically skilled work force" necessary to support the enrichment process. LEU from France, 66 Fed. Reg. 65884.

"(2) the [United States International Trade] Commission determines that—

"(A) an industry in the United States—

"(i) is materially injured, or

"(ii) is threatened with material injury, or

"(B) the establishment of an industry in the United States is materially retarded, by reason of imports of that merchandise or by reason of sales (or the likelihood of sales) of that merchandise for importation,

"then there shall be imposed upon such merchandise an antidumping duty, in addition to any other duty imposed, in an amount equal to the amount by which the normal value exceeds the export price (or the constructed export price) for the merchandise. . . ."

See also § 1677(1) (designating the Secretary of Commerce as the "'administering authority'"); § 1677(2) (explaining that the term "'Commission'" refers to the United States International Trade Commission).

The Tariff Act's antidumping provision derives from similar terms in the Anti-Dumping Act, 1921, 42 Stat. 11, which were adopted to "protec[t] our industries and labor against a now common species of commercial warfare of dumping goods on our markets at less than cost or home value if necessary until our industries are destroyed. . . ." H.R.Rep. No. 1, 67th Cong., 1st Sess., p. 23 (1921).

Following the USEC charges, the Commerce Department opened an investigation into the practices of respondents, a French enricher, Eurodif, S.A., its owner, Compagnie Général des Matiéres Nucleaires (now AREVA NC), its U.S. subsidiary, COGEMA (now AREVA NC, Inc.), and United States utilities that consume LEU (Eurodif collectively). Eurodif conceded that EUP contracts were for the sale of LEU, but argued that SWU contracts involved only the sale of uranium enrichment services, and were therefore outside the scope of § 1673. LEU From France, 66 Fed. Reg. 65882-65883.

In its final determination, the Commerce Department concluded that LEU from France, including LEU acquired under SWU contracts, was being sold, or likely to be sold, in the United States at less than fair value.[4] *Id.,* at 65878. In deciding that SWU contracts are for a sale of LEU, not enrichment services, the Department stressed several features of the transactions. First, because the enrichment process accounts for approximately 60 percent of the value of LEU and works a "substantial transformation" on uranium feedstock, *id.,* at 65881, enrichment creates "the essential character" of LEU, *id.,* at 65884. Second, "enrichers not only have complete control over the enrichment process, but in fact control the level of usage of

4 The Commerce Department concluded in a separate determination that LEU from the United Kingdom, Germany, and the Netherlands was not being sold, or likely to be sold, at less than fair value. Notice of Final Determinations of Sales at Not Less Than Fair Value: Low Enriched Uranium from the United Kingdom, Germany and the Netherlands, *id.,* at 65886.

the natural uranium provided." *Ibid.* Third, the utilities themselves take no part in the manufacture of LEU and are the sole purchasers of the product. *Ibid.*

The Commerce Department also rejected the argument that LEU transferred pursuant to SWU contracts should not be considered "sold" in light of a "tolling" regulation then (but no longer) in effect. *Ibid.* The regulation stated that a "toller," a subcontractor who sells processing services in, or material for incorporation into, subject merchandise, would not be considered a manufacturer or producer "where the toller or subcontractor does not acquire ownership, and does not control the relevant sale, of the subject merchandise." 19 CFR § 351.401(h) (2000) (withdrawn in Import Administration, Withdrawal of Regulations Governing the Treatment of Subcontractors, ("Tolling" Operations), 73 Fed. Reg. 16517 (2008) (hereinafter Tolling Operations)). This regulation, the Commerce Department explained, was intended to apply in situations where a good is first sold by a manufacturer and then resold by an exporter or reseller. LEU from France, 66 Fed. Reg. 65880. The regulation provides that in such a situation the second sale should be used to calculate the U.S. price and normal value of the manufactured good; however, the Commerce Department concluded, the regulation was not meant to preclude anti-dumping duties where a manufacturer makes the only relevant sale that can be used to establish U.S. price and normal value. *Ibid.; id.,* at 65884–65885.

Finally, the Commerce Department reasoned that language in SWU contracts speaking of the transactions as the sale of enrichment services could not control, lest deferring to the parties' characterizations allow them to "convert trade in goods into trade in so-called `manufacturing services,' . . . thereby exposing industries to injury by unfair trade practices without the remedy of the [antidumping] laws." *Id.,* at 65881. In economic reality, the Commerce Department said, "the contracts designated as SWU contracts are functionally equivalent to those designated as EUP transactions." *Id.,* at 65885.[5]

Eurodif challenged the Department's determination before the Court of International Trade (CIT), which remanded for "a more persuasive explanation" of the tolling regulation. *USEC Inc. v. United States,* 259 F. Supp. 2d 1310, 1326 (2003). On remand, the Commerce Department repeated that the tolling regulation governed which price should be used to calculate antidumping duties, not whether imports are subject to the antidumping provision in the first instance. Final Remand Determination, USEC Inc. and United States Enrichment Corporation v. United States (June 23, 2003), App. G to Pet. for Cert. 211a (hereinafter Final Remand Determination). The Department further explained its conclusion that SWU contracts lead to transfers of LEU for consideration. The contracts and other evidence

5 In February 2002, the International Trade Commission found that imports of LEU from France materially injured the enrichment industry in the United States, allowing the imposition of antidumping duties. U.S. Int'l Trade Comm'n, Low Enriched Uranium from France, Germany, the Netherlands, and the United Kingdom (Pub. No. 3486).

in the record convinced the Department that "enrichers own, and hold title to, all the LEU they produce," *id.,* at 217a, a conclusion grounded on findings that "enrichers hold inventories of uranium from various sources, including uranium owned by the enricher itself, and produce LEU without relying solely upon the input from a particular customer." *Id.,* at 221a. Finally, the Department emphasized that the enrichers "have complete control over the enrichment process and control the amount of uranium and energy actually used in producing the LEU." *Id.,* at 231a.

The CIT was unconvinced and reversed, relying on what it candidly recognized as a "legal fiction" expressed in SWU contracts, "that the very feed uranium delivered by a utility to an enricher is enriched and then returned as LEU to the utility." *USEC Inc. v. United States,* 281 F. Supp. 2d 1334, 1339 (2003). The CIT reasoned, because "nothing in the record support[ed] a determination that the enricher has any ownership rights," the Commerce Department's determination was "unsupported by substantial evidence and not in accordance with law." *Id.,* at 1340.

USEC challenged this conclusion in an interlocutory appeal to the Court of Appeals for the Federal Circuit, which affirmed. *Eurodif S.A. v. United States,* 411 F.3d 1355 (2005) *(Eurodif I).* The court approached the issues much as the CIT had, with the observation that "the SWU contracts in this case do not evidence any intention by the parties to vest the enrichers with ownership rights in the delivered unenriched uranium or the finished LEU." *Id.,* at 1362. It recalled that in a previous case, *Florida Power & Light Co. v. United States,* 307 F.3d 1364 (C.A.Fed.2002), it had accepted the Government's position that SWU contracts were for services, not for "'disposal of personal property,'" and so were outside the cause of action provided by the Contract Disputes Act of 1978, 41 U.S.C. § 601 *et seq. Eurodif I, supra,* at 1363, and n. 3 (quoting *Florida Power & Light Co., supra,* at 1373). While the court conceded that SWU agreements "do 'not fall neatly' either into the category of contracts for services or the category of contracts for the sale of goods," 411 F.3d, at 1364 (quoting *Florida Power & Light Co., supra,* at 1373–1374), it still concluded that "even under the deferential standard of review that we apply in this case, we choose not to ignore our previous holdings." *Eurodif I, supra,* at 1363.

Shortly after this decision, we held in *National Cable & Telecommunications Assn. v. Brand X Internet Services,* 545 U.S. 967, 982–983, 125 S. Ct. 2688, 162 L.Ed.2d 820 (2005), that a court's choice of one reasonable reading of an ambiguous statute does not preclude an implementing agency from later adopting a different reasonable interpretation. On rehearing, the Federal Circuit responded to *National Cable & Telecommunications Association* by explaining that it had not rejected the Commerce Department's position because it conflicted with the prior interpretive choice that carried the day in *Florida Power & Light. Eurodif S.A. v. United States,* 423 F.3d 1275, 1277–1278 (2005) *(Eurodif II).* The Circuit, rather, saw no statutory uncertainty to be resolved: "the antidumping duty statute unambiguously applies to the sale of goods and not services" and "it is clear that [SWU] contracts are contracts for services and not goods." *Id.,* at 1278. After final judgment was entered, *Eurodif S.A. v. United States,* 506 F.3d 1051, 1053 (C.A.Fed.2007) *(Eurodif III),* we granted certiorari 553 U.S. ___, 128 S. Ct. 2056, 170 L.Ed.2d 792 (2008), to consider whether transactions under SWU contracts may be subjected to antidumping duties under the Tariff Act. We now reverse.

II.

The issue is not whether, for purposes of 19 U.S.C. § 1673, the better view is that a SWU contract is one for the sale of services, not goods. The statute gives this determination to the Department of Commerce in the first instance, § 1677(1), and when the Department exercises this authority in the course of adjudication, its interpretation governs in the absence of unambiguous statutory language to the contrary or unreasonable resolution of language that is ambiguous.[6] *United States v. Mead Corp.,* 533 U.S. 218, 229–230, 121 S. Ct. 2164, 150 L.Ed.2d 292 (2001) (citing *Chevron U.S.A. Inc. v. Natural Resources Defense Council, Inc.,* 467 U.S. 837, 104 S. Ct. 2778, 81 L.Ed.2d 694 (1984)). This is so even after a change in regulatory treatment, which "is not a basis for declining to analyze the agency's interpretation under the *Chevron* framework." *National Cable & Telecommunications Assn.,* 545 U.S., at 981, 125 S. Ct. 2688. "'[T]he whole point of *Chevron* is to leave the discretion provided by the ambiguities of a statute with the implementing agency.'" *Ibid.* (quoting *Smiley v. Citibank (South Dakota), N. A.,* 517 U.S. 735, 742, 116 S. Ct. 1730, 135 L.Ed.2d 25 (1996)).[7]

In approaching the Department's position on the application of § 1673, two threshold propositions must be taken as given. First, we think the Department reasonably concluded that § 1673 is not limited by its terms to cash-only sales. Otherwise, any sale of a manufactured product could be exempted from the operation of § 1673 by a contractual term stating part of the purchase price in terms of a commodity.[8]

---

6 The specific factual findings on which an agency relies in applying its interpretation are conclusive unless unsupported by substantial evidence. 5 U.S.C. § 706(2)(E).

7 Respondents' assertion that the Commerce Department's prior tolling regulation is inconsistent with its position in these cases is therefore beside the point. For the reasons given by the Department in its remand determination, we are not convinced that the tolling regulation precludes viewing SWU transactions as the sale of LEU; but even if it did, it has since been withdrawn, Tolling Operations, 73 Fed. Reg. 16517, and cannot now constrain the Commerce Department's interpretive authority under *Chevron. National Cable & Telecommunications Assn.,* 545 U.S., at 981, 125 S. Ct. 2688 ("Unexplained inconsistency is, at most, a reason for holding an interpretation to be an arbitrary and capricious change from agency practice under the Administrative Procedure Act"). Likewise, even if the position taken by the Department of Energy in *Florida Power & Light Co. v. United States,* 307 F.3d 1364 (CA Fed.2002), was inconsistent with the Government's position here, it would not speak to the deference owed the Commerce Department under *Chevron.*

8 Respondents argue that, after determining that SWU contracts involved the sale of LEU, the Commerce Department employed an impermissible methodology by constructing the normal value of the LEU based on the combined costs to Eurodif of obtaining feed uranium

Second, in applying § 1673, the Commerce Department is not bound by the "legal fiction [created by SWU contracts] that the very feed uranium delivered by a utility to an enricher is enriched and then returned as LEU to the utility." *USEC,* 281 F. Supp. 2d, at 1339. The parties are free to contract as they wish, and they may genuinely regard SWU agreements as contracts for the sale of enrichment services. But, whatever the significance of such a term in a contract dispute, cf. *Florida Power & Light Co.,* 307 F.3d 1364, it is well settled that in reading regulatory and taxation statutes, "form should be disregarded for substance and the emphasis should be on economic reality." *Tcherepnin v. Knight,* 389 U.S. 332, 336, 88 S. Ct. 548, 19 L.Ed.2d 564 (1967). See also *Frank Lyon Co. v. United States,* 435 U.S. 561, 573, 98 S. Ct. 1291, 55 L.Ed.2d 550 (1978) ("'In the field of taxation, administrators of the laws, and the courts, are concerned with substance and realities, and formal written documents are not rigidly binding'" (quoting *Helvering v. F. & R. Lazarus & Co.,* 308 U.S. 252, 255, 60 S. Ct. 209, 84 L.Ed. 226 (1939))). Surrender to private contractual terms is especially uncalled for in dealing with international tariffs, as Congress saw when it amended the Tariff Act to say that the sale of foreign merchandise includes "the entering into of any leasing arrangement regarding the merchandise that is equivalent to the sale of the merchandise." Trade and Tariff Act of 1984, § 602(b)(2), 98 Stat. 3024, 19 U.S.C. § 1673.

Since public law is not constrained by private fiction, the test of the Department's position turns first on whether the statute clearly excludes a transaction involving mixed payment for LEU that may and almost certainly will be produced from uranium feed distinct from what the utility provides. No one disputes that § 1673 applies to the sale of goods, not services, LEU From France, 66 Fed. Reg. 65882–65883. Nor do we think anyone would deny that the exchange of cash combined with a commodity for a product that uses that very commodity as a constituent material is sometimes a sale of services and sometimes a sale of goods, the distinction being clear at the extremes. A customer who comes to a laundry with cash and dirty shirts is clearly purchasing cleaning services, not clean shirts. And a customer who provides cash and sand to a manufacturer of generic silicon processors is clearly buying computer chips rather than sand enhancement services.

But the line blurs when the facts get more complicated, and SWU contracts exemplify a class of transactions that the Federal Circuit recognized does "'not fall neatly' either into the category of contracts for services or the category of contracts for the sale of goods." *Eurodif I,* 411 F.3d, at 1364 (quoting *Florida Power & Light*

---

and enrichment. Brief for Respondent Eurodif S.A. et al. 48–50. These calculations, respondents argue, "were a charade, underscoring that the antidumping laws cannot be applied to these SWU contracts." *Id.,* at 48. To the degree respondents' argument is that antidumping duties may never be applied to mixed cash-commodity sales, it is doomed by implausibility. If respondents are contending that the Commerce Department's dumping determination improperly assessed the normal value of LEU, they are raising an issue well outside the scope of our grant of certiorari.

Co., supra, at 1373–1374). The agreement is not like the laundry ticket, which says that the same shirts are supposed to come back, just minus the dirt around the collar. And it is not on all fours with the agreement of the chip buyer and the manufacturer, in which it is inescapable that the silicon processors delivered are a separate good from the sand provided. Section 1673 simply does not speak with the precision necessary to say definitively whether it applies to the LEU and the agreement that gives the utility a right to get it.

This is the very situation in which we look to an authoritative agency for a decision about the statute's scope, which is defined in cases at the statutory margin by the agency's application of it, and once the choice is made we ask only whether the Department's application was reasonable. As to that, the Commerce Department relied on two related characteristics of these transactions in deciding SWU contracts should be treated as a sale of LEU. It stressed that the utility in a SWU contract provides cash plus a fungible commodity that is not tracked after its delivery to the enricher, in exchange for a product owned by the enricher.[9] And it recognized that the enrichment process results in a substantial transformation of the unenriched uranium.

The combination of these characteristics reasonably captures a common understanding of the sale of a good. Because an individual's shirts are not fungible, they are tracked during the cleaning process and returned to the same customer who brought them in; there are no good reasons to treat them as owned for a time by the laundry, and no one does. And without any transfer of ownership, the salient feature of the transaction is the cleaning of the shirt, a service. Conversely, where a constituent material is untracked and fungible, ownership is usually seen as

9 Eurodif argues that the Commerce Department erred in concluding that enrichers own LEU prior to its delivery under a SWU contract. *Id.,* at 36–37. While the precise form of this argument is unclear, it fails under any reading. Respondents seem to mean that the Commerce Department's interpretation of § 1673 is impermissible as being inconsistent with the formal terms of SWU contracts, an argument we rejected above. The argument could also be read to suggest that the Commerce Department lacked substantial evidence to conclude that, contractual formalities aside, enrichers in fact own the LEU provided under SWU contracts prior to its delivery. But the evidence in the record not only supports the Department's conclusion, it compels it. It is undisputed that the LEU delivered under a SWU contract is not actually derived from the feed uranium provided as consideration; as CIT observed, the notion that the same feed uranium delivered by a utility to an enricher is enriched and then returned as LEU to the utility is "a legal fiction." *USEC Inc. v. United States,* 281 F. Supp. 2d 1334, 1339 (2003). Moreover, the enricher is free to vary the amount of feed uranium used to produce an order of LEU, either stockpiling feed uranium or supplementing its stores from other sources. Finally, the SWU contracts at issue provide that the utility retains title to the feed uranium until delivery of the LEU, at which point it obtains title in the LEU. In light of this process, some entity must own the LEU prior to delivery and obtain title to the feed uranium after delivery, absent some modern analog to the abhorrent possibility of an abeyance of seizen; the enricher is the only serious candidate.

transferred, and the transaction is less likely to be a sale of services, as the Court explained years ago in distinguishing a common-law bailment from a sale:

> "[W]here logs are delivered to be sawed into boards, or leather to be made into shoes, rags into paper, olives into oil, grapes into wine, wheat into flour, if the product of the identical articles delivered is to be returned to the original owner in a new form, it is said to be a bailment, and the title never vests in the manufacturer. If, on the other hand, the manufacturer is not bound to return the same wheat or flour or paper, but may deliver any other of equal value, it is said to be a sale or a loan, and the title to the thing delivered vests in the manufacturer." *Powder Co. v. Burkhardt,* 97 U.S. 110, 116, 24 L.Ed. 973 (1878).[10]

And when the manufacturer is not only free to return different material, but also substantially transforms the material it uses, it is even more likely that the object of the transaction will be seen as a new product, not work on enduring material of primary interest to the buyer. After all, what makes the hypothetical exchange of sand for silicon processors so obviously a sale of goods is the extreme transformation brought about by the chip manufacturer.

These are good analytical grounds to show that SWU transactions are reasonably placed within the ambit of sale of goods, and the Department's reliance on them is reinforced by practical reasons aimed at preserving the effectiveness of antidumping duties. There is no dispute that LEU sold under an EUP contract at less than fair value must be subjected to antidumping duties under § 1673, there being a clear sale of goods when a domestic utility pays a single sale price in cash for the feed uranium and enrichment components represented by LEU. If foreign enrichers set this price below the fair value of LEU, the domestic enrichment industry is obviously open to material injury, the very threat the antidumping statute was meant to counter, see H.R.Rep. No. 1, at 23. But the same injury would occur if a SWU contract were untouchable. Under a SWU contract, the domestic utility pays cash to a third party for unenriched uranium and provides this along with additional cash in exchange for LEU; any EUP contract could be structured as a SWU contract simply by splitting the transaction in two, one contract to buy unenriched uranium and another to enrich it.[11] And the restructuring would not stop with uranium; contracts for imported pasta would be replaced by separate contracts for wheat and wheat processing services, sweater imports would give way to separate contracts for wool and knitting services, and antidumping duties

---

10 Common law definitions do not necessarily control the meaning of terms in modern trade laws; we merely mean to show the long pedigree of the distinction relied upon by the Commerce Department.

11 This would be particularly easy in these cases, since COGEMA, Eurodif's parent company, "is a major world supplier of natural uranium for the production of LEU." Final Remand Determination, App. G to Pet. for Cert. 221a, n. 38. In fact, many SWU contracts provide that if a utility fails to deliver feed uranium, the enricher will substitute feed uranium of its own, which may then be purchased from the enricher. App. 13-14, 185–186, 537 (Sealed).

would primarily chastise the uncreative.[12] The Commerce Department's attempt to foreclose this absurd result by treating SWU transactions as sales of goods is eminently reasonable.

III.

Where a domestic buyer's cash and an untracked, fungible commodity are exchanged with a foreign contractor for a substantially transformed version of the same commodity, the Commerce Department may reasonably treat the transaction as the sale of a good under § 1673. We therefore reverse the judgment of the Federal Circuit and remand the cases for further proceedings consistent with this opinion.

It is so ordered.

---

12 Eurodif suggests the Commerce Department could combat such circumvention of antidumping duties by taxing domestic downstream sales of such products. Brief for Respondent Eurodif S.A. et al. 53–54. But this ignores the substantial number of manufactured goods that are not resold. More fundamentally, this argument fails to explain why the Commerce Department should be required to chase after downstream resellers when the first sale has the same economic substance.

UNION STEEL
v.
UNITED STATES

645 F. Supp. 2d 1298 (C.I.T. 2009)
Decided September 28, 2009

Troutman Sanders LLP (Donald B. Cameron, Brady W. Mills, Jeffrey S. Grimson, Julie C. Mendoza, Rudi W. Planert, and Mary S. Hodgins) for plaintiff.

Tony West, Assistant Attorney General, *Jeanne E. Davidson,* Director, *Patricia M. McCarthy,* Assistant Director, Commercial Litigation Branch, Civil Division, United States Department of Justice (Claudia Burke); *Jonathan Zielinski* and *Daniel J. Calhoun,* Office of the Chief Counsel for Import Administration, United States Department of Commerce, of counsel, for defendant.

Skadden Arps Slate Meagher & Flom, LLP (Ellen J. Schneider, Jeffrey D. Gerrish, Jared R. Wessel, John J. Mangan, Robert E. Lighthizer, and Luke A. Meisner) for Defendant-Intervenor United States Steel Corporation.

Wiley Rein, LLP (*Timothy C. Brightbill, Alan H. Price,* and *Robert E. DeFrancesco, III*), Washington, DC, for Defendant-Intervenor Nucor Corporation.

OPINION AND ORDER

STANCEU, Judge.

Plaintiff Union Steel ("Union") contests the final determination ("Final Results") issued by the International Trade Administration, U.S. Department of Commerce ("Commerce" or the "Department"), in a periodic administrative review of an anti-dumping duty order on imports of certain corrosion-resistant carbon steel flat products (the "subject merchandise") from the Republic of Korea ("Korea"). *See* Certain Corrosion-Resistant Carbon Steel Flat Products from the Republic of Korea: Notice of Final Results of the Thirteenth Admin. Review, 73 Fed. Reg. 14,220 (Mar. 17, 2008) ("Final Results"). Union, a producer and exporter of subject merchandise and a respondent in the review, brings two claims. Union challenges Commerce's "model match" methodology, by which Commerce compared Union's U.S. sales of painted corrosion-resistant carbon steel flat products to Union's home market sales, which included not only painted products but also "laminated" products, i.e., products that are coated with a plastic film rather than paint. Second, plaintiff challenges Commerce's construction of 19 U.S.C. § 1677(35) (2006), according to which Commerce concluded that it was permissible to apply "zeroing," i.e., the deeming of the sales a respondent makes in the United States at prices above normal value to have individual dumping margins of zero rather than negative margins.

Without confessing error, defendant requests that the court order a partial voluntary remand to allow Commerce to reconsider its denial, made during the review, of plaintiff's request to revise the model match methodology. Plaintiff responds that a remand on this issue is required but submits that the court, in issuing a remand order, should consider plaintiff's substantive arguments, make certain findings with respect to Commerce's model match determination, and issue specific instructions governing the scope and substance of the remand redetermination. Defendant-intervenors Nucor Corporation ("Nucor") and United States Steel Corporation ("U.S.Steel") argue that the Department's model match methodology is supported by substantial evidence and otherwise consistent with law and, in the alternative, oppose the specific remand instructions sought by Union. For the reasons discussed herein, the court grants defendant's request for voluntary remand and declines to issue a remand order in the form that plaintiff advocates.

Based on applicable precedent, the court affirms the Department's use of zeroing in the Final Results. Accordingly, the court denies relief on plaintiff's second claim.

I. Background

In September 2006, Commerce initiated the thirteenth administrative review of an antidumping duty order on certain corrosion-resistant carbon steel flat products from Korea for the period of August 1, 2005, through July 31, 2006 (the "period of review"). *Initiation of Antidumping and Countervailing Duty Admin. Reviews,* 71 Fed. Reg. 57,465 (Sept. 29, 2006). In conducting the review, Commerce sent Union and other respondents a questionnaire detailing twelve model-match criteria, the first of which was termed "TYPE." *Letter from U.S. Dep't of Commerce to Union Steel Manufacturing Co., Ltd.* (Sept. 13, 2006) (Admin.R.Doc. No. 7); *Letter from U.S. Dep't of Commerce to Dongbu Steel Co., Ltd.,* App. IV at 1 (Sept. 13, 2006) (Admin.R.Doc. No. 9); Br. in Supp. of the Mot. of Pl. Union Steel for J. upon the Agency R. 2-3 ("Pl.'s Br."). The questionnaire listed four possible types of corrosion-resistant carbon steel flat products: (1) "Clad (metals bonded by the hot-rolling process), less than 3/16" in thickness"; (2) "Coated/plated with metal: Painted, or coated with organic silicate, Polyvinylidene Flouride (PVDF)"; (3) "Coated/plated with metal: Painted, or coated with organic silicate, All Other (*i.e.,* other than PVDF)"; and (4) "Not painted, and not coated with organic silicate." Pl.'s Br. 3; *Letter from U.S. Dep't of Commerce to Dongbu Steel Co., Ltd.* at B-7 (Sept. 13, 2006); *Letter from U.S. Dep't of Commerce to Union Steel Manufacturing Co., Ltd.* (Sept. 13, 2006). Respondents were asked to classify their sales of subject merchandise made during the period of review into one of these four types. Pl.'s Br. 3; *Letter from U.S. Dep't of Commerce to Dongbu Steel Co., Ltd.* at B-7 (Sept. 13, 2006); *Letter from U.S. Dep't of Commerce to Union Steel Manufacturing Co., Ltd.* (Sept. 13, 2006).

During the period of review, Union did not have sales of subject merchandise that consisted of clad products but had sales in the United States and in Korea of unpainted products, products painted with PVDF, and products in the "All Other" painted category. Pl.'s Br. 3. In addition, Union made sales in Korea of corrosion-resistant steel flat products that were laminated with a plastic film but had no sales of laminated products in the United States during the period of review. *Id.* at 3–4. In responding to Commerce's questionnaire, Union reported its sales based on the four types Commerce had described but also proposed, and reported sales based on, a product type not specified in the questionnaire: "Coated/plated with metal: Laminated with film." *See Letter from Kaye Scholer LLP to Sec'y of Commerce,* Attach. 1 at 5–6 (Nov. 20, 2006) (Admin.R.Doc. No. 52) (*"Union's Section B Resp."*); *see also Letter from Kaye Scholer LLP to Sec'y of Commerce*, Attach. 1 at 20–21 (Feb. 2, 2007) (Admin.R.Doc. No. 99) (*"Union's Supplemental Resp."*). Union advocated that Commerce recognize this proposed new type category by explaining that its laminated products underwent a different production process than its painted products, were physically different from its painted products because they were coated with plastic film and not with paint, and were costlier than its painted products. *See Union's Section B Resp. 6; see also Union's Supplemental Resp.* 20-21.

In calculating Union's antidumping duty margin for the preliminary results of the administrative review, Commerce rejected Union's proposed new type category and grouped within the type category of "All Other" painted products the home market sales of products Union had categorized as laminated. Pl.'s Br. 5; *see also Mem. from Case Analysts, AD/CVD Operations, Office 3, to The File* 4 (Aug. 31, 2007) (Admin.R.Doc. No. 230). Using Union's information grouped according to Commerce's type categories, Commerce assigned Union a preliminary antidumping duty margin of 4.35%. *Certain Corrosion-Resistant Carbon Steel Flat Products from the Republic of Korea: Notice of Prelim. Results and Partial Rescission of Antidumping Duty Admin. Review,* 72 Fed. Reg. 51,584, 51,588 (Sept. 10, 2007).

Commerce issued the Final Results of the thirteenth administrative review on March 17, 2008. *Final Results,* 73 Fed. Reg. 14,220. As explained in the Issues and Decision Memorandum ("Decision Memorandum") that was incorporated into the Final Results, Commerce once again classified as "All Other" painted products the sales of laminated subject merchandise that Union had proposed for a separate type category. *See Issues and Decisions for the Final Results of the Thirteenth Admin. Review of the Antidumping Duty Order on Certain Corrosion-Resistant Carbon Steel Flat Products from the Republic of Korea (2005–2006) (Final Results)* 14–15 (March 10, 2008) ("*Decision Mem.*"); Final Results, 73 Fed. Reg. at 14,221 (adopting the Decision Mem.). Commerce also rejected an argument, made by Union and by other respondents, that Commerce should cease "zeroing" in its administrative reviews, including the current review. *Decision Mem.* 3-5. Based on these decisions, Commerce assigned Union a final antidumping duty margin of 4.35%. *Final Results,* 73 Fed. Reg. at 14,221.

In the instant action, Union advances two claims against the United States, Compl. ¶¶ 7–16, and moves for judgment upon the agency record pursuant to USCIT Rule 56.2. Pl. Union Steel's Mot. for J. upon the Agency R.; *see also* Pl.'s Br. Union's first claim is that Commerce failed to explain how the model match criteria utilized by the agency could be reasonable or supported by substantial evidence. Compl. ¶¶ 15–16; *see also* Pl.'s Br. 13. Plaintiff's second claim is that Commerce's construction of 19 U.S.C. § 1677(35) to allow zeroing, as applied in the subject review, is contrary to law. Compl. ¶¶ 7–14; Pl.'s Br. 29-39. Pursuant to plaintiff's motion, the court held oral argument on April 24, 2009. Mot. for Oral Argument 1.

II. Discussion

The court exercises jurisdiction under 28 U.S.C. § 1581(c), pursuant to which the court reviews actions commenced under 19 U.S.C. § 1516a (2006), including an action contesting the final results of an administrative review that Commerce issues under 19 U.S.C. § 1675(a) (2006). 28 U.S.C. § 1581(c) (2006). The court will uphold the Department's determination unless it is unsupported by substantial evidence on the record or otherwise not in accordance with law. *See* 19 U.S.C. § 1516a(b)(1)(B)(i).

A. A Voluntary Remand Is Appropriate to Allow Commerce to Review and Reconsider the Model Match Methodology It Applied to Union's Sales

In support of its first claim, plaintiff argues that laminated corrosion-resistant carbon steel flat products are distinct from painted (both PVDF painted and "All Other" painted) corrosion-resistant carbon steel flat products with respect to cost, price, commercial identity, and use. *See* Pl.'s Br. 3-4, 16–29. Union points to record evidence that its laminated products have physical properties that cannot be achieved by painting, such as the unrestricted expression of various patterns, superior durability, and the use of environmentally-friendly material. *Id.* at 3. Citing these claimed distinctions, plaintiff argues that Commerce's classifying of the laminated products as "All Other" painted products is unsupported by substantial evidence of record. *Id.* at 14–29. According to Union, Commerce improperly relied on its analysis from the previous (twelfth) administrative review to justify grouping within the same type category two distinctly different classes of products and failed to provide an adequate explanation for its decision. *Id.* at 13, 20–23. As relief on its first claim, plaintiff proposed a remand to Commerce with instructions that the agency revise the model match criteria to classify laminated corrosion-resistant carbon steel flat products as a separate product type. *Id.* at 40.

Nucor and U.S. Steel responded to plaintiff's brief by arguing that the court should uphold the model match methodology the Department applied in the thirteenth administrative review. Mem. in Opp'n to Pl.'s Mot. for J. on the Agency R. Filed by Def.-Intervenor United States Steel Corporation 14-27 ("U.S. Steel Resp."); Resp. Br. of Nucor Corp. 7-17 ("Nucor Resp."). Defendant, however, acknowledges that Commerce relied on the analysis applied in the twelfth administrative review, rather than on data on the record of the subject thirteenth administrative review, to justify use of its model match methodology. Def.'s Resp. to Pl.'s Mot. for J. upon the Agency R. 10 ("Def.'s Resp."). Defendant requests a partial remand "[t]o permit Commerce to consider Union Steel's reported data during this administrative review and to determine whether this reported data would justify a revision in the model match methodology." *Id.*

While favoring a partial remand to allow Commerce to reconsider its earlier decision not to change its model match criteria, Union also requests that the court "first consider Union's arguments prior to remanding the case" and "instruct Commerce as to the appropriate criteria to consider and apply on remand." Reply Br. of Pl. Union Steel in Supp. of its Mot. for J. upon the Agency R. 1-2 ("Pl.'s Reply"). Plaintiff maintains that doing so "will reduce the likelihood of the need for multiple remands." *Id.* at 2. Union also requests that the court first consider Union's arguments prior to remanding the case because "Union has already expended substantial resources in briefing the model-match issue." *Id.* at 1. In a submission filed after oral argument,[1] Union explained that while it "agrees with Defendant that a remand is necessary in this case, Union believes that the Court should not grant Defendant's request for voluntary remand without also making specific findings as to the legal errors in the original determination and providing instructions as to the scope and substance of the analysis to be conducted on remand."[2]

---

1 At oral argument, plaintiff requested the opportunity to clarify the relief it seeks in this case by submitting a revised draft remand order and an explanation of its contents. Oral Argument Tr. 10, Apr. 24, 2009. Defendant did not oppose plaintiff's request but sought the opportunity to file a response. *Id.* at 39. Defendant-intervenors also sought the opportunity to respond to plaintiff's clarification. *Id.* at 54–55, 127. At oral argument, the court granted plaintiff's request and invited the other parties to respond to plaintiff's proposal. *Id.* at 127.

2 Plaintiff proposes the following three remand instructions:

> 1. "Commerce shall determine the appropriate classification of laminated CORE within the 'Type' category in its model match hierarchy. In particular, Commerce shall determine whether laminated CORE is appropriately classified as a separate 'Type' category or whether laminated CORE should be classified together with 'other painted' CORE within a single 'Type' category."
>
> . . . .
>
> 2. "If Commerce determines to classify laminated CORE within the same 'Type' category as 'other painted' CORE, it must support that determination with substantial evidence and persuasively explain why such a determination is reasonable in view of the record evidence that laminated CORE is coated with plastic whereas 'other painted' CORE is coated with paint; cost and price differences exist between laminated and painted CORE; and

Post-Oral Argument Submission Addressing Proposed Voluntary Remand Order 1-2 ("Pl.'s Post-Oral Argument Submission"). Plaintiff proposes that the court reach two conclusions identifying legal errors in the Final Results. First, plaintiff would have the court conclude that the Department's decision "to classify Plaintiff's laminated corrosion-resistant carbon steel flat products ("CORE") as painted CORE is unsupported by substantial evidence." *Id.* at 2–3. Second, plaintiff urges the court to hold that the model match criteria applied by Commerce in the Final Results "are not reflective of the subject merchandise because they fail to address the appropriate classification of laminated CORE." *Id.* at 3 (quotation marks omitted).

Defendant opposes Union's proposed remand instructions. Def.'s Resp. to Pl.'s Post-Oral Argument Submission Addressing Its Proposed Voluntary Remand Order 1 ("Def.'s Post-Oral Argument Submission"). Defendant proposes that the court instead issue an order stating that "Commerce's determination regarding plaintiff's request to revise the model match methodology is remanded to Commerce for further consideration." *Id.* at Attach. 1. Nucor and U.S. Steel also object to Union's proposed remand instructions; in addition, U.S. Steel submits that it does not believe a remand is necessary in this case. Def.-Intervenor's Resp. to Pl.'s Proposed Voluntary Remand Order; Resp. of Def.-Intervenor United States Steel Corporation to Union Steel's Proposed Remand Order and Comments 1-5 ("U.S. Steel's Post-Oral Argument Submission").

The court considers defendant's request for a voluntary remand under the framework established by the Court of Appeals in *SKF USA Inc. v. United States*, 254 F.3d 1022, 1027–30 (Fed. Cir. 2001), which addresses the various types of voluntary remand situations that may arise. One such situation occurs when there are no "intervening events," *i.e.,* legal decisions that would affect the outcome of the agency's determination, but when the agency nonetheless requests "a remand (without confessing error) in order to reconsider its previous position." *Id.* at 1029. The Court of Appeals opined that, under these circumstances, a reviewing court has discretion over whether to grant a voluntary remand and that remand is generally appropriate "if the agency's concern is substantial and legitimate" but may be refused "if the agency's request is frivolous or in bad faith." *Id.*

> Commerce's model match hierarchy separately breaks out PVDF painted products from 'other painted' products."
>
> . . . .
>
> 3. "If Commerce cannot present substantial evidence to support including laminated CORE in the same 'Type' category in its model match hierarchy as 'other painted' products, it shall assign laminated CORE its own 'Type' category and recalculate Plaintiff's dumping margin using this revised model match hierarchy."

Post-Oral Argument Submission Addressing Proposed Voluntary Remand Order 4–5.

The court is aware that both defendant-intervenors, at varying times during this litigation, have opposed the issuance of a remand order on the model match issue. *See* U.S. Steel's Post-Oral Argument Submission 1 (stating that "U.S. Steel does not believe that remand is warranted in this case"); U.S. Steel Resp. 14-26 (arguing that Commerce properly denied Union's request to revise the established model-match criteria); Nucor Resp. 24 (arguing that Commerce should affirm the portions of the Final Results challenged by plaintiff). The court, however, will not overlook the salient point that defendant itself has called into question an aspect of the Final Results, i.e., the Department's basing its model match decision on an analysis applied in the prior review and not on a consideration of the body of evidence on the record of this review.

The court rejects the proposed conclusions and remand instructions urged by plaintiff. Such a remand could not be described as a "voluntary" remand, and Union essentially requests that the court, prior to issuing a remand order, review the Department's model match determination on the merits. *See* Pl.'s Reply 1-2, 15; Oral Argument Tr. 17-18, April 24, 2009; Pl.'s Post-Oral Argument Submission 1-2 (stating that the court "should not grant Defendant's request for a voluntary remand without also making specific findings as to the legal errors in the original determination and providing instructions as to the scope and substance of the analysis to be conducted on remand"). The court, in its discretion, declines to review on the merits a determination that defendant has described at oral argument as "at best confusing," Oral Arg. Tr. 42, and with respect to which defendant indicated that it could not "tell [the court] why it's reasonable in this administrative review . . . and that is the reason why we asked for the remand." *Id.* at 47. Defendant acknowledges that "Commerce's final decision lacks any analysis of the record evidence of the thirteenth administrative review and lacks any analysis of the model match issue, except to refer to the final decision in the twelfth administrative review." Def.'s Post-Oral Argument Submission 4. Defendant thus raises the question as to whether Commerce acted properly in relying on data from a previous review, rather than the current review, for its decision to deny Union's request to change the model match methodology. *See id.* at 2 (explaining that Commerce is requesting remand to "reconsider Union's request to revise the model match methodology during the thirteenth administrative review" because the Final Results "failed to address record information regarding Union's proposed classification of laminated CORE in a separate category from painted CORE"). Defendant's reason for requesting a remand is "substantial and legitimate." *See SKF USA Inc.*, 254 F.3d at 1029. Under these circumstances, judicial review of the model match decision in the Final Results would not serve the goal of judicial economy.

Contrary to Union's arguments, the court is not in a position to presume that an additional remand will be necessary. It is axiomatic that the remand redetermination the Department files with the court must stem from a good faith reconsideration of the model match decision. It must be supported by findings of fact grounded in substantial evidence on the record of this review, and it must adhere to statutory requirements, including the requirement that the Department achieve accurate dumping margins through lawful comparisons of the sales of subject merchandise with home market sales of foreign like products. A conclusion by Commerce that the model matches made during the thirteenth review were not lawful necessarily would require redetermination of Union's margin upon remand. Although the court does not adopt plaintiff's proposed remand instructions and exercises its discretion to grant defendant's request for a voluntary remand, the court, in adopting the substance of defendant's proposed remand language, effects certain modifications appropriate to the circumstances of this case.

B. Commerce's Use of Zeroing in the Final Results Was Lawful

Plaintiff's second claim challenges the method Commerce used to calculate Union's weighted-average dumping margin. To calculate a weighted-average dumping margin in an administrative review, Commerce first must determine, for each entry of subject merchandise falling within the period of review, the normal value and the export price (or the constructed export price if the export price cannot be determined). 19 U.S.C. § 1675(a)(2)(A)(i). Commerce then determines a margin for each entry according to the amount by which the normal value exceeds the export price or constructed export price. 19 U.S.C. §§ 1675(a)(2)(A)(ii), 1677(35)(A) (2006); *Decision Mem.* 4. If the export price or constructed export price on a particular entry is higher than normal value, Commerce, in calculating a weighted-average margin, assigns a margin of zero, not a negative margin, to the entry. *See Decision Mem.* 4. Finally, Commerce aggregates these individual margins in determining a weighted-average dumping margin. 19 U.S.C. § 1677(35)(B).

Plaintiff argues that Commerce's construction of 19 U.S.C. § 1677(35), pursuant to which Commerce engaged in zeroing in this administrative review, *see Decision Mem.* 4, is unreasonable and therefore not in accordance with law. Pl.'s Br. 34-39. Union acknowledges that the Court of Appeals and the Court of International Trade consistently have upheld Commerce's practice of zeroing in administrative reviews. *Id.* at 29. Union argues, however, that a determination Commerce issued under Section 123 of the Uruguay Round Agreements Act, 19 U.S.C. § 3533(g) (2006), to implement recommendations of the World Trade Organization Dispute Settlement Body ("Section 123 Determination") has adopted a new interpretation of § 1677(35) that "justifies a fresh review of this issue by this Court." *Id.* at 30 (citing *Antidumping Proceedings: Calculation of the Weighted-Average Dumping Margin During an Antidumping Investigation; Final Modification,* 71 Fed. Reg. 77,722 (Dec. 27, 2006) ("*Section 123 Determination*")). According to Union's argument, in issuing the Section 123 Determination "Commerce for the first time has interpreted [19 U.S.C. § 1677(35)] to mean one thing with respect to antidumping investigations (that weighted average dumping margins should be calculated without zeroing negative dumping margins), and to mean the exact opposite with respect to antidumping administrative reviews (that weighted average dumping margins should be calculated by zeroing negative dumping margins)."

Id. at 30. Referring to the second step of the Supreme Court's analysis in *Chevron U.S.A. Inc. v. Natural Resources Defense Council, Inc.*, 467 U.S. 837, 104 S. Ct. 2778, 81 L.Ed.2d 694 (1984), Union submits that "[t]o the best of our knowledge, no court has yet considered the question of whether Commerce's new statutory interpretation-that [19 U.S.C. § 1677(35)] provides for zeroing in reviews but not in investigations-is reasonable within the meaning of step two of *Chevron*." *Id.* at 30–31 (footnote omitted). Union argues that Commerce's construction of 19 U.S.C. § 1677(35) is not reasonable.

According to Union, the upholding of zeroing by the Court of Appeals in *Timken Co. v. United States*, 354 F.3d 1334 (Fed. Cir. 2004), and *Corus Staal BV v. Department of Commerce*, 395 F.3d 1343 (Fed. Cir. 2005) ("*Corus I*"), "was expressly premised on the fact that *the same statutory provision* governed the weight-averaging element of [Commerce's] dumping margin methodology and that [Commerce] was applying that provision consistently in both types of proceedings." Pl.'s Reply 12-13. According to Union, the Section 123 Determination removed this underlying premise of the holdings of the Court of Appeals affirming the use of zeroing, and for this reason the court should conduct a new Chevron step-two analysis of Commerce's current statutory interpretation to determine whether those prior holdings are still valid. *Id.* at 13–14. Union argues that an "interpretation of the identical statutory provision to have two diametrically opposite meanings is unreasonable and directly contrary to the previous holding of the Federal Circuit in *Corus I*, 395 F.3d at 1347, and *Timken*, 354 F.3d 1334, 1341–42." *Id.* at 11.

Relying on *Corus Staal BV v. United States*, 502 F.3d 1370 (Fed. Cir. 2007) ("*Corus II*"), defendant responds that the Court of Appeals has held unequivocally that Commerce's decision to discontinue zeroing in investigations did not affect administrative reviews. Def.'s Resp. 11-12. Defendant also argues that *Corus I* and *Timken* do not require Commerce to interpret 19 U.S.C. § 1677(35) consistently in antidumping investigations and administrative reviews, *id.* at 13, and that Commerce may interpret a statutory provision differently in different contexts. *Id.* at 16–17. Defendant-intervenors, relying on 19 U.S.C. § 1677f-1(d) (2006), contend that zeroing is required by statute in all antidumping proceedings. U.S. Steel Resp. 27-33; Nucor Resp. 17-19. In the alternative, defendant-intervenors argue that zeroing is permissible under the statute. U.S. Steel Resp. 33-39; Nucor Resp. 19-23.

Ruling on Union's claim challenging the use of zeroing in the thirteenth administrative review requires the court to decide, initially, whether one or more of the Court of Appeals decisions that address the question of zeroing are controlling in this case. Only if no such decision is controlling is the court free to conduct what is, in Union's formulation, "a fresh review of this issue." *See* Pl.'s Br. 30. In other words, Union's argument is, first, that the question of statutory construction presented by this case is one of first impression and, second, that the court must conclude that Commerce's statutory construction was unreasonable.

Commerce discussed its construction of 19 U.S.C. § 1677(35) in the Decision Memorandum:

> Section 771(35)(A) of the Act [19 U.S.C. § 1677(35)(A)] defines "dumping margin" as the "amount by which the normal value exceeds the export price or the constructed export price of the subject merchandise." (Emphasis added). Outside the context of antidumping investigations involving average-to-average comparisons, the Department interprets this statutory definition to mean that a dumping margin exists only when normal value (NV) is greater than export or constructed export price (CEP). As no dumping margins exist with respect to sales where NV is equal to or less than export or CEP, the Department will not permit these non-dumped sales to offset the amount of dumping found with respect to other sales.

Decision Mem. 4. As the quoted language indicates, Commerce applied in this administrative review a construction of § 1677(35)(A) that it applies generally but that it does not apply in the specific situation in which it conducts an average-to-average comparison in an antidumping investigation. The exception Commerce makes for average-to-average comparisons in investigations stems from U.S. action to implement certain decisions of the World Trade Organization ("WTO") concluding that zeroing as applied in various U.S. antidumping investigations was inconsistent with U.S. international obligations under Article 2.4.2 of the Agreement on the Implementation of Article VI of the General Agreement on Tariffs and Trade. It was for this purpose that Commerce issued the Section 123 Determination on December 27, 2006, announcing that "the Department will no longer make average-to-average comparisons in investigations without providing offsets for non-dumped comparisons." Section 123 Determination, 71 Fed. Reg. at 77,722. In the *Section 123 Determination*, Commerce stated that it was declining to adopt in any other segment of an antidumping proceeding the change it announced to its procedure for average-to-average comparisons in investigations. *Id.* at 77,724. Commerce set an effective date of February 22, 2007 for that change.[3]

In *Corus II*, the Court of Appeals upheld as reasonable Commerce's use of zeroing in the second administrative review of an antidumping duty order on hot-rolled steel from the Netherlands. *See Corus II*, 502 F.3d at 1372. The plaintiff in *Corus II* argued that a number of events subsequent to Commerce's issuing final results in the second administrative review "demonstrate that Commerce had abandoned the policy of zeroing." *Id.* at 1373. Those events included Commerce's action to implement instructions from the U.S. Trade Representative, issued April 23, 2007 under Section 129 of the Uruguay Round Agreements Act, 19 U.S.C. § 3538 (2006), in response to a WTO decision with respect to eleven specific anti-dumping investigations. Corus II, 502 F.3d at 1374; *Implementation of the Findings*

---

3 Although the Section 123 Determination announced an effective date of January 16, 2007, Commerce later announced a delay in the effective date to February 22, 2007. *Antidumping Proceedings: Calculation of the Weighted-Average Dumping Margins in Antidumping Investigations; Change in Effective Date of Final Modification,* 72 Fed. Reg. 3783 (Jan. 26, 2007).

of the WTO Panel in US-Zeroing (EC): Notice of Determinations Under Section 129 of the Uruguay Round Agreements Act and Revocations and Partial Revocations of Certain Antidumping Duty Orders, 72 Fed. Reg. 25,261 (May 4, 2007). In rejecting the argument made by the plaintiff in Corus II, the Court of Appeals also discussed the relevance of the Section 123 Determination to that plaintiff's claim:

> When Commerce announced the elimination of zeroing in conjunction with the use of average-to-average comparisons to calculate dumping margins in antidumping investigations, it stated that the new policy did not apply to any other proceedings, including administrative reviews. Antidumping Proceedings: Calculation of the Weighted-Average Dumping Margin During an Antidumping Investigation; Final Modification, 71 Fed. Reg. 77772, 77722–24 (Dec. 27, 2006). Thus, Commerce's new policy has no bearing on the present appeal, just as it had no effect on the final determination of Corus's fourth administrative review.

Id. at 1374. The Court of Appeals addressed the effect of the Section 123 Determination and the related developments by stating that "[t]o the extent recent developments have changed the current scheme, Commerce has made it clear that those changes do not apply retroactively to administrative reviews. Thus, our previous determination [in *Corus I*, 395 F.3d at 1349] that Commerce's policy of zeroing is permissible under the statute applies to the challenged administrative review." *Id.* at 1375. In this way, the Court of Appeals in *Corus II* made it amply clear that it did not consider Commerce's decision to discontinue zeroing when performing average-to-average comparisons in antidumping investigations while continuing zeroing in administrative reviews to be a sufficient basis to disturb its precedents, under which it had held zeroing to be permissible in administrative reviews based on the reasonableness of the Department's construction of 19 U.S.C. § 1677(35). Because the holding of the Court of Appeals in *Corus II* is controlling on the question presented by Union's zeroing claim, the court must uphold as reasonable the construction of 19 U.S.C. § 1677(35) that Commerce set forth in the Decision Memorandum. Union's argument that the Section 123 Determination marked the first time that Commerce has interpreted 19 U.S.C. § 1677(35) "to mean one thing with respect to antidumping investigations . . . and to mean the exact opposite with respect to antidumping administrative reviews," Pl.'s Br. 30, does not suffice to distinguish the zeroing claim it makes in this case from the precedent established by *Corus II*.

In *NSK Ltd. v. United States*, 510 F.3d 1375 (Fed. Cir. 2007), the Court of Appeals followed an approach similar to that of *Corus II*, rejecting the argument that it should hold Commerce's use of zeroing unlawful based on a decision of the WTO Dispute Settlement Body and on statements by the United States indicating that the United States would comply with that decision. *NSK*, 510 F.3d at 1379–80. The Court of Appeals explained that

> until Commerce abandons zeroing in administrative reviews such as this one, a remand in this case would be unavailing. Therefore, because Commerce's zeroing practice is in accordance with our well-established precedent, *until Commerce*

> *officially abandons the practice pursuant to the specified statutory scheme, we affirm its continued use in this case.*

Id. at 1380 (emphasis added).

Union argues that *Corus II* and *NSK* are distinguishable from this case because the administrative reviews in those prior cases had been completed prior to the publication of the Section 123 Determination. Pl.'s Reply 11; Oral Argument Tr. 100. This argument is unconvincing. In *Corus II*, the Court of Appeals reasoned that the Section 123 Determination did not bear on the question of the reasonableness of Commerce's construction of 19 U.S.C. § 1677(35) to allow zeroing in administrative reviews, noting that the Section 123 Determination, by its language, did not apply to administrative reviews. *See Corus II*, 502 F.3d at 1374–75. Because of the breadth of the holding in *Corus II* and the reasoning on which that holding is based, the fact that the subject administrative review was completed on March 17, 2008, a date that was after the issuance of the Section 123 Determination and the February 22, 2007 effective date thereof, does not place this case outside of the precedent that *Corus II* establishes.

Nor does the court find merit in Union's argument that the upholding of zeroing by the Court of Appeals in *Timken* and *Corus I*, "was expressly premised on the fact that *the same statutory provision* governed the weight-averaging element of [Commerce's] dumping margin methodology and that [Commerce] was applying that provision consistently in both types of proceedings." *See* Pl.'s Reply 13. Plaintiff's interpretation of the holdings in *Timken* and *Corus I* does not withstand scrutiny when considered according to the holdings in *Corus II* and NSK, with which plaintiff's interpretation is plainly inconsistent.

The court's conclusion on Union's zeroing claim is in accord with the decision in *Corus Staal BV v. United States*, 32 CIT __, 593 F. Supp. 2d 1373 (2008) ("*Corus III*"), in which the Court of International Trade also considered the issue of whether it is permissible for Commerce to interpret 19 U.S.C. § 1677(35) to allow zeroing in reviews despite the discontinuation of zeroing in average-to-average comparisons in investigations. The plaintiff in Corus III argued that "Federal Circuit decisions upholding the use of zeroing are not binding because Commerce's interpretation of § 1677(35)(A)-(B)-which prohibits zeroing in investigations, but not in administrative reviews-is inconsistent and, therefore, unreasonable." *Corus III*, 32 CIT at __, 593 F. Supp. 2d at 1383. The Court of International Trade applied a Chevron step-two analysis to conclude that Commerce's interpretation of 19 U.S.C. § 1677(35) is reasonable and in accordance with law, emphasizing that "[t]he Federal Circuit has repeatedly found Commerce's use of zeroing in administrative reviews to be reasonable." *Id.* at __, 593 F. Supp. 2d at 1384.

III. Conclusion and Order

With respect to the model match issue, the court concludes that granting defendant's request for voluntary remand is appropriate in the circumstances of this case. Also, the court concludes that the Final Results must be affirmed with respect to the Department's use of zeroing based on precedent of the Court of Appeals. Therefore, upon consideration of all proceedings and submissions herein, and upon due deliberation, it is hereby

ORDERED that defendant's request for a partial voluntary remand of *Certain Corrosion-Resistant Carbon Steel Flat Products from the Republic of Korea: Notice of Final Results of the Thirteenth Administrative Review* 73 Fed. Reg. 14,220 (Mar. 17, 2008) ("Final Results") be, and hereby is, GRANTED with modifications to defendant's proposed remand instructions as set forth herein; it is further

ORDERED that Commerce, upon remand, shall review and reconsider its "model match" methodology, including its decision in the Final Results to deny Union Steel's request for a revision of that model match methodology, by which Commerce compared the types of subject merchandise in plaintiff's U.S. sales with the types of foreign like products in plaintiff's sales in its home market; it is further

ORDERED that Plaintiff's Motion for Judgment upon the Agency Record, as filed on August 21, 2008, be, and hereby is, GRANTED only to the extent that a remand is hereby ordered under which Commerce is directed to review and reconsider its model match methodology, DENIED to the extent that plaintiff's motion requests a remand detailing the specific findings and instructions contained in plaintiff's Post-Oral Argument Submission Addressing Proposed Voluntary Remand Order, and DENIED to the extent that such motion seeks to have set aside the Department's Final Results with respect to the zeroing methodology used therein; it is further

ORDERED that the requests of defendant-intervenors Nucor and U.S. Steel that the Final Results be affirmed with respect to the model match methodology used therein be, and hereby are, DENIED; it is further

ORDERED that the Department shall issue upon remand a redetermination that responds to Union Steel's request that Commerce revise the model match methodology and that such redetermination shall comply with this Opinion and Order, be supported by substantial record evidence, and be in all respects in accordance with law; it is further

ORDERED that the Department shall have ninety (90) days from the date of this Opinion and Order to file its redetermination upon remand in this proceeding, that plaintiff and defendant-intervenors shall have thirty (30) days from the filing of the redetermination upon remand to file comments thereon with the court, and that defendant shall have fifteen (15) days thereafter to file any reply to such comments; and it is further

ORDERED that the Final Results be, and hereby are, affirmed with respect to the Department's use of zeroing methodology therein.

ACCIAIERIE VALBRUNA S.p.A
v.
UNITED STATES

Court No. 08-00381, 2009 Ct. Intl. Trade LEXIS 84 (C.I.T. 2009)
Decided July 23, 2009

White & Case LLP, (Gregory J. Spak, Yohai Baisburd, and Sarah O. O'Neal), for Plaintiffs Acciaierie Valbruna S.p.A. and Valbruna Stainless, Inc.

Tony West, Assistant Attorney General; *Jeanne E. Davidson*, Director; *Patricia M. McCarthy*, Assistant Director, Commercial Litigation Branch, Civil Division, United States Department of Justice (*Claudia Burke*); *Rachael Wenthold*, Office of the Chief Counsel for Import Administration, United States Department of Commerce, Of Counsel, for Defendant United States.

Before: Judith M. Barzilay, Judge.

OPINION

JUDITH M. BARZILAY, Judge.

The case presents an issue that has been before this Court and the Federal Circuit many times—whether the relief provided under Section 129 of the Uruguay Round Agreements Act ("URAA") is retrospective, prospective, or both.[1] *See, e.g., Corus Staal BV v. United States*, 502 F.3d 1370, 1374 (Fed. Cir. 2007); *Corus Staal BV v. United States*, 32 CIT ___, ___, 593 F. Supp. 2d 1373, 1382–83 (2008). This particular action concerns the effect of a determination made by Commerce under Section 129 on certain stainless steel bar manufactured in Italy and imported into the U.S. by Plaintiffs Acciaierie Valbruna S.p.A. and Valbruna Stainless, Inc. (collectively, "Plaintiffs") from March 1, 2006 through February 28, 2007. Plaintiffs contest the U.S. Customs & Border Protection ("Customs") decision to liquidate and assess antidumping duties on entries made during the period of review.

1 The plain language of Section 129 of the URAA provides that a determination made under that provision has prospective effect, thereby applying only to entries made on or after the date the United States Trade Representative directs the U.S. Department of Commerce ("Commerce") to implement the decision. 19 U.S.C. § 3538(c)(1)(B).

Compl. ¶¶ 40–47. Plaintiffs also challenge the instructions from Commerce to Customs which subjected those entries of stainless steel bar from Italy to antidumping duties. Compl. ¶¶ 48–54. Pursuant to USCIT R. 12(b)(1) and (b)(5), Defendant United States moves to dismiss Plaintiffs' claims for (1) the Court's lack of subject matter jurisdiction under both 28 U.S.C. § 1581(a) and § 1581(i), and (2) Plaintiffs' failure to state a claim upon which relief may be granted. The court grants Defendant's Motion to Dismiss for the reasons explained herein.

I. Background

In 2002, Commerce issued an antidumping duty order on the subject merchandise. *Notice of Antidumping Duty Order: Stainless Steel Bar from Italy,* 67 Fed. Reg. 10,384, 10,384 (Dep't Commerce Mar. 7, 2002). In its final determination, Commerce employed the zeroing methodology to calculate the weighted-average dumping margin for the subject merchandise.[2] *Issues and Decision Memo for the Antidumping Duty Investigation of Stainless Steel Bar from Italy; Final Determination,* A-475-829 (Jan. 23, 2002), *available at* 2002 WL 171499, at 4–6 (discussing Commerce's use of the zeroing methodology in Comment 1).[3] Commerce calculated a final weighted-average dumping margin of 2.50% for Plaintiffs' entries of the subject merchandise. *Notice of Final Determination of Sales at Less Than Fair Value: Stainless Steel Bar From Italy,* 67 Fed. Reg. 3,155, 3,158 (Dep't Commerce Jan. 23, 2002).

The European Communities thereafter challenged Commerce's use of zeroing in several antidumping investigations and administrative reviews before the World Trade Organization ("WTO"), including the investigation that resulted in the imposition of an antidumping duty order on the subject merchandise from Italy. *See* Request for Consultations by the European Communities, *United States—Laws, Regulations and Methodology for Calculating Dumping Margins (Zeroing),* at

---

2 A dumping margin ("DM") is expressed functionally as DM = NV - (EP or CEP). The normal value, or "NV," is the price charged for the subject merchandise in the home market, an appropriate third country market price, or the cost of production of the goods subject to statutorily permitted adjustments. 19 U.S.C. § 1677b(a)(1)(B)(i)-(ii), (a)(4). The export price, or "EP," is the price at which the subject merchandise is sold by the producer or exporter to an unaffiliated purchaser in the U.S. or for exportation to the U.S. 19 U.S.C. § 1677a(a). However, if the foreign producer or exporter is affiliated with the importer of the subject merchandise, then a constructed export price, or "CEP," may be used. § 1677a(b). The CEP is the price, as adjusted pursuant to section 1677a, at which the subject merchandise is sold in the U.S. to a buyer unaffiliated with the producer or exporter. § 1677a(b). The weighted-average dumping margin expresses the DM as a percentage, and is determined by dividing the aggregate DMs of a specific exporter or producer by the aggregate EPs or CEPs of that same exporter or producer. 19 U.S.C. § 1677(35)(B).

3 Zeroing is a practice whereby Commerce gives the sales margins of merchandise sold at or above fair value prices an assumed value of zero. *See Corus Staal BV v. Dep't of Commerce,* 395 F.3d 1343, 1345–46 (Fed. Cir. 2005). With zeroing, Commerce uses only the sales margins of merchandise sold at less than fair value prices to calculate the final weighted-average dumping margin. *See id.*

4–5, WT/DS294/1 (June 19, 2003). On October 31, 2005, a WTO Panel found Commerce's use of zeroing in investigations involving comparisons of weighted-average normal values to weighted-average U.S. prices to be inconsistent with U.S. obligations under the WTO Antidumping Agreement ("*AD Agreement*"). *See* Panel Report, *United States—Laws, Regulations and Methodology for Calculating Dumping Margins ("Zeroing")*, ¶¶ 8.2–8.4, WT/DS294/R (Oct. 31, 2005) ("*Panel Report*"). More specifically, the WTO Panel found that zeroing violates the AD Agreement as such and as applied in the specific investigations at issue.[4] *Id.* The Appellate Body upheld the WTO Panel's determination on appeal and went further, stating that Commerce's use of zeroing in certain administrative reviews was also inconsistent with the AD Agreement. *See* Appellate Body Report, *United States—Laws, Regulations and Methodology for Calculating Dumping Margins ("Zeroing")*, ¶¶ 132–35, 263(a)(i), WT/DS294/AB/R (Apr. 18, 2006).

In response to the *Panel Report,* Commerce announced that it would no longer give negative value dumping margins an assumed value of zero in antidumping investigations involving comparisons of "average-to-average" prices.[5] *Antidumping Proceedings: Calculation of the Weighted-Average Dumping Margin During an Antidumping Investigation; Final Modification,* 71 Fed. Reg. 77,722, 77,722 (Dep't Commerce Dec. 27, 2006) ("*Section 123 Determination*"). Throughout its pronouncement, Commerce explicitly stated that the central purpose of the *Section 123 Determination* was to conform the agency's practices with the international trade obligations of the United States, as they are outlined in the *Panel Report. See id.* at 77,722. Commerce explained that the department's new policy would apply in (1) the recalculation of the dumping margins in the "specific antidumping investigations challenged by the [European Communities] in [the *Panel Report*]" and (2) all then current and future investigations involving comparisons of average-to-average prices. *Id.* at 77,725. Notably, the Section 123 Determination did not

---

4 A law, regulation, or measure of a WTO Member that violates a WTO agreement "as such" means that the "Member's conduct—not only in a particular instance that has occurred, but in future situations as well—will necessarily be inconsistent with that Member's WTO obligations." Appellate Body Report, *United States—Sunset Reviews of Anti-Dumping Measures on Oil Country Tubular Goods from Argentina,* ¶ 172, WT/DS268/AB/R (Nov. 29, 2004). In contrast, a law, regulation or measure that violates a WTO agreement "as applied" means that the WTO Member's "application of a general rule to a specific set of facts" is inconsistent with that Member's WTO obligations. *Id.* at ¶ 6 n.22.

5 In Sections 123 and 129 of the URAA, Congress established two procedures by which an adverse decision from the WTO Dispute Settlement Panel or Appellate Body may be implemented into domestic law. A Section 123 determination amends, rescinds, or modifies an agency regulation or practice that is found to be inconsistent with any of the Uruguay Round Agreements. 19 U.S.C. § 3533(g)(1). A Section 129 determination amends, rescinds, or modifies the application of an agency regulation or practice in a specific antidumping, countervailing duty, or safeguards proceeding that is found to be inconsistent with U.S. obligations under the WTO *AD Agreement*, the Agreement on Subsidies and Countervailing Measures, or the Safeguards Agreement. 19 U.S.C. § 3538(a)(1), (b)(2).

embrace all of the findings of the WTO Appellate Body, stating instead that the change in policy applied only to investigations where Commerce uses average-to-average comparisons and did not extend to any other kind of investigation or administrative review. *Id.* at 77,724.

Commerce subsequently applied its policy change to the particular investigations that were at issue in the *Panel Report. Implementation of the Findings of the WTO Panel in US—Zeroing (EC): Notice of Determinations Under Section 129 of the Uruguay Round Agreements Act and Revocations and Partial Revocations of Certain Antidumping Duty Orders*, 72 Fed. Reg. 25,261, 25,262 (Dep't Commerce May 4, 2007) ("*Section 129 Determination*"). In applying the *Section 123 Determination*, Commerce recalculated the weighted-average dumping margin for the subject merchandise without the use of zeroing, finding that it decreased from 2.50% to zero. *Id.* at 25,262–263. The agency noted that it would revoke the antidumping order on stainless steel bar from Italy, effective for entries of the subject merchandise made on or after April 23, 2007. *Id.* at 25,263. During this proceeding, Plaintiffs argued that Commerce should not impose antidumping duties on unliquidated entries of the subject merchandise, irrespective of the date that the goods entered the United States. *See Issues and Decision Memorandum for the Final Results of the Section 129 Determinations,* A-122-838, A-421-807, A-427-820, A-428-830, A-475-829, A-412-822, A-401-806, A-469-807, A-475-820, A-423-808, A-475-824, A-475-818 (Apr. 9, 2007), Def. Br. App. B at 15 ("*Section 129 Determination Issues and Decision Memorandum*"). However, Defendant rejected that notion, stating that "these [S]ection 129 proceedings will not apply to entries made before [April 23,2007]." *Id.* at 17. Importantly, while Plaintiffs commented on Commerce's preliminary determination in the Section 129 proceeding, they did not challenge the final results contained in the *Section 129 Determination*.

On April 2, 2007, Plaintiffs filed a request with Commerce to review the antidumping duty order for entries of the subject merchandise made during the period of review, the time frame corresponding to the sixth administrative review of the antidumping duty order. *See Initiation of Antidumping and Countervailing Duty Administrative Reviews,* 72 Fed. Reg. 20,986, 20,986 (Dep't Commerce Apr. 27, 2007). However, Plaintiffs withdrew that request on June 25, 2007. *Stainless Steel Bar from Italy: Notice of Rescission of Antidumping Duty Administrative Review,* 72 Fed. Reg. 45,223, 45,223 (Dep't Commerce Aug. 13, 2007). Commerce ultimately rescinded the sixth administrative review, noting that it would instruct Customs to assess antidumping duties on all entries of the subject merchandise "at rates equal to the cash deposit of estimated antidumping duties required at the time of entry. . . ." *Id.* Accordingly, Customs liquidated Plaintiffs' entries of the subject merchandise at the cash deposit rate, as instructed.[6]

---

6 *See* Def. Br. App. A (containing Protest Nos. 1704-08-100050, 0901-08-100100, 1601-08-100175, 5301-08-100199, 2704-08-101095, 4601-08-100679, 4601-08-100658, 1401-08-100127).

On March 19, 2008, Plaintiffs filed sixteen protests challenging Custom's liquidation of entries they made during the period of review. *See* Def. Br. App. A. Plaintiffs argued that Customs lacked the authority to assess antidumping duties on the subject merchandise because, at the time of liquidation, there was no valid antidumping duty order in place. Customs denied eight of the original sixteen protests between May and October 2008, explaining that a challenge to the calculation of antidumping duties was not a protestable decision and that the agency had correctly liquidated those entries pursuant to Commerce's instructions. *Id.*

II. Standard of Review

When deciding a motion to dismiss based upon either lack of subject matter jurisdiction or failure to state a claim for which relief may be granted, the Court assumes that all undisputed facts alleged in the complaint are true and it must draw all reasonable inferences in the plaintiff's favor. *See Henke v. United States*, 60 F.3d 795, 797 (Fed. Cir. 1995); *Gould, Inc. v. United States*, 935 F.2d 1271, 1274 (Fed. Cir. 1991).

A fundamental question in any action before the Court is whether subject matter jurisdiction exists over the claims presented. *See Steel Co. v. Citizens for a Better Environment*, 523 U.S. 83, 94–95 (1998). Subject matter jurisdiction involves the Court's power to hear a case and declare the law, and when it ceases to exist, "the [C]ourt must dismiss the complaint in its entirety." *Arbaugh v. Y&H Corp.*, 546 U.S. 500, 514 (2006). The party invoking the Court's jurisdiction bears the burden of establishing it. *See Norsk Hydro Can., Inc. v. United States*, 472 F.3d 1347, 1355 (Fed. Cir. 2006).

Finally, assuming that all of the factual allegations are true, "a complaint must contain sufficient factual matter, accepted as true, to 'state a claim to relief that is plausible on its face.'" *Ashcroft v. Iqbal*, 129 S. Ct. 1937, 1949 (2009) (citing *Bell Atl. Corp. v. Twombly*, 550 U.S. 544, 570 (2007)). "A claim has facial plausibility when the plaintiff pleads factual content that allows the [C]ourt to draw the reasonable inference that the defendant is liable for the misconduct alleged," thereby raising the plaintiff's right to relief above the speculative level. *See Iqbal*, 129 S. Ct. at 1949 (citing *Twombly*, 550 U.S. at 556). Though detailed factual allegations are not required, the plaintiff's complaint must contain more than labels and conclusions or a formulaic recitation of the elements of a cause of action to provide the defendant with fair notice of its claims and survive a motion to dismiss for failure to state a claim upon which relief may be granted. *See id.* at 1949; *Twombly*, 550 U.S. at 555.

III. Discussion

A. Subject Matter Jurisdiction

Defendant argues that the court lacks subject matter jurisdiction over Plaintiffs' claims under both § 1581(a) and § 1581(i). Defendant notes that it was Commerce, and not Customs, who conducted the Section 129 proceeding, calculated the weighted-average dumping margin, and revoked the antidumping duty order for particular entries. Accordingly, Defendant claims that Customs's role in liquidating Plaintiffs' entries was merely ministerial in nature, and that those acts do not constitute a protestable decision under § 1514. Def. Br. 7-9. Defendant also argues that § 1581(i) is not a proper basis for the court to establish jurisdiction over Plaintiffs' claim against Commerce because § 1581(c) would have provided Plaintiffs with an adequate remedy had the Plaintiffs (1) challenged Commerce's *Section 129 Determination* or (2) maintained the sixth administrative review and challenged the final results thereof. Def. Br. 9-12.

In contrast, Plaintiffs aver that Customs's act of liquidating and assessing antidumping duties on its entries of the subject merchandise made during the period of review, despite the revocation of the antidumping duty order on those goods, is a protestable action that is reviewable under § 1581(a). Pl. Br. 7-10. Specifically, Plaintiffs claim that they are challenging Customs's assessment of antidumping duties on the subject merchandise because Commerce determined that no dumping occurred and, thus, there was no valid antidumping order in place at the time of liquidation. Pl. Br. 8. Plaintiffs also argue that the court may review Commerce's application of "an invalid dumping order" to entries of the subject merchandise made during the period of review under § 1581(i). Pl. Br. 10. Plaintiffs allege that Commerce's application of antidumping duties to those entries "exceeded the scope of [the agency's] authority and contravened 19 U.S.C. § 1673." Pl. Br. 11. Finally, Plaintiffs note that § 1581(c) did not provide them with an adequate remedy because they had "no reason" to either challenge the *Section 129 Determination* or complete the sixth administrative review given that the *Section 129 Determination* allegedly invalidated the antidumping duty order for all unliquidated entries of the subject merchandise, irrespective of the date of entry. Pl. Br. 12-14.

Chapter 95 of Title 28 of the United States Code contains Congress's jurisdictional grant to the Court. The first section of Chapter 95, § 1581, is titled "Civil actions against the United States and agencies and officers thereof," and consists of subsections (a) through (j). Each subsection of § 1581 "delineates particular laws over which the Court . . . may assert jurisdiction." *Nat'l Corn Growers Ass'n v. Baker*, 840 F.2d 1547, 1555 (Fed. Cir. 1988).

1. Plaintiffs' Claim Against Customs & 28 U.S.C. § 1581(a)

Section 1581(a) provides the Court with "exclusive jurisdiction of any civil action commenced to contest the denial of a protest, in whole or in part," arising under 19 U.S.C. § 1515. § 1581(a). Congress outlines the rules for Customs's review of a protest in § 1515, with the filing of a protest by an aggrieved party under 19 U.S.C. § 1514 being a condition precedent for Customs to exercise that authority. § 1515(a). Customs must either grant or deny the protest before a party may sue under § 1581(a). *Mitsubishi Elecs. Am., Inc. v. United States*, 44 F.3d 973, 976 (Fed. Cir. 1994).

Section 1514(a) sets forth the categories of Customs decisions that an aggrieved party may protest. § 1514(a). Specifically, Customs may review protests challenging

> (1) the appraised value of merchandise;
>
> (2) the classification and rate and amount of duties chargeable;
>
> (3) all charges or exactions of whatever character within the jurisdiction of the Secretary of the Treasury;
>
> (4) the exclusion of merchandise from entry or delivery or a demand for redelivery to customs custody under any provision of the customs laws, except a determination appealable under [19 U.S.C. § 1337];
>
> (5) the liquidation or reliquidation of an entry, or reconciliation as to the issues contained therein, or any modification thereof, including the liquidation of an entry, pursuant to either [19 U.S.C. § 1500] or [§ 1504];
>
> (6) the refusal to pay a claim for drawback; or
>
> (7) the refusal to reliquidate an entry under [19 U.S.C. § 1520(d)];

§ 1514(a). Importantly, these categories are exclusive, "and if Customs' underlying decision does not relate to any of these seven categories, [then] the court may not exercise § 1581(a) jurisdiction over an action contesting Customs' denial of a protest filed against that decision." *Am. Nat'l Fire Ins. Co. v. United States*, 30 CIT 931, 939–40, 441 F. Supp. 2d 1275, 1285 (2006) (citing *Playhouse Imp. & Exp., Inc. v. United States*, 18 CIT 41, 44, 843 F. Supp. 716, 719 (1994)); *see also Mitsubishi Elecs. Am., Inc.*, 44 F.3d at 976.

Although Plaintiffs construct their claim against Customs as one that falls within the purview of § 1581(a), it is in essence tantamount to a challenge to an antidumping decision. Plaintiffs describe the central focus of their claim against Customs as a challenge to the agency's "assessment upon liquidation of antidumping duties at any rate in a case in which Commerce has determined [that] no dumping occurred." Pl. Br. 8. Plaintiffs note that their claim against Customs definitively centers on the agency's "authority to take steps to enforce an antidumping order [that was subsequently] determined [to be] invalid within the meaning of 19 U.S.C. § 1673." Pl. Br. 11. According to Plaintiffs, § 1514(a)(5) therefore provides the court with jurisdiction over their claim.[7] Pl. Br. 8.

However, it is well settled that Commerce, and not Customs, conducts antidumping proceedings to (1) calculate and determine antidumping rates and (2) issue antidumping orders, where appropriate. *See Mitsubishi Elecs. Am., Inc.*, 44 F.3d

---

7 Customs may review a protest challenging "the liquidation or reliquidation of an entry, or reconciliation as to the issues contained therein, or any modification thereof, including the liquidation of an entry, pursuant to either [19 U.S.C. § 1500] or [§ 1504]." § 1514(a)(5).

at 976. "Customs cannot 'modify . . . Commerce's [antidumping] determinations, their underlying facts, or their enforcement.'" *Id.* at 977 (brackets & citation omitted). Indeed, Customs has no discretion in the matter, and merely liquidates entries of the subject merchandise according to Commerce's instructions. *See id.* Customs' role in the liquidation of subject merchandise is ministerial in nature, "and those actions do not amount to antidumping 'decisions' under 19 U.S.C. § 1514." *Am. Nat'l Fire Ins. Co.*, 30 CIT at 940, 441 F. Supp. 2d at 1285–86. Thus, because Customs does not make an antidumping decision under § 1514(a), the court may not hear Plaintiffs' claim here under § 1581(a). *See Mitsubishi Elecs. Am., Inc.*, 44 F.3d at 977.

2. Plaintiffs' Claim Against Commerce & 28 U.S.C. § 1581(i)

Section 1581(i) provides the Court with broad residual jurisdiction over civil actions that arise out of import transactions. *See Conoco, Inc. v. United States Foreign-Trade Zones Bd.*, 18 F.3d 1581, 1588 (Fed. Cir. 1994). However, Congress's grant is subject to an important caveat, namely that the Court may not exercise jurisdiction pursuant to § 1581(i) where jurisdiction "is or could have been available" under another subsection of § 1581. *Consol. Bearings Co. v. United States*, 348 F.3d 997, 1002 (Fed. Cir. 2003) (quotations & citation omitted). This principle holds true for an antidumping proceeding that is otherwise reviewable under 19 U.S.C. § 1516a(a).[8] § 1581(i). In other words, the subsections of § 1581 must be read in concert and a litigant may invoke the Court's jurisdiction under § 1581(i) only if (1) jurisdiction is unavailable under all other subsections of § 1581, or (2) jurisdiction is available under another subsection of § 1581, but the relief provided by that subsection is manifestly inadequate. § 1581(i); *Consol. Bearings Co.*, 348 F.3d at 1002.

Plaintiffs argue that Commerce exceeded its authority when it issued liquidation instructions to Customs to assess antidumping duties on entries of the subject merchandise made during the period of review, a claim that the court may hear under both § 1581(i)(2) and (i)(4).[9] Pl. Br. 10-14. More specifically, Plaintiffs note that they do not challenge Commerce's liquidation instructions to Customs,[10] but instead contest Commerce's authority to enforce the antidumping duty order on

---

8 Section 1516a provides for the judicial review of, among other determinations, the final results of an administrative review and of a Section 129 proceeding. § 1516a(a)(2)(B)(iii), (vii).

9 Under those provisions, the Court has exclusive jurisdiction over "any civil action commenced against the United States, its agencies, or its officers, that arises out of any law of the United States providing for," among other measures, "tariffs, duties, fees, or other taxes on the importation of merchandise for reasons other than the raising of revenue" or the administration and enforcement of matters referred to in § 1581(a)-(h) and § 1581(i)(1)-(3). § 1581(i)(2), (4).

10 The Court has subject matter jurisdiction over a challenge to Commerce's liquidation instructions pursuant to the "administration and enforcement" language of § 1581(i)(4) as that subsection relates to § 1581(i)(2). *Consol. Bearings Co.*, 348 F.3d at 1002. That kind of claim "essentially contends that the instructions do not accurately (i.e., lawfully) reflect the results

entries made during the period of review in light of the order's subsequent revocation in the *Section 129 Determination*. Pl. Br. 11. Plaintiffs also aver that they had "no reason" to either appeal the *Section 129 Determination* or complete the sixth administrative review because they instead took issue with Commere's "enforcement of the order" that was revoked by the *Section 129 Determination*. Pl. Br. 13. Citing § 1581(i), Plaintiffs therefore ask the court to find jurisdiction over their claim here because the antidumping duties assessed on the subject merchandise not only provided for duties on the importation of merchandise for reasons other than the raising of revenue, but also concerned the administration and enforcement of a matter referred to in § 1581(c). Pl. Br. 10.

Despite Plaintiffs' quixotic assertions to the contrary, § 1581(c) could have provided them with the ability to seek adequate relief, and their failure to choose a remedy thereunder does not permit the court to find jurisdiction here under § 1581(i). The core of Plaintiffs' claim against Commerce takes issue with the scope of the *Section 129 Determination*, namely Commerce's decision not to make the revocation of the antidumping duty order apply retroactively to all then unliquidated entries of stainless steel bar from Italy. However, Plaintiffs had a meaningful opportunity to challenge that decision by making a case against the final results of two proceedings that are judicially reviewable under § 1581(c). In particular, Plaintiffs could have contested the scope of the *Section 129 Determination* under § 1516a(a)(2)(B)(vii). Alternatively, Plaintiffs could have waited for Commerce to complete the sixth administrative review, and dispute the final results of that proceeding under § 1516a(a)(2)(B)(iii). However, Plaintiffs declined to avail themselves of either option, and Commerce rightly instructed Customs to assess antidumping duties at "rates equal to the cash deposit of, or bond for, estimated antidumping duties . . . required on that merchandise at the time of entry" after Plaintiffs withdrew their request for the sixth administrative review. 19 C.F.R. § 351.212(c)(1)(i). Moreover, that Plaintiffs participated in both administrative proceedings, but had "no reason" to challenge the final results of the *Section 129 Determination*, or to complete the sixth administrative review, does not satisfactorily demonstrate to the court that the remedy provided by § 1581(c) is manifestly inadequate. *See Am. Air Parcel Forwarding Co., Ltd. v. United States*, 718 F.2d 1546, 1550–51 (Fed. Cir. 1983). Thus, jurisdiction is unavailable here under § 1581(i) precisely because Plaintiffs could have sought relief under § 1581(c) and because Congress did not intend for subsection (i)—and in particular paragraph (4)—"to circumvent the exclusive method of judicial review of those antidumping . . . determinations listed in [19 U.S.C. § 1516a]. . . ." H.R. Rep. No. 96-1235, at 48 (1980), *reprinted in* 1980 U.S.C.C.A.N. 3729, 3759.

Plaintiffs also contend that changed circumstances—*i.e.,* (1) a recent clarification by the WTO Dispute Settlement Body and (2) the inconsistent positions held by

---

of the underlying administrative proceeding." *DentalEZ, Inc. v. United States, Slip Op.* 07-98, 2007 WL 1847615, at 2 (June 28, 2007) (citation omitted).

the United States at that forum—warrant reconsideration of the Court's interpretation of the prospective effect of a Section 129 proceeding in § 3538(c). Pl. Br. 17-22. It is well known that decisions from the WTO are "not binding on the United States, much less this court." *Timken Co. v. United States*, 354 F.3d 1334, 1344 (Fed. Cir. 2004). That the United States interprets a domestic statute differently in separate cases at the WTO, with each action concerning distinct facts and unique legal issues, is more indicative of the Government's astute lawyering than suggesting to the court that the text of § 3538(c) is ambiguous. Therefore, Defendant's advocacy at the WTO does not convince the court that it should reconsider the plain meaning of the text of § 3538(c).

Finally, because the court finds that it does not have jurisdiction over the claims presented, it need not decide whether Plaintiffs have stated a claim upon which relief may be granted. *See Arbaugh*, 546 U.S. at 514.

IV. Conclusion

For the reasons discussed herein, Defendant's Motion to Dismiss is granted. Section 1581(a) does not provide the court with jurisdiction here because Plaintiffs' claims do not fit within one of the seven specifically enumerated categories of protestable decisions in § 1514(a). Moreover, because § 1581(c) could have provided Plaintiffs with adequate relief, § 1581(i) is not the proper basis for the court to exercise its jurisdiction.

ZHEJIANG NATIVE PRODUCE & ANIMAL BY-PRODUCTS IMPORT & EXPORT CORP.
v.
UNITED STATES

637 F. Supp. 2d 1260 (C.I.T. 2009)
Decided August 19, 2009

Grunfeld, Desiderio, Lebowitz, Silverman & Klestadt LLP (*Bruce M. Mitchell, Andrew T. Schutz, Elaine F. Wang*, and *Ned H. Marshak*) for the plaintiff.

Tony West, Assistant Attorney General; *Jeanne E. Davidson*, Director, *Reginald T. Blades*, Jr., Assistant Director, Commercial Litigation Branch, Civil Division, U.S. Department of Justice (*Jane C. Dempsey*); *Sapna Sharma*, Office of the Chief Counsel for Import Administration, U.S. Department of Commerce, of counsel, for the defendant.

Kelley Drye & Warren LLP (*Michael J. Coursey* and *R. Alan Luberda*) for the defendant-intervenors.

OPINION

RESTANI, Chief Judge.

This matter is before the court on the motion of plaintiff Zhejiang Native Produce & Animal By-Products Import & Export Group Corp. ("Zhejiang") for judgment on the agency record pursuant to USCIT Rule 56.2. Zhejiang, an exporter of packaged honey from the People's Republic of China ("PRC"), challenges the final determination of the United States Department of Commerce ("Commerce") in the fifth administrative review of the antidumping duty order on honey from the PRC. *See Honey from the People's Republic of China: Final Results and Rescission, In Part, of Aligned Antidumping Duty Administrative Review and New Shipper Review*, 73 Fed. Reg. 42,321 (Dep't Commerce July 21, 2008) ("*Final Results*"). Zhejiang contests Commerce's decision not to review Zhejiang individually as a respondent and Commerce's calculation of Zhejiang's dumping margin. For the reasons stated below, the court grants Zhejiang's motion and remands this matter to Commerce to determine a company-specific dumping margin for Zhejiang.

BACKGROUND

In 2001, Commerce issued an antidumping duty order on honey from the PRC. *Notice of Amended Final Determination of Sales at Less Than Fair Value and Antidumping Duty Order; Honey From the People's Republic of China*, 66 Fed. Reg. 63,670 (Dep't Commerce Dec. 10, 2001). Zhejiang requested that Commerce review Zhejiang's honey sales to the United States during the fifth administrative period of review ("POR 5"), December 1, 2005 to November 30, 2006. (App. to Pl.'s Mem. in Supp. of Rule 56.2 Mot. for J. Upon the Agency R. ("Pl.'s App.") Tab 1, at 1.) Commerce initiated an aligned administrative review of Zhejiang and thirty other companies for POR 5 and new shipper review for QHD Sanhai Co., Ltd. ("QHD Sanhai") in February 2007. *See Honey from the People's Republic of China: Initiation of New Shipper Antidumping Duty Reviews*, 72 Fed. Reg. 5265 (Dep't Commerce Feb. 5, 2007); *Initiation of Antidumping and Countervailing Duty Administrative Reviews and Request for Revocation in Part*, 72 Fed. Reg. 5005 (Dep't Commerce Feb. 2, 2007). The administrative review was rescinded as to twenty-two companies for which the petitioners, the American Honey Producers Association and the Sioux Honey Association, withdrew their request for review. *Honey from the People's Republic of China: Notice of Partial Rescission of Antidumping Duty Administrative Review*, 72 Fed. Reg. 24,561 (Dep't Commerce May 3, 2007).

Of the remaining companies, only four—Inner Mongolia Altin Bee-Keeping ("IMA"), Qinhuangdao Municipal Dafeng Industrial Co., Ltd. ("QMD"), Dongtai Peak Honey Industry Co., Ltd. ("Dongtai Peak"), and Zhejiang—submitted quantity and value ("Q & V") questionnaire responses and claimed shipments for the period of review. *Antidumping Duty Administrative Review of Honey from the People's Republic of China: Selection of Respondents*, A-570-863, POR 12/01/2005-11/30/2006, at 2 (Apr. 17, 2007) ("*Respondent Selection Memorandum*"), *available at* App. to Def.-Intervenors' Br. in Resp. to Pl.'s Rule 56.2 Mot. for J. on the Agency R. Tab 5. On April 17, 2007, Commerce issued a memorandum concluding that review of all four companies was not practicable because of resource constraints arising from the "significant workload" Commerce faced in other antidumping proceedings. *Id.* at 2–3. Commerce selected IMA and QMD, the two companies whose exports represented "the overwhelming proportion of the total export volume under review," as the mandatory respondents. *Id.* at 4. In a letter dated April 23, 2007, Zhejiang asked Commerce to reconsider its decision and to select Zhejiang as a mandatory or voluntary respondent.[1] (*See* Pl.'s App. Tab 2.) During a telephone call on May 25, 2007, a Commerce official informed Zhejiang's counsel that Commerce had considered the letter, but "the resource constraints identified in the . . . respondent selection memorandum resulted in

1 Dongtai Peak did not challenge Commerce's decision to limit the number of mandatory respondents and is not a party here.

[Commerce's] being required to invoke its statutory authority to limit the number of respondents it examined individually in this review." (*Id.* Tab 5.)

IMA subsequently withdrew from the administrative review on August 15, 2007. (*See id.* Tab 6, at 1.) On August 21, 2007, Zhejiang's counsel asked Commerce whether Zhejiang would be selected as a mandatory respondent in light of IMA's withdrawal. (*Id.* Tab 8.) Commerce responded "that it would not be selecting Zhejiang as a mandatory respondent as it is too late in the proceeding and Zhejiang had not filed responses to [Commerce's] questionnaire as a voluntary respondent by the appropriate deadline." (*Id.*) QMD withdrew from the administrative review on October 18, 2007. (*See id.* Tab 9.)

Commerce's January 2008 preliminary determination assigned a de minimis dumping margin for QHD Sanhai; individual margins of 45.46% ad valorem to Zhejiang and Dongtai Peak as non-examined, cooperative separate rate exporters; and a PRC-wide margin, based on adverse facts available, to all other companies in the review. *See Honey From the People's Republic of China: Preliminary Results and Partial Rescission of Antidumping Duty Administrative Review*, 73 Fed. Reg. 2890, 2893–97, 2899 (Dep't Commerce Jan. 16, 2008) ("*Preliminary Results*").[2] Zhejiang submitted a case brief, arguing that Commerce should have reviewed Zhejiang as a mandatory or voluntary respondent. (*See* Pl.'s Confidential App. Tab 20, at 6–9.) Commerce again rejected Zhejiang's argument. See Issues and Decision Memorandum for the Final Results in the Aligned Fifth Administrative Review and Tenth New Shipper Review of Honey from the People's Republic of China, A-570-863, POR 12/01/2005-11/30/2006, at 13–15 (July 14, 2008) ("*Issues and Decision Memorandum*"), *available at* http://ia.i ta.doc.gov/frn/summary/PRC/E8-16624-1.pdf. For its July 2008 Final Results, Commerce arrived at an ad valorem rate of 104.88%, which it converted to a per-kilogram cash deposit and assessment rate, and imposed a rate of $0.98/kg on Zhejiang and Dongtai Peak and an otherwise applicable PRC-wide rate, based on total adverse facts available, of $2.06/kg. *See Final Results*, 73 Fed. Reg. at 42,322–23.

JURISDICTION AND STANDARD OF REVIEW

The court has jurisdiction under 28 U.S.C. § 1581(c) and 19 U.S.C. § 1516a(a)(2)(B)(i). The court must uphold Commerce's final determination in an antidumping review unless it is "unsupported by substantial evidence on the record, or otherwise not in accordance with law." 19 U.S.C. § 1516a(b)(1)(B)(i).

2 The 45.46% margin was assigned to the non-examined, cooperative separate rate exporters in the original investigation, based on the weighted average of the rates calculated for the mandatory respondents. *See Notice of Final Determination of Sales at Less Than Fair Value; Honey From the People's Republic of China*, 66 Fed. Reg. 50,608, 50,609 (Dep't Commerce Oct. 4, 2001), *amended by* 66 Fed. Reg. at 63,672. Commerce preliminarily applied the 45.46% margin here because it was "the separate rate margin calculated in the most recent segment of Honey from the People's Republic of China in which a separate margin was calculated." *Preliminary Results*, 73 Fed. Reg. at 2893.

DISCUSSION

Zhejiang claims that Commerce should have selected Zhejiang as a respondent in the review and calculated an individual dumping margin for Zhejiang. (Br. in Supp. of Pl.'s Rule 56.2 Mot. for J. Upon the Agency R. ("Pl.'s Br.") 10–15.) This claim has merit.

The antidumping statute states that as a general rule, Commerce "shall determine the individual weighted average dumping margin for each known exporter and producer of the subject merchandise." 19 U.S.C. § 1677f-1(c)(1). If, however, "it is not practicable to make individual weighted average dumping margin determinations . . . because of the large number of exporters or producers involved in the . . . review, [Commerce] may determine the weighted average dumping margins for a reasonable number of exporters or producers." *Id.* § 1677f-1(c)(2). The statute thus grants Commerce authority to limit the number of mandatory respondents only where a large number of exporters or producers are involved in the review.

Here, Commerce concluded that four was a large number of respondents in the context of "the various administrative circumstances" Commerce was confronting during the review and that individual examination of all four exporters and producers was not practicable because of its significant workload arising from other antidumping reviews and investigations. *Issues and Decision Memorandum* at 13–14. Commerce stated:

> The office to which this administrative review is assigned . . . does not have the resources to examine all such exporters/producers. This office is conducting numerous concurrent antidumping proceedings which place a constraint on the number of analysts that can be assigned to this case. Not only do these other cases present a significant workload, but the deadlines for a number of the cases coincide and/or overlap with deadlines in this antidumping proceeding. In addition, because of the significant workload throughout Import Administration, we do not anticipate receiving additional resources to devote to this antidumping proceeding.

Respondent Selection Memorandum at 2–3.

The court rejects Commerce's conclusion. The statute focuses solely on the practicability of determining individual dumping margins based on the large number of exporters or producers involved in the review at hand. *See* 19 U.S.C. § 1677f-1(c)(2). Accordingly, Commerce may not rely upon its workload caused by other antidumping proceedings in assessing whether the number of exporters or producers is "large," and thus deciding that individual determinations are impracticable. Commerce cannot rewrite the statute based on its staffing issues.

Longkou Haimeng Machinery Co. v. United States, 581 F. Supp. 2d 1344 (CIT 2008), does not support deference to Commerce's conclusion here. In that case, Commerce had selected three of the fifteen exporters and producers as mandatory respondents. *Id.* at 1348. Longkou upheld Commerce's decision not to examine two of the plaintiffs, who were non-selected exporters, as voluntary respondents. *Id.* at 1349–54. Although the court stated that "[t]he authority to limit the number of respondents for examination rests 'exclusively' with Commerce," *id.* at 1352, this statement apparently refers to Commerce's authority to select the number of respondents to review when individual review of all producers and exporters is not practicable because the number of producers and exporters is large. Whatever "exclusive authority" connotes, the statute actually vests Commerce with "exclusive[]" authority only with regard to the selection of "averages and statistically valid samples." 19 U.S.C. § 1677f-1(b). Commerce, however, has no authority to limit the number of mandatory respondents it reviews unless there is a large number of exporters or producers. *See* 19 U.S.C. § 1677f-1 (c)(2). If that precondition is met, it may then either use sampling or select entities "accounting for the largest volume" of the subject merchandise from the exporting country that can reasonably be examined. *Id.* Commerce chose the second option; it did not use sampling in either *Longkou* or this case.

Further, although the *Longkou* court determined that Commerce's careful examination of resource constraints arising from other antidumping proceedings supported its decision to review three rather than five of the fifteen exporters and producers, the court merely recognized that Commerce has broad discretion in allocating its resources where the statute permits Commerce to limit its review. *See Longkou*, 581 F. Supp. 2d at 1353–54. The issue of whether the number of exporters and producers was sufficiently large to render individual review impracticable was not before the court, as the plaintiffs conceded that Commerce had the authority to limit the number of mandatory respondents to less than fifteen. *See id.* at 1350.

By contrast, the number of exporters and producers initially involved in this review, four, does not appear to satisfy the requirement that the number be "large" under any ordinary understanding of that word. In any event, not even four exporters or producers were involved here because the two mandatory respondents withdrew from the review. Only one exporter, Zhejiang, preserved its request for individual review. One is not a large number. *Cf. Zenith Elecs. Corp. v. United States*, 770 F. Supp. 648, 660 (CIT 1991) (holding that where "Commerce had before it the exact production data relating to a single United States sale" and made only three adjustments to the price, Commerce could not calculate a weighted average under a former version of 19 U.S.C. § 1677f1 (a)(1), which granted Commerce authority to use averages "only where 'a significant volume of sales is involved or a significant number of adjustments to price is required'"), *vacated in part by* 865 F. Supp. 890 (CIT 1994).

Commerce cited two reasons for its decision not to select Zhejiang as a respondent after the two mandatory respondents withdrew: "it [was] too late in the proceeding and Zhejiang had not filed responses to [Commerce's] questionnaire as a voluntary respondent by the appropriate deadline." (Pl.'s App. Tab 8.) The statute itself did not impose a time bar to review, and the court need not determine the limits of Commerce's discretion to decline any individual review after the selected mandatory respondents have withdrawn but others have requested a review. Here, Commerce's reasons are not persuasive.

First, Commerce could have timely reviewed Zhejiang's data, as Commerce, acting within the statutory deadlines, released its *Preliminary Results* in January 2008, five months after IMA withdrew and three months after QMD withdrew, and its *Final Results* in July 2008, eleven months after IMA withdrew and nine months after QMD withdrew. *See* 19 U.S.C. § 1675(a)(3)(A). Second, and perhaps most importantly, Zhejiang timely filed its separate rate certification and Q & V questionnaire response but did not file a response to questionnaire section C (U.S.sales) or D (factors of production) for reasons not of its own making. *See Preliminary Results*, 73 Fed. Reg. at 2890–91; *Issues and Decision Memorandum* at 13 n. 16. The section C and D responses for the mandatory respondents were not due until at least June 7, 2007, but by then, Commerce had informed Zhejiang's counsel that Commerce would not accept Zhejiang as either a mandatory or a voluntary respondent.[3] *See Preliminary Results*, 73 Fed. Reg. at 2892; (Pl.'s App. Tab 5). Commerce did not leave open the possibility that it would consider Zhejiang as a voluntary respondent if Zhejiang timely filed its questionnaire responses, contrary to Commerce's practice of not discouraging voluntary respondents. *See Statement of Administrative Action accompanying the Uruguay Round Agreements Act*, H.R.Rep. No. 103-316, at 872 (1994), *reprinted in* 1994 U.S.C.C.A.N. 4040, 4201 ("Commerce, consistent with Article 6.10.2 of the [Antidumping] Agreement, will not discourage voluntary responses."). Thus, Commerce should not have penalized Zhejiang for failing to file its section C and D responses after indicating to Zhejiang that it would be futile to do so.

CONCLUSION

Accordingly, Commerce's decision not to select Zhejiang for review was not supported by substantial evidence or in accordance with law. Zhejiang's motion for judgment on the agency record is granted. The court hereby remands this matter to Commerce to determine an individual dumping margin for Zhejiang based on Zhejiang's sales and factors of production data during POR 5.[4]

---

3 Commerce must calculate an individual dumping margin for any voluntary respondent who submits the information requested from the mandatory respondents "by the date specified" for the mandatory respondents if "the number of exporters and producers who have submitted such information is not so large that individual examination of such exporters or producers would be unduly burdensome and inhibit the timely completion of the investigation." 19 U.S.C. § 1677m(a)(1)(A), (a)(2).

4 Because Commerce must determine an individual dumping margin for Zhejiang, it is premature for the court to consider Zhejiang's alternative argument that it is entitled to a de minimis margin, rather than the $0.98/kg cash deposit and assessment rate. (*See* Pl.'s Br. 15–19.)

Commerce shall request any missing information and file its remand determination with the court within sixty days of this date. Zhejiang, the American Honey Producers Association, and the Sioux Honey Association have eleven days thereafter to file objections, and Commerce will have seven days thereafter to file its response.

Printed and bound in the UK by
CPI Antony Rowe, Eastbourne

The manufacturer's authorised representative in the EU for product
safety is Oxford University Press España S.A. of El Parque Empresarial
San Fernando de Henares, Avenida de Castilla, 2 - 28830 Madrid
(www.oup.es/en or product.safety@oup.com). OUP España S.A. also acts
as importer into Spain of products made by the manufacturer.
Printed and bound by CPI Group (UK) Ltd, Croydon, CR0 4YY
14/09/2026
02216290-0016